Cryptocurrency

Cryptocurrency

*How Bitcoin and Digital Money are
Challenging the Global Economic Order*

PAUL VIGNA

and

MICHAEL J. CASEY

THE BODLEY HEAD
LONDON

Published by The Bodley Head 2015

2 4 6 8 10 9 7 5 3

First published in Great Britain in 2015 by
The Bodley Head
Random House, 20 Vauxhall Bridge Road,
London SW1V 2SA

www.bodleyhead.co.uk
www.vintage-books.co.uk

Addresses for companies within The Random House Group Limited can be found at:
www.randomhouse.co.uk/offices.htm

The Random House Group Limited Reg. No. 954009

A CIP catalogue record for this book
is available from the British Library

ISBN 9781847923448 (Hardback)
ISBN 9781847923325 (Trade Paperback)

Printed and bound in Great Britain by Clays Ltd, St Ives plc

For Elizabeth
—PV

For Mum and Dad
—MC

Contents

Cryptocurrency

Introduction

DIGITAL CASH FOR A DIGITAL AGE

Money won't create success, the freedom to make it will.
—Nelson Mandela

Even though Parisa Ahmadi was in the top of her class at the all-girls Hatifi High School in Herat, Afghanistan, her family was initially against her enrolling in classes being offered by a private venture that promised to teach young girls Internet and social-media skills—and even pay them for their efforts. "Here in Afghanistan a woman's life is limited by her room's walls and school," she wrote in an e-mail. In Afghanistan, girls are not exposed to the Internet, not at home and not at school. That's the way it might have stayed, too, if Ahmadi hadn't persisted. She was a top student, and she wanted to take even more classes. In her mind, that was reason enough. She pressed her family, by her own admission, "a lot."

The venture backing these classes is the Film Annex, a U.S.-based arts group that uses social media and an online site to pay the three hundred thousand bloggers and filmmakers who contribute their work. Film Annex ended up in Afghanistan by way of its direct affiliation with the Women's Annex, a digital literacy program set up in conjunction with Afghan businesswoman Roya Mahboob, which now educates fifty thousand girls in schools across Afghanistan. Mahboob is something of a celebrity; named one of the one hundred most influential people in the world by *Time* magazine, she runs a software company called Afghan Citadel, is one of the few female CEOs in Afghanistan, and has made education for Afghan women her central cause. The Women's Annex sets up its classrooms in local high schools, and the classes are taught by women. Because of this last feature, Ahmadi's family finally relented and let her sign up.

Ahmadi started taking classes in 2013. She and her classmates were learning about the World Wide Web, social media, and blogs. A movie lover who also loved to write about the movies that moved her, she began posting on a blog, and its members responded positively to her reviews, earning her the first real income of her young life.

Still, one of the other things most girls don't have in Afghanistan is a bank account. If the Afghan teen ever had any money, she had to transfer it into her father's or brothers' bank accounts, and that's simply the way it is for most girls where she lives. In this sense, she was lucky—for many women from her background male family members block them from access to their funds and treat the money as their own.

Ahmadi's luck would change in early 2014. The Film Annex's New York–based founder, Francesco Rulli, aware of the difficulty faced by women like Ahmadi and frustrated by the transaction costs he incurred in sending relatively small amounts of money around the world, implemented a sweeping change to the Film Annex's payment system. He would pay his bloggers in bitcoin, the digital currency that had seemed to come out of nowhere in 2013, with a small, fiercely dedicated band of tech-minded, libertarian-leaning digital utopians acting as its standard-bearers, and swearing to anybody who'd listen that it was going to change the world.

Rulli, driven by a philosophy that's a sort of bootstrap capitalism, soon "got" bitcoin and gleaned the advantages it could have for people like Ahmadi, who was one of more than seven thousand young Afghan women listed as paid contributors to the Film Annex. Bitcoins are stored in digital bank accounts or "wallets" that can be set up at home by anyone with Internet access. There is no trip to the bank to set up an account, no need for documentation or proof that you're a man. Indeed, bitcoin does not know your name or gender, so it allows women in patriarchal societies, at least those with access to the Internet, to control their own money. The importance of this cannot be overstated. These women are building something that is theirs, not their fathers' or brothers'. While not a panacea, this blast of cutting-edge, twenty-first-century technology offers real promise as a way to help unshackle an entire swath of the human population.

Many Film Annex contributors in the United States, the United Kingdom, Italy, and other rich countries grumbled about the inconvenience of the digital currency. Few businesses, online or otherwise, accepted it for payment, and to many the whole thing seemed dodgy. The complaints aren't unique to Film Annex contributors; to many people bitcoin seems like a half-baked scam, some scheme to sucker fools out of their money. Moreover, Ahmadi contends with the same issues related to bitcoin that her peers in other countries had grumbled about, in particular that the options for spending it are still limited, especially in an economy as underdeveloped as Afghanistan's. To deal with such problems, the Film Annex set up an e-commerce site in 2014 allowing its members to trade bitcoins for gift cards from global sites such as Amazon that will ship to Kabul, Herat, and other Afghan cities. In effect, Film Annex is creating its own self-enclosed bitcoin economy, an approach it reinforced by changing its trade name to BitLanders.

Ahmadi used her bitcoins to buy a new laptop. Only a few years ago, this would have been impossible. She credits bitcoin with "teaching us how to be independent and how to decide by our own, and best of all, how to stand on our own feet." It's allowed her to ponder a future in which she isn't merely an appendage to the men in her life, a future in which she can chart her own course. "I see myself an educated and active female doctor in the future," she said.

You don't typically read stories like Ahmadi's in press coverage of bitcoin. Most of it has focused on the roller-coaster ride of what's seen as a suspect monetary concept. Ask people on the street what they know about bitcoin, and if they can answer anything at all, they'll likely cite the most prominent of those press reports. They'll say something about drug dealers who were busted using bitcoin on the illicit Silk Road Web site. Or they'll refer to volatile price movements and utter the word *bubble*. Or they might recall the sudden vanishing of a large number of bitcoins from a thing with the Dr. Seuss–esque name of Mt. Gox, knowing little more than that it was an obscure online exchange in Tokyo. Perhaps they know of the search for Satoshi Nakamoto, the shadowy figure who created bitcoin.

All of these elements of the circus sideshow that has arisen around bitcoin are both colorful and important to understanding its story. But to dismiss it as a con because of them is to turn your back on something that may well change your life. Bitcoin is a groundbreaking digital technology with the potential to radically change the way we conduct banking and commerce, and to bring billions of people from the emerging markets into a modern, integrated, digitized, globalized economy. If it works—and that's still a big if—an awful lot of things that today seem like part of the natural state of the world are going to look as antiquated as Gutenberg's printing press.

The system we use now for managing exchanges of currency and assets dates back to the time of the Medici family of the Florentine Renaissance, when banks first assumed dominance in the monetary economy of Europe. These guys were the ultimate technological disrupters, radical thinkers who discovered a vital need in society and then filled it. In essence, they figured out how to intermediate between savers and borrowers, bringing in the excess capital of the former and parceling it out to those among the latter who needed it—all for a fee. This was a dramatic version of what a Silicon Valley investor would these days call a network efficiency. By bringing society's myriad debts and claims into the central ledger of a single bank, the bankers created a powerful, new centralized system of trust. With the help of their specialized intermediating services, strangers that previously had no way of trusting each other enough to do business could now do so. In effect, the Medici created a high-powered system of money creation—money being not a physical currency but a system for organizing, expanding, and sharing society's debts and payments. It made way for an explosion in mercantile trade, which in turn created the wealth and capital that would finance the projects from which great civilizations would grow and conquer the world.

But . . . by creating this centralized system of trust and then putting themselves in the middle of it, banks became extremely powerful—eventually, too much so. Since strangers could not do business with each other without the banks, the world's increasingly complex and interconnected economies became utterly dependent on the bankers' intermediation. The ledgers they kept inside their institutions became the vital means through which societies kept track of the debts and payments that arose among their citizens. Thus the banks created the ultimate rent-seeking business, positioning themselves as fee-charging gatekeepers, managers of the financial traffic that made economies tick. Anyone sitting at the sending or receiving end of that traffic had no choice but to deal with a bank—much as Parisa Ahmadi did before the Film Annex changed its payment policy. As this new finance business grew and became more complex, other rent-seeking middlemen installed themselves as specialized providers of intermediated *trust*—from early bond and securities brokers, to insurance agents, to financial lawyers, to the payment processors and credit-card companies of our modern day. As it currently works, our high-charged global economic system would collapse if these middlemen stopped doing what they do. All of this has simply made the banks at the center of it all even more powerful, so much so that eventually a system that first empowered people has fostered a dangerous dependence upon them. This is what gave rise to the behemoths of Wall Street, which would ultimately take the world to the brink of disaster in 2008.

Enter cryptocurrency—the category to which bitcoin belongs. The simple genius of this technology is that it cuts away the middleman yet maintains an infrastructure that allows strangers to deal with each other. It does this by taking the all-important role of ledger-keeping away from *centralized* financial institutions and handing it to a network of autonomous computers, creating a *decentralized* system of trust that operates outside the control of any one institution. At their core, cryptocurrencies are built around the principle of a universal, inviolable ledger, one that is made fully public and is constantly being verified by these high-powered computers, each essentially acting independently of the others. In theory, that means we don't need banks and other financial intermediaries to form bonds of trust on our behalf. The network-based ledger—which in the case of most cryptocurrencies is called a blockchain—works as a stand-in for the middlemen since it can just as effectively tell us whether the counterparty to a transaction is good for his or her money.

By eliminating middlemen and their fees, cryptocurrency promises to reduce the costs of doing business and to mitigate corruption inside those intermediating institutions as well as from the politicians who are drawn into their prosperous orbit. The public ledgers used by cryptocurrencies can bring into the open the inner workings of an economic-political system that was previously hidden within impenetrable, centralized institutions. Indeed, the technology's potential as a force for transparency and accountability goes far beyond money and payments, as it can strip out information-controlling middlemen from many other forms of human exchange—in elections, for example, where cryptocurrency enthusiasts see the capacity to end vote-rigging. At its core, this technology is a form of social organization that promises to shift the control of money and information away from the powerful elites and deliver it to the people to whom it belongs, putting them back in charge of their assets and talents.

If we listen to Mike's neighbor, Scott Robbins—the same Scott of Pelham, New York, whose Middle American skepticism toward globalization also helped ground the introduction to *The Unfair Trade*—it's clear that many middle-class Westerners struggle to grasp how all this might improve their own lives. "I just don't understand why I should give a damn about bitcoin," Scott said one evening. And sure, if we focus narrowly on, say, the 2 or 3 percent savings that bitcoin offers on each credit-card transaction fee—a benefit that would typically go to merchants—it's hard to get excited about a "cryptocurrency revolution." But when we consider that world economic output runs to $87 trillion a year, and think of how much of that is hived off by the same banks and financial toll-collectors that cryptocurrencies bypass, it's possible to imagine many trillions of dollars in savings. Each of us can stake a claim on those funds, indirectly via the employment and income opportunities that businesses might create with what they save on financial costs, or directly via the lower interest rates, bank fees, and transaction charges by our bank and credit-card accounts. The day you started earning and spending money is the day you began repeatedly handing over slices of that money to these middlemen, often adding up to millions of dollars over a single person's lifetime. Cryptocurrency promises to stop that outflow and put the money back in your pocket. This, in the most basic way, is bitcoin's value proposition—the "Why should I care?" that Scott was looking for.

Cryptocurrency is certainly not without flaws and risks. Some fear that if we follow bitcoin's model, its mechanism for incentivizing computer owners to maintain and manage the public ledger—which drives them to compete for batches of newly issued bitcoins every ten minutes—could encourage a politically disruptive concentration of computing power. So, even as bitcoin aims to decentralize monetary power, capitalism's innate monopolizing tendencies could lead some players to accumulate enough computing power to seize control of the network and revert a trustworthy, decentralized system back to one where self-interested, centralized institutions are in control. Bitcoin is not currently under such a threat, and many believe it would never arise because computer owners who profit from owning bitcoins have no interest in destroying it. Still, the threat cannot be fully eliminated.

Also, bitcoin and crime have been associated, as seen in the Silk Road case, where users sought to exploit the digital currency's anonymity to sell drugs and launder money. Some worry, too, that bitcoin could foment economic crises because it strips government policymakers of the capacity to adjust the money supply and to offset people's instinct to hoard it at times of mass panic. We will examine these important concerns and show how the community of people working on bitcoin is already addressing them.

There's no getting around that cryptocurrency is a highly disruptive technology. All else being equal, technological disruption makes an economy more efficient and creates more wealth overall. But it is never painless. That will clearly be evident if cryptocurrency takes hold. It will unleash political tensions as millions who've made their living from the old system wake up to find their jobs are at risk. That backlash is already building, even before the technology is properly established, as we'll witness in the struggles and debates that arise in the chapters to follow. The political conflict is not only between those who cling to the old system and those who support the new one, but also within the ranks of the latter group, as idealists, pragmatists, entrepreneurs, and opportunists compete to control cryptocurrency's future.

When disruption is driven by a technology associated with money, these clashes can be especially intense. However, when the knives are out—metaphorically; we're not yet aware of any bitcoin-related assassinations—it's often a good sign that something big is happening.

Former U.S. treasury secretary Larry Summers has grasped this. "If you think about what a modern economy is all about, it basically involves ever more exchange," he told us. "And exchange, unless it can be literally simultaneous, always has real issues of trust. So, what the breakthrough in communications and computer science represented in bitcoin does is to support deeper exchange at lower price. And that matters both within countries for the traditionally excluded and it also matters across international borders."

The "issues of trust" to which Summers refers are the core problem that the Medici bankers first sought to solve, the dilemma that strangers face when they seek to do business with each other. When Summers talks of "the traditionally excluded," he's making an oblique reference to the "unbanked," the Parisa Ahmadis of the world, the roughly 2.5 billion people from Afghanistan to Africa to even America who have been shut out of the modern finance system, who don't have bank accounts with verifiable balances, or credit histories, or any of the requirements banks impose for us to do business through them. Without access to banking, they are essentially shut out of the modern economy.

At its core, cryptocurrency is not about the ups and downs of the digital currency market; it's not even about a new unit of exchange to replace the dollar or the euro or the yen. It's about freeing people from the tyranny of centralized trust. It speaks to the tantalizing prospect that we can take power away from the center—away from banks, governments, lawyers, and the tribal leaders of Afghanistan—and transfer it to the periphery, to We, the People.

So, what exactly is bitcoin? It gets a little confusing because people refer to two different things when they talk about bitcoin. The first is the feature that has got the most attention: *bitcoin the currency*, the digital units of value that are used by people in exchange for goods and services or other currencies, and whose price tends to swing wildly against traditional government-issued currencies. But that narrow definition distracts from a broader one that captures bitcoin's far more important contribution, and that is *bitcoin the technology*—or, as some prefer to write it in text,

Bitcoin, with a capital B (with the currency always referred to with a lower-case *b*).*

At its core, *bitcoin the technology* refers to the system's protocol, a common phrase in software terminology that describes a fundamental set of programming instructions that allow computers to communicate with each other. Bitcoin's protocol is run over a network of computers that belong to the many people around the world that are charged with maintaining its core *blockchain* ledger and monetary system. It provides those computers with the operating instructions and information they need to keep track of and verify transactions among people operating within the bitcoin economy. The system employs encryption, which lets users key in special passwords to send digital money directly to each other without revealing those passwords to any person or institution. Just as important, it lays out the steps that computers in the network must perform to reach a consensus on the validity of each transaction. Once that consensus has been reached, a payee knows that the payer has sufficient funds—that the payer isn't sending counterfeit digital money.

Now, here's what gets techies, economists, and futurists most excited about bitcoin the technology. They see its open-source protocol as a foundation on which to develop new tools for doing commerce and for managing exchanges. You can think of it as an operating system. (Because it's based on open-source software, we'd use the analogy of Linux for PCs or Google's Android for smartphones rather than Microsoft's Windows or Apple's iOS.) The difference is that bitcoin's operating system is not providing instructions to a single computer on how to run itself but to a network of computers on how to interact with each other. Its core features are its decentralized model of "trustless" proof and an automatically generated database that contains every transaction ever completed, is made available to everyone in real time, and can never be tampered with. Just as mobile-app makers are busy building applications on top of Android, developers are building specialized applications on top of bitcoin that

---

* In some cases, bitcoin will refer to both the currency and the technology. But for convenience and consistency with the style at *The Wall Street Journal,* we stick with lowercase in all references. To a large extent, context will clarify the distinction being made.

exploit those key features. These applications might merely make exchanges of bitcoin the currency more fluid and user-friendly, such as the mobile digital-wallet apps that allow smartphone users to zap digital money to each other, or their objectives might be much more expansive. The bitcoin protocol's rules for sharing information allow these developers to fashion a set of software-based instructions to manage decision-making across companies, communities, and societies. Because it comes with a fully verifiable, transparent record of ownership that requires no centralized registry, this "trustless" system allows people to exchange all sorts of digitized items of value and any manner of useful data with confidence that the information is accurate. This all comes without the costly intervention of banks, government agencies, lawyers, and the many other intermediaries required to make our current, centralized system function. That's the power of bitcoin the technology.

Because of its rapid price rise, high-profile missteps, and passionate, occasionally messianic legions of believers and critics, bitcoin has inspired volumes of heated debate that have tended to overwhelm serious efforts to explain it and its potential. This book is an effort to restore balance to the subject in a way that will allow readers of various levels of expertise and understanding to get a grip on what it is, how it works, and what it might mean for all of us.

We're journalists, not futurists. Our intent is not to outline some definitive case for what the future will look like. But if we've learned anything since the arrival of the Internet, it's that technology does not wait for us to catch up. From threshing machines and power looms to electricity and assembly lines to mainframe computers and e-mail, individuals and governments who haven't paid significant attention to new technologies have been in for a nasty shock. We believe bitcoin, and more specifically the breakthroughs that have made it and other cryptocurrencies particularly effective tools for monetary exchange, have the potential to be an important force in finance. Just consider this: control of a currency is one of the most powerful tools a government wields; ask anybody in Ireland, Portugal, Greece, or Cyprus who lived through those countries' recent financial crises. Bitcoin promises to take at least some of that power away from governments and hand it to people. That alone augurs significant political, cultural, and economic clashes.

You see hints of those clashes to come in the fervor of the pro and con crowds. The bitcoiners we spoke to in researching this book and talked to during our day jobs at *The Wall Street Journal* have a passion that borders on fervor. Bitcoin takes on the look of a religious movement: the meetups that are reminiscent of church socials, the cultlike crowds that sing bitcoin's praises on social forums such as Reddit and Twitter, the movement's evangelists—people such as Barry Silbert, Nicolas Cary, Andreas Antonopoulos, Charlie Shrem, and Roger Ver (whose nickname is Bitcoin Jesus). At the top of it all, ensconced firmly in a creation myth that inspires and nurtures the faithful, is Satoshi Nakamoto, the godhead of bitcoin.

But cryptocurrencies could flame out entirely—like the Betamax video format (for those of you old enough to remember it). Or they could have only marginal real-world application, much as the once heavily hyped Segway has had. No less a dedicated bitcoiner than Gavin Andresen, the software engineer whom Satoshi Nakamoto effectively appointed to become the lead developer of bitcoin's core software, articulates it this way: "Every time I give a talk, I emphasize that bitcoin really is still an experiment; every time I hear about somebody investing their life savings in it, I cringe." And that's the guy responsible for keeping the whole thing running. More convinced in their doubt are mainstream business leaders such as JP Morgan Chase's chieftain, Jamie Dimon, who called bitcoin "a terrible store of value," and legendary investor Warren Buffett, who called it simply a "mirage."

These are not unusual reactions, actually. Most people, we found, react about the same way when they first start to think about bitcoin and cryptocurrencies. Some get past the initial gut reaction, some don't. We expect you'll go through a sort of Kübler-Ross model of cryptocurrency recognition before this book is over. It would go something like this:

Stage One: Disdain. Not even denial, but disdain. Here's this thing, it's supposed to be money, but it doesn't have any of the characteristics of money with which we're familiar. It's not tangible. It's not issued by a government or forged from precious metal.

Stage Two: Skepticism. You read the paper every day, and enough stories have appeared to convince you that bitcoin is real, that some entrepreneurs, including the Winklevoss twins of Facebook fame, expect to make a lot of money from it. But the details don't add up. You get it by doing math problems? No? By having your computer do math problems? How can that possibly work? At this stage, phrases like *Ponzi scheme* and *tulip mania* enter your mind.

Stage Three: Curiosity. You've kept reading. It becomes clear that many people, even some seemingly sensible people such as Internet pioneer Marc Andreessen, people with a track record for being right about this stuff, are genuinely excited by it. But why all the fuss? Okay, it's digital money, it may work, but what difference is that going to make to regular people? And why are people so heated up about it?

Stage Four: Crystallization. This is the critical one. Choose whatever metaphor you like—call it the jaw-drop moment, the lightbulb moment, the mind-now-officially-blown moment—it is a point of realization that hits just about everybody who spends any time around digital currencies, even if they remain skeptical about the hurdles to their acceptance. Some people we spoke with talked about being unable to sleep for days, scouring every word they could find on bitcoin. In one fell, digitized swoop, an entire new way of doing things crystallizes in your mind.

Stage Five: Acceptance. It's not an easy thing to get your head around, but big ideas never are. The bottom line is that even if bitcoin doesn't keep growing, even if none of the other "altcoin" cryptocurrencies catch on—and several hundred of these bitcoinlike cryptocurrencies with their own features and quirks exist—we've seen a way of doing business that is faster and cheaper, that cuts out the middleman and the rentier, brings in millions of "unbanked" people, and gives everyone a measure of control over his or her finances and businesses that has not existed before. Once you see this, there is no way to unsee it.

For sure, reasons exist to doubt the success of this grand experiment. Bitcoin tends to attract headlines about scandals and security breaches, and while these are not yet as big as those occurring within the dominant, bank-centric system of finance and credit-card payments, they create an image problem. Imagine the PR blow if reports emerge that bitcoin has been used to finance a major terrorist attack. Public anxiety over such risks could prompt an excessive response from regulators, strangling the project in its infancy. This legal reaction could be especially restrictive if officials sense that bitcoin is starting to impinge on governments' capacity to control their monetary and payments system—which is the stated goal of many of its more impassioned, libertarian-minded supporters. The first serious regulatory efforts are now under way as officials in Washington, New York, London, Brussels, Beijing, and various other financial and political capitals formulate rules for users of digital currencies to follow. If well designed, these could bolster cryptocurrencies by making people feel better protected from their more dangerous elements. But the bureaucrats may go too far and quash innovative start-ups' ability to make full use of this technology's potential to empower individuals, break down monopolies, and reduce cost, waste, and corruption in our financial system.

Meanwhile, other emerging technologies could evolve to provide better competition. For example, in China, people currently have few incentives to use it in payments because ubiquitous new mobile smartphone-based applications already allow them to make renminbi-denominated payments without the risk of bitcoin's volatility. The legacy systems that are coming under attack will surely work to improve the services they offer, lower their costs, and support regulation designed to dull bitcoin's competitive advantage.

The biggest wild card in all of this is people. Cryptocurrency's rapid development is in some ways a quirk of history: launched in the throes of the 2008 financial crisis, bitcoin offered an alternative to a system—the existing financial system—that was blowing itself up and threatening to take a few billion people down with it. Within a few years, an entire counterculture movement formed around cryptocurrencies, and it has continued to revolve around them. Without that crisis painfully exposing the flaws of the world's financial system, it's hard to say where bitcoin would be today. As that crisis recedes, will the impetus to adopt a digital currency recede with it?

No one can claim to know how all of this will shake out. So, while we won't be making predictions, we will speculate on the prospects for cryptocurrency, examining *what might be* while recognizing and detailing reasons why it might *not* be.

•   •   •

You may be skeptical. That's fine; we were, too. We both started covering the markets in the 1990s. We saw the dot-com boom, and the dot-com bust. We saw the housing boom, and the housing bust. We saw the financial crisis, and the global recession, and the euro crisis, and Lehman Brothers, and Long-Term Capital Management, and Cyprus. We interviewed any number of true believers from the tech world who thought they had the next big thing. You go through enough of that, and you're instinctively skeptical.

So we were both doubters when we first heard of bitcoin. Money that isn't backed by a government? That's crazy! (In our experience, that is the single biggest sticking point for most doubters; they simply can't get past it.) But our curiosity got the better of us. We started writing about it, and talking to people about it, and writing some more. Eventually, the enormity of bitcoin's potential became apparent to us, and in some ways this book mirrors our own trip through the world of cryptocurrencies. It's an extension of our curiosity.

We are telling the story of bitcoin, but the thing we're really trying to do is to figure out exactly where cryptocurrencies fit into the world, to put this big puzzle together. It's a big story, one that spans the globe, from the high-tech hub of Silicon Valley to the streets of Beijing. It includes visits to the mountains of Utah, the beaches of Barbados, schools in Afghanistan, and start-ups in Kenya. The world of cryptocurrencies comprises venture-capital royalty, high school dropouts, businessmen, utopians, anarchists, students, humanitarians, hackers, and Papa John's pizza. It's got parallels with the financial crisis, and the new sharing economy, and the California gold rush, and before it's all over, we may have to endure an epic battle between a new high-tech world and the old low-tech world that could throw millions out of work, while creating an entirely new breed of millionaires.

Are you ready to jump down the bitcoin rabbit hole?

One

FROM BABYLON TO BITCOIN

The eye has never seen, nor the hand touched a dollar.
—Alfred Mitchell Innes

For any currency to be viable, be it a decentralized cryptocurrency issued by a computer program or a traditional "fiat" currency issued by a government, it must win the *trust* of the community using it. For cryptocurrency advocates, as we'll learn in the chapters ahead, the whole point is to offer an alternative model for that trust. They tout a system of payments in which the payee no longer has to trust "third-party" institutions such as banks or governments to assure that the payer can deliver the agreed-upon funds. Instead, cryptocurrency systems imbue trust in an inviolable, decentralized computer program that is, in theory, incapable of defrauding people. None of this, however, gets cryptocurrencies off the hook. They, too, must win people's trust if they are to become relevant.

Trust is at the core of any system of money. For it to work, people must feel confident that a currency will be held in the right esteem by others. So before we get into bitcoin's dramatic arrival on the scene and its bid to change the way we think about such things, we need to explore that notion of trust in more depth as it has evolved through history. This chapter will takes us on a journey through the evolution of money, one of society's most remarkable yet poorly understood inventions.

Let's start with some basic questions. What is money? What does it represent? How did society come to develop such a system for exchanging goods and measuring their value? As is the case in any field of study, figuring out how something functions is often best approached by examining cases where the system hasn't worked.

One contemporary example of failure is in Zimbabwe, whose defunct multibillion-denominated notes now sit on the desks of financial reporters and currency traders as reminders of how unhinged things can become with money. But the strongest lesson Western societies have learned comes from farther back: the 1920s Weimar Republic. The German government then, unwilling to court military conflict with its European neighbors but also reluctant to upset the public by raising taxes, instead printed money to cover its debts and sent the German mark into an uncontrollable downward spiral. As inflation soared beyond anything anyone could imagine, children would arrange stacks of worthless 50-million-mark notes into playhouses. The greatest caution from all this comes from the knowledge that this monetary and governmental chaos opened a door to Adolf Hitler.

Germany was eventually converted into a functioning, generally peace-loving nation, showing that it's possible for democratic societies to restore order after a bout of financial and political chaos. The same goes for Brazil, which, through tough monetary-policy reforms, put the 30,000-plus percent inflation rates and the dictatorship of the 1980s behind it. But some places live with monetary dysfunction almost permanently, and for this they pay a formidable price. We learn from their experience that the core problem is not irresponsible policy decisions by money-printing central banks, though this is the mechanism through which hyperinflation is created. Rather, the problem stems from a deep-seated breakdown of trust between the people who use a currency and the monetary authority that issues it. Since those monetary authorities are ordinarily national governments, this breakdown reflects a society's flawed relationship with its government. It's an instructive way to think about what a cryptocurrency, with its "trustless," math-based system of monetary exchange, offers as an alternative.

If citizens don't trust a government to represent their interests, they won't trust its currency—or better put, they won't trust the monetary system around which their economy is organized. So when given a chance, they will sell that currency and flee it for something they regard as more trustworthy, whether it's the U.S. dollar, gold, or some other safe haven. When this dysfunction is entrenched, such beliefs are self-fulfilling. The loss of value in its currency depletes the government's financial resources, which leaves money-printing as the only means to pay its debts and ensure political survival. Pretty soon, the excess money in circulation further undermines trust, which can give way to a vicious cycle of spiraling inflation and plummeting exchange rates.

Argentina has lived with this broken relationship for a long time. A century of failure to resolve the trust problem explains why Argentina has been through many, many currency crises and why it has fallen from the world's seventh-richest country at start of the twentieth century to rank around eightieth in mid-2014.* That puts Argentina, which for many years portrayed itself as a beacon of European sophistication in a continent of New World backwardness, more or less on par with Peru.

Mike knows a thing or two about Argentina. He picks up the story from here:

My family and I spent six and a half happy years in Buenos Aires. Sunshine, steak, Malbec wine, all rounded out the experience. The best part was the friends we made, people who would give you bear hugs, who would always go out of their way to help you, and who thought nothing of taking a four-hour lunch to engage in intense conversation about the state of the world.

But mine was a love-hate relationship with their country. For all of Argentines' passionate embrace of friends and family, their society is in permanent war with itself. This is manifest in the dog feces littering Buenos Aires' sidewalks, the graffiti defacing the city's once-beautiful Parisian architecture, and the interminable traffic jams caused by drivers' unwillingness to yield. The country's bitterly divided politicians espouse competing, outdated ideologies, but in truth their loyalty lies with a unifying, corrupt political machine installed by Juan Domingo Perón half a century ago. Peronism's system of Machiavellian power has trapped Argentine politics in a vicious cycle of shortsightedness and corruption, a failure that has left Argentines with zero faith in their governments.

---

* Based on nominal Argentine GDP in pesos, converted into dollars at the going black-market rate in August 2014.

Skipping taxes is the norm—why, people reason, would you pay crooks who will steal your money? In this environment, self-interest constantly asserts itself, and the country's deep pool of natural resources is squandered. Bucketloads of money will be made in short multiyear bursts by those savvy enough to ride the pump-and-dump schemes that masquerade as policies, but that only means the economy rushes toward an oncoming cliff every ten years or so.

I arrived in Argentina in early 2003, right when the last such crisis was barely subsiding. Banks, which were still keeping people's savings frozen in accounts that the government had forcibly converted from dollars to devalued pesos, had enclosed their downtown branches in steel plates to protect their windows from the barrages of bricks hurled by protesting depositors. When I left, in 2009, the next crisis was brewing. Inflation was pushing toward 30 percent a year, but the government was openly lying about it, an act of bad faith that only made Argentines mistrust their currency further and led businesses to hike prices preemptively in a self-reinforcing cycle. People were slowly withdrawing pesos from banks again, and the government was putting restrictions on purchases of foreign currencies, which, predictably, further undermined confidence in the national currency. This cat-and-mouse game, as Argentines knew too well, was destined to end badly.

It also complicated our departure. A year after we left, we finally sold the lovely apartment we'd bought in the leafy Buenos Aires suburb of Palermo. But when I returned to the city to close the deal, it was now difficult to get our money out of the country.

Residential property in Argentina has historically been sold in dollars—literally, physical greenbacks. History has made Argentines wary not only of their own currency but also untrusting of checks, money orders, and anything else that requires the provision of credit. Cold, hard dollar notes can cut through all that. That's what our buyers wanted. Reluctant to wire money to our U.S. bank account, they wanted to do things in that old, traditional way. They suggested we complete the deal at a *casa de cambio* in Buenos Aires' financial district, one of numerous exchange houses that help Argentines manage their complicated financial affairs. The *casa* would take our newly obtained cash and credit our U.S. bank account. Easy. What could possibly go wrong?

With shiny lobbies, Victorian-style insignia, and names conveying integrity and security, these exchange houses can look similar to bank branches, but they operate outside the banking system. In addition to swapping dollars for pesos, they manage a network of accounts to shift money overseas at lower costs than bank wires. Now that the government was placing strict constraints on offshore bank wires, these places were in demand as convenient, extra-official money transmitters.

I was uncomfortable with this seemingly shady option, but Miguel, my closest friend in Buenos Aires, told me that this *casa de cambio* handled his business weekly in fully legal transactions with his associates overseas. He trusted them fully and I trusted him. This was the way things worked in Argentina: you trusted whom you knew, and to resolve your business affairs you frequently leaned on those relationships more than you relied on the legal protection of a corrupt judicial system.

To be certain, however, I had an initial meeting with the *casa de cambio,* in which I was assured that the overseas transfer would be fully verifiable and legal since we would have the real estate contract as backing documentation. Satisfied, I agreed to the buyers' plan. Days later, eight people gathered in one of the firm's sealed rooms to complete the closing: two staff members; the couple buying our apartment; one of their fathers, who was paying for it; an official *escribano,* or notary public, required by law to authenticate the settlement; Miguel; and I.

A man entered carrying ten or so stacks of bills and gave them to me. I'd never had my hands on so much cash, but was still struck by how small $280,000 packed down to. It was counted by staff from the *casa de cambio,* after which the signing of the transfer papers began. Once the *escribano* had ascertained that all was aboveboard and fair, he and the father bid their farewell, and arrangement of the international transfer began.

Suddenly, a staff member rushed in, hurriedly yelling, "You can't do it! This has to go through the banking system!" I looked at Miguel and it sank in. The staff had misunderstood a key documentation requirement under the ever-changing Argentine foreign-exchange laws. Or perhaps—the conspiratorial Argentine in me was now kicking in—we'd been set up. Why did this happen after the *escribano* had left and signed over the property? Either way, we were stuck.

These were my options: I could gather up the money, our life savings, and take them across town—in what? A backpack? In my socks?—and hope the local bank branch at which I'd maintained a mostly inactive account to pay my electricity bills would happily accept a massive stack of dollars, convert them into pesos for a fee and at a confiscatory exchange rate, and then immediately convert them back into dollars for another fee and at another expensive exchange rate before wiring the money to my bank for a bigger fee. We were facing security risks and some $15,000 more in costs, assuming the plan would fly with the bank's compliance officers. Or, the *casa de cambio* offered, I could complete the deal with them but without the documentation I'd been promised. The institution would take my money, and an agent overseas would deposit the equivalent amount in our account—but I would receive no paper record of ever having handed over any money. I would have to trust—*that word again*—that twenty-four hours later I could call my bank and ascertain that the money was en route to my account, although it would take three days before the credit actually registered.

I thought hard about it. Tens of thousands of Argentines did such transactions every day. To them, it was, ironically, a more trustworthy method of exchanging value than dealing with a banking system that had repeatedly robbed them of their savings. More important, Miguel, the man I trusted more than anyone else in Argentina, trusted this group of people to look after his accounts. He did so in a more transparent, aboveboard way than I was contemplating, but he dealt with them regularly. Indeed, the *casa de cambio* needed to maintain Miguel's trust. The confidence of their customers was the foundation of their business. On the other hand, I was unlikely to be a repeat customer.

I reluctantly agreed to the unofficial transaction. All the exchange house could give me as a "record" was a cutoff piece of ticker tape from a basic, receipt-printing calculator that simply showed numbers in text: the total amount transferred, minus the fee, and nothing else. I misplaced it that very evening.

The next day, Miguel and I returned to the *casa de cambio* to get a special code with which my bank could trace the payment. The gentleman we were supposed to meet wasn't there, or so we were told by the security guard looking after the heavily fortified entrance to the back offices. As my blood pressure spiked, I asked to see another staff member. The guard called him, then relayed his message: the money was already deposited in my account. I was incredulous. It was supposed to take three days. My heart raced. Were they lying? Had I been swindled? Nervous beyond belief, I went outside to the street and called an agent at my bank. The reply came back: "Yes, Mr. Casey, the money is in your account." Miguel and I bear-hugged.

We tell this story because it illustrates the link between trust and money, which is in turn critical for understanding cryptocurrencies and the notion that they substitute trust in a government money-issuer with trust in a computerized algorithm. (In this sense, calling bitcoin "trustless" is inaccurate, even though it's a convenient descriptor all the time.) You need some kind of model of trust to run a monetary system. Bitcoin seeks to address this challenge by offering users a system of trust based not on human beings but on the inviolable laws of mathematics. Its own trust challenge lies in the fact that not many people are filled with confidence by the overall image of bitcoin—its sense of insecurity, its volatility. To many, too, math is kind of scary, as is the notion that computers, rather than human beings, are running things—though applying such concerns to bitcoin alone would betray an ignorance of how computerized our fiat-currency-based financial markets have become.

In places such as Argentina, where confidence in political institutions is weak, the trust problem is resolved by elevating the trust that society holds in families, friends, and reputation-based relationships. Unfortunately, this is exceedingly inefficient. Such circles of trust are too small for any economy that has a complex network of economic interactions outside of small communities, let along one that purports to be integrated with the rest of the world. What's more, the system gets stretched to the breaking point when a crisis prompts everyone to rush for the exits and dump their untrustworthy pesos.

Solving this problem is what cryptocurrencies purport to do. They are marketed as such because no government-run monetary system is perfect. Argentina might be an extreme case, but as the events of 2008 showed, every other nation's model is also vulnerable to breakdowns of trust.

To comprehend why trust is so important to money, and before we delve into the workings and grand promise of cryptocurrency, let's take a trip through history and explore competing theories of money that have developed over the centuries. We hope that by its end you will have an idea of what money actually *is*. You'd think the answer to that would be simple by now, with people having used the stuff for millennia. But in reality, the practice of exchanging money lies so deep in the cultural evolution of society that we give it little thought.

In his recent and provocative book, *Money: The Unauthorized Biography*, Felix Martin argues that to focus on money as a "thing"—the commodity, or "metallist," conception of money, which we will come to later—is to miss the powerful, civilization-building force that this invention unleashed. Calling money a "social technology," he declares that "currency is not itself money. Money is the system of credit accounts and their clearing that currency represents." Conceived this way, we see how money allowed for a new form of social organization beyond tribalism. It provided a universal value system, which meant that power structures in prehistoric tribal communities, where order was maintained through the threat of violence at the hands of whoever was the most brutally powerful, could give way to something that allowed all members of society, not just the physically powerful or connected, to thrive. Wealth as defined by the accumulation of this new, abstract measure of value would become the benchmark of power. It completely changed the rules of the game.

Martin takes us to the Micronesian island of Yap to make his point. He describes a unique currency system that baffled early European visitors, consisting of stone wheels known as *fei*. These were quarried three hundred miles away and were as large as twelve feet in diameter. After an exchange, it was frequently too inconvenient to transport these giant limestone rocks to their new owner, so they were often left in the possession of the previous owner. Yet the mutual understanding throughout Yapese society was that ownership rights to these hefty symbols of wealth could pass from one person to another in a series of transactions, thereby providing a means of settling outstanding debts. Martin cites an account by the young American adventurer William Henry Furness III of how one *fei* sank into the ocean en route from Babelthuap but was still recognized as an exchangeable unit of currency for its new owner.

The *fei* system shows how far society can come in creating abstract notions of value and power. This concept plays out to varying degrees as societies come to recognize the universal, if fictional, value of money and is incredibly powerful. So we see the arrival of money in ancient Greece and its groundbreaking system of democracy coinciding with a break from the society that preceded it, where the power structures were far more brutal and limiting. Money opened up the world, created possibilities.

But as powerful as this communal act of accepting the abstraction has been to the development of civilization, it's a struggle for our individual minds, which prefer material explanations for how the world works and especially for understanding value. We see this now as an older generation that grew up with bricks-and-mortar stores and physical goods struggles to comprehend why someone would buy "virtual goods"—such as those sold in online games such as Second Life—much less pay for them with "virtual currency." We can intellectually have the "What is money?" discussion, but we have a hard time getting past this deep-seated notion of a dollar or a euro—or even a bitcoin—as being a thing of material value in its own right.

Go ahead and remove a dollar bill from your wallet—or do the same with a euro or a pound or a yen—whatever you're carrying (assuming you still carry cash). Take a good hard look at it. Now, ask yourself, what's it worth?

Your first answer, no doubt, would be something like "Duh, one dollar." But ask yourself again. What's it really worth? What intrinsic value does that *thing* in your hand, that 2.61-inch-by-6.14-inch piece of paper, hold?

Well, you could write on it if you so desired, turning it into a note-keeping device, albeit one extremely less efficient than a perfectly good notepad. Drug users have found it to be a useful tool for snorting cocaine, though that's possibly more of a "because you can" statement than a reflection of the dollar bill's special utility for this purpose. The point is, as a material object little is unique about a dollar, or about any country's banknote. It's not a table or a hammer or a car or a source of food, or even a service rendered such as a haircut or a taxi ride.

To some extent, this piece of paper is similar to those other pieces of paper that play an important role in our society: written contracts. Contracts are not valuable for the material they are written on, but because a court will recognize the words contained on them as evidence of an enforceable agreement. They are proof of a deal between two parties and afford each party an optional claim on our legal system to get the other one to abide by its terms. But what exactly is the contractual agreement conveyed by a dollar? Sitting there in your hand, it contains a rather obscure promise, an affirmation from the U.S. government that it owes you the value of that dollar. Uncle Sam promises to accept those IOUs and net them off against the debts that you in turn owe him—your tax bill, fees, fines, etc.—but for all the excess dollars after that, your take-home pay, he's never going to make good on that debt. When you think about it, how could he?

In a strict legal sense, a dollar constitutes a claim on the banking system and, by extension, on the U.S. Federal Reserve, which establishes the rights of all future holders of that banknote when it first issues it to a bank. The bank and the Fed are obligated to recognize your claim according to the value it purports to represent. Put simply, if you deposit a dollar note in your account, the bank acknowledges that it owes you that dollar. But this really doesn't resolve the problem of what gives the dollar its value. In a practical sense, its value depends entirely upon everyone else consensually recognizing that your dollar can be redeemed for an agreed-upon measure of goods and services. If that consensus were to disappear, your dollar's value would fall away very quickly, as Argentines know from the frequent phases of hyperinflation they have endured. By this measure, a dollar's value does not reside in the fact that a bank acknowledges a liability to you or that the bank registers a claim on it with the Fed; rather, it hinges on society's willingness to accept it in settlement of a debt. This consensus measure of value is very different from saying the dollar note has any *intrinsic* value.

Here the gold bugs, as the finance world affectionately calls advocates of gold-based monetary systems, step up to the plate, promising to solve our intrinsic-value problem. Gold, they say, is real currency, for it is hard, tangible, durable, and intrinsically valuable. Under their beloved gold standard, you could indeed take your dollar to the U.S. government and insist that it make good on a debt to you, by demanding the return of the same value in gold.

But that raises another question: What is a bar of gold truly worth? What indeed is *its* intrinsic value? The gold bugs point to myriad uses for this highly durable, fully fungible metal. Its properties are impressive: It is both malleable and enduring. It can be melted down and re-formed but never loses any of its luster. Its electrical conductivity is used in circuit boards, while dental implants have drawn on its strength and resistance to tarnishing. But let's be clear: these uses are not why we assign value to gold. Indeed, they account for only a tiny portion of its supply. No, the assigned value has much more to do with its perceived beauty, exemplified by its traditional use in jewelry, in architecture, and in housewares. Here, though, we still end up in a circular argument about gold's value: it's hard to distinguish our innate appreciation for gold's beauty—as we might appreciate a flower, for example—from our idea that a gold ornament conveys value, that it signifies wealth, prosperity, and prestige.

Gold is scarce. It's been said that all the gold mined throughout history would fill up only two Olympic-size swimming pools. But scarcity is relative, and relevant only if there is demand. Countless material objects could be deemed scarce, but they don't have value because they are not in demand. All that matters is that people want gold. But why?

We're going around in circles. The only conclusion we can reach is tautological: gold is valuable as a currency or investment because we believe it is valuable (which is the same reason for valuing money itself). Gold's value as currency is an abstract social construct. Yet—that value itself is real. It has a real impact on the world. Through history, blood has been spilled, lands have been conquered, and nations have been built and destroyed in the pursuit of this shiny material thing. All of that illustrious and at times ugly history stems from the fact that societies from very early on recognized gold as an excellent, practical currency and store of value, one that fulfilled a host of key qualities needed for that monetary purpose: it was scarce, durable, divisible, portable, easily verified, and fungible—i.e., its qualities did not change from unit to unit, such that one store of gold was substitutable for another of the exact same weight. Those qualities led societies everywhere to collectively agree that gold would be acceptable as currency. It's that agreement that gives it its value. Once again, though, this does not mean gold has *intrinsic* value.

The centuries-long debate over the nature of money can be reduced to two sides. One school sees money as merely a commodity, a preexisting thing, with its own inherent value. This group believes that societies chose certain commodities to become mutually recognized units of exchange in order to overcome the cumbersome business of barter. Exchanging sheep for bread was imprecise, so in our agrarian past traders agreed that a certain commodity, be it shells or rocks or gold, could be a stand-in for everything else. This "metallism" viewpoint, as it is known, encourages the notion that a currency should itself be, or at least be backed by, some tangible material. This orthodox view of currency is embraced by many gold bugs and hard-money advocates from the so-called Austrian school of economics, a group that has enjoyed a renaissance in the wake of the financial crisis with its critiques of expansionist central-bank policies and inflationary fiat currencies. They blame the asset bubble that led to the crisis on reckless monetary expansion by unfettered central banks.

The other side of the argument belongs to the "chartalist" school, a group that looks past the thing of currency and focuses instead on the credit and trust relationships between the individual and society at large that currency embodies. This view, the one we subscribe to and which informs our understanding of cryptocurrencies, recognizes the presence of an implicit, societywide agreement that allows monetary exchange to perpetuate and debt and credit to be issued and cleared. This negotiated solution, a project that's inherently political, *is* money. It's not the currency. The currency is merely the token or symbol around which this complex system is arranged. (*Chartalist* comes from the Latin *charta*, which means "token.") This conception of money has naturally attracted economists who believe policymakers have a role to play in managing the economy for the betterment of society, a group most prominently represented by apostles of John Maynard Keynes. Yet it is also ingrained into the rigid structure of any cryptocurrency monetary system, one that allows no room for Keynesian interventionists yet depends just as much on a collective agreement that the digital currency can be accepted in the settlement of debts.

This philosophical division sustains a core debate over cryptocurrencies and how or whether to regulate them. The rise of bitcoin has attracted many with the metallist mind-set, a group led by libertarians and anarcho-capitalists, who want government to get its greedy mitts out of the money supply. Overlooking the intangible nature of bitcoin, they've treated the digital currency as a scarce commodity, a *thing* to be "mined" and stored, a thing whose mathematically proven finite supply ensures that its value will rise and outstrip that of unlimited fiat currencies such as the dollar. Yet many other cryptocurrency believers, including a cross section of techies and businessmen who see a chance to disrupt the bank-centric payments system, are de facto chartalists. They describe bitcoin not as a currency but as a payments protocol. They are less concerned about its appeal as an intrinsically valuable thing and more with the underlying computer network's capacity to rearrange the rules of trust around which society manages exchanges of value. They see money as a system for settling and recording debt obligations.

These distinctions will prove important as we examine in later chapters the future for cryptocurrencies, but for now let's take a step back into the millennia-old past and trace the events that brought us to this point.

When did money begin? The answer to that question depends on which camp you belong to. Discussing the history of money almost inevitably veers toward a discussion of the *historicity* of money because it's impossible to describe its evolution without also describing how it has been conceived.

On that basis, the metallism crowd views the beginnings of money through the eyes of Aristotle, who wrote, "When the inhabitants of one country became more dependent on those of another and they imported what they needed, and exported what they had too much of, money necessarily came into use." This view, that once trade became so complex that barter would no longer cut it, was resurrected two millennia later by Adam Smith in *The Wealth of Nations*. Smith described the New World communities of Peru and elsewhere as burdened by barter until the genius of European coinage was introduced. Smith's view was critical to the conventional wisdom that we've sequenced from barter to money to debt. He argued that as human beings divided labor according to their talents, they produced surplus goods to trade but were trapped by the failure to meet what economists call a "coincidence of wants." In other words, there was no guarantee that the next guy wanted to swap his sheep for all the arrowheads you needed to off-load. So, an easily exchangeable, clearly distinguished commodity was chosen to function as the agreed-upon standard to facilitate exchange. This commodity became money, and by this thinking it was a *thing* in its own right, carrying an intrinsic value. Once we thrust it into this role, money opened the doors to all other tools for exchanging value, including the creation of debt.

If you're a chartalist, your historical starting point is very different. First, you dismiss the barter story as myth. You draw on the writings of dozens of twentieth-century anthropologists who have visited places where currencies weren't used; anthropologists who claim to have found no evidence that these peoples ever engaged in barter, at least not as the primary system of exchange. Instead, these societies came up with elaborate codes of behavior for sorting out their various debts and obligations. Debt, in other words, came first. The anthropologist David Graeber hypothesizes that specific debt agreements likely evolved out of gift exchanges, which generated the sense of owing a favor. After that, codified value systems may have emerged from the penalties that tribes meted out for various wrongdoings: twenty goats, say, for killing someone's brother. From there human beings started to think about money as a system for resolving, offsetting, and clearing those debts across society.

Given this wide divide in their worldviews, the metallists and the chartalists ascribe very different motivations to the prominent role played by the state in the minting of currency through the ages. To the metallists, governments simply played an endorsement role, authenticating the quality and quantity of metal in each coin. But to the chartalists, the state evolved to become the ultimate clearinghouse for debts and credits through its monopoly power over taxes, which could only be paid in the coin of the realm.

Regardless of where loyalties lie across this divide, most agree that the first recorded monetary system appeared in Mesopotamia, modern-day Iraq, around 3000 B.C., when the Babylonians began using silver and barley as universal mediums of exchange and units of value. It coincided with development of the Code of Hammurabi, one of the oldest surviving pieces of writing and the first example of a ruler setting down laws, also in Mesopotamia. That code included a set of payment rules by which debts could be settled with either silver or barley. Based on those instructions, early-day Mesopotamian accountants would keep records of transactions in society, doing so via specialized indents in clay tablets. Their record-keeping employed a relatively easily understood cuneiform style that supplanted hieroglyphics, an ancient writing system that had been limited to royalty and high priests.

Over time, people's standing in society would become defined by a monetary measure of their ability to obtain items of value, more so than by a record of their capacity to inflict suffering. Money, then, made human settlements less vulnerable to bloodletting and chaos. As the world became more orderly, it was also more conducive to trade. From there developed the great ancient civilizations: Mesopotamia, Greece, and, most successfully, Rome.

The rise and fall of these civilizations coincided with money, and whether one fueled the other or vice versa is impossible to disentangle. The Roman Empire's vast reach was synonymous with its coins being legal tender across huge swaths of Europe and the Middle East. The political instability that ultimately weakened it and led to its collapse was in part generated by the deterioration of that currency's purchasing power, as Rome succumbed to repeated bouts of raging inflation, worsened by Emperor Diocletian's flawed attempts at price controls. After Rome's fall, the Dark Ages descended on Europe and the continent lost its feel for money. Some fitful efforts to revive the practice didn't find traction until the Renaissance. As the historian Niall Ferguson reminds us, the return of money at that time and the related invention of banking by the Medici families of Florence financed an explosion in world trade and helped pay for the architectural and artistic revival of the era. This put Europe on track to the modern era, in which money and finance have long been at its center.

For most of its history, currency has been issued by those who rule, be they kings or democratically elected governments. Consistently, those rulers have stamped their authority—both figuratively and literally—on their currency, reminding citizens of the deep connection between money and power.

Staters, the gold-and-silver-alloy coins thought to be the first minted currency, from the kingdom of Lydia in what is now western Turkey, are notable for bearing a lion's head. This insignia makes King Alyattes, presumed to be the sovereign behind these coins, likely the author of a millennia-long association between artwork and currency—a practice that has lent these otherwise impractical, inanimate objects great power, significance, and perceived value.

Look at your dollar bill again. Note on its face side the ornate borders and leafage running along the edge and enclosing George Washington's head, as well as the seals of the issuing regional Federal Reserve Bank and the U.S. Treasury Department. See on the reverse the even more elaborate border designs engulfing the words *ONE* and *In God We Trust,* along with the two sides of the great seal of the U.S. government, the outstretched eagle on the right and the Eye of Providence perched above a pyramid on the left. This baroque intricacy is difficult to replicate and so helps keep counterfeiters at bay, as do embedded fibers, watermarks, and metallic strips. But just as important, the compelling imagery is simply impressive. It's filled with semiotic noise that denotes authority and order.

Artistic imagery on currency helps us engage in the metallist fiction that a money token has intrinsic value. Yet neither can we escape the symbolism of state power associated with it. Countless monarchs after King Alyattes used similarly dramatic symbols to put their stamp on coinage. It gave the coin authenticity but also functioned as a kind of royal branding, an advertisement of the omnipresence of the realm. We are reminded that money and power are inseparable.

The sovereign's capacity to issue money afforded one specific benefit: the creation of seigniorage, the ability to profit directly from the issuance of currency. These days, seigniorage arises because of the interest-free loan that a government obtains by printing money on comparatively worthless pieces of paper. But when currencies were associated with particular weights of precious metals, monarchs exploited this power through more overt methods. Many would "clip" gold or silver coins to melt down and redeem the value of the shavings. Before coins were assigned specific numerical values, rulers would "cry down" the arbitrarily assigned value of a specific coin—by declaring that it could now buy less of a certain useful commodity or contribute less than previously to the settlement of a tax bill. In effect, the monarch was recanting on a promise to honor IOUs at a certain rate and so got to write off his or her debts in accordance with the size of the cry-down. By the same token, the crown's subjects were forced to come up with more money to meet *their* debts. Needless to say, this irritated the moneyed classes—the nobles and aristocrats, and later the bourgeoisie, for whom the periodic, arbitrary depreciations could amount to significant reductions in wealth. As their resistance to this abuse of power grew, it gave rise to some of the great liberal ideas upon which modern democracy is based, ideas behind the founding of America and the French Revolution. Now, this same spirit of resistance is found among bitcoin evangelists.

Well before the medieval European monarchs even had coins to tinker with, Chinese emperors were taking money into its next phase of technological development. In the ninth century A.D., when regions such as Szechuan experienced shortages of the bronze they'd used for coins, government officials began experimenting with letters of credit that functioned as a form of paper money. Then, in 1023, the Song dynasty issued full-blown sovereign-issued paper money across the kingdom.

Centuries earlier, China had already staked out the intellectual position that money was a part of the "machinery" of government, as imperial scholars put it. They described it as a means "to preserve wealth and goods and thereby regulate the productive activities of the people, whereupon they brought peace and order to the Subcelestial Realm." This is diametrically opposed to the metallists' commodity view of money. But it's not far from the modern central bankers' approach to money-supply management. The difference is that the Chinese rulers' responsibility came not from legislation but by a moral code made possible by the Confucian view of the emperor as the benevolent apex of a coherent "Middle Kingdom" society. Today, China grapples with competition to its sovereign currency, the yuan, due both to its citizens' demand for foreign national currencies such as the dollar and to a fledgling but potentially important threat from private, digital currencies such as bitcoin. As it navigates these shifts and exerts itself on the world economic stage, the country's leaders still appear constrained by this ancient concept of state-run money, which in modern societies has ceased to sound so enlightened.

In Europe, the struggle between the private and the public sectors for control over money has a much deeper history. While many complained about the sovereign's constant debasement of the currency, some developed work-arounds that created de facto private money.

The most impressive of these was the *écu de marc,* a form of currency developed and used by the merchant bankers who emerged out of the Italian Renaissance and which allowed them to expand their business internationally. Based on an exchange rate jointly agreed upon by the merchants, the *écu de marc* allowed the exchange of bills of trade from different banks in different countries. The sovereigns in each land kept tight control over their currencies, but this banking class was developing its own international exchanges through the wonder of credit creation. The bills financed shipments—say of shoes made in Venice to an importer in Bruges—that enriched the manufacturer, but the real profit spinner lay in trading the paper, a lesson that would be passed down through generations of bankers to the present day. For the first time, a private-sector community had come up with a de facto money-creation machine. This direct threat to the sovereignty of monarchs gave rise to a political clash as the kings and queens of Europe feared that their monopoly powers were being eroded.

But the bankers didn't want political power per se. They were pragmatic businessmen, as they would prove to be for centuries afterward. They would use the leverage of private money to strike deals with governments, sometimes as a threat but mostly to wheel and deal their way to more wealth.

This negotiation between the sovereign and these new private generators of money would find its ultimate expression in the royal charter that founded the Bank of England in 1694. The BOE, as bond traders in London's City now call it, was formed at the behest of King William III, who wanted to build a world-class navy to take on France, then the dominant power on the high seas. The privately owned bank—the BOE was not nationalized until after the Second World War—would lend the Crown £1.2 million, a massive sum for its time, and could then issue banknotes against that debt, effectively relending the money. Then, to give the banknotes value as a de facto currency, the sovereign agreed to accept them in payment of taxes. In one fell swoop, the agreement created a form of paper money effectively endorsed by the sovereign, established fractional-reserve banking—a guiding principle of modern banking that allows regulated banks to relend most of the money they take in as deposits—and conceived the idea of a central bank. The Bank of England had, in effect, been given a license to print money.

This was the dawn of modern banking, and it had a profound impact on England's economy. The new financial architecture not only helped the kingdom develop a top-class naval fleet with which it would rule the world from pole to pole, but also financed the industrial revolution. Bank credit effectively became money, since it was deemed to be backed by the sovereign. This new definition of money has prevailed ever since. Eventually the new British system extended to the point where ordinary citizens had checking accounts and companies could draw upon all manner of bank-based credit instruments to finance everything from day-to-day operations to large-scale projects. With the banks now able to lend their good names to a borrower as guarantors, these instruments became tradable, which quickly gave rise to a bond market.

This financial leap gave an exponential boost to liquidity in the economy, but also to risk. While it created prospects for entrepreneurship and capital creation never before imagined, it also gave rise to what we now refer to as systemic risk. Losses in one institution could ripple out and destabilize many others through the interconnections of the financial system. It made that system vulnerable to swings in that all-important social commodity: trust. The ever-expanding web of interlinking credit relationships meant that textile mills could finance their expansion and, later, steam engines could be built, but not every textile mill made money and not every businessman was good for his debts. While debt defaults and bankruptcies in isolation were a normal part of risk-taking, once the financial system became so interconnected, they could have domino effects. If a lender began to worry that a large debtor might not meet its payments, that lender might withhold funds from other borrowers, who would now face financing troubles, breeding even wider concerns. Thus flimsy public trust could break down. When it evaporated, credit could suddenly dry up, leaving perfectly good debtors unable to make good on their loans, which would in turn make their creditors' finances shaky, further depleting the public pool of trust. This is how financial crises were made. Money had been liberated but it had also become more dangerous.

This financial instability gave rise to fierce debates over how to control it, and over how to define the very nature of money. The debates would continue over time and would shape our modern monetary and financial systems. It all came down to different views on how best to protect trust in the monetary system.

On one side sat the believers in gold. Based on the ideas of liberal thinkers such as the great English philosopher John Locke, the gold standard was promulgated in the late-seventeenth century. People felt it was necessary to tie money to this tangible *thing* to prevent governments and their new partners in a profiteering banking sector from destroying the public's money. The model succeeded in keeping inflation down, which helped protect the savings of the wealthy. However, the monetary constraints and the elevated value of gold typically also led people to hoard money in crises, which shut down credit growth, generated bankruptcies, and led to unemployment. At such times, the biggest victims were inevitably the poor.

As financial systems lurched from crisis to crisis, a competing conception of what constituted the money supply and of what made it grow or contract emerged. It focused not on how to constrain the ability of a government to issue currency, but on how to manage banks in their unique role as creators of private, credit-fueled money. Spearheaded by Walter Bagehot, the nineteenth-century editor of *The Economist,* this thinking led to the development of modern central banking. Backed by sovereigns that could never go bankrupt, central banks such as the Bank of England were to be the "lender of last resort" to overcome crises of confidence. They would agree to freely lend to solvent banks if their access to liquidity dried up in periods of financial stress. Although Bagehot's rule was that such loans would carry a penalty interest rate and were to be secured with good collateral, the commitment turned central banks into a critical backstop to help overcome financial panics. The gold standard still existed, but this expansive new role for central banks alarmed its advocates, who had an aversion to unfettered banking power and freewheeling debt.

Such concerns rang strong in the United States and made it slow to enter the central-banking game. The country went through a century and a half of changing currency regimes—sometimes centrally issued, other times with multiple, competing currencies circulating under issuance from commercial banks under various state and federal arrangements. Eventually the dollar became dominant, but not until a series of severe financial panics in the late nineteenth and early twentieth centuries did Americans decide they needed a central bank; the Federal Reserve was founded in 1913. A hundred years later, the Fed is still a source of controversy and derision from some quarters, blamed by its detractors for creating asset bubbles and inflation, but applauded by its supporters, who claim, for example, that without its massive interventions the crisis of 2008–9 would have been much worse.

Clearly, the Fed's record in keeping the financial system on the straight and narrow is far from perfect. Exhibit A: the Great Depression. Exhibit B: Lehman Brothers. Still, the twentieth century has also shown the dangers of constraining central-bank discretion. During the Depression, the gold standard tied the Fed's hands at the worst moment by limiting its ability to create new money and offset a deep-frozen banking sector's aversion to issuing loans. This exacerbated the downturn. Eventually, the gold peg was abandoned, freeing central banks of that straitjacket and helping to restore liquidity to a financially starved global economy.

After World War II, governments again professed a longing for a firm monetary anchor and, in particular, a central pole of stability for a distressed international economy. Britain—led by the economist John Maynard Keynes—wanted an internationally based solution to be run by the newly created International Monetary Fund. But in the end, the United States, as the only major power not devastated by war and with its currency now globally dominant, called the shots. The U.S. dollar became the central pole around which the global economy would function. It remains so today.

The pact signed at the Bretton Woods Conference in 1944 repegged the dollar to gold and then got the rest of the world to peg their currencies to the dollar. Foreign governments holding reserves in dollars were given the right to redeem them in gold at a fixed rate. It worked as a financial stabilizer for two and half decades, but by the late 1960s the system's own constraints—in this case imposed directly on the Fed—made it unsustainable. America, hobbled by the cost of the Vietnam War and unable to compete with cheaper foreign producers, couldn't bring in enough foreign currency with which to restock its gold reserves and so started to run out of them as countries such as France demanded that their dollars be redeemed for the precious metal. Feeling trapped, President Richard Nixon took the stunning step on August 15, 1971, of taking the dollar off the gold peg. He did so with an executive order that was designed in consultation with just a handful of staffers from the Treasury, the Fed, and the White House.

The "Nixon Shock" rendered the Bretton Woods agreement pointless. By 1973, once every country had taken its currency off the dollar peg, the pact was dead, a radical change. Governments could now decide how big or small their country's money supply should be. Finally, it seemed, the chartalists' moment had come. In this new age of fiat currencies, trust in money would become a relative and fluctuating thing: Do you trust the dollar more than the pound, or vice versa?

Nixon's audacious move had one desired effect: it drove down the dollar's exchange rate and sparked a revival in U.S. exports. It also created huge new opportunities for Wall Street to develop foreign-exchange trading. Now that the dollar was no longer pegged to gold, banks could take their credit-creation business global, setting the stage for the globalization of the world economy. It also paved the way to the multinational megabanks that would become too big to fail . . . and all the problems these would create.

The happy experience of American manufacturing's post-1971 revival was quickly marred by a new, entirely predictable scourge. Coupled with the oil blockade imposed by petroleum-exporting nations in 1973, the weaker and unhinged dollar immediately generated inflation; as the value of the world's most important currency sank, the price of all the goods and services it bought rose. (It's always useful, we feel, to remember that prices are two-way concepts; there's the value of a good in dollar terms, but there's also the value of a dollar in terms of how much of a good it can buy. When the value of one falls, the other by definition must rise. That's the essence of inflation.) This time the inflationary outbreak was accompanied by high unemployment, confounding economists and adding a new, ugly word to their lexicon: *stagflation*.

Raging prices continued through the 1970s, paving the way for a new financial hero: six-foot-seven Paul Volcker. The feisty chairman of the Federal Reserve vowed to break the back of inflation even if it meant driving the economy back into recession, and with a series of painful interest-rate hikes that's exactly what he did. Memories of that period, where inflation drastically eroded the value of the dollars in people's pockets and then forced them into a painful economic contraction, are still so strong among a certain generation that they feed the appeal of scarce, independent "currencies" such as gold and, as we shall see, bitcoin.

After Volcker's tough love, things improved enormously, at least for a time. A period known as the Great Moderation set in for industrialized countries, with low, predictable inflation and steady growth marred only by the occasional, short-lived recession. Europe embarked on a truly bold new experiment to create a currency union, one that for the first ten years of its existence seemed to be a rip-roaring success, as the euro miraculously conveyed Germany's sound credit rating to once backwater countries such as Ireland and Spain, which enjoyed a tremendous influx of capital and an unprecedented housing boom. Emerging markets such as Brazil, Russia, and Indonesia took in a flood of investment, albeit tinged with periodic crises. This was the brave new world of fiat-currency global finance. But, as we now know, it contained within it a destructive flaw.

On Wall Street, new technologies and a mantra of deregulation encouraged by the free market's apparent victory over communism pushed a financial-engineering machine into overdrive. Here the gremlins were being hatched. All looked good on the macro front—inflation was low, growth was solid—but economists were focused on the wrong things. The real buildup of risks didn't appear in the mainstream economic numbers. Heck, the risks weren't even in the routine banking system of deposits and residential and commercial loans. They were hiding in an obscure and hard-to-comprehend realm known as the shadow banking system.

There, as we now know, weirdly bundled pools of mortgages and credit-derivative contracts, all with a nominal value in the hundreds of trillions of dollars, left hedge funds, banks, pension funds, and other institutions on the hook to each other in a complex, intertwined network that no one could ever hope to comprehend. As if learning from the Renaissance merchant bankers, Wall Street had again found an effective way to take sovereign money and multiply it many times over through a form of private money built on debt. But it was happening in an area that was far more thinly regulated than the traditional banking system. When it finally dawned on people how important this shadow system was, it was too late. With the collapse of Lehman Brothers, this fragile edifice came tumbling down.

The Great Moderation had carried a curse. Not only did it foster a false sense of security, but also it caused us to forget our responsibilities as a society to use our political process to change unwelcome economic circumstances. Everyone from voters to Wall Street traders to congressmen to the president wanted to believe the financial system could be left in the hands of the Fed. The highly respected Paul Volcker gave way to the "maestro," Alan Greenspan, who was equally revered, until he wasn't. In 1999, we turned a blind eye to the repeal of the Glass-Steagall Act, which had barred the merging of commercial and investment banks ever since the Depression, and so blessed the emerging banking behemoths to hijack every lever of power. When the system blew up in their faces, they pulled their last lever: taxpayer-funded bailouts.

Six years on, we are still a long way from fixing this system. Wall Street's lobbyists continue to finance a huge part of Congress's political campaign needs, giving them undue influence over reform. In part that's because we are still letting central bankers do our dirty work, allowing the drug of easy money to keep things afloat while Washington locks itself in acrimonious, self-interested gridlock. The Fed's zero-interest-rate policies and more than $3 trillion in bond-buying, along with similar actions from its counterparts in Europe and Japan, have forestalled disaster. But little has been done to resolve the long-term fiscal imbalances in the United States or to restructure a financial system dominated by the same TBTF (too big to fail) banks. The structural flaws of the European monetary system, with its untenable split between its political and monetary functions, are still firmly in place even after having been exposed when Greece, Ireland, Portugal, Spain, and then Italy all plunged into crisis from 2010 on.

Meanwhile, in an entirely globalized economy in which the dollar is the currency of the world, not merely that of the United States, the limitations of a monetary policy dictated by domestic political imperatives have also been exposed. So much of the money created by the Fed's relentless bond-buying, all of it intended to boost the U.S. economy, simply escaped overseas to create unwelcome bubbles in developing countries' housing markets and to fuel tensions over what some described as a "currency war." All might appear calm, as it did at the time of this writing, but make no mistake: our global monetary system still has serious problems.

The history of money reveals a central challenge: how to design a system that most effectively facilitates the exchange of goods and services and generates prosperity while preventing the institutions that manage that system from abusing the trust that comes with that role. Whether bitcoin or other cryptocurrencies represent a viable solution to this challenge remains to be seen. The first step will be for them to be accepted widely as viable money; that is, to become trusted themselves as a means of expanding exchange and prosperity.

One familiar benchmark says that for a currency to become money it must function as a medium of exchange, a unit of account, and a store of value. Dollars can be used to buy things all around the world; they are used to measure the value of pretty much anything; and most, if not all, people believe their savings will be more or less protected over time if they are denominated in dollars. While bitcoin is currently used as a medium of exchange by various people to buy and sell things, few use it as a unit of account. Merchants that accept bitcoins invariably list their products' prices in the national currency of the country in which they are based. As for a store of value, the speculators who've bought bitcoin in the hope of future gains certainly believe it has this feature, but for most people its volatility precludes it. Bitcoin's price in dollars soared 8,500 percent in the first eleven months of 2013, but then lost two-thirds of its value in the following six months. Who would put their life savings in that thing?

But the more important question is whether cryptocurrencies can *become* money. That's where the insistence that money must be backed by something "real" must be put away. What matters is whether it has utility. Ultimately, does it enhance our ability to engage in exchange, commerce, and human interaction? By that score, bitcoin has something to offer: a remarkable capacity to facilitate low-cost, near-instant transfers of value anywhere in the world. We think this will eventually make this technology—if not bitcoin itself—widely sought after. Maybe then it will become money.

You could say a currency is money when everyone agrees it is money. To achieve that rather difficult, tautological proof, bitcoin must attract believers. Its earliest adopters have employed strategies straight out of our monetary history. These range from choosing a symbol that resembles those of other currencies—most commonly shown as a *B* with dollarlike lines through it—to, as anthropologist Bill Maurer has noted, imbuing the digital currency with the myth of physical, tangible value by using the term *mining* to describe the work done to mint bitcoin.

But the early adopters have a bigger challenge, and that's to build a much larger community of users around bitcoin. The community that has embraced bitcoin, initially consisting of as few as two people, has already grown substantially in numbers as well as in motivations for embracing it. If we apply the chartalists' view that money is a social phenomenon, then this ongoing community expansion represents nothing less than a currency's endeavoring to *become* money.

Two

GENESIS

What is needed is an electronic payment system based on cryptographic proof instead of trust.

—Satoshi Nakamoto

October 31, 2008, 2:10 P.M., New York time. The several hundred members of an obscure mailing list comprising cryptography experts and enthusiasts receive an e-mail from somebody calling himself Satoshi Nakamoto.* "I've been working on a new electronic cash system that's fully peer-to-peer, with no trusted third party," he writes flatly. His brief text directs them to a nine-page white paper posted at a new Web site that he had registered two months earlier, which describes a currency system he calls bitcoin.

The paper explains, in clear but dry text accompanied by illustrations, equations, code, and footnotes, this system of digital "currency." It's certainly not a currency as almost anybody in mainstream society would understand the word. "We define an electronic coin as a chain of digital signatures," Nakamoto writes. "Each owner transfers the coin to the next by digitally signing a hash of the previous transaction and the public key of the next owner and adding these to the end of the coin. A payee can

---

* The true identity of this person, or even group of people, is a well-kept secret. For simplicity's sake, we'll refer throughout the book to the founder of bitcoin as a single male person and by the name chosen by that founder.

verify the signatures to verify the chain of ownership." (If, like most people, you're not familiar with the science of computer encryption, that might sound like gobbledygook—although by the time you're done with this book we hope such phrases will sound less daunting—but it was familiar stuff to the cryptography enthusiasts Nakamoto was targeting.) He explains the various features, including the clever way he gets around the necessity of a third-party intermediary, a bank or other financial institution, to stand behind and guarantee transactions.

He's describing a system of online exchange that uses encryption to allow two parties to exchange tokens of value without divulging vulnerable information about themselves or their financial accounts. It is intended to operate outside the traditional banking structure and allows people to send digital money directly to each other—peer to peer, as the concept of middleman-free commerce is known. No banks or credit-card companies are needed. No payments processors or other "trusted" third parties are involved. In effect, it is a form of digital cash. The bitcoin revolution has begun. Most of those first invited to join it don't realize it.

Among the close-knit cryptography community invited to review Nakamoto's work were members of the Cypherpunk movement, a loose association of tech-minded activists who had first gained notoriety in the 1990s with their efforts to use cryptographic privacy tools to force radical political and cultural change. This effort bore some fruit: transparency crusader Julian Assange and his activist publishing organization, WikiLeaks, grew out of this movement. To the Cypherpunks, the idea of an anonymous digital cash system was nothing new. It had been one of their first big ideas, but no one had yet turned it into something viable. Several had attempted to build digital cash systems, one had even got tantalizingly close, but ultimately no system had reached any kind of critical mass, and the cause had fizzled out.

At first glance, bitcoin seemed similar to its predecessors. Its software protocol—the guiding set of communications instructions that underpin the system—followed the same basic ideas of those earlier iterations. Like them, it used public-key encryption to allow people to safely share valuable strings of code. A transfer could take place whenever a person used a secret, private key—a string of closely guarded code—to digitally authenticate a paired, publicly available key attached to a store of the currency. Also like those predecessors, it sought to establish a set of unbreakable rules by which a decentralized network of computers would collaborate to maintain the monetary system's integrity. Similarly, anyone with a computer could become part of the network, help to maintain its integrity, and pay and get paid in a common digital currency. It pursued the same goal as its predecessors: to dispense with the existing model for global payments and currency issuance and replace it with one where individually owned computers, rather than banks, were in charge of keeping the system honest.

All other attempts to do this had failed. Was there any reason to believe that Nakamoto's system would be better at generating mass appeal? Most members of the group who bothered to read the white paper didn't see such a reason. San Francisco programmer Ray Dillinger's dismissive response reflected the views of many within the cynical community: "People will not hold assets in this highly inflationary currency if they can help it."* James A. Donald, a cryptography enthusiast who writes a libertarian-leaning blog, applauded the attempt to achieve the "old Cypherpunk dream" and allowed that the world "very, very much needed such a system." But he predicted that Nakamoto's system would never be sufficiently robust or scalable to support transactions from "hundreds of millions of people." John Levine, a subscriber to the cryptography list best known as the author of *The Internet for Dummies* book, said hackers would ultimately be the "killer" of Nakamoto's system since "the good guys have vastly less computational firepower than the bad guys."

Nakamoto was undeterred. He knew the system contained two major breakthroughs: an inviolable universal ledger, which he dubbed the blockchain, against which anyone could verify the validity of transactions, as well as a unique set of monetary incentives to encourage the network's

---

* Dillinger's characterization of bitcoin as "highly inflationary" is the opposite of how it is generally now, more than six years later, described; because it is programmed with a hard-fixed, finite supply of bitcoins over time and a diminishing rate of issuance, it's mainly thought of as a deflationary currency.

computer owners to keep that ledger up-to-date. This is what would keep his system honest while fighting off hackers.

Nakamoto had already set up a new Web site at bitcoin.org, a domain he'd purchased around the time of the release of his white paper. But to take his system to the next level, he knew he would have to crank up the software program that he'd also quietly developed and thus generate the very first bitcoins. Come the New Year, he turned on the computer algorithm and started "mining" his new currency. As we'll learn in chapter 5, *mining* is a bit of a misnomer because the most important activity that these networked computer "miners," or nodes, do is to confirm transactions. The "mined" bitcoins are a reward for being the first miner to solve a randomly generated, mathematically complex puzzle that must be completed before transactions can be confirmed. That reward gets increasingly difficult to attain as miners add ever more computational power to the network.

Nakamoto, "Node Number One," loaded the software onto his desktop computer and started the program, its simple interface laying out the results of his efforts in a grid. Since no one else was on the network but him, with no giant string of third-party transactions to work through and confirm, indeed no transactions at all, he could just let his PC sit there and deliver bitcoins into the digital "wallet" he'd created for himself. Today, the network comprises users all over the world, and the computational difficulty in mining has so risen that it requires vast, expensive, dedicated machines in special warehouses to do the job profitably. But back in those early days of 2009, producing bitcoins for his own account was as easy as downloading a copy of, say, Microsoft Outlook and running it on a desktop.

In firing up the software, Nakamoto created the Genesis Block, the first-ever fifty-coin "block" of bitcoins. Over the following six days he would mine many more bitcoins—as many as forty-three thousand if the software worked to its inbuilt schedule of a block every ten minutes. As of August 2014, a haul that size would be worth about $21 million, but back then they were worth exactly zero, since Nakamoto had no one else to transfer them to, no way to "spend" them. If a hallmark of a currency is utility, at this early point bitcoin had absolutely none. He had to get others to join.

So, six days after the Genesis Block, Nakamoto went back to the same cryptography mailing list and told its readers that the program was ready: "Announcing the first release of bitcoin, a new electronic cash system that uses a peer-to-peer network to prevent double-spending."

And then the sales pitch: "It's completely decentralized with no server or central authority."

The people on that list, who'd heard claims like this before, had no evidence yet that Nakamoto had overcome the challenge that had felled his predecessors: preventing fraudulent transactions—the so-called double-spending problem—when no central authority is charged with authenticating transactions. As much as these people hated to admit it, you seemed to need a central authority like a bank to do that.

Once again, the response to Nakamoto's overtures was tepid. Some immediately homed in on a criticism of bitcoin that would become common: the energy it would take to harvest "bitbux" would cost more than they were worth, not to mention be environmentally disastrous. Jonathan Thornburg, an astronomy professor at Indiana University, saw a larger political challenge: "No major government is likely to allow bitcoin in its present form to operate on a large scale."

Even within such a small group, the people on that initial mailing list constituted an eclectic readership: an astrophysicist, a software engineer, a security consultant, and a science-fiction writer. They were not all fixated on the idea of digital cash. Some were focused on computer-security issues. A clutch of them were trying to perfect encrypted e-mail. Most simply weren't interested in what seemed to be a reprise of an old, failed idea.

"We were all saying, 'Uh-huh, yeah, sure, fine,'" said Levine, laughing, five years later. "We had no idea bitcoin would be a big deal." In fact, until we asked him to reflect on that exchange, Levine had forgotten he'd been on the mailing list at all, forgotten he was present at the launch of bitcoin, and forgotten that he was among those doubting the now-legendary and still-unidentified Satoshi Nakamoto. Still, he can take comfort in that he wasn't the only one. What's clear from the debate is that many felt that Nakamoto was digging for a bone they'd long ago given up on finding.

It probably didn't help that nobody had any idea who Nakamoto was. The members of the Cypherpunks and cryptography communities were preoccupied with anonymity, but they weren't anonymous to each other. Most of them used their real names, and those who didn't were typically well known by a nickname. As in their real-world counterparts, in online communities reputations are built up by sustained involvement. Before October 2008, nobody had ever heard of Satoshi Nakamoto—he simply showed up one day—which may be one reason he wasn't taken seriously. "He was just a name on a mailing list," notes says Russ Nelson, an engineer from Clarkson University, who recalls having no impression at the time about whether bitcoin would succeed, or the impact it would have.

"It might make sense just to get some in case it catches on," Nakamoto suggested to one underwhelmed observer. As marketing goes, this was a subdued pitch but it spoke to a crucial objective. Nakamoto's masterpiece would come to nothing unless others used it. It had to start somewhere. Nakamoto had been bitcoin's first adopter. Now, he needed a second. Thankfully for him—and for bitcoin—somebody raised his hand.

Hal Finney, then fifty-three, was a top developer at PGP Corp., a company founded by Phil Zimmermann, a legendary crypto-activist whose ironically named Pretty Good Privacy software helped popularize public-key encryption systems for e-mail. An early and prominent member of the Cypherpunk movement, Finney is credited with various cryptographic innovations himself, including anonymous remailers, which allow people to send e-mail without revealing its origins. In 2004, Finney had unveiled his own version of e-money. Like bitcoin, Finney's model used the "proof of work" coding functions introduced in 1997 by British cryptographer Adam Back to verify and quantify the processing power needed to create and underpin the value of a digital currency. (This is a critical concept—albeit a rather complicated one—for understanding how computer owners "mine" cryptocurrencies, bring them into existence, and imbue them with value by expending resources on their creation—hence "proof of work." For now, it's enough to understand the basic concept: in return for the valuable privilege of creating a currency, a computer must be required to perform a task, in this case a difficult computational undertaking. We will come back to it, gently, when we explore how cryptocurrencies work in chapter 5.)

Finney's connection to digital cryptography locates him within the core scientific endeavor behind bitcoin and all cryptocurrencies, as well as with their philosophical underpinnings. For much of history since its beginning in ancient Egypt, the essence of cryptography—which takes its name from the Greek words for "hidden" and "writing"—lay in encoding language to keep a message secret. Cryptography systems were mostly used by governments and militaries to protect state secrets and deceive enemies. But in the digital era, when the science was exponentially enhanced by computing machines that could develop elaborate algorithms to perform ever-more-complex encryption tasks, it found much broader application, evolving into a way to protect personal, corporate, and government information. In this era, the fraternity of cryptographers developed varying, if not divergent, political strains. Some treat the practice as a commercial endeavor, finding employment in companies and government. But others seem to find it a higher calling, associating it with a struggle for freedom and individual rights. The anarchic, libertarian-leaning Cypherpunks were among the more radical of these activists; others were more subdued and communal. But all those who used their knowledge in a bid to enact social change saw cryptography as a tool to enhance individual privacy and to shift power from big, central institutions to the human beings who live in their orbit. Hal Finney belonged to this tradition—his prior exploration of cryptocurrency demonstrated this. So did Satoshi Nakamoto, at least from what we know of his/her/their writings. So does bitcoin.

Thus perhaps naturally, Finney was intrigued by Nakamoto's system. He soon wrote to this unfamiliar newcomer to the mailing list via the e-mail address Nakamoto had supplied. (The bitcoin founder has used at least three e-mail addresses publicly; naturally, all are encrypted and untraceable to the person who set them up.) By January 10, 2009, the pair had begun working together in what would be a two-week, intensive project. They would collaborate and share notes by e-mail as they strove to get the bitcoin protocol up and running. Following the founder's instructions, Finney downloaded the software, created a wallet, and started mining a block of fifty bitcoins. That made him Node Number Two. As a test, Nakamoto also transferred a store of ten coins to his new correspondent's wallet. Finney became the first person to receive bitcoins from someone else.

The early e-mail exchanges between this pair provide a fascinating look into the dawn of bitcoin. At the same time, it's striking how mechanical their interactions are. No personal information is exchanged, no details that might provide clues to Nakamoto's identity, just the matter-of-fact back-and-forth of two experienced coders who also understand monetary systems.

Finney started off trying to download version 0.1.0 of the bitcoin software—and it crashed. His interlocutor was surprised—he hadn't experienced such problems. Nonetheless, Nakamoto went back in, "reproduced the bug," as he put in one e-mail response, and found the faulty lines of code. "It was absolutely the last piece of code to go in," he wrote. "I'm really dismayed to have this botch up the release after all that stress testing."

They pressed on through version 0.1.2, encountering a problem when Finney's "node" stopped replying to messages from Nakamoto's computer, which required more debugging. Back and forth it went, with both running their computers heavily, pushing the new software to find its flaws. Version 0.1.2 crashed, version 0.1.3 crashed. Nakamoto was running through the code, finding problems, getting error messages, and then rewriting and retooling the code all over again.

"It definitely looks like 0.1.3 solved it," Nakamoto writes back after another crash. He then makes an interesting comment that's difficult to decipher without him or Finney to provide context, but which could, intriguingly, suggest others had secretly downloaded the software and were also trying to mine bitcoin but weren't communicating with these two early adopters. "It was getting so there were so many zombie nodes, I was having a hard time getting a reply to any of my messages," Nakamoto said. Then the system crashed again.

Finney kept his computer mining bitcoin for a week or so and ended up with a stash of about a thousand coins. But the software was no Microsoft Word program. It required constant, intense data-crunching, and he feared it might harm his computer. What's more, the device's loud fan, pushed to the extreme, was beginning to get on his nerves. So he stopped mining and never tried it again.

In March 2013, when his coins were worth around $60,000, Finney would look back on his decision to stop mining: "In retrospect, I wish I had kept it up longer, but on the other hand I was extraordinarily lucky to be there at the beginning. It's one of those glass half-full, half-empty things. . . . Hopefully [those coins] will be worth something to my heirs." Finney's future estate had become important ten months after he had first made contact with Nakamoto when he was diagnosed with ALS— amyotrophic lateral sclerosis, or Lou Gehrig's disease, a degenerative condition that slowly destroys the body. Bound to a wheelchair when we made contact, he was by then completely dependent upon machines to keep him alive, and on his wife, Fran, and son, Jason, for help with daily living. Then, in August 2014, he died. One of bitcoin's pioneers was gone. In keeping with his wishes and with Fran Finney's description of her husband as having "always been optimistic about the future," Finney's bitcoin stash is now funding the cryogenic freezing of his body at a facility in Arizona, all in the hope he might one day be revived if and when ALS is eradicated.

In truth, no matter how many references bitcoiners make to "Big Bang" events or "Genesis" moments, this project did not just explode in a void. Like any brilliant invention, it is built on the backs of prior inventors. Writ large, cryptocurrencies can trace their roots through centuries of innovations that have enhanced human communication and exchange, from the printing press through the telegraph to the Internet. But, as noted above, the most direct precursor came from the Cypherpunks. The group had got its start in the early 1990s as a loose affiliation of cryptography wizards who shared a common concern about the creeping erosion of privacy and individual disempowerment in modern society. (This was long before anybody had used the term Big Data, had heard of Edward Snowden, or had an inkling the U.S. National Security Agency was spying on everybody.) One of this group's first ideas was a digital currency.

The movement was founded in September 1992, when a mob of ponytailed coders were invited to the Oakland home of cryptography enthusiast Eric Hughes. In the United States, Arkansas governor Bill Clinton was about to defeat President George Bush in the November election, ending twelve years of Republican rule. In Europe, the Maastricht Treaty was in the middle of a messy and contentious ratification, though its passage that year would eventually lead to the formation of the European Union in 1993 and the euro six years later. The founding of the Cypherpunks

also came on the cusp of the Internet age, with the group's de facto headquarters appropriately located in the San Francisco Bay Area, which would
become the hub of the online revolution. E-mail and Web sites had not
yet gone mainstream, but Apple and Microsoft were laying the necessary
groundwork as new, easy-to-use personal computers found their way into
American homes. The moment was ripe for this new movement, an evolutionary offshoot of the sixties counterculture, but one more singularly
focused on matters of individual liberty than the social causes of that era.

The coders at the inaugural meeting were greeted by Tim May, a
bearded anarcho-libertarian and former Intel physicist who, when he
wasn't reading or writing sci-fi, spent most of his waking hours conceiving of new cryptographic tools of rebellion. May read them his "Crypto-
Anarchist Manifesto," which opened with a play on Karl Marx's famous
manifesto: "A specter is haunting the modern world, the specter of crypto-
anarchy." The essay went on to predict that "just as the technology of printing altered and reduced the power of medieval guilds and the social power
structure, so too will cryptologic methods fundamentally alter the nature of corporations and of government interference in economic transactions." This, in these coders' minds, was all positive. It would subvert
the nexus of power they believed central banks and government agencies
maintained in the service of their clients in corporate America. It would
re-empower citizens.

May's essay would become the Cypherpunks' founding document.
Despite their common core beliefs, they were an eclectic bunch. Some held
day jobs at U.S. tech firms and used anonymous identifiers to keep their
online lives separate. Others, such as May, had dropped out of mainstream
employment. The group's name was partly drawn from *cipher,* which in
cryptography refers to an algorithm used for encryption or decryption,
and partly a play on *cyberpunk*, the sci-fi genre and popular generic pro-
tagonist character of that era. But *Cypherpunk* was also intended to
sound more nuanced and subtle, distinguishing the group's behind-the-
scenes movement from the brash hackers of William Gibson's novels,
though they were no less radical in their intent for change.

Guided by the principle that in the digital age protecting privacy
would be crucial for maintaining an open society, the Cypherpunks set
their active minds to creating tools to allow people to maintain

anonymity. They would share these ideas via a common e-mail list, whose archive is now a vital artifact in the history of cryptographic activism. One product they developed was the Cypherpunk version of an anonymous message remailer, which hid the identity of a person sending an e-mail and prevented the recipient from replying to it, all in the name of stopping governments or corporations from snooping on people's daily communications. Other products had more subversive objectives—for example, May's audacious BlackNet project, a precursor to WikiLeaks, which solicited secret information with the promise of encryption and payments in untraceable digital money. A few products were downright scary. Jim Bell, who like May was formerly employed by Intel, proposed an anonymous market for assassinations. The idea was that people could anonymously contribute to a bounty that they would pay to have a particular influential person killed, the assumption being that the market would put a greater price on the heads of those most egregiously abusing a position of authority.

All of this—the good, the bad, and the ugly of the Cypherpunks' idea bank—would go into the intellectual soup from which bitcoin would emerge. The currency's and its supporters' embrace of anonymity and of the libertarian principles of freedom from central authority were almost a reincarnation of this nineties movement's principles. Notably, it would also attract some of the dark, antisocial strains that ran through the Cypherpunks' mailing list. In November 2013, bitcoin was featured as the in-house unit of exchange for a new, encrypted Web-site-based assassination market set up by someone under the samurai pseudonym of Kuwabatake Sanjuro. Upon its launch the public figure with the biggest bounty on his or her head was Fed chairman Ben Bernanke.

But most significant, at least in retrospect, the Cypherpunks themselves were some of the earliest purveyors of cryptocurrency ideas. In the exchanges on Cypherpunk bulletin boards around that time are various references to such ideas and the occasional full-blown project. As mentioned, Hal Finney dabbled in designing such a system. So too did another Cypherpunk mailing-list subscriber to whom Nakamoto would reach out years later: Wei Dai, a cryptography expert and enthusiast whose interests run from math to cryptography to philosophy. Six years after that first meeting of the Cypherpunks, Dai released b-money. As with bitcoin, it would highlight anonymous peer-to-peer transactions, and a ledger shared with each participant in the network would keep track of the transactions. Around the same time, Adam Back, another Cypherpunk, came up with a proof-of-work system called hashcash. It was designed in response to the first wave of Internet spam—the purveyors of which had, ironically, been given cover by the anonymous remailers developed by Hal Finney and others. These spammers were starting to fill people's in-boxes with ads for Viagra and penis enlargement. Back's solution was to force computers to do expensive work before giving them permission to send information, requiring any that sought to flood a network with messages to incur heavy operational costs, all without applying a monetary fee.

Nakamoto would explicitly use Back's proof-of-work system as the foundation for bitcoin's mining computational-difficulty program and would cite Wei Dai's work in his white paper. The bitcoin founder was clearly impressed by b-money, but was determined to overcome its limitations, including its punitive system for enforcing honesty among the network of computer owners. In b-money's model, each contributor to the network had to deposit money into a special account that could be used for fines or rewards for proof of misconduct. It's not hard to imagine this solution having drawbacks in incentivizing cooperation. How does a community mete out punishment without a central enforcement agency to do so? Who would adjudicate? Bitcoin's solution was to make it all about rewards, not punishment.

Nakamoto makes no mention, however, of bit-gold, another cryptocurrency developed by Nick Szabo, a computer scientist, law scholar, and all-around Renaissance man. Szabo's wide-ranging interests are laid out in his *Unenumerated* blog, where an eclectic trove of essays draws from economics, computer science, politics, anthropology, and law. Wei and Szabo had communicated and worked off each other's ideas. But although Wei says he told Nakamoto of Szabo's project, the latter is never mentioned in the bitcoin white paper, nor in the subsequent e-mails and chat-room postings by its author. That, along with some linguistic forensic work that finds similarities between Szabo's and Nakamoto's writing styles, has led some to speculate that the blogger and the presumably pseudonymous bitcoin founder are the same person. Whether Szabo's ideas, which are shaped by a libertarian bent common to the bitcoin subculture, directly connect him to Nakamoto in one way or another, they deserve recognition within the broad body of intellectual thought upon which the first truly successful cryptocurrency was built.

None of the pre-bitcoin e-money proposals came as close to being put into practice as those of David Chaum, the highly innovative and influential cryptographer who was something of a high priest to the Cypherpunks in their heyday in the 1980s and 1990s—even though he didn't share their anarchist tendencies. Even before the Cypherpunks had got started, this former professor at New York University and the University of California at Santa Barbara had claimed at least seventeen patents, was the author of dozens of groundbreaking papers on the use of digital technology and cryptography to revolutionize everything from money to voting, and was the founder of the International Association for Cryptologic Research. Chaum's worldview evolved through this period to combine a classic cryptographer's mistrust of centralized systems with a pragmatic assessment that the only way to change the world was to deal with the powers that be. Much of what has gone into bitcoin—the idea of a universal ledger, of encrypted accounts, and systems to prevent double-spending—have their earliest traces in Chaum's work. But what he is most known for is founding DigiCash, a company that almost took anonymous cryptocurrency into the mainstream, way back in 1990.

Based in Amsterdam, DigiCash drew from some of Chaum's breakthrough ideas on how to share monetary information, transmit information wirelessly, and manage the degree to which different people's identities could be encrypted. It came up with a digital currency system that at one point seemed to be on the verge of revolutionizing money in Europe. Chaum's brain wave was a cryptographic structure that would protect the identity of the payer while enabling that payer to irrefutably identify the payee if needed. In an interview, Chaum explained to us the great promise of this form of money, an idea that he pitched to government officials, central bankers, commercial bankers, technology leaders, and financial policymakers, anyone who'd listen. Here was a way to end corruption, organized crime, kidnappings, extortions, and bribes. "What politician would take a bribe from someone knowing they could later blackmail them?" Chaum explained. DigiCash shared some of the middleman-bypassing qualities later found in bitcoin, the same principle of peer-to-peer payments without third-party mediation. But this bitcoin predecessor's unique treatment of anonymity, not to mention Chaum's unabashedly political approach, made his project fundamentally different from the model Satoshi Nakamoto would introduce to the world in the following decade. Whereas DigiCash's anonymity powers were asymmetrical, bitcoin's were symmetrical, allowing both sides of a transaction to hide their identity behind an alphanumeric code. This lets bitcoin function as a "pirate currency," Chaum now says.

As he developed his ideas through the 1990s, Chaum deliberately sought to market them to governments and central banks—an approach that may have unsettled some of the anarchist Cypherpunks who'd positioned themselves as Chaum disciples. The ambitious cryptographer didn't care. He reasoned that central banks or their centrally regulated commercial counterparts could deliver the efficiencies and official imprimaturs needed to turn DigiCash into the groundbreaking technology it deserved to become. What's more, he could make money from doing so. He would sell DigiCash licenses to these institutions, which would issue this new digital form of money, denominated in their national currencies. Servers at those central institutions—the trusted third parties—would confirm transactions, prevent double-spending, and keep the system honest. He hoped that these institutions' embrace of his model would foster a more honest monetary system and reduce intermediary costs such as credit-card fees. That government- and bank-focused approach separates him from both the anarchy-inclined Cypherpunks of the 1990s and the libertarian bitcoiners of our age. It's why those who believe David Chaum is Satoshi Nakamoto are likely wide off the mark.

DigiCash emerged when the computer revolution was getting started. The Internet wasn't big yet, but enterprise networking was getting big, with businesses laying out interlinking cables to hook up their internal and external computer networks. In this environment, and with banks rolling out international networks of ATMs and integrated accounting systems, many leading minds in technology and finance thought the world of payments was ripe for a digital form of money that would travel across these connections. They foresaw a new way of transferring value that would tap the privacy and directness of cash but overcome that centuries-old system's security and criminality risks. Governments and central banks as well as large commercial banks and corporations all saw the promise of this new system, and Chaum quickly gained their ear. He signed a contract with the Dutch government to have drivers make toll-road payments with untraceable DigiCash; a clutch of major banks, including Deutsche Bank in Germany, Advance Bank of Australia, Credit Suisse in Switzerland, and Sumitomo in Japan, took out licenses, and the first two even began issuing DigiCash as pilot projects. Chaum had talks with Microsoft and Visa and various other big companies intrigued by how they might use the new payments system or even buy a strategic stake in it. A group called Conditional Access for Europe (CAFE), a nonprofit dedicated to creating privacy-enhanced electronic payments, engaged Chaum's company to explore a Europe-wide system to achieve that goal—this, almost a decade before the arrival of the euro. To cap it off, the investment bank Credit Suisse First Boston provided his team with a corner office on a high floor in its midtown-Manhattan offices, which Chaum would use on periodic trips to New York to discuss how stakes in DigiCash could be packaged and sold to investors. In this era, the mid-1990s, the initial public offering became the prime badge of entrepreneurial achievement. Few doubted that DigiCash would go down that same IPO route.

But then, just as quickly as it had grown, DigiCash fell apart. The IPO never happened; the talks with Microsoft and Visa subsided; the banks stopped issuing DigiCash and just let their licenses subside. Without a functioning banking system behind it, DigiCash could no longer function as an anonymous payment means for drivers on the toll roads of the Netherlands. In the end, the noncash solution for toll roads went to a model of centrally controlled, prepaid services such as the E-ZPass system in America's Northeast. This created a new monitoring tool for police officers.*

Why did a project with such promise fall apart? "I really don't know," says Chaum when asked now. However, he does believe that the new

---

* Mistrust of that system must at least be one reason that so many drivers wait in long cash-only queues at New York tollgates rather than go through an E-ZPass lane. DigiCash would have liberated them.

management that took over in 1997 contributed to the decline. That's when a team of venture-capital investors installed Michael Nash, a former senior manager at Visa, as the new CEO and moved Chaum aside. Eighteen months later, with the business opportunities that Chaum had lined up slipping from the company's grasp, Nash himself was forced out. Six months after that, DigiCash filed for Chapter 11 bankruptcy. Another view, conveyed in a 1999 report in the Dutch magazine *Next!*, holds that Chaum was an obsessive micromanager and unable to close deals, simply too difficult to deal with as the founder and main proprietor. Chaum says such views were perpetuated by his enemies and that his record of deals before the management change stands on its own.

The search for personal blame misses a bigger point, however. DigiCash, more than a simple electronic-payments solution, was cutting-edge in its cryptographic features. It protected user privacy; it removed payment-processing intermediaries and the costs that went with them; it even promised to upend power structures and end corruption. These ideas were ahead of their time. Society wasn't ready for them—or, more accurately, the banks and other interest groups that managed the plumbing of the financial system weren't ready for them. Would they ever be? These institutions didn't see the problems that David Chaum was tackling as the primary challenges of the moment. In fact, it's safe to assume that they also saw in some of DigiCash's features the kernels of a subversive threat to the system from which they prospered—banks, politicians, both.

What most interested bankers and businessmen at that time was finding an efficient way to do e-commerce, the great disruptive business model that the Internet was poised to deliver. DigiCash offered a solution to that, but it was far from the only option. There was Mondex, a U.K. company developing smart-card technology to store cashlike units on a digital chip embedded in credit- or debit cards. It was abandoned after an underwhelming pilot on New York's Upper West Side by both Chase Bank and Citibank. Credit-card companies also formed a consortium called Secure Electronic Transactions, or SET, to figure out how to make online credit-card purchases safe from hackers. And then, in 1998, PayPal was launched by Elon Musk, the serial entrepreneur now best known for his Tesla electronic car. The service allowed people to open up online accounts with the digital equivalent of dollars and send them to other PayPal users, including the new breed of low-overhead vendors using e-marketplaces such as eBay. None of these could do what DigiCash could do, but they didn't need to. The market, at least as defined by the banks that controlled the financial system, simply wanted the existing system of payments and finance to translate into an e-commerce environment. The right to privacy and the need to re-empower individuals didn't factor in this—then again, they had never done so.

The race for an e-commerce fix would be won by the same payments model run by big banks like those with which Chaum was negotiating. In other words, they ended up having no use for him. With the aid of new Web-site security solutions and third-party ratings to give consumers confidence, the infrastructure of the credit-card payment networks, with the intermediaries and transaction costs that went with it, was just bolted onto that of the Internet. Some alternatives, such as PayPal, would create a bridge for those retailers with no means of accepting card payments, but over time most would simply migrate to cards. It would provide an enormous jolt of new business for the two big bank-issued card associations, Visa and MasterCard. The banks that owned them—both card companies were at that time controlled by different consortia of banks—would enjoy a huge rush of new revenue through their payment processing and revolving-credit businesses.

Many expected the banks to control the system that would make online payments safe and fast. What's not as well known is that even within these institutions a competition was under way throughout the 1990s to determine the future of money in the digital age. How it played out would set the stage for the great crisis of 2008 and in turn foment a public backlash that would underpin the rise of bitcoin. The best example of that internal struggle was found right inside the archetypal too-big-to-fail bank, a giant institution whose problems would come to define that final crisis: Citibank.

In the 1990s, before Citibank's holding company, Citicorp, merged with Travelers Group to create a controversial multipurposed bank called Citigroup, it was led by John Reed, an MIT graduate with an affinity for technology. Under Reed's leadership Citibank had pioneered the ATM and built a state-of-the-art electronic-information service to link its vast global network of branches and customer accounts. Much of that innovation had been led by an in-house research lab whose manager, a tech whiz named Paul Glaser, reported directly to Reed. In 1990, Glaser was replaced by Colin Crook, a Brit known for developing Motorola's 68000 microchip, then used by the Apple Macintosh. Embodying the same spirit of inventiveness, the cutting-edge lab would then embark on what was perhaps its most audacious project ever: the reinvention of money.

The man who drove this project was Sholom Rosen, a technologist with a yen for cryptography who'd been hired by Glaser. Like many finance-based techies of the time, Rosen was obsessed with how to bring money into the consumer-focused digital realm that companies such as Hewlett-Packard, Microsoft, Intel, Apple, and Sun Microsystems were creating. The Internet had not yet taken off, and applications such as Napster, iTunes, and Kindle were still far off in the future, but Rosen was already imagining an era in which people would buy and use digitized music files and other forms of entertainment over their computers. How to digitize money, then, was the challenge.

Rosen came to Crook with a plan whose breadth was captured in its authoritative name: the Electronic Monetary System. This wasn't just about creating a new tool for Citibank; this would be a new form of money for the United States, for the whole world, perhaps. Crook was taken by it. So too was Reed, it seemed, who assured it a healthy budget. Top technology academics from MIT, Berkeley, and Stanford were contracted to help out, including public-encryption pioneer Ron Rivest, the R in the legendary, MIT-spawned company RSA. Consultations were made and agreements struck with major technology companies—Intel and Sun Microsystems in the United States, Acorn Computers in the United Kingdom. Rosen even paid a visit to David Chaum in Amsterdam, but decided he couldn't work with him, which only encouraged Rosen more to develop his own e-cash system from scratch.

As with DigiCash and later with bitcoin, Citi's e-cash model would be composed of independent currency units. Users wouldn't merely be transferring balances between accounts within a closed system such as PayPal's, but could exchange full-fledged digitized dollars with anyone, anywhere, as if they were cash. Also like bitcoin and other cryptocurrencies, Rosen's project ran off a permanent ledger of transactions and allowed for the digital dollar to be cut into smaller pieces so that commerce could occur in whatever denomination was required. Citi's e-cash was in this sense a disruptive, disintermediating, peer-to-peer currency. It wouldn't need the extensive network of communications that underpins credit-card payments, so transaction costs would be kept low, providing gains for both consumers and businesses and making micropayments viable.

But this is not to say Rosen wanted to cut banks out from the system as, say, Satoshi Nakamoto did. Far from it. Banks would sit at the heart of his system, reflecting a deep-felt view that he'd developed on the theory of money by reading the likes of Milton Friedman and the nineteenth-century financial journalist Walter Bagehot. "You can't divorce banking from money, especially modern money," Rosen said in an interview for this book. "The actual creation of money is done by the banking system, under the guidance and the control of the Fed. When you go to borrow a thousand dollars from a bank, the bank creates that thousand dollars, not the Fed."

In fact, Rosen would take the existing model a step further. Commercial banks wouldn't merely create secondary money by lending out deposits; they would also take over the primary role of issuing actual currency, which in the United States has been handled for the past hundred years by the Fed via its twelve Federal Reserve banks. His system "was like a model from the Civil War, when the government first set up the national banking system, which made it so that every individual bank issued currency," Rosen said. The difference was that in this late-twentieth-century version, banks would be issuing digital dollars, not paper money.

Rosen and his seven or so staffers perfected their model through the 1990s. Working mostly out of closely guarded rooms in Citibank's New York offices, team members were given detachable hard drives that were locked in safes at the day's end. They used biometric-reading devices to open doors and installed infrared communications devices on their portable computers. The team, some dressing in the mode of rebellious hackers of the day, made for an oddball crew against the buttoned-down bankers they'd share elevators with. But for the close-knit group, it was an exciting time. "I felt like I was working on something really big," recalls Sandeep Maira, who joined Rosen's team shortly after graduating with a computer-science degree from Cornell.

Over time, they developed twenty-eight patents. These would describe features for Citi's e-cash that were very different from DigiCash and the cryptocurrencies such as bitcoin that would come later. For one, the digital dollars would expire after a certain time, requiring the holder to contact the bank and have them replaced—a trick designed to prevent money laundering. To keep the system secure, computers that used e-cash would be installed with specialized chips that would keep track of the monetary system.

Rosen's big break came in 1997, when the U.S. Treasury Department agreed to test this system. The U.S. government, as the biggest spender in the country, was as eager as Rosen and his employer bank to figure out where payments technology was going in the rapidly developing e-commerce environment. As part of the research into that process led by the head of a special electronic-commerce division, Gary Grippo, the Treasury ran an extensive pilot program until 2001. From what we can tell, the program has not been reported until now. Over the life of the program, the government bought some thirty thousand personal computers from Dell and accepted millions of dollars in excise-tax payments from tobacco company Brown & Williamson, completing around $350 million in transactions, all of it in Citi's e-cash. For some of those involved it would have seemed that the United States was en route to a digital dollar.

But then, just like DigiCash, Sholom Rosen's edgy project was abruptly shut down, a direct outcome of the creation of Citigroup Inc. This landmark event in U.S. banking history would presage financial disaster a decade later and set the stage for bitcoin's arrival.

In 1998, John Reed struck a deal with Sanford Weill, then CEO of financial conglomerate Travelers Group, for it to merge with Citi's mostly commercial-banking operation and form a single, universal bank—a financial supermarket, as the concept was then described by its backers. It would combine the global commercial-banking reach of Citicorp with the investment-banking prowess of Travelers' Salomon Smith Barney, as well as the latter's comprehensive insurance offerings.

One problem: the deal was essentially illegal. By any reading it ran afoul of the Depression-era Glass-Steagall Act, which decreed that commercial banks and investment banks must remain separate. The law's intent was that commercial depositors' funds should not be put at risk by an investment bank that could use them to finance speculative investments rather than the more reliable residential or commercial loans that commercial banks pursued. But Weill and Reed convinced both Congress and the Clinton administration that America needed bigger, more expansive banks to compete in the era of globalization. So, on November 12, 1999, President Clinton signed a bill sponsored by three Republicans—Senator Phil Gramm of Texas, Representative Jim Leach of Iowa, and Representative Thomas Bliley of Virginia—that put the nail in Glass-Steagall's coffin. This "historic legislation," Clinton said at the time, "will modernize our financial services laws, stimulating greater innovation and competition in the financial services industry. America's consumers, our communities, and the economy will reap the benefits of this." Clinton's signature would set things up for the biggest financial crisis the world had seen in eighty years.

Nine years later, Citigroup would symbolize that failure when it needed a $45 billion bailout from the U.S. government. But in 1999, Sandy Weill could bask atop the most powerful bank in the United States, if not the world. And his power was just beginning. The brash Wall Street dealmaker clashed with the geeky technology-lover with whom he'd agreed to a cochairman relationship. So, in February 2000, just four months after Congress had blessed their union, Weill arranged an internal coup. Reed was forced out and the requisite management shake-up was ordered.

With Reed gone, Weill set out to mark his territory and find cost savings to pay for the $70 billion tab that shareholders had incurred in the merger, at its time the biggest in U.S. corporate history. In that context, it meant nothing to shut down a quirky John Reed experiment with electronic money—especially given that credit-card payments were now being widely used online, seemingly negating the need for e-cash. By the second half of 2001, the Electronic Monetary System project was wound down. Rosen, then sixty, took early retirement. Colin Crook went off to pursue academic interests as a Wharton Fellow. Citi's e-cash idea withered and died.

Members of Rosen's team describe the decision to shutter the Electronic Monetary System project as mostly bureaucratic, a way to save money on a project that simply didn't interest Weill. But it also reflected a philosophical difference between believers in innovative projects who seek to profit by being first to market with new, cost-cutting business models, and believers in the prevailing ethos of Wall Street that Sandy Weill embodied. Wall Street banking is, if nothing else, a rent-seeking exercise. It would be inclined to preserve and strengthen centralized revenue streams such as credit-card transaction fees rather than expunge them. With the repeal of Glass-Steagall, and the waves of commercial-and-investment-bank mergers that followed Citigroup's lead—Chase Manhattan with JP Morgan, Bank Boston with Fleet Bank and later with Bank of America—this ethos was now seizing control of the American financial system. It assumed that as much money could be made from brawn, bucks, and bullshit as from brains.

Sure, these giant, new supermarket banks would hire hordes of math geeks in the following years, but rather than seeking to make the financial system more efficient, their innovations were used to monopolize information and extract excessive profits from clients who were kept ignorant about what they were buying. These math "quants" took the giant pools of home loans now sitting on their employers' balance sheets and repackaged them into highly complex, opaque, and difficult-to-value securities that were sold as safe bets. As more and more of these risky securities were purchased by pension funds, insurance firms, and other stewards of the global public's savings, the quants' securitization machine demanded more loans, which in turn led to a massive expansion of dubious lending to low-income American households.

The rest is history. Once it was shown that the underlying mortgage assets were of far poorer quality than the valuations implied by the re-packaged securities, a house of cards collapsed. Because the banks had become so very, very large and interconnected within the global financial system, governments worldwide felt compelled to put up trillions of taxpayer dollars, pounds, and euros to avoid bringing down that entire system. The rise of cryptocurrencies can properly be understood only in relation to those cataclysmic events.

On the Wednesday after the September 15 collapse of Lehman Brothers in 2008, Mohamed El-Erian, then co-CEO of the massive asset manager Pacific Investment Management Co. and at that time working around the clock to try to extract his firm from the swirling financial maelstrom, took the time to call his wife from PIMCO's headquarters in Newport Beach, California. She should go to an ATM and withdraw as much money as she could. She didn't understand why. Because, he told her, there was a chance U.S. banks wouldn't open the next day.

That frightening prospect—complete paralysis of the most important financial system in the world—was the price we paid for letting Wall Street deepen its model of centralized, rent-seeking power. The final social tab is still being tallied, but its costs go beyond what any book-keeper can put into dollars and cents. One place it is felt is in the bitter taste that's left in the mouths of citizens forced to prop up these banks. That has translated into a loss of trust in institutions generally, those of both Wall Street and Washington.

Into this world of broken trust Satoshi Nakamoto placed his bitcoin project, just one month after the Lehman collapse.

Did he choose the release date because of those events? It's impossible to know for sure. His public writings are guarded. In one forum post, Nakamoto said he'd been working on bitcoin since 2007. However, a few clues suggest that at the very least he saw in the crash an opportunity to highlight his system's advantages.

In a February 11, 2009, post on a forum for developers, he wrote, "The root problem with conventional currency is all the trust that's required to make it work. The central bank must be trusted not to debase the currency, but the history of fiat currencies is full of breaches of that trust. Banks must be trusted to hold our money and transfer it electronically, but they lend it out in waves of credit bubbles with barely a fraction in reserve." It's about as direct an indictment of the existing system as he makes. In another post, he writes with unusual élan, "Escape the arbitrary inflation risk of centrally managed currencies!"

Another clue is embedded in the code of the Genesis Block. To authenticate the time stamp of that creation, Nakamoto referenced a headline from the front page of *The Times* of London on January 4, 2009: "Chancellor on Brink of Second Bailout for Banks."

The chancellor in question was Alistair Darling, then the United Kingdom's chancellor of the exchequer, who was struggling to prevent outright collapse of the British banking system. His government had pumped

£500 billion in loans and guarantees into the banks, including £50 billion to purchase majority stakes in three giant, teetering institutions: the Royal Bank of Scotland, Lloyds, and HBOS. It wasn't enough. On January 19, the U.K. government announced another £50 billion bailout package.

These were dark days. In addition to Lehman Brothers' bankruptcy, Merrill Lynch had been rescued by Bank of America on that same weekend. Days later an implosion in insurer AIG led to a government bailout that would swell to $182 billion. Western economies began hemorrhaging jobs, stock markets collapsed, world trade ground to a halt. If somebody was ever looking for a moment to launch an alternative monetary system, the person could not have picked a better time.

Let's not forget, also, that Nakamoto launched his project with a reminder that his new currency would require no government, no banks, and no financial intermediaries, "no trusted third party." It offered the antithesis to the core problem of that moment in history. For all the technical and legal wizardry employed by Wall Street's denizens, for all the financial innovation practiced by the Street's bankers, trust was the most important element of capital markets—trust that counterparties were good for the money they pledged; trust that market prices really did reflect all available information at the time; trust that if an asset was represented on the balance sheet as being worth X amount of dollars, it actually was worth X amount of dollars. The collapse of Lehman and AIG shattered all that. Nobody trusted asset valuations, nobody trusted price quotes. Nobody trusted the banks' balance sheets. The entire machinery of the global capital markets seized up, coming to a grinding, smashing, disastrous halt, because nobody trusted anyone anymore.

In the months and years that followed, an increasing number of people would decide that perhaps Satoshi Nakamoto's idea offered a better alternative to all that.

While we have no proof that the for-profit-company-led cash initiatives of the 1990s and the 2008 banking crisis shaped Nakamoto's thinking, both underscored the reasons that cryptocurrency designers were eager for change. The message in each case was that the centralization of money is destructive and that attempts to change that from within would fail. The solution could only be true decentralization, by coming up with a brand-new, rebel monetary system. In the mind of the libertarian-inclined techies who believed in these models, it was not enough to build the kind of anonymity functions that Chaum created. Cryptocurrencies needed a purely independent model. Yet until bitcoin came along no one could figure out how to build it, mostly because it was hard to replace a centralized corporate structure in which rules can be enforced from on high with a decentralized community in which no one is nominally in charge. In the absence of a central authority, how do you get everyone in the network to cooperate? And if you can't create a collective authority, how do you stop people from gaming the system, from spending bitcoins they don't have?

Nakamoto came up with a twofold solution. One component was his breakthrough blockchain ledger. Under its design, transactions are arranged in chronologically arrayed blocks that give miners the ability to verify their contents by comparing them to the historical ledger of account balances. Once satisfied, they acknowledge their approval by moving on to create the next block and chaining it to the now-approved predecessor. This verification and chaining of the blocks, and the acceptance of each new one as the legitimate base on which to build future blocks, constitute a de facto consensus on the validity of the underlying transactions. That made it effectively impossible for a single person to "double-spend" a coin. Digital counterfeiting could at last be ruled out.

The second solution lay in the mining rewards algorithm, which created exactly the alignment of incentives needed to get the owners of the networked computers to commit the electricity and computing resources needed so that their machines would help maintain the blockchain ledger. Together, these features laid the foundation for a decentralized mechanism of trust.

But there was still a problem: Nakamoto had to create a sense of ingrained value in bitcoins, which came down to figuring out the right supply-and-demand dynamics. He addressed this by fiddling with the time schedule for the future release of coins. In the first four years, the protocol would set a fixed amount of fifty coins to be released more or less every ten minutes. It would then reduce the issuance to twenty-five coins at the end of 2012 and keep halving it again every four years after that until the supply petered out to zero in 2140, by which time a total of 21 million coins would have been released. This preprogrammed, diminishing release of a finite supply of coins created a sense of scarcity, which built a base of support for bitcoin's price that would incentivize miners to keep working with it. He knew that the ever-thinning supply of bitcoins would eventually require an alternative carrot to keep miners engaged, so he incorporated a system of modest transaction fees to compensate them for the resources they contributed. These fees would kick in as time went on and as the payoff for miners decreased. In all, it was an elegant, free-market solution to a dilemma that has dogged societies for centuries: how to align people's pursuit of self-interest with the needs of their community.

This achievement was critical for philosophical and practical reasons. Decentralization carries real benefits for a currency system that presents itself as an alternative to the dominant system that's controlled by governments and run by banks. Since there is no single point of control, no central server to coordinate the diffusely and globally spread network of computers, there is no way to shut the alternative system down. The Chinese government might bar its banks from handling bitcoin-related transaction services or declare that only the yuan be used within the nation's borders, but it can't shut down bitcoin, which resides nowhere and everywhere. The same challenge faces any government. This was appealing to a marginal but not insignificant subculture of passionate, highly motivated activists who are skeptical of central-bank-run fiat money. More broadly, it was consistent with a trend toward decentralization and individual empowerment in the broader economy, a world in which people are renting out their sofas to paying guests, selling solar-generated power back to the grid, and drawing their news from decentralized forums such as Twitter.

In this environment and faced with what Nakamoto had proposed, an increasing number of people came to trust that his system worked. Many decided it was better to trust this inviolable-algorithm-based system than the error- and fraud-prone human beings that run the large institutions at the center of the old monetary system.

Hal Finney's departure from the network of two that he and Nakamoto formed in January 2009 proved no setback for bitcoin, as others with the clarity to glean its significance quickly started to get interested. That year it would attract new users who downloaded the software to become new nodes to manage the network and mine bitcoins. To communicate, many used an IRC channel that Nakamoto had set up on the bitcoin.org site. By October, a new coder-focused IRC room had been set up online with the handle #bitcoin-dev, and the next month it was formalized under the name Bitcoin Forum. A community of bitcoiners was forming.

Every time a new person signed his or her computer up to the network, it increased the combined amount of computational power being applied to the hunt for bitcoins, as well as the total electricity consumed, the main variable input for bitcoin mining. It also meant that competition intensified for the fifty-coin batches that the system was then programmed to release, meaning that each computer node's chances of winning one would decline. Over time, this increase in network-wide computing power would also induce the core program to automatically ratchet up the difficulty of its mathematical puzzle. This was so that the increase in the combined puzzle-solving power wouldn't discover the solution too quickly and force a premature release of bitcoins. That way, the ten-minute release schedule could be adhered to over time.

For bitcoin to develop, however, it needed an alternative to mining as a way to acquire the coins. You had to be able to buy them with dollars or other fiat currencies. But at what price? So, by October of 2009, some in the community took it upon themselves to quote a dollar-based exchange rate and post it on a new Web site called New Liberty Standard. Using a calculation based on the cost of electricity for mining, its first quote was listed as BTC1,309.03 for $1. Put differently, one bitcoin was worth 0.08 of a cent. Some thought New Liberty Standard was overcharging, but at least they now had a place to buy and sell this experimental virtual asset. In what would be a hallmark of its trading in years to come, bitcoin's volatility immediately showed itself, as the price leapt 70 percent to 0.14 of a cent on November 13, only to plunge to 0.06 the next month. Still, it was fun trading these tiny tokens. Since the community was still relatively small and no one had yet figured out how to crank up his or her computer to beat everyone else in the math puzzle, the payouts were relatively evenly shared among all the miners. It was all very communal.

This would change in the New Year as Laszlo Hanyecz, a software engineer in Florida, figured out he could write software that would instruct his computer's graphics card, or GPU, to take over the mining task, which had until then been done by each miner's CPU. Engaging this more narrowly focused, higher-performance tool ramped up the computing power that Hanyecz could apply to the mathematical puzzle and exponentially increased his chances of being awarded one of the fifty-bitcoin blocks.

This caught a lot of attention. Even though each bitcoin was worth so little, the growing community began to believe that their rising value presaged future gains. Coinciding with the release of a more robust version 0.2 of the core bitcoin software and with the creation of a second currency exchange called Bitcoin Market, news that this Hanyecz guy was creaming in so many bitcoins for himself was like news of the gold find at Sutter's Mill in 1848. New hobbyists quickly joined the fray. An arms race ensued, as people turned their graphics-card-loaded home computers into mini digital-currency mints. Once these electricity-gorging machines cranked up, the network started to heat up with energy—both literally and figuratively.

As things got more frenzied and bitcoin edged slowly out of the geeky fringes of techie society to embrace a new tier of early digital gold digger, Nakamoto must have looked with wonder at what was happening. Did he celebrate or lament what he had wrought? We may never know. A year later he would disappear from the world of bitcoin.

Three

COMMUNITY

Money is like muck, not good except it be spread.

—*Francis Bacon*

On December 12, 2010, the following post appeared on the Bitcoin Forum: "There's more work to do on DoS [denial of service], but I'm doing a quick build of what I have so far in case it's needed, before venturing into more complex ideas. The build for this is version 0.3.19." It would be Satoshi Nakamoto's last message.

That was it. There wasn't any good-bye message, no noble speech. He simply stopped writing. The founder kept communicating with some of the software developers who were helping him improve and maintain the bitcoin system, but by April 2011, he'd also sent them his last e-mail. As far as we know, the last one went to Gavin Andresen, a coder based in Amherst, Massachusetts, who'd joined the group a year earlier and on whom Nakamoto had bestowed a leadership role. Much like his final Bitcoin Forum post, indeed like everything else Nakamoto ever wrote, that last e-mail was perfunctory, purposeful, lacking in virtually all sentimentality.

But if the bitcoin founder's written legacy is a body of dry, utilitarian words, his other big legacy is found in the fervent community of true believers he left in his wake. This passionate group would grow around the ideas that Nakamoto developed and the code he implemented. It is arguably his greatest creation, for, as we've argued, a currency cannot

Two versions of the bitcoin "B"

(Left) *Source: Wikipedia*
(Right) *Source: bitcoinsymbol.org*

exist without a community. In the case of an independent, decentralized currency, with no central authority to impose order on the monetary system, the human bonds that define that community are doubly important.

The markers of this community are found in much more than its members' willingness to send bitcoins to each other or to collectively mine them and maintain the blockchain ledger. They are embedded in a distinct "bitcoin culture," a way of talking and thinking and relating to each other and outsiders. The culture is burnished by phenomena similar to those that underpin more established cultures. Just as cultural signifiers such as flags, anthems, and the rousing speeches of founding fathers help people imagine an abstract sense of national identity, so, too, do icons and memes encourage members of this community to self-identify as bitcoiners and as followers of a certain, if ill-defined, belief system. Bitcoin also has its symbols—the bitcoin *B* being the most ubiquitous, although community members have debated whether it should look like a currency symbol (for example, $) or a marketing logo. Like other cultures, bitcoin also has its art, its music, even its poetry. It has also cultivated larger-than-life personalities who are recognized as "community leaders."

Tellingly, these personalities are often described as "evangelists." Similarly religious undertones are everywhere in the language and concepts attached to bitcoin: the Genesis Block label pinned on Nakamoto's first mined batch of coins; the nickname Bitcoin Jesus given to Roger Ver, now one of the community's most prominent representatives; the very idea of a "believer"; and the notion that one has an epiphany once the "truth" of bitcoin's solution is revealed. The most important of these quasi-religious ideas, however, lies in the core cultural building block that Nakamoto himself laid with his mysterious appearance in the world of cryptocurrencies in 2008 and then with his equally mysterious disappearance from it three years later. Whoever he/she/they are, Nakamoto gave bitcoin its creation myth.

The quintessential creation myth is that of Genesis, and look how far that took both Judaism and Christianity. In a far less spiritual vein, marketers have come to realize the power of creation myths and narratives. The notion that a particular business was born out of the brilliant idea of someone working against the odds helps to personalize the product and boost appeal. Such allusions are everywhere in business: Ford Motor's Model T, Coca-Cola's secret recipe, Bill Hewlett and Bob Packard's garage, Steve Jobs and the first Apple computer.

"In business, creation stories reinforce the role of the individual as a societal agent of change and speak to a core audience of customers," wrote Nicolas Colas, chief market strategist for brokerage ConvergEx, in a research piece reflecting on the importance of the mystery surrounding bitcoin's founder. "They are the bedrock for what marketers call 'brand' and the source waters for Wall Street's 'shareholder value.'"

Bitcoin's "brand" is undoubtedly tied to the founder and the mystery surrounding him, her, or it. Homages to Satoshi appear throughout bitcoin culture: the smallest denomination of a bitcoin is called a Satoshi, numerous meetups are held in places dubbed Satoshi Square, various bitcoin businesses have used the founder's name, including the high-profile gambling site SatoshiDice.

Assuming Nakamoto is a single person, you could argue that as public figure he or she no longer holds human form and has morphed into total myth. No physical person stands in front of us or is available in a YouTube video. Nobody is sitting across the table from Charlie Rose, getting interviewed by the news channels. Nobody to write a book or sign away the movie rights to his story. All we have is the specter of a reclusive genius, and a hint at the godhead of bitcoin.

Who is Satoshi Nakamoto? Techies, hobby investigators, and journalists have found this tantalizing question impossible to ignore. In pursuing it, they've all helped to further burnish bitcoin's creation myth and to imbue the cultural core of its community with a sense of wonder, genius, and greater purpose.

For all that's been written about Nakamoto, for everything he (or she or they) has written, for all the snoops who've tried to ferret him out, we know astonishingly little about him. He communicated through encrypted channels that have so far proven untraceable. His public writings are completely guarded; at no point does he divulge any personal information; at few moments does he offer anything that appears like an opinion. On occasion, he slips a British spelling into a post, which has led some to assume he's from the United Kingdom. But the spelling isn't consistent—which has led some to surmise it's more than one person writing, and therefore Nakamoto isn't a person at all but a group. Trying to grasp him through his writing is like trying to catch an eel. A body is there, but nothing to grab on to.

When we journalists come searching for Nakamoto, bitcoiners inevitably tell us to leave this person alone, to respect his or her desire for privacy. This position is ideologically both consistent and inconsistent with the founding principles of the Cypherpunks. That movement's philosophy valued privacy completely, but also expected that your identity would be sought out, which is why encryption was created in the first place.

It might even be better for bitcoin if Satoshi's identity is eventually revealed. Initially, the absence of an identifiable founder meant enforcement agents couldn't find Satoshi and shut down his fledgling project before it gained traction. Now it's at a different phase. More than six years into bitcoin's existence, with a global economy having formed around it, the project is looking to undertake the ultimate community-expansion exercise and embrace the wide, all-encompassing "mainstream." For that exercise, the lack of transparency over bitcoin's founding is a hindrance. It feeds doubts in the minds of government officials and lawmakers, making friendly regulation that might smooth bitcoin's development a harder sell for cryptocurrency lobbyists. The same goes for the general public. Coming clean would put to bed conspiracy theories that bitcoin was created by the CIA or the NSA or the IMF, or that the whole thing is an elaborate scam. Nakamoto's anonymity in bitcoin's early days may have helped deflect attention away from the leading figure and onto the project, but now that secrecy is itself a distraction. Whereas the initial problem was that early adopters might have mistrusted a founder thought to be pumping his or her own currency, now the problem is that the average joes targeted by bitcoin advocates see the mystery as a reason *not* to trust it. "Mysterious in the case of money is not so good," says Jeremy Allaire, founder of bitcoin financial firm Circle.

What's more, Nakamoto himself has a dilemma. He is believed to be the owner of about 1 million bitcoins, or around $500 million worth at the time of this writing. That's the estimate that cryptographer Sergio Lerner came up with after analyzing the movements into addresses that he identified for Nakamoto from the Genesis Block and subsequent mining hauls over the two or so years that he was involved in the bitcoin network. Since Lerner identified those addresses, the world has been watching them like a hawk. (Even though their owner can't be identified, the wallet addresses in which the coins reside can easily be seen, along with all other bitcoin addresses, using tools that track the blockchain.) Now might be the time for Nakamoto to fulfill what private-exchange SecondMarket's CEO, Barry Silbert, describes as one of his personal "dreams for bitcoin"—that Nakamoto outs himself and makes a high-profile donation of his giant bitcoin holdings to an extremely worthy cause.

Regardless of what transparency on this issue might mean for bitcoin, people will continue hunting for Satoshi Nakamoto. Bitcoiners can protest, but they can't quash a desire to know. As journalists we perhaps experience this instinct stronger than most, but most people are naturally curious. We see it in our own children, of which we have three between us, all eager to know what their fathers are doing. One of them, a fifth-grade girl, has become intrigued by the bitcoin stories she keeps hearing her dad talking about. "Have you found out who Satoshi is yet, Dad?" she asks from time to time. She seems to view it a bit like that popular children's video game *Where in the World Is Carmen Sandiego?*

Since Nakamoto went silent in 2010, dozens of names have been presented as candidates, starting with the obvious ones from the Cypherpunk and cryptography community who'd previously dabbled in cryptocurrency: people such as Wei Dai, Hal Finney, David Chaum, and the odds-on favorite, Nick Szabo, whose writings, the forensics linguists tell us, make a pretty close match to the word and phrase choices of bitcoin's founder. All, in one forum or another, have denied being Nakamoto.

Other investigators have gone off on interesting but equally fruitless tangents. Writing for *The New Yorker,* Joshua Davis fixated on some of the British spellings in Nakamoto's writings and headed to the British Isles to find their author. He zeroed in on Michael Clear, a Dublin-based computer-science student who'd worked for Allied Irish Banks on peer-to-peer technology and who responded to Davis's inquiries with the enticing line "I'm not Satoshi, but even if I was I wouldn't tell you." Davis's work was inconclusive, but Clear's comment, which he later said was intended as a harmless joke, meant the Irishman was inundated with e-mails. He has since vehemently denied creating bitcoin and has pleaded with people to leave him alone.

Convinced that Davis was caught out by a probable disinformation campaign by the founder—as if Nakamoto's Britishisms and *The Times* of London reference were planted to throw trackers off the scent—New York University journalism professor Adam Penenberg turned his attention elsewhere. In an article for *Fast Company* he pointed to three names who'd jointly filed cryptocurrency-relevant encryption patents around the time of bitcoin's release: Neal King and Charles Bry, who both resided in Germany, and Vladimir Oksman, living in the United States. He got explicit denials from them, including one from King in which he criticized bitcoin for having "no intrinsic value." Penenberg was undeterred by this and speculated that King's statement could have been a red herring, but Penenberg's evidence was circumstantial and inconclusive, and he conceded that.

Next came Ted Nelson, an information theorist famous for coining the term *hypertext* in the 1960s. In a rambling, videoed monologue in which he adopted faux-British accents to mimic Sherlock Holmes, Nelson declared that the bitcoin inventor was Japanese mathematician Shinichi Mochizuki and dared him to deny it. Not only did Mochizuki have the kind of mind capable of devising such a scheme, Nelson said, he also had the suspicious habit of quietly leaving his mathematical discoveries on the Internet for people to find. The mathematician has not publicly responded to Nelson's challenge, but others have found holes in the argument, pointing out that Mochizuki is not a cryptographer and seems to have no extensive experience writing code.

Then, on March 6, 2014, the U.S. magazine *Newsweek* relaunched its print edition, and for its cover story it went for a big scoop. "Bitcoin's Face" was the title, with an artful image of a single person hidden in black, a mask in the form of bitcoin's *B* currency symbol being peeled away. Reporter Leah McGrath Goodman declared she'd found Satoshi Nakamoto hiding in plain sight, a Japanese American man living in a suburb of Los Angeles whose name had been Satoshi Nakamoto before he changed it to Dorian Nakamoto. To say the story went viral would be an understatement.

For several hours, *Newsweek* owned the story, but it was top news everywhere, on cable TV, on Reddit, on Twitter, on the Bitcoin Forum, at newspapers such as our own. Everybody was amazed by this tale, everybody was amazed that *Newsweek* had flushed out the real Nakamoto. What a scoop! What a coup! Goodman made the rounds on the media circuit, explaining how the magazine had pulled it off. The intense reaction to the story showed just how much pull this Nakamoto myth had in the public eye. Then it got weird.

Dorian Nakamoto eventually emerged—hours after the magazine hit newsstands—to confront the throng of journalists who'd taken up positions on his front lawn. He denied any involvement in bitcoin and did so in such an idiosyncratic way that it suggested he was a poor match for the bitcoin founder's character profile. He stood next to his front door and promised an exclusive interview to the first reporter to offer him a free lunch. An AP reporter quickly did so and whisked him off in a car to a sushi place. The other reporters followed, with at least one, the *Los Angeles Times'* Joe Bel Bruno, live tweeting the "chase" in a scene oddly reminiscent of the infamous O. J. Simpson chase.

Most intriguing was a posting later that day on a relatively obscure online message board owned by the P2P Foundation, a nonprofit that seeks to build peer-to-peer applications through cryptography and software tools. The post was made to a thread that dated back to February 12, 2009, which had been dormant for years, a thread started by Satoshi Nakamoto when he was spreading the word on bitcoin. The new message was simple, but it was the first anybody had heard from him in years.

It simply said, "I am not Dorian Nakamoto."

At best the *Newsweek* report was inconclusive, and at worst, sloppy journalism. Still, the media circus it generated demonstrated how much bitcoin was now inserted into public consciousness and how the Satoshi mystery had energized people's fascination, a fascination that says a lot more about the people seized by it than about the source of their fascination.

What do we think? Well, bitcoin's founder almost certainly is not Dorian Nakamoto. What does seem most likely to us is that, at least initially, one person dreamed it up. Seeing as Wei, Szabo, Finney, and Chaum all came up individually with digital-currency systems, it seems reasonable to assume that bitcoin could also be the project of one person. Indeed, most of the elements for a digital currency had already been laid down; in essence, Nakamoto took an existing puzzle, found the few missing pieces, and put it together. We also think it's quite possible this person came out of the Cypherpunk movement, and that it's just as possible that upon conceiving of it he or she soon enlisted other Cypherpunks to help with the project. Inconsistencies in the writing style—the occasional insertion of British spellings, for example—lend weight to the idea that a small group was behind it. That would most likely put bitcoin's founder or founding group somewhere in the San Francisco/Silicon Valley region. That's about the best we can do for you. Likely one guy, quite possibly a group.

The group idea is enticing to us, partly because a pact like that would give each member plausible deniability, the capacity to say "*I* am not the founder of bitcoin" when nosy journalists come snooping around. Just as important, though, even if one person did have the original idea of a decentralized, networked currency, its development ultimately had to become a group effort—as we've discussed, it needed to grow into a community. Befitting that notion is a saying that you sometimes hear among bitcoiners that addresses the mystery of the founder's identity. It's a rallying cry of sorts, and it seems that in the symbiotic relationship between bitcoin and its community, the way the one strengthens the other, it really does explain the reality behind the myth.

"We are all Satoshi."

To some extent, the earliest development of the bitcoin community was a natural outgrowth of the decentralized and open-source nature of its source computer code. Open-source projects have a distinguished history of attracting smart people to join communities dedicated to perfecting and evangelizing, as with the community that has supported the open-source Linux operating system for decades. Similarly, bitcoin's open-source software has been essential to the widening of its community.

You don't buy bitcoin's software as you would other products, which means you're not just a customer. What's more, there's no owner of the software—unlike, say, PayPal, which is part of eBay. Because of that, everybody who uses it has a delineated relationship with the bitcoin program. Although eBay sells a service, it owns the product. The end user never has any ownership of the product. Bitcoin eliminates that distinction.

Anybody can go on the Web, download the code for no cost, and start running it as a miner. Congratulations, you are now a "node," one of thousands responsible for keeping the network running by confirming transactions and generating coins. The community of people who have taken this step run bitcoin. Everybody who's invested time and computing power is, in a real sense, the system. This gives you a stake in its future. It helps build a community of dedicated users.

That community grew slowly at first, with word spreading in cryptography circles and on various online forums. Handfuls at a time were downloading the code through 2009. The forums that Nakamoto had set up at bitcoin.org were attracting a couple of dozen new users every month. Some of these were serious computer programmers and coders, the kind who are incessantly drawn to new and interesting ideas. One such person was Gavin Andresen, who in May 2010 stumbled across an article about interesting open-source software projects in which bitcoin was mentioned. "It piqued my interest," says Andresen, but his skeptical nature forced him to do some heavy due diligence. "At first, I thought this couldn't possibly work, but I read Satoshi's white paper and then basically everything that had been written about bitcoin to that point. Then I read the source code . . . and convinced myself that it wasn't going to infect my computer with some nasty virus if I ran it, and then I decided that it could actually work." On May 28, he registered as a user on the Bitcoin Forum.

To get his "feet wet," Andresen started a project he called Bitcoin Faucet, which was literally a giveaway plan. He bought ten thousand bitcoins on Bitcoin Market, one of the early bitcoin exchanges, for $50 and gave them all away, the intent being to expand the usage, grow the community, and build up the currency. Andresen believed that bitcoin needed people using it and spreading it around if developers were to be encouraged to build useful tools around it. In this way he saw Bitcoin Faucet as "key to bootstrapping the infrastructure" of the bitcoin ecosystem. As Andresen inserted himself into the community via the bitcoin chat rooms, his calm, careful demeanor soon attracted the attention of Nakamoto. Bitcoin's creator was still active in the community, still working with people and still answering questions. Andresen became a key partner of Nakamoto's in the development work, and today—with the founder gone from the public airwaves—he is bitcoin's lead developer.

Yet, right at the beginning, Andresen was a sideline player. When he first discovered bitcoin in May 2010, other, earlier adopters beyond Nakamoto were having far more influence on the community's development. One in particular would change the trajectory of bitcoin.

We first met Laszlo Hanyecz in the previous chapter. He's the coder whose discovery of GPU-based mining would quickly change how bitcoin's all-important mining network functioned. Hanyecz's contribution to bitcoin development—and in particular to the burnishing of its community and culture—goes well beyond that to his place in one of the community's key founding stories.

On May 21, 2010, Hanyecz ate a cheese pizza from Papa John's. Nothing about the pizza itself was extraordinary. What was extraordinary was the way he paid for it.

A little more than a year into bitcoin's existence, the Jacksonville, Florida–based coder had already mined a bunch of bitcoins. His graphics-card discovery had ramped up over eight hundred times the computing capacity he could apply to mining, giving him virtual dominance over the rewards that the bitcoin protocol was then paying out; he was getting about half of all the bitcoins mined. "I had a lot," he says, so many that his problem was what to do with them. "If nobody will take them, they're worthless," he thought. So Hanyecz struck upon an idea.

"I'll pay 10,000 bitcoins for a couple of pizzas, like maybe two large ones so I have some left over for the next day," he wrote on May 18 on the Bitcoin Forum, which had only about 230 members. He had no reason to think anyone would take him up on it. Nobody had ever used bitcoins in the real world. Certainly no pizza places in his patch of Florida would accept bitcoin as payment. Hanyecz needed a middleman and figured ten thousand—worth about $41 based on the prices being quoted on some rudimentary bitcoin markets—would get him the two pies and compensate his middleman for the trouble.

After three days, a bitcoiner in England, who went by the chat-forum name jercos, stepped up. Jercos placed an order online with a Papa John's in Jacksonville and paid over the Web with a credit-card. Hanyecz transferred the bitcoins from his own wallet to the sender in England. Shortly after that, a confused deliveryman arrived at Hanyecz's house with the two pies and a puzzled look on his face. "Fresh pizza," he said, "from London." It was the currency's first step toward becoming real money, and by one compelling metric, it has traveled a long way since. If we value the bitcoins that Hanyecz spent in 2010 according to their August 2014 market price, those two pizzas cost him $5 million.

In the year and a half since Nakamoto had first launched his trial balloon, the bitcoin community had grown slowly. Back then, Hanyecz says, it "was like a ham radio club." Close-knit, they were united by their interest in bitcoin, but uncertain about its future. In March of 2010, for example, one of the earliest members of the forum who went by the moniker SmokeTooMuch offered to auction ten thousand bitcoins. His starting bid was $50. There were no takers.

New members, often confused about what they were doing and prone to mistakes, found a welcoming group. "So, I finally got my client to start generating," a user named AgoraMutual wrote, after downloading the software to his laptop computer. "My first transaction completed resulting in +50 coins. Yay!" But he wasn't sure if his computer was still generating

Laszlo Hanyecz's pizzas, paid for with bitcoin

(Courtesy of Laszlo Hanyecz)

coins. It appeared the program had simply stopped working. He soon got an answer. He was reading the program wrong. He was still generating coins. The respondent? Satoshi Nakamoto. "Back then, it was a lot of people helping each other," Hanyecz said—one of them being Nakamoto.

Hanyecz described a community in which people helped each other overcome the technical bumps in the road that accompanied efforts to figure out this new technology. As they learned more themselves, the new people would become helpers and start experimenting with the bitcoin code. One of Hanyecz's other early contributions included writing a version that could run on Mac computers.

The pizza sale and the rise of GPU mining would soon change the experience. Hanyecz left the offer standing, figuring that if he could mine enough bitcoins to get a pizza a week, he was making out fine. At first his new, high-powered machines—which he says "sounded like a vacuum cleaner when they were busy"—were easily achieving that. He did several more pizza deals, but then noticed a problem: he wasn't mining as many bitcoins as he had been. His offer, which showed the outside world that bitcoins had actual value, had attracted attention online. That in turn attracted competition in mining, with all the newcomers setting up the GPU strategy that Hanyecz had pioneered and with faster and many more graphics cards deployed. Nakamoto's algorithm released only a finite number of bitcoins each day; more people, with more powerful hardware at their disposal, ramped up the difficulty of the mathematical puzzles, making mining increasingly time-consuming, and less rewarding.

"In one week, the difficulty shot up so high, regular people couldn't mine," Hanyecz said. Where he was previously getting tens of thousands of coins a month, he was soon mining just a single bitcoin a day, and he was exhausting his supply buying Papa John's pizzas. He says he went through with the pizza offer four or five times, spending about 40,000 BTC in total.

Nakamoto wasn't too happy about this change, said Hanyecz, recalling the founder's interactions in the chat room. The founder wanted a system that could be accessed by regular people using common equipment. It was becoming impossible to mine without powerful computers. Whereas two weeks earlier the CPU on a normal computer could deliver the owner several hundred bitcoins, now it would earn one or two if the owner was lucky. In no time, mining had become more expensive—the energy costs had shot up. It was no longer a costless enterprise for a ham-radio hobbyist. Costwise, it seemed to some more sensible to buy bitcoins. In time people started doing so, which is why Hanyecz's remaining stash of bitcoins still ended up being worth a decent sum.

The pizza stunt had more than proven Hanyecz's original point. It generated new interest in bitcoin, and the community of users started expanding. In June, 55 people signed on to the Bitcoin Forum. In July, 370 did. The price was moving, too. Over five days, bitcoin's exchange rate jumped nine-fold, from $0.008 to $0.08 on July 18. A single bitcoin was now for the first time worth more than a cent. In the summer of 2010, as Hanyecz was winding down his pizza venture, this rapidly expanding interest was about to give rise to other ventures that would greatly expand the community, albeit in ways that attracted great controversy. On that same July 18 date of bitcoin's cyclical price peak, a new user showed up on the Bitcoin Forum. "Hi everyone," he wrote, "I just put up a new bitcoin exchange." The user's name was mtgox.

•   •   •

The forum user was an unemployed coder named Jed McCaleb. McCaleb was a different breed from the early bitcoiners, the hobbyists and tinkerers. He was among the first of a new group that would soon be drawn to bitcoin: the entrepreneur. With their arrival would come both great growth and the problems that can bring.

In 2007, McCaleb had started an online platform for trading cards related to the game *Magic: The Gathering,* which is itself a trading-card game with millions of players. He named it Mt. Gox, an amalgam of "Magic: The Gathering Online Exchange." The trading-card platform didn't take off as he'd hoped, but McCaleb held on to the domain name. In 2010, he'd become aware of bitcoin and realized that it lacked an intuitively easy-to-use trading application for people to buy and sell the cryptocurrency. So he created one and placed it under the old Mt. Gox domain name, from which his new exchange would also take its name. It attracted a lot of interest, catching the eyes of a few notable new investors looking to get into this exciting new market. Trading ramped up quickly. On the first day of trading, July 17, volume was 20 BTC. On October 10, it hit 187,000 BTC. Volume was erratic, but by the fall, the exchange had seen volume spike to as high as 200,000 BTC, and 50,000 days were common. By November 2011, trading would be averaging 27,541 BTC a day.

The growth was exciting, but McCaleb has a history of starting projects and soon after losing interest. This would be no different. In March 2011, he told the forum that while it had been "fun and interesting" to set up Mt. Gox "on a lark" and watch it grow, he no longer had enough time to manage it so had sold it to "someone better able to take the site to the next level." That someone was the French programmer Mark Karpelès, known to some on bitcoin chat forums as MagicalTux. A lover of Japanese manga and cosplay pastimes, Karpelès promptly moved Mt. Gox's headquarters to Tokyo.

Mt. Gox was the first major bitcoin exchange, and in those early days it was virtually the only place to trade coins. As the first really visible business in the bitcoin world, it further validated that this digital currency was so much more than just a toy for techies. It would bring many new bitcoiners into the community. Whereas the Bitcoin Forum had added new members at an average rate of 36 per month in its first eight months of existence to bring its total membership to 286 in June 2010, onward from July, the month that McCaleb launched his site, the forum added several hundred new users every month and at an increasing rate. By February 2011, monthly additions crossed 1,000 for the first time, and in June of that year, with Karpelès in charge at Mt. Gox, 14,483 members joined the Bitcoin Forum to bring total membership to 31,247.

For most of Mt. Gox's customers, it was their first gateway into bitcoin, their first experience with cryptocurrency. But the exchange had been built quickly, on a lark, and it was ill equipped to handle the challenges of a global currency-trading platform. Karpelès found himself struggling to bring the platform up to speed, as bitcoin's value surged from $1 in April to $30 in June; during that same period, accounts on Mt. Gox rose from six thousand to sixty thousand. June would also bring the first major challenge to bitcoin's survival.

Around June 13, 2011, people began to notice that bitcoins were missing from their Mt. Gox accounts. It seemed that a hacker had gained access to the exchange's system and pilfered a large number of coins—reports put the amount at anywhere from two thousand to half a million coins; Karpelès said it was a thousand. Soon after, the coins started showing up on the exchange for sale—at one penny. These sell orders were met, and the result? Bitcoin's prices plunged to meet it, the value of the currency dropping from $17 to mere cents. Worse, passwords and other client information began circulating, indicating that the breach was about more than just one or two hacked accounts.

The situation would eventually stabilize. But before then, Karpelès had to take the unprecedented step of shutting the exchange down, and unwinding the trades. This calmed the situation, but people didn't have much choice but to trust the site. In July 2011, Mt. Gox was handling 80 percent of all bitcoin trading. This first crisis at Mt. Gox—an even bigger one was to come three years later—showed the vulnerability that could come with fast growth in the bitcoin world.

The episode also revealed the importance of that key element of currency development that we keep coming back to: trust. While Karpelès's name is well known today, in 2011 few outside of the coding community who'd interacted with MagicalTux on chat forums knew who was running Mt. Gox. The exchange's customer service was notoriously poor. In a bitter irony, a currency predicated on trustless exchange was now be-ing controlled by an exchange that people didn't trust but were compelled to use.

The first major Mt. Gox crisis heralded the start of bitcoin's Wild West phase. The community had morphed from a clique of early techie geeks to one in which a new breed of adventurers saw all manner of get-rich-quick schemes—all inside what seemed like a lawless haven. The most extreme manifestations of that idea would come into existence when another new member of the forum posted on March 1, 2011, "Silk Road is into its third week after launch and I am very pleased with the results." Referring to the new site as an "anonymous online market," he or she asked community members what they thought of the site. With the Bitcointalk forum now boasting 5,343 members, the Silk Road post got hundreds of replies. Some liked the idea, some hated it, and some, immediately understanding its implications, made jokes about getting busted by the cops just for replying.

Silk Road, which allowed buyers and sellers to disguise their identi-ties, was run by a person who used the handle Dread Pirate Roberts (a character from the book and movie *The Princess Bride*). It made use of the Tor network, a sophisticated encryption system and Web browser that makes Web traffic nearly impossible to track, to keep its buyers' and sell-ers' identities hidden. Critically for our purposes, Silk Road used bitcoin as its medium of exchange.

While Silk Road ostensibly allowed the sale of just about anything, its central product quickly became drugs. Absolutely any drug imaginable was available from sellers all over the world, as well as many other illicit substances and services. The Web site *Gawker*, in June 2011, likened it to Amazon, "if Amazon sold mind-altering drugs." In truth, it was more like eBay, where buyers and sellers were matched up. Regardless, its rep-utation spread like wildfire.

"The site went mainstream way faster than we were hoping and we weren't prepared for the traffic," the poster, who went by the moniker silk-road, wrote on the forum. "We really didn't expect all of the media to catch on so quickly, and we should have been prepared with a semi-closed sys-tem. We'll do our best to get out of the spotlight and hopefully the merits

Shop by Category

Drugs *8,670*
  Cannabis *2,066*
  Dissociatives *165*
  Ecstasy *660*
  Opioids *591*
  Other *455*
  Precursors *50*
  Prescription *2,146*
  Psychedelics *981*
  Stimulants *1,102*
Apparel *264*
Art *127*
Biotic materials *1*
Books *861*
Collectibles *5*
Computer equipment *32*
Custom Orders *68*
Digital goods *509*
Drug paraphernalia *305*
Electronics *77*
Erotica *540*
Fireworks *2*
Food *9*
Forgeries *81*
Hardware *23*
Herbs & Supplements *8*
Home & Garden *8*
Jewelry *54*
Lab Supplies *71*
Lotteries & games *77*
Medical *57*

1g MDMA 82%+ High
Quality -Made in Germany-
฿1.30

50 gr. Crystal MDMA Rocks
฿23.33

Kamagra Jelly (India), 1 week pack | TheBen

Kamagra jelly (India), 1
week pack
฿0.98

10 grams ketamine crystals
฿7.15

3g XxX AAA QUALITY
WEED,AMAZING
฿0.98

Valium 10mg/ Diazepam
(100 Pills)
฿2.32

Honeycomb Wax (85+%
THC) Fully Purged
฿1.45

1 gram ✕ Moroccan Hash ✕
DUTCH QUALITY
฿0.27

FinestKiwiBuds

[3g] Greenstone NZ Hash (B
Grade)
฿2.49

Mr. Shab

Citalopram 10x 20mg table
฿0.10

-SR

300x 25i/25c-NBOMe Liqui
Dropper 1200μg
฿4.14

+++ 100 x 25i-NBOMe
Strawberry Snuff Caps +++
฿3.80

(*Source:* Business Insider)

Silk Road

of Bitcoin will become the focus." That didn't happen. Other news sites picked up on the story. Some provided instructions on how to find the site. This was noticed not only by your average pothead, but by law enforcement, and politicians. New York Senator Chuck Schumer called it "the most brazen attempt to peddle drugs online that we have ever seen" and called for it to be shut down.

The response on the Bitcoin Forum was mixed. Some worried about DEA agents infiltrating the Silk Road site. Others were keeping watch to see if the site was even still up. Some wanted to band together; Silk Road and Mt. Gox were the two most prominent bitcoin businesses. "An injury to one is an injury to all," one poster wrote. But others were worried about fallout. One poster responded with typically cynical humor: "I guess they're climbing up in our windows now!"

Despite the heat from the Feds, Silk Road would operate encrypted, shielded, and totally out in the open for more than two years after that, with thousands of listings for drugs, hacking services, pirated media, and even forgers' services. It had nearly 1 million accounts. Estimates of its sales varied. In August 2012, *Forbes*'s Andy Greenberg estimated that it was doing $22 million in annual sales, double that of six months earlier. The FBI estimated that between February 6, 2011, and July 23, 2013, over 1.2 million transactions on the site generated sales of 9.5 million bitcoins. (Given the wild fluctuations in price during that time, it's hard to extrapolate how much that is in dollars.)

It would come to an end in October 2013 when the FBI arrested a Texas native named Ross Ulbricht in a San Francisco library. The agency charged him with money laundering and conspiracy to traffic narcotics—to which Ulbricht has, as of the time of writing, pleaded not guilty; his lawyer has said he is not Dread Pirate Roberts. The agency also said he solicited six murders-for-hire, though there was no evidence anybody was killed. It also seized tens of thousands of bitcoins worth millions of dollars, turning the FBI into a bitcoin wallet holder, one of the biggest and most unlikely new members of the bitcoin "community." Those later events would bring another turning point in bitcoin's development, heralding an era of government regulation. But in the early years on which we are focused here, Silk Road, for all its notoriety, played a key role in developing bitcoin—by expanding its community of users.

Much as online porn was one of the first big profitable businesses in the early days of the Internet, thus proving that there was a business model there, Silk Road was the first big bitcoin business. So while the site's products might have been morally offensive to many, as with porn, it did prove that bitcoin could operate as a legitimate currency. Along with Mt. Gox, which over the same period provided proof of a speculative and investing interest in the currency, it helped put bitcoin in the hands of thousands of newcomers, many of whom were now looking to use it for things other than drugs. Silk Road was a critical catalyst for this particularly rapid phase of community formation.

Even as its community expanded rapidly, bitcoin was still far from being a household name through 2011 and 2012. Wall Street and Washington mostly ignored it. Still, that expansion enticed other entrepreneurs to follow McCaleb's and Dread Pirate Roberts's lead. New ideas began to pop up for businesses that would create the financial, technical, and social infrastructure to sustain bitcoin's growth. Critically, it was a global affair.

During this period, new exchanges sprang up as competitors to Mt. Gox, among the earliest and most notable being Tradehill in the United States, formed by Jered Kenna, and Britcoin in London. Others would follow. Trading platforms for bitcoin started appearing for every currency from the Polish zloty to the Brazilian real. Mainstreaming would require easier interfaces. Just as Microsoft Outlook and Hotmail made e-mail accessible to the average person, so, too, would bitcoin require more user-friendly digital wallets. Sure enough, new businesses began offering them, highlighted by the founding of London-based Blockchain.info, the now high-profile wallet and analytics firm, in August 2011. Whereas Nakamoto's wallet was clunky and difficult for outsiders to decipher, Blockchain's prettier interface helped newcomers more easily conceive of a digital version of the physical wallets they kept in their pockets.

Another problem needed resolving: the interminably long wait to get traditional fiat money into, out of, and between bitcoin exchanges. To fix this, Charlie Shrem, a Brooklyn-based twenty-one-year-old college senior with an e-commerce background, teamed up with fellow bitcoin trader Gareth Nelson of the United Kingdom to found the bitcoin transfer service BitInstant in August 2011. The service would, for a fee, forward money on credit to speed up the transfer of funds between exchanges. Professional payment-processing services also emerged in this era, with BitPay and Coinbase coming on the scene in anticipation of offering easy interfaces for merchants to receive bitcoins and, if they desired, to convert them into dollars. Meanwhile, SatoshiDice, an online bitcoin gambling service that used bitcoin technology to offer a "provably fair" betting model so that users could trust that its computer-driven game of chance wasn't rigged, took off. By mid-2012, SatoshiDice, whose internal system required the generation of thousands of tiny transactions, would account for half of all bitcoin transfers in volume terms, if not value. As all these developments and opportunities for new businesses arose, early investors started conceiving of ways to encourage more innovation. One of the first was Peter Vessenes, who late in the summer of 2011 set up CoinLab, a Seattle-based incubator to develop new talent and start-ups dedicated to bitcoin products.

Other symbols of the community's coming of age appeared, too. The first press articles touching on bitcoin began, and *Bitcoin Magazine*, founded by Mihai Alisie and Vitalik Buterin in 2011, began publishing a print edition in May 2012, becoming the first serious publication dedicated to cryptocurrencies. Bitcoin conferences became more common, with New York, London, and Prague featuring in the early circuit. In September 2012, the Bitcoin Foundation was founded in Seattle. Founded by lead bitcoin developer Andresen, BitInstant's Shrem, Mt. Gox's Karpelès, CoinLab's Vessenes, the investor and "evangelist" Roger Ver, and lawyer Patrick Murck, it aimed to represent the growing bitcoin community internationally and, in its founding document's words, to help "standardize, protect and promote the use of Bitcoin cryptographic money for the benefit of users worldwide."

At that time, the Bitcoin Forum had about sixty-eight thousand members, up from about thirty-one hundred at the end of 2010. But the community was growing not only in a cyberspace setting. All around the world, the phenomenon of the bitcoin "meetup" took off, with cryptocurrency enthusiasts forming informal groups that would meet in bars and cafés everywhere from Buenos Aires to Beijing. In this way, the bitcoin community was given a physical foundation, but one that, importantly, had no central base.

More ominous events, too, challenged the growing community's re-solve and solidarity. The first major bitcoin thefts were reported. Beginning in March 2012, thefts totaling more than $500,000 occurred from Bitcoinica, a company that allowed investors to speculate on bitcoin with derivative contracts. The company said its account at Mt. Gox had been compromised by hackers. Bitcoin's core software remained untouched, but companies were showing vulnerabilities. Meanwhile, various start-ups were already facing trouble, particularly because of awkward relationships with reluctant banks and payment-processing services, denying them a link to the fiat-currency world and highlighting a problem that would continue in the years ahead. Kenna's Tradehill exchange was forced to shut its doors in February 2012, just eleven months after its founding.

Yet all the while, the bitcoin price went up, up, and up. There were hiccups, for sure, especially those associated with Mt. Gox in mid-2011, but between the start of 2011 and the end of 2012, anyone who'd invested would have made a 5,000 percent return, with the price going from $0.25 to $6 at the end of 2011, and then on to $13 another year later. Despite the fact that on November 28, 2012, bitcoin's core software had, as programmed, halved the bitcoin payout for miners to twenty-five per block, the interest in mining bitcoins continued to surge. People geared up for the onset in January of high-powered, dedicated mining rigs running ASIC (application specific integrated circuit) chips. It was a boom period. The community tent was getting wider and wider.

In fact, the tent was widening in different and confusing ways. One was that by 2011, bitcoin was inspiring imitators—some outright copies, others clear attempts to remove what were seen as some of bitcoin's flaws. Altcoins, as they came to be known, would use the same or similar aspects of bitcoin's system, all made possible because of bitcoin's open-source protocol and its lack of an owner. Anybody can download the software, copy it, and build something new from it. Lawsuits for copyright or patent infringement are simply not a concern.

As of this writing, several hundred of these digital coins exist, most too small to be worth mentioning, but a few with sizable followings. They all fall well short of bitcoin in ranks. Litecoin, the oldest and largest of the altcoins, had a market cap of about $150 million at the time of writing.

Bitcoin's was around $6.5 billion. Some are dubious-looking projects, quite blatant pump-and-dump schemes. Some aren't really competitors to bitcoin at all because they exist for the purpose of creating new forms of decentralized commerce through blockchain technology—we'll explore some of them in chapter 9. But a good many are legitimate attempts to create another form, and possibly a better form, of cryptocurrency-based money.

Some of these have developed loyal followings, contributing to the impression of a more varied cryptocurrency community than just that of bitcoin. Many bitcoiners welcome these projects as new elements of the same cryptocurrency revolution in which they are engaged. But others are openly hostile to what they see as interlopers, fearing that the nascent movements gathering around them could detract from the broader mission of change.

At the same time, the community development around some of these altcoins is instructive to the broader question of how communities develop around cryptocurrencies. Bitcoiners can learn from how passions have been stirred by some of them. Case in point: dogecoin, an altcoin that started out as a joke by Billy Markus and Jackson Palmer in December 2013 that quickly took on a life of its own. The "doge" was appropriated from an Internet meme that started with a 2005 puppet show on YouTube, in which one of the puppets misspells *dog* as *doge,* and the other mispronounces it as "dohj." That name was then applied by someone else to a picture of a Shiba Inu dog that appeared to be smiling. For its software, dogecoin borrowed some of the ideas of litecoin's founder, Charlie Lee, who had tweaked the mining system for his coins so that miners weren't so incentivized to build up energy-hungry computing power in competition with each other as they were with bitcoin. But just as important, if not more, to dogecoin's appeal were the two main goals that its emerging community set for itself: dogecoin was going to be fun, and its members were going to use their currency to do good deeds. Dogecoin was going to be philanthropic.

Interest in the currency rose, as did its price on cryptocurrency markets, where it traded against bitcoins, which could then be sold for dollars. This meant that dogecoins had real value and could be used to raise money for causes. One member of the Dogecoin Foundation read about the Jamaican bobsled team's being short of funds for a trip to the Sochi Olympics in 2014 and proposed raising money for their trip. Through campaigns launched on Reddit and elsewhere, with instructions about which wallet to send dogecoins to, they quickly raised the equivalent of $25,000 in their currency. Next, somebody suggested clean-water wells in Kenya. They raised $30,000 for wells in Kenya. They raised money for a coffee shop in Manchester, England. Our favorite dogecoin endeavor had more to do with marketing than philanthropy, though. Somebody read about a young NASCAR driver, Josh Wise, who was racing without a sponsorship. The person suggested—again, on a lark—that they raise money to buy a sponsorship with Wise, in order to spread the word. In short order, the dogies rallied around the idea, transferred coins to the designated wallet, and raised more than $55,000 (about 67 million dogecoins), enough to get their beloved Shiba Inu pictured on the hood of Wise's #98 Moonrocket, which made its debut in May 2014 at the Talladega Superspeedway.

"Doge is an Internet cryptocurrency," the Fox announcer said on national television. "It's not traded in dollars, but a win here would pay 596,664,147 dogecoins."

In roughly four months, a community of thousands materialized. Their passion and zeal for their brand has catapulted dogecoin from a joke based on a meme to what may turn out to be a relatively legitimate cryptocurrency. When GoCoin decided that it would start offering payment-processing services in dogecoin as well as bitcoin and litecoin, Chairman Brock Pierce explained that it was driven by the power of its community. "Community is everything for a currency," he said.

The question is whether the emergence of altcoin communities such as this one undercuts the wider bitcoin community or benefits it. Some wonder whether these imitators will simply take market share away from bitcoin—though with bitcoin's market capitalization more than ten times that of the combined ninety-nine next biggest altcoins, no such threat had arisen as of September 2014. Others think that by expanding both the range of technological innovation and the branding and cultural production associated with cryptocurrency, these alternative communities are helping a wider cryptocurrency community to fulfill a grander, shared purpose.

The philanthropy component to dogecoin provides a valuable lesson to bitcoiners on the power of good deeds to breed support. Within the bitcoin community, a similar ethos has developed on its own. Many bitcoiners have sought to live out their forebears' hope that cryptocurrencies could play a role in creating a less caustic and more humane society. Andreas Antonopoulos, chief security officer at wallet provider Blockchain.info and a prominent bitcoin personality, raised about $21,000 via bitcoin in a dedicated fund for Dorian Nakamoto, the man fingered, incorrectly it seems, in March 2014 by *Newsweek* magazine as Satoshi Nakamoto. *Forbes* writer Andy Greenberg started an effort to raise bitcoin for Hal Finney, the coder who'd helped Nakamoto set up bitcoin, and who was faced with significant medical bills for his debilitating ALS. Sean's Outpost is a homeless shelter in Pensacola, Florida, that's almost entirely funded by bitcoin donations. These efforts and others like them show the unmistakable fingerprint of the early bitcoiners, who wanted their currency to be used as a tool for empowering communities and helping the less fortunate within them. But they're also consciously part of the broader community-building effort. If such efforts can help improve bitcoin's image, more adherents can be won over, and in time that means bitcoin can truly be turned into a currency.

Philanthropy helps to physically spread bitcoin around and create a positive image for it, all of which works directly at expanding the community. But it's also important that those who've joined the core of believers sustain *their* passion. In this part of community formation and reaffirmation, those who create cultural product have a role to play. Just as songs that are sung at football games, artwork depicting the Stars and Stripes on the back of Jeeps, and stirring recitals of the Declaration of Independence help to burnish Americans' faith in their nation's greatness, so, too, can cultural production help strengthen other communities—even one formed around a currency. And so we find bitcoin literature, bitcoin poetry, bitcoin artwork, bitcoin photography, and bitcoin songs. It's a striking demonstration of how much this idea has captured people's imagination. Nobody writes songs about PayPal.

"Oh, bitcoin, I know you're gonna reign, gonna reign," John Barrett sings in his bluegrass "Ode to Satoshi," recorded in a studio in East Nashville, Tennessee. "Till everybody knows, everybody knows, till everybody knows your name." He's not alone in his choice of song topic: "10,000 Bitcoins" is a love song by Laura Saggers; "Bitcoin Barons" is a rap piece by YTCracker; and there are a handful of others. Meanwhile, the German artist Kuno Goda painted *200 Bitcoins,* with the bitcoin logo repeated two hundred times on a canvas—a play on Andy Warhol's *200 One Dollar Bills.* L.A. photographer Megan Miller did a whole series of pieces showing bitcoin in daily life. Oakland, California, artist Dave Kim was fascinated by the story of Dorian Nakamoto and chose him as the subject of his painting *Free Lunch.*

All of this speaks to another aspect of what bitcoin represents. More than just a currency and a technology, it's a countercultural movement. But like all countercultural movements, it will go nowhere as a force for societal change unless it moves beyond that definition of itself and finds a foothold in popular culture, in the mainstream. And doing so takes more than songwriters and poets to sing the praises of a new idea; it also needs ordinary people to find something appealing in it and, through their contacts with others, spread that idea around.

Dave Kim's *Free Lunch*
(Courtesy of Dave Kim)

As much as a decentralized community can have no central leader, to grow it still needs individuals to take the lead. Without first movers, there can be no community. We've already met a few of these early adopters—the coders, entrepreneurs, and evangelists who took to bitcoin and promoted it. But its growth has also depended on lower-profile individuals who've simply sought to use the cryptocurrency, to make it function as an element of everyday life. People like Austin and Beccy Craig of Provo, Utah.

The Craigs were unlikely proselytizers. She was a graphic artist; he made corporate videos. Neither is a coder or an entrepreneur. They weren't Cypherpunks. But Austin, a young man with a libertarian bent who had a background in video production, had heard about bitcoin in 2011 and was intrigued by its democratizing potential—and also had a creative idea about planting bitcoin's flag in the popular culture.

After proposing to Beccy, he made a second proposal: after their honeymoon, they would conduct an experiment—they would live for ninety days on nothing but bitcoin and film the whole thing for a documentary. It was the kind of on-a-lark thing only young people could do, and to his surprise, Beccy readily accepted the challenge. As if all that wasn't challenging enough, the Craigs added another wrinkle: they would drive across the United States, fly to Europe, fly to Asia, and then fly back to Utah. They would pay for every stage of this round-the-world trip with bitcoin.

They launched a Kickstarter project to fund the film, raised $72,000, bought themselves a little publicity, and hired a film crew. While it is reasonably feasible today, in 2015, to spend nothing but bitcoin for three months, this was mid-2013—just before a parade of well-known businesses announced they would accept bitcoin, as we'll discuss in the next chapter. At that time, the Craigs' quest seemed quixotic at best. Few businesses took bitcoin, and most vendors hadn't even heard of it. They had to convince a whole host of people in their town to accept the currency—their landlord, their employers, a local grocer. The grocer, who ran LoLo's Fresh Food Warehouse, was converted when they explained to him the difference in fees between bitcoin and credit-cards. At each stop, they perfected their pitch, in effect becoming bitcoin evangelists. Their experiment started on July 25, 2013.

The hardest part about living on bitcoin in Provo turned out to be finding a gas station. "For the first two weeks," Austin said, "we had no place to fill up." So they barely used the car. They were fortunate that Jeremy Furbish, an overnight gas-station clerk and bitcoin enthusiast known to the community as Furb, heard about their quest. He invited the Craigs to his station. "Driving an hour out there on a Friday night at ten became part of our routine," Beccy said. In early October, they hit the road.

We met up with the Craigs that month at a pizza parlor in Brooklyn called Lean Crust Pizza on Fulton Street. On this unusually warm day,

Fulton Street was in full, hot, noisy New York bloom. The owner, Dan Lee, is a bitcoin enthusiast, and Lean Crust had begun accepting bitcoin shortly before, as had his two other stores in the neighborhood. But that a business accepted bitcoin did not mean that the people who worked there knew how to take it.

Austin stood in front of the counter, waiting to pay. In his hand he had not his wallet, but a phone.

"That comes to thirty-four dollars," said the young woman behind the counter.

"Okay," Austin said. "Can we pay in bitcoin?"

"In what?"

"In bitcoin. Can we pay in bitcoin?"

"Bit . . . what?"

Eventually, Austin was able to pay for his meal with bitcoin, but only after the girl at the counter called Lee, who sent an employee from one of his other stores to process the transaction. Once this happened, it went smoothly. Austin took the address of Lean Crust's bitcoin account, typed it into his own account, entered the amount, and hit send. The transaction took about five seconds.

The exchange summed up quite a lot about bitcoin: the confusion over what it is; the initial difficulties in using it; and then the simplicity of it once the system is set up. As we ate our pizza out on the sidewalk, the cashier walked by, obviously interested in figuring out what she had just seen. She stopped to talk for a minute, apologizing for her earlier misunderstanding, and telling the Craigs if they wanted anything else, she would help them with it.

A few weeks later, while gathering facts for a story about the Craigs, we got back in contact with the young cashier, Nadia Alamgir, and discovered she'd been converted. The chance encounter with bitcoin had piqued her interest, she'd gone off and done some research and had become more interested, and before she knew it, she was going to bitcoin meetups in Brooklyn.

This is how bitcoin grows, by word of mouth and chance encounters. For a system that is decentralized, one that isn't being run by a for-profit enterprise, where nobody is going to put any money into marketing or advertising, it's the only way the community can grow. In the Craigs' case, word of their project had filtered out, on the forums and through the loose confederation of meetups. At every stop on their trip, in the United States and overseas, they met up with at least one bitcoiner who wanted to lend a hand. "It was largely because of the bitcoin community that we made it," Austin said.

In the end, the Craigs lived for 101 days spending nothing but bitcoin. They proved that it was possible to do so, if not practical. The community embraced them, and they became minor bitcoin celebrities before their film had even been released. A year later, when Dish Network was looking for a "bitcoin face" to help launch its bitcoin payment options, it picked the Craigs. What their trip really showed, though, was that a project that had begun nearly five years earlier with just one person, Nakamoto, had mushroomed into a global community whose members had been able to form strong connections without the aid of a centralized authority.

Four

Money . . . ranks with love as man's greatest joy. And it ranks with death as his greatest source of anxiety.

—John Kenneth Galbraith

If community is one important part of growing a currency, the other part is comparative advantage. It has to be fundamentally more useful than that which it hopes to replace. In the following chapters, we'll explore the various ways in which cryptocurrency could reshape the global economy beyond just how we send money to each other. But the core pitch, especially to users in the developed world, must for now focus on the capacity to make electronic payments cheaper and more efficient. To see how that's the case, we must first look at how the traditional payment system works and the many costs it generates. So, let's go out and buy a cup of coffee.

You're in a Starbucks in New York, where a grande latte costs $4.30. You might hesitate for a moment at the price (unless you're from Oslo, where the same size goes for $9.83), but once you've decided to go ahead with the purchase, you're not going to think twice about handing over a credit-card to the cashier (an increasingly outdated job title). Within seconds, and without even signing for it, your card has been swiped and is back in your wallet as you head for the door, sipping from a cup of foamy coffee. Who needs to carry cash anymore? Who needs the risk of dropping a twenty on the floor, or the hassle of frequent ATM visits?

And that absurd latte price tag? It would be no different if you'd paid cash. All this extra, modern convenience of electronic payment costs you nothing . . . or so it seems.

Now let's take a closer look at what happens when the cashier swipes your card. With that action, the personal information contained in its magnetic strip—your account number, the expiration date, the billing address's zip code, and the CVV (credit-card validation value) code—is sent to something called a **front-end processor**. That firm, one of hundreds now in operation worldwide, specializes in handling payment information on behalf of its merchant client—in this case Starbucks—and for the bank into which the coffee vendor's sales receipts are deposited, an institution that's referred to within the transaction chain as the **acquiring bank**. For now, both Starbucks and its bank simply need to know whether the credit-card account attached to your card has enough funds in it to cover the payment. (They'll deal with whether it's actually your card and your account a bit later.) The front-end processor's job is to check that out, and quickly. So it forwards along the information contained on the card to the network of the relevant **card association**—MasterCard, Visa, American Express, or one of the others—which figures out which **issuing bank** your card came from. Having left imprints of itself on multiple databases already, it's now time for your personal information to move along to a separate **payment processor** representing the issuing bank, the one whose name is on your card and manages your account. Once your bank has verified the validity of the information and checked for sufficient credit, the signal goes back the other way. The bank tells its processor to give the all clear to the association, which conveys it back to the front-end processor so that Starbucks and the acquiring bank can be satisfied . . . for now. The cashier is notified of the approval via an "authorized" message that appears on the card-reader display. This long series of electronic communications has all occurred within seconds.

You're now walking down the street, cup in hand. But the payment system is far from being done with either you or Starbucks. For one, the café still hasn't been paid for delivering the coffee. For that, it must send a follow-up request to its acquiring bank, usually in a batch of receipts at day's end. The acquiring bank will pay the merchant for those receipts, but it will need to place a request for reimbursement from the issuing bank, using an automatic clearinghouse (ACH) network managed by either the regional **Federal Reserve** banks or the Electronic Payments Network of the **Clearing House Payments Co.,** a company owned by eighteen of the world's biggest commercial banks. Still, your bank won't release the funds if it's not convinced that it was really you who bought the latte. So before it even gets the request for payment, its antifraud team has been hard at work analyzing the initial transaction, looking for red flags and patterns of behavior outside your ordinary activity. If the team is not sure about who was swiping the card, it will call your cell and home phone numbers, text you, and e-mail you, trying to get you to confirm that it really was you there in New York. After all, years of transaction activity on your account show that you usually buy your morning coffee from a diner in your hometown of Seattle, unless you're in San Francisco for your monthly team meetings at the employer cited on your credit-card application. Once your bank is satisfied that all is aboveboard, it will release the ACH settlement payment and register a debit on your credit-card account. The money then flows to Starbucks' acquiring bank, which credits Starbucks' account. This process typically takes up to three business days to complete.

If you've been counting the boldfaced words above, you'll know that seven different entities in addition to you and the café had a hand in this transaction, five of which, in addition to Starbucks, had access to the identifying information on your card (account number, zip code, CVV code). Each demands a cut for its part of the operation, adding up to total transaction fees of between 1 percent and 3 percent of every sale, depending on whether a debit or credit-card is used. The biggest piece of the pie goes to the banks, which have in recent years turned payment processing into one of their most important sources of profits—and in some cases, *the* most important. Those fees are paid by the merchant. That's in addition to chargebacks the acquiring bank will impose if a customer disputes a charge, requiring the merchant to forfeit both the money and merchandise. Other fines and fees may also be levied to reimburse banks when fraud occurs.

In the United States, most merchants simply absorb all these transaction costs, with only a few, such as some gas stations, charging a premium for card transactions in place of cash, and most banks reimbursing the customer for fraudulent transactions. Still, it's an illusion to think you are not paying for any of this. The costs are folded into various bank charges: card issuance fees, ATM fees, checking fees, and, of course, the interest charged on the millions of customers who don't pay their balances in full each month. And then there's that crazy $4.30 price tag for the latte. Starbucks has to cover its costs somehow.

Let's imagine you're buying that latte in a café in Paris or a hotel resort in Cancún. In that case, a host of other intermediaries are roped in to facilitate the exchange of dollars for euros or pesos: foreign-exchange trading banks and brokers, foreign-currency settlement and clearinghouse operators, and currency messaging services such as SWIFT. This time, direct costs are imposed on you through foreign-transaction fees, and you'll incur hidden costs via the unfavorable foreign-exchange "spread" between the price at which you are charged for acquiring dollars and the price it costs your bank to obtain them. These mostly hidden costs can add up to as much as 8 percent on a single transaction—fees that are coming out of your pocket in addition to those levied on the French café owner or Mexican hotelier.

If this seems like a drag to you as an individual, think about the burden it places on the whole economy. Extrapolating from the 2 percent estimated average fee for credit- and debit-card payments and from the whopping $11 trillion in payments that Visa and MasterCard processed in 2013—about 87 percent of the global market—we estimate these operations cost merchants $250 billion that year. Benefiting from a global explosion in e-commerce, which is projected to double between 2013 and 2017, total payment-card volumes are increasing by about 10 percent each year. Add in the cost of fraud, and you can see how this "sand in the cogs" of the global payment system represents a hindrance to growth, efficiency, and progress.

Of course, hundreds of thousands of people are employed by banks, payment processors, and credit-card companies worldwide to keep this system running. We need these middlemen because the world economy still depends on a system in which it is impossible to digitally send money from one person to another without turning to an independent third party to verify the identity of the customer and confirm his or her right to call on the funds in the account. They help create the institutional trust on which our exchanges of value depend. If we could find a way to perform those transactions without having to trust these intermediary institutions, hordes of people would be out of a job. Doing away with the system, then, wouldn't be entirely costless for every member of society. But the bigger point is that by removing them, and the fees that are charged for the work they do, by allowing one person to compensate another for delivering a good or service without a host of financial institutions taking a cut, we would also free up funds for investment in new businesses, new products, *and* new jobs.

In letting the existing system develop, we've allowed Visa and MasterCard to form a de facto duopoly, which gives them and their banking partners power to manipulate the market, says Gil Luria, an analyst covering payment systems at Wedbush Securities. Those card-network firms "not only get to extract very significant fees for themselves but have also created a marketplace in which banks can charge their own excessive fees," he says. Other than American Express, which functions as an independent bank, the top ten credit-card issuers in the world are giant multinational banks such as Barclays, HSBC, Wells Fargo, and Citibank, which release them under association and licensing agreements with either Visa or MasterCard. The same banks also work under acquiring-bank licenses with the card companies so that they can process payments received by merchants such as Starbucks. This is how those two firms and their banking partners have sewn up the global payment system. It's how they get to set the terms by which it functions.

The entire architecture of electronic payments is built on the assumption that banks belong in the middle of global money flows. As we saw, economists treat the creation of debt by banks as fundamental to the creation of private money—without them, they say, cash would just be circulating through the economy without turning on the multiplier effect of credit creation. Whenever you swipe your credit-card during your shopping rounds, you are participating in that money creation. The problem is not debt per se—credit is a vital lubricant for the economy—it's the complexity of the system for clearing that debt. By handing Starbucks your card, you're not so much transferring money as creating a series of IOUs between you, your bank, Starbucks' bank, and Starbucks. Once checks and wire transfers are added into the mix, this constant sharing and offsetting of credits and debits leaves banks with giant balances to be reconciled and settled at the end of each day. For that, still more service providers get involved: clearinghouses, settlement agencies, custodial banks that look after the collateral used to secure loans, and money-market dealers peddling short-term investments and loans. In the United States, this netting process is coordinated by the Fed's Fedwire service, which handles $3.5 trillion a day in electronic wire transfers between banks.

Underpinning these transactions are the traditional mainstays of the economy and symbols of national power: banknotes and coins. Banks are required by their regulators—the Fed in the United States, the European Central Bank in the euro zone, the Prudential Regulation Authority in the United Kingdom—to carry a minimum ratio of cash reserves to deposits in case depositors demand their funds back in paper form. Fractional reserve banking, which allows banks to relend funds and "create" private, credit-fueled money, means the amount of debt in the economy is actually many times these cash balances. Nonetheless, the law requires that there be a proportional amount of cash held dormant within the financial system to sustain all that debt.

In sum, our high-tech "electronic" payment system depends on the presence of a minimum amount of paper, which must be secured in vaults with alarm systems, security guards, armored cars, and so on. Securing and distributing all this cash costs countries between 0.5 percent and 1.5 percent of their GDP, says Ajay Banga, CEO of MasterCard Inc., offering an estimate that runs as high as $1.4 trillion when applied to the entire world. Banga drops these big numbers to argue for further advancing electronic payments, the kind that would, presumably, run over Master-Card's network. But as we've seen, that cumbersome system, as it is currently designed, is tightly interwoven into the traditional banking system, which always demands its cut.

As the calendar progressed through 2013 a vanguard of retail businesses began to spot the advantages of cryptocurrency's lower-cost, faster payment system and started signing up for payment-processing services offered by Silicon Valley–funded bitcoin start-ups such as BitPay, Coinbase, and GoCoin. These firms touted a new model to break the paradigm of merchants' dependence on the bank-centric payment system described above. These services charged monthly fees that amounted to significantly lower transaction costs for merchants than those charged in credit-card transactions and delivered swift, efficient payments online or on-site.

In these new cases, the customer uses bitcoin to make the payment but merchants have the choice to be paid in dollars or their home currency. This is possible because those larger bitcoin payment processors absorb the bitcoins, then manage their risk by actively trading on digital-currency exchanges.

Given this option, there's no shortage of merchants now taking it up. They're the ones who save the money, not the customer—few, so far, are opting to pass on cost savings to the shopper. Many see they have nothing to lose since customers are still free to pay with credit-cards, debit cards, cash, and all other payment methods associated with the legacy system. So a number of high-profile U.S. businesses have now added bitcoin as a payment option. From the end of 2013 through the summer of 2014, firms such as online retailer Overstock.com, the Sacramento Kings basketball team, cable provider Dish Network, Dell computers, and travel site Expedia had added their names to a list of merchants accepting bitcoin that, by *CoinDesk*'s count, had reached sixty-seven thousand merchants by the end of June 2014.

The challenge for bitcoin's salesmen now lies not in convincing merchants of the cryptocurrency's benefits, but in convincing customers of them. So far those results are mixed. The good news is found in the steady expansion in the adoption of digital wallets, the software needed to send and receive bitcoins, with Blockchain and Coinbase, the two biggest providers of those, on track to top 2 million unique users each at the time of writing. Blockchain cofounder Peter Smith says that a surprisingly large majority of its accounts—"many more than you would think," he says cryptically—are characterized as "active." The bad news is that other figures, especially the sluggish growth in network-wide transaction volumes, indicate that many of those users are just tinkering at the margins. For the first eight months of 2014, around $50 million per day was passing thought the bitcoin network (some of which was just "change" that bitcoin transactions create as an accounting measure), compared with the combined $30 billion—with a *b*—that was processed daily by Visa and MasterCard in 2013. In numbers of transactions, the median daily amount stood at around sixty-five thousand, and although that's ten times what it was two years ago, the trend seems to have plateaued from a spike to above one hundred thousand during the peak surge in bitcoin's price versus the dollar. Again, this is a tiny fraction of credit-card transactions. Moreover, it's not clear how many of those transactions comprise trading and how many comprise actual commerce. The former is mainly speculation, and as we will soon see, that can be quite destructive. Only the latter would clearly demonstrate that bitcoin is being adopted as currency.

We've already discussed the uptick in entrepreneurial activity designed to make bitcoin more attractive and easier to use as currency, and we'll see this in more depth in chapter 7. Some of the fruits of their labor have been rolled out and are constantly being updated: more user-friendly, smartphone-based wallets to make payments easier; better and more trustworthy online exchanges for buying and selling bitcoins; bitcoin ATMs that make it easier for ordinary people to cash in and out of their local currency; gift cards and other tricks that allow bitcoin holders to buy goods from major merchants such as Amazon that don't accept the cryptocurrency; and tools such as bitcoin-loaded debit cards that will work with regular point-of-sale card-swipe machines and banks' ATMs.

But all the technology in the world won't drive people into this if the incentives aren't strong enough. For now, the benefits simply aren't obvious to people in places such as the United States and Europe. Unless they're contemplating all the hidden costs we outlined above and see themselves as activists seeking to lead the world to a more efficient, fairer system for everyone, typical customers can't appreciate the cost savings from bitcoin. That's because the costs are borne, at least directly, by merchants. Some clever payment processors, such as Santa Cruz, California–based PayStand, have figured out ways to give merchants the option of passing on their transaction-costs savings to bitcoin customers. If that catches on, presumably as a competitive tool, it could spur more bitcoin spending. But for now, end users are not seeing a clear advantage in using cryptocurrency over, say, a credit-card. Instead, they're focused on the risks, of which there are two main ones.

The first is security. Remember, bitcoin functions very much like cash. Once it is sent, it is sent; there's no way to get it back, no chargebacks like those that credit-card companies impose on merchants when they discover they've sold goods to someone with a stolen card. As with cash, if your bitcoins are stolen, that's it. You can't retrieve them—unless, of course, the thief is caught.

How might you lose them? It could happen if you divulged the all-important "private key," or password, needed to open a bitcoin address that's assigned to you. If you keep your bitcoins in a "hot wallet" that's sitting on a computer hooked up to the Internet, a hacker could enter through that connection to gain access to your private key and steal the coins. Just as important, if you lose your private key—literally the string of code needed to unlock bitcoins from a "cold wallet" that has been taken offline—or if you forget the password to your hot wallet and you are the only person with it, there's no way of getting back your coins. They are as good as lost. This risk arises if you use a service that leaves you solely in charge of your passwords, such as the generic wallet offered by the bitcoin core development team or with the product provided by Blockchain.info.

This all sounds alarming, particularly because so much more value can and will be held in a bitcoin wallet than the cash that's stuffed into a regular wallet. But remember also that hacking and identity theft are commonplace in credit-card systems, with fraud numbers in aggregate far and above those in bitcoin. Also, with a few simple precautions, you can make it much harder for someone to hack into your bitcoin digital wallet. You should use only an alphanumeric password and combine that with a double-factor authentication service via smartphone or SMS messages. And if you have significant bitcoin holdings, you can shift the bulk of those into a "cold wallet," in which you keep the private key on a piece of paper in a safe place—lose it and you've lost access to your bitcoins—while keeping the coins you use day to day in a "hot wallet" with an easily accessible key stored on your computer.

Thankfully, more sophisticated solutions than these are being developed, which enhance protection but allow for ease of use and less risk of losing a key. These include multiple-signature wallets, which require the application of at least two out of at least three possible keys held by different people or institutions for the bitcoins to be released. Some new businesses also offer high security and insurance. Most prominently represented by Circle Financial and Xapo, these start-ups are offering wallets and highly sophisticated custodial services combined. For now, these firms make no charge to cover costs of insurance and security, betting that enough customers will be drawn to them and pay fees elsewhere—for buying and selling bitcoins, for example—or that their growing popularity will allow them to develop profitable merchant-payment services as well. But overall, these undertakings must add costs back into the bitcoin economy, not to mention a certain dependence on "trusted third parties." It's one of many areas of bitcoin development—another is regulation—where some businessmen are advocating a pragmatic approach to bolstering public confidence, one that would necessitate compromises on some of the philosophical principles behind a model of decentralization. Naturally, this doesn't sit well with bitcoin purists.

Still, until the security problem is resolved, stories of bitcoin hacks will continue to hurt bitcoin's image. At least once a month, it seems, a new report emerges of several thousands of dollars' worth of bitcoins being stolen. After Bitcoinica lost almost half a million dollars in bitcoin from two hacks, thefts kept popping up elsewhere—a hacker hijacked an Internet service provider's computers to steal $83,000 worth of bitcoins from miners; a Greece-based botnet used Facebook to infect 250,000 computers with malware to steal bitcoins; Mt. Gox, by its own account, had been hacked twice in three years and ultimately lost 650,000 bitcoins. Bitcoin was also indirectly implicated in the hacking attack that released dozens of celebrities' naked photos to the public in August 2014. Although in this case it was accounts on Apple's iCloud service that suffered the security breach, the fact that the hacker requested payment for those photos in bitcoin created a negative association with the digital currency. It was yet another red flag for a general public already wary of an unfamiliar technology.

Still, perspective is needed. You can easily make the case that legacy payment systems are actually more prone to fraud than bitcoin. That's because credit-card networks and banking systems require the sharing of private information, which fosters identity theft, sometimes on mass scales, such as the $148 million attack on Target in December 2013 and the subsequent breach at Home Depot, where early estimates were that 56 million credit-card swipes were stolen in August 2014. Smaller versions of such thefts happen all the time. What's different from bitcoin is that the initial charges in legacy systems are borne by merchants. Other than the inconvenience of lost credit-cards, consumers don't notice the burden, even though, as we discussed above, it eventually reaches them in the form of higher prices and interest rates. Bitcoiners need to do a much better job of educating people about those hidden costs if they are to properly incentivize average joes to use bitcoin.

Another big concern is price volatility. Nobody wants to go to the grocery store week to week and see her bill change 10 percent or more just because the underlying bitcoin exchange rate is fluctuating. Until we live in a bitcoin-based economy, where the digital currency is the unit of account in which prices are quoted, this exchange-rate fluctuation will be unavoidable in everyday life for bitcoin-using payers and payees. Let's compare the average U.S. price of a gallon of gasoline in dollars to that of bitcoin over the seven-month period between September 2013 and the end of March 2014. In the first three months of that period you would have seen your gas bill plunge 90 percent, only to see it jump by 50 percent over the following four months. By contrast, the price of gasoline dropped and rose by no more than 12 percent in dollar terms over the same period.

Extrapolating from the three-part textbook definition of "money" that we referenced in chapter 2, a currency must exhibit price stability if it is to function properly as a *medium of exchange*—in addition to proving itself a reliable *store of value* and an accepted *unit of account*. It's hard to suggest that bitcoin now has anywhere near the price stability that's needed. That's a direct result of its fluctuation versus other currencies. In an extensive study of bitcoin's price performance against various other currencies and assets, New York University professor David Yermack concluded that bitcoin is much better viewed as a commodity than as a currency. Not only does it fluctuate wildly versus the dollar, he found, but it also shows no strong positive or negative correlations with any of the other major currencies, such as the euro, yen, or Swiss franc, or even against the price of gold. This lack of a predictable pattern against other measures of value makes it much harder for a businessperson or an investor to design an effective hedging strategy that could guard against a loss of value in his bitcoin holdings. Whereas you can hedge against a fall in the dollar by owning gold, it's not clear what you could buy to protect against a fall in bitcoin.

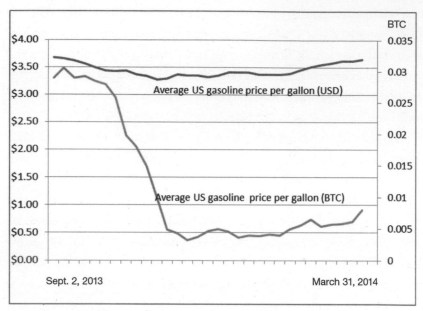

A gallon of gasoline, priced in dollars and bitcoin, weekly
(Source: EIA, CoinDesk)

This is just another way of saying that bitcoin is a volatile asset. You need look no further than its twelve-month dollar-based price chart from September 2013. Over the first three months, bitcoin rose 800 percent from $129.46 to a November 30 peak of $1,165.89, as U.S. regulators made some welcoming comments about digital-currency technology and as a surge of speculative buying took hold in China. At that stage, anyone holding bitcoin would have been whooping it up. But someone who'd off-loaded coins back in September to, say, buy a car might have been disappointed. Seller remorse in a rising market is a normal feature of investing in stocks or other volatile assets, but for a currency you want both sides in a transaction to feel satisfied that they're not giving up too much. Regret is not a constructive emotion when it comes to currencies, which should ultimately be viewed not as investments but as tools for making payments. In any case, a little more than four months after that November peak, the price was plumbing the depths of $344.24 following the collapse of Mt. Gox and amid news in early April of a crackdown by Chinese authorities. Things stabilized somewhat over the summer, but with frequent bouts of what would still be regarded as extreme volatility

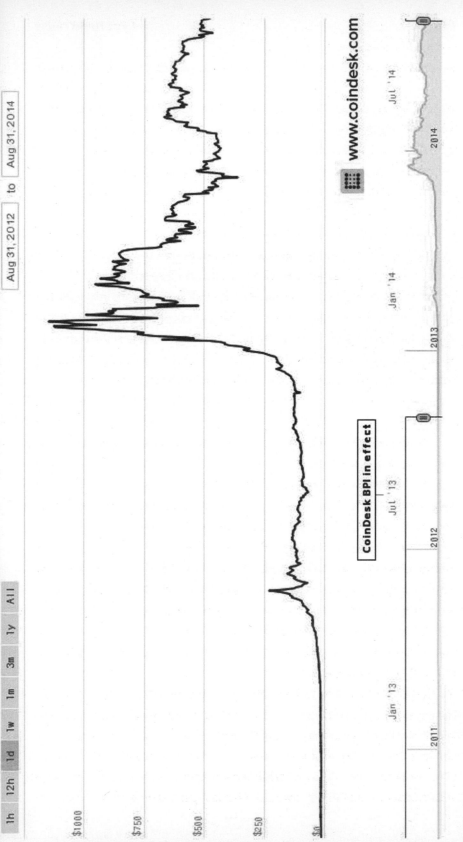

CoinDesk's Bitcoin Price Index

(*Courtesy of CoinDesk*)

in any other currency market. This included a harrowing "flash crash" that occurred in mid-August solely on the Bulgaria-based exchange, BTC-e, where the price plunged from $500 to $309 in three minutes before bouncing most of the way back.

A case can be made that bitcoin's volatility is unavoidable for the time being. Earning respect and widespread adoption as a currency is a process; it can't be achieved overnight. As that process plays out, bitcoin advocates say, stability will come once it attracts a sufficiently large number of people will have bought into bitcoin's promise as an effective new way to send money around the world. It's worth noting that over its six-year life, regardless of the big price swings, bitcoin has performed extremely well as an investment, as more and more people have bought into this idea. "The Honey Badger of Money" is how bitcoin's fans describe its tenacious ability to bounce back from adversity. Even after the big sell-off in early 2014, bitcoin was still about forty times higher than where it was at the end of 2012, a hundred times where it was on December 31, 2011, and almost seventeen hundred times more than where it was a year before that.

Critics such as Boston University economist Mark Williams, a strong skeptic of bitcoin's prospects, see these gains in a negative light. In a scathing presentation to the New York Department of Financial Services, Williams said it was a sign of "extreme hoarding" that will deny bitcoin the possibility of ever becoming a "useful transactional currency." But its proponents say you can't stop enthusiasts from buying and holding bitcoin and that this investment mind-set is part of an unavoidable, indeed necessary, transitional phase. "I wouldn't say hoarding is a bad thing," says BTC China CEO Bobby Lee, who has witnessed the intense speculative approach to bitcoin of Chinese investors. "Once its price has risen far enough and bitcoin has proven itself as a store of value, then people will start to use it as a currency."

Gil Luria, the Wedbush analyst, even argues that volatility is a good thing, on the grounds that it draws profit-seeking traders into the marketplace. Their presence encourages the development of sophisticated exchanges and more reliable mechanisms for swapping bitcoins into fiat currencies, he says, noting that bigger, more high-tech, and better-regulated trading exchanges were already coming online in 2014 to service a growing Wall Street–based clientele. The argument is that this build-out will in turn lead to stability—eventually. To understand this argument we must recognize the role played in markets by traders, that special breed of investors who buy and sell assets in a short period to profit from price moves in either direction. In placing these short-term bets, traders provide much-needed "liquidity" to markets—defined as the degree to which investors can easily find buyers of an asset they want to sell or sellers of one they want to buy. As more traders enter the market, creating more prospective buyers and sellers, liquidity increases and prices stabilize. Ironically, though, it's the volatility, not price gains, that first draws traders in, since that's what creates profits. If prices are swinging around, traders can make more money being on either side of the trade. We saw this in the 1970s, when the collapse of the Bretton Woods system sent exchange rates haywire and banks rushed to set up highly profitable foreign-exchange trading desks. Over time, the expansion of these desks, and the development of more and more sophisticated trading tools, delivered so much liquidity that exchange rates became relatively stable. Luria is imagining a similar trajectory for bitcoin. He says bitcoiners should be "embracing volatility," since it will help "create the payment network infrastructure and monetary base" that bitcoin will need in the future.

Then there's the argument that for bitcoin to fulfill its real potential—and here we're talking about *bitcoin the technology*, not *bitcoin the currency*—the exchange rate itself doesn't matter. The idea is that someday consumers and businesses won't hold bitcoins for their account but will unknowingly access the bitcoin network whenever payments are made. Already, bitcoin payment processors such as BitPay and Coinbase shield merchants from exchange-rate risk by immediately converting the incoming bitcoins into dollars. It's expected that the mirror version of this will in time be set up for consumers to convert their dollars into bitcoins, which will then immediately be sent to the merchant. Eventually, we could all be blind to these bitcoin conversions happening in the middle of all our transactions.

Still, someone will have to absorb the exchange-rate risk, if not the payment processors, then the investors with which they trade. Until volatility comes down, these players will charge for doing so, either directly via fees or in the discounted prices they quote to buy bitcoins or dollars. There's no magic bullet. Volatility must eventually be contained for bitcoin to live up to its promise as a low-cost, efficient way for people to exchange money.

At this point, it is simply not clear how all this will play out. It's not hard to imagine bitcoin and other cryptocurrencies becoming victims of their instability, never escaping from the chicken-and-egg problem of volatility. Moreover, as the memory of the 2008 crash fades, the necessity of finding an alternative payment model fades as well, especially one that appears so unpredictable. On the other hand, cryptocurrency's potential to upend a cumbersome centralized payment system is clear.

The problem with all this analysis is that we don't have an up-to-date historical model for gauging how an independently issued currency is supposed to evolve, let alone one that also functions as a unique payment-processing system and a protocol for decentralizing social relationships. None of the benchmarks that people use both to laud and to critique bitcoin—"currency," "commodity," "payment protocol"—quite fit. Bitcoin has features from all of them, but none in entirety. So, while it might seem unsatisfying, our best answer to the question of whether cryptocurrency can challenge the Visa and MasterCard duopoly is "maybe, maybe not."

The price volatility of bitcoin in 2013–14 certainly thrust it into the public eye. Ironically, this rise to a new level of mania—even beyond that of bitcoin's first four years of existence—would eventually force bitcoin's supporters to confront the challenges of its Wild West days and contemplate how it might mature.

The mania's starting point was in March 2013, with what we'll call the Cypriot bump. The tiny island nation of Cyprus, split between Greek and Turkish states, fell into the grip of a financial crisis because its banks, their cash balances swollen with deposits from wealthy Russians seeking a tax haven, had invested heavily in the bonds of neighboring Greece. That larger neighbor had become the basket case of the European Union, which had just forced the government in Athens to impose a "haircut," or mandated losses, on its investors. The EU did this to ensure that private-sector investors who'd made risky bets on Greece shouldered some of the burden of the bailout that German and other euro-zone taxpayers were bearing. Cyprus's overleveraged banks were an unintended casualty of that and were now faced with the terrifying threat of a bank run by their large Russian depositors.

The dramatic solution, one endorsed by Germany and its EU partners, who were equally reluctant to bail out Russian oligarchs, was that the government in Nicosia would freeze deposits and confiscate 10 percent of them to pay for a bank bailout. This unprecedented step sent shock waves around the world. "If they can do that there, they can do it anywhere," yelled Mark McGowan, a London cabbie famous for his profanity-laced YouTube videos, where he rants about topical matters under the moniker chunkymark, all delivered from his cab. The Cyprus rant is one of his all-time classics. *If they can do that there, they can do it anywhere.* He wasn't the only one thinking that.

Suddenly, bitcoin's "value proposition" was clear. The government might be able to take money out of your local bank account, but it couldn't touch your bitcoin. The Cyprus crisis sparked a stampede of money into bitcoin, which was now seen as a safe haven from the generalized threat of government confiscation everywhere. The price went from $33 at the end of February to $230 on April 9, pushing bitcoin's total market capitalization through $1 billion for the first time, but also setting off one of the wildest yearlong rides that any financial asset has ever seen.

Then there was some bad news. New technical problems at the trouble-prone Mt. Gox emerged, this time compelling it to suspend trading for two days on April 11, which then morphed into bigger legal problems. The bitcoin price plunged to $68 on April 16, where it seemed to find a floor, even though a month later the U.S. government froze Mt. Gox's U.S. bank account in one of the first signs that Washington wanted to regulate this lawless, new digital currency. Throughout the summer, the price stabilized, sort of, oscillating within "only" a range of $65 to $130.

Then U.S. law enforcement first arrived on the cryptocurrency scene. In late June 2013, reports emerged that the FBI had seized 11 bitcoins (then worth $800) from a drug dealer in what was seen as an initial "honeypot sting" on Silk Road. A month later, the Securities and

Exchange Commission filed charges against Trendon Shavers, a Texan accused of running a bitcoin Ponzi scheme under the moniker pirateat40. That the Feds were now taking bitcoin seriously was an alarming yet exhilarating proposition for bitcoiners, who were divided between those who wanted its lawlessness to continue and those who believed its growth depended on the legitimacy of regulation and enforcement against criminality.

While the news of drug busts and Ponzi schemes bred some mainstream suspicion about this unfamiliar, anonymous currency, it also spurred curiosity among some who hadn't yet cottoned on to bitcoin's possibilities. What was the fuss about? Inquiries led to discoveries, which led to investments. Silicon Valley investors started putting money into new exchanges and digital-wallet providers, and some prominent names declared themselves believers. Moneyed investors came, following in the footsteps of Cameron and Tyler Winklevoss— the twin brothers famous for their legal tussles with Facebook founder Mark Zuckerberg—who had announced back in April that they had acquired a massive stock of bitcoin then worth $11 million. As bitcoin's price began to rise, rise, and rise further, the twins' investment started looking well timed indeed. Not even the dramatic October 2 news that the Federal Bureau of Investigation had arrested Ross Ulbricht, the alleged Dread Pirate Roberts mastermind of the Silk Road site, and had seized 26,000 bitcoins, then worth $3.6 million, would pose much of a setback. The price went from $125 at the end of September to $198 a month later, even as word spread on October 26 that the FBI had hauled in an additional 144,000 bitcoins (then $28 million) from its Silk Road operation.

But then in November, things really went bananas, prompted by the outcome of some anxiously anticipated Senate hearings. Although Treasury Department Financial Crimes Enforcement Network director Jennifer Shasky Calvery announced new guidelines on the rules the bitcoin industry needed to follow, she said her organization "recognizes the innovation virtual currencies provide, and the benefits they might offer society." She had essentially given Washington's blessing, a cause for celebration in bitcoinland. The party was nowhere more evident than in the currency's price, which got above $1,150 on November 30.

All this was great news for bitcoin miners, who were continually accumulating bitcoins on their computers. However, their activity was changing, rapidly becoming industrialized. In January of 2013, a Chinese company called Avalon, set up by two students, Ng Zhang and Yifu Guo, had started delivering a new, stand-alone, specially dedicated mining computer using an ASIC (application-specific integrated circuit) chip. Over the coming months, ever faster, energy-hungry ASIC machines would come on the market, spurring a relentless arms race among miners chasing the finite supply of newly issued bitcoins; by the end of the year, the only way to win that race and stay profitable was by creating giant, data-center-based mining farms. Bitcoin had evolved into a worldwide industry, its expansion fueled by the rising price of the currency.

The price gains gave rise to the "bitcoin barons," many of them in their twenties, who became the public face of the brash new industry. In a watershed moment, *Bloomberg Businessweek* ran a story on April 10, 2013, with the title "Meet the Bitcoin Millionaires," featuring photos of Jered Kenna, founder of bitcoin exchange Tradehill, BitInstant's Shrem, and Avalon's Yifu Guo—all of them under thirty years of age. Other instantly rich bitcoiners started making it into the news—such as Roger Ver, the Bitcoin Jesus, so nicknamed for his enthusiasm for giving bitcoins away to promote the currency, and Mark Karpelès, the Frenchman who'd presided over the evolution of Mt. Gox into a virtual if crumbling monopoly. These were joined by more established bitcoin backers, including the Winklevoss twins and Internet pioneer Jeremy Allaire. Some of these people would become regulars at bitcoin conferences, which had by now evolved from the low-budget affairs of the early years to packed-house events in conference centers in Las Vegas, Amsterdam, and Toronto.

By December, bitcoin was over $1,100 and its total market capitalization was just shy of $14 billion. But at that lofty peak the signal for the party to wind down came—from China. Chinese speculators had played a key role in driving up the price of bitcoin, mostly through Bobby Lee's BTC China exchange, which at one point even surpassed Mt. Gox in volume. Bitcoiners looked with great hope at China. With more than 1 billion citizens living in an economy that was still only partially opened to the free market and whose government imposed strict controls over how much money they could send overseas, bitcoin might provide a work-around. Chinese officials seemed not to care; they had said nothing. Then suddenly word was leaked and duly reported by the Chinese press that the People's Bank of China was not happy about banks dealing with Chinese bitcoin exchanges. The ruling was vague but enough to scare people away. Bitcoin's price began to fall.

By January 2014, the price was down to $770. The 35 percent move from its peak twenty-nine days prior would have been a historic decline if it were, say, the dollar versus the yen. But that price left intact most of the fortunes made by people who'd got into bitcoin in mid-November or earlier. So when the community descended on Miami for yet another bitcoin conference at the end of January, the mood was still celebratory. That would change quickly.

The day after the conference, Charlie Shrem, one of *Businessweek*'s "bitcoin millionaires" and the vice chairman of the Seattle-based industry group the Bitcoin Foundation, was arrested in New York upon his return from a payments conference in Amsterdam. The high-profile, outspoken twenty-four-year-old was charged with helping a drug dealer from Silk Road launder money through his BitInstant service. Shrem pleaded not guilty at first but seven months later agreed to plead guilty to a markedly lesser charge of aiding and abetting an unlicensed money transmission. At the time of this writing he was yet to be sentenced. Although Shrem continued to play a vocal role in the community while under house arrest at his parents' place in Brooklyn, the charges against a person once viewed as a community spokesman left yet another stain on bitcoin.

Things would get worse. Mt. Gox, which had struggled with its finances ever since the seizure of its U.S. bank accounts and had stopped letting people withdraw dollars, reached its breaking point when it announced that it would also no longer allow customers to send bitcoin overseas. It would blame a bug in bitcoin's core software, a charge that was refuted by developers, who suspected that CEO Karpelès was deflecting blame, only to find that there was indeed a bug—one that hackers would exploit, almost bringing the network to a standstill as they tried to obtain fraudulent payments with thousands of fake transactions. Meanwhile, Mt. Gox spiraled out of control. Whatever the cause of its problems, it was unable to resolve them, and on February 28 it announced that it would file for bankruptcy and added the stunning revelation that it had outright lost 850,000 bitcoins,* 650,000 of which belonged to customers—gone, just like that. The amount was worth about $500 million at the time. Clients were outraged. The general public was bemused. And investors dumped bitcoins en masse.

Around the world more governments, among them Russia's and Australia's, started laying down the law to varying degrees. To all but the most doctrinaire bitcoiners, the question was not whether there should be regulation—most saw positive effects from the acknowledgment of bitcoin's importance and thought it could potentially quell users' fears—but whether regulatory overreach would constrain innovation. China cemented that concern with a more formal ruling in April banning banks from having anything to do with bitcoin businesses. Coupled with that, exchanges in the United States were having a hard time opening accounts with banks, which were wary of dealing with them, leaving some of the industry's main players without a key financial lifeline. On April 11, the bitcoin price touched an intraday low of $344.24, less than a third of where it was at its peak four months earlier. Was this the end? some wondered.

A far bigger concern than China was what might happen in Washington or New York, whose regulators had the most power to dictate cryptocurrency development. That's because the dollar's role as the world's dominant reserve and commercial currency puts its financial system at the center of everything. The Internal Revenue Service came out with a much-awaited ruling, declaring that bitcoin was not a currency but property and so would be taxed for capital gains. This wasn't the worst announcement for cryptocurrency enthusiasts, but it did create a headache for users, who, according to the initial IRS guidelines, would have to keep track of every bitcoin they spent to determine whether they'd made a gain or loss since buying it. Many feared this would provide yet another excuse for mainstream users to steer clear of bitcoin. Meanwhile, the New York Department of Financial Services proposed establishing a "BitLicense," which would regulate digital-currency businesses and overcome some of the ambiguity surrounding state money-transmitter licenses.

---

* The total lost was later downgraded to 650,000 after Mt. Gox management announced that it had rediscovered 200,000 coins in its possession.

Although Financial Services superintendent Benjamin Lawsky described the plan during hearings in February as a constructive effort to regulate bitcoin without quashing innovation, the draft he released in July came as a significant disappointment for bitcoiners. It seemed far more draconian than expected and prompted an immediate backlash from a suddenly well-organized bitcoin community. Lawsky indicated he was willing to change some of the clauses and that some were being misconstrued, but at the time of writing it was unclear what shape those changes would take.

Regulators weren't the only ones responding to the scroll of bad headlines with measures to get bitcoin's chaotic anarchy under control. Many of the more business-inclined entrepreneurs wanted to put the Mt. Gox era behind them, too. This didn't sit well with the radical antigovernment types who'd made bitcoin their personal cause, but it did spur some of the innovation that Gil Luria predicted would come in the trading arena. Various firms with Wall Street pedigrees moved to build high-tech exchanges that could accommodate sophisticated investors such as hedge funds and which would be heavy on classic compliance procedures. These would be the antidote to the loss of confidence spurred by Mt. Gox, they argued. But until they came online, trading conditions remained thin, which meant that some of the innovations that *were* brought to bitcoin trading and which might otherwise have helped foster two-way flows of buyers and sellers simply exaggerated the one-way moves in times of panic. These included high-frequency, automated trading "bots" used in some of the mainland-Chinese exchanges, margin-trading facilities introduced by Hong Kong exchange Bitfinex for customers to buy bitcoin with loans, facilities for futures, and short-sale bets on a bitcoin decline. Amid the angst created by Lawsky's unpopular BitLicense proposal, these edgy trading strategies, coupled with an illiquid market and more market conniptions in August, revived people's concerns about volatility until the price stabilized toward the end of the summer around $500.

Through all these highs and lows, all this joy and anxiety, bitcoin continued to grow its ecosystem. Many merchants put their hands up to accept bitcoin. More and more people opened wallets (more than 5 million as of this writing). This story of expanded adoption offered a compelling counterpoint to the impression of criminality, incompetence, and regulatory crackdown that had dominated mainstream press coverage in 2014.

Meanwhile, innovation in cryptocurrency technology powered on. If anything, it accelerated as developers around the world became increasingly enamored with the prospect of total economic disruption and the profits this augured. Not only did they put their minds to developing a host of new services making it easier for people to buy, sell, and transact in bitcoin, but techies also dreamed up new "Bitcoin 2.0" projects that promised to decentralize every corner of the economy. It was all a mark of the enormous respect that many had developed for the core invention of Satoshi Nakamoto and its myriad potentials: the blockchain. This is the machine inside the bitcoin machine. In the next chapter, we go inside it.

Five

BUILDING THE BLOCKCHAIN

The love of money grows as the money itself grows.
—*Juvenal*, A.D. *60–140*

As noted above, a big question dogged early cryptocurrency efforts: How do I know the person sending me a digital token hasn't sent a copy of it to someone else? I can't check the watermark, magnetic strip, or physical fibers in the note, as I can with paper currency. Herein lies the threat of "double-spending," the great vulnerability of digital money. Satoshi Nakamoto solved it, not by strengthening the security of a currency token, but by a real breakthrough in social technology, in the system of credits, debits, and balances that the chartalists recognize to be the true nature of money. The blockchain, the all-important ledger that functions as bitcoin's central nervous system, was Nakamoto's signature achievement. While technical in nature, it reflected important insights about the psychology of money and community, and what's needed to create rules that make individuals act in the interest of the group.

We've hinted that one of cryptocurrencies' great advantages is that they are decentralized. What does this mean? It comes down to the use of a common, fully public ledger.

Until now monetary systems have been built on centralized ledger-keeping, whether by banks or by central banks operating über-economy-wide ledgers. This has provided efficiency and security for communities that have had no other way to trust each other's accounts about who owes what to whom. The problem has always been, however, that this model confers too much power and excessive profit on those central record-keepers. The challenge lay in finding a compromise solution: a trustworthy, decentralized system for keeping society's tabs in order without losing the efficiency and security that centralization had delivered.

To create a less centralized system, you had to figure out a way to assign the shared record-keeping task to a group of individuals or institutions connected by a network, and to give them some incentive to perform those duties. You also needed to ensure that their common ledger was managed in such a way that no one record-keeper could tamper with it and introduce errors that the others wouldn't notice. Finally, you had to imbue the whole group with a sense of *trust* in its own rules, or at least trust that barriers to bad behavior were sufficient.

Early warning: the nitty-gritty of how this works can be a little complicated. It draws from mathematical concepts that are unfamiliar to most people. One way out of this would be to acknowledge that you don't *need* to understand the workings of cryptocurrencies. Neither of us has a handle on how an internal combustion engine works, but we still drive cars and entrust our families to their mechanisms. It's quite possible that you can't properly explain the workings of the U.S. banking system, but you still entrust your money to a bank. Even so, it's completely understandable, indeed laudable, that potential users of this new, untested monetary system want to understand its internal plumbing. It's a key reason that we chose to write this book, and perhaps one of the reasons you picked it up. So, let's press on. We'll take it slow, try to bring it down to the basics. Onward.

First, to help us get our heads around the model that Nakamoto established as the benchmark, we'll borrow an idea developed by software engineer Yevgeniy Brikman. It draws from the story referenced in chapter 2 of how *fei* stones were used to track and clear debts in the nineteenth-century Micronesian society of Yap. Imagine, Brikman wrote, that as trade and transactions expanded, one Yapese tribe had difficulty keeping track of who owned and owed *fei* stones. It became impossible to determine whether a person who claimed to have a sufficient store of stone currency actually had enough to settle a debt. After fights broke out and tensions rose, the tribal elders appointed one person to take charge of a shared written record of *fei* holdings and transactions. But that record-keeper started charging fees for recording each transaction, applying arbitrary distinctions that favored one tribe member over another, and rewarding his cronies. And he wasn't the only one who began to use the system for his advantage: the chiefs soon pressured him to cook the books.

Finally, one group of concerned tribespeople took matters into their hands. They would do away with the record-keeper and his central ledger. Instead, every family would maintain its own ledger. Every time a transfer of *fei* occurred, the person making the payment would go to the village center and announce to everyone that a transfer had been made—in fact, making the announcement constituted the payment. Everyone would update his or her ledger, introducing a debit entry in the payer's account and making an equivalent credit to the payee's. If a majority of homes recognized a transaction as legitimate, the others would have to go along with that ruling.

Until recently, it was impossible to create such a decentralized system in the vast scope of the global economy. But then the Internet solved a big part of the problem by creating a network for instant universal communication. The next steps were (1) creating a mechanism to publicly display each record-keeper's work and to maintain the integrity of the one common ledger that everyone agrees to be accurate, and (2) providing the right incentives for enough individuals or firms to dedicate resources to the upkeep of that ledger. Bitcoin neatly handled both of these challenges.

We've mentioned that bitcoin's software is preprogrammed to generate a consistent amount of new bitcoins over a 130-year period, and that these are issued as rewards to computer owners known as miners for their work confirming transactions. Of course, this doesn't mean people won't be able to keep using bitcoins, which can each be divided into tiny fractions. They will still be shared back and forth, their value shifting according to what price the market places on the goods and services they can buy. But for now the release of those rewards is what ensures that bitcoin's public ledger, its blockchain, is updated, maintained, and preserved. Over time, as the generation of new bitcoins slows, the reward system will shift to one in which miners are compensated with modest transaction fees imposed on anyone making payments.

Bitcoin's blockchain ledger is a long chain of blocks, or groupings, of transactions occurring around the same time. The chain will continue to grow indefinitely so long as the system keeps operating. This chronological structure is crucial because it confers legitimacy on the oldest transactions, the idea being that later-dated attempts by a user to re-spend the same bitcoin balance is treated as illegitimate. By creating a time-stamped sequence of expenditures and receipts among every participant in the bitcoin economy, the system keeps track of where everybody's balances are at any given moment, as well as the identifying information attached to every bitcoin—and fraction of bitcoin—ever created, spent, or received. If James uses a bitcoin wallet app on his smartphone to, say, buy a cup of coffee at Coupa Café in Palo Alto, the network will be notified of a request to send BTC0.008 from an address that's uniquely attached to his wallet to one controlled by Coupa Café's digital wallet. At this moment, the purchase stands as a "pending transaction," one awaiting confirmation. But after the miners have completed the tasks required to arrange a new block of transactions and insert it into the blockchain, James's and a host of other transactions occurring within the same ten minutes will be permanently recorded into that ledger. That establishes his coffee purchase as authenticated and irreversible. (Note: the blockchain won't actually know or even care that it was for coffee, or that James and the Coupa Café were involved; all it needs are the special passwords and identifying addresses associated with James's and Coupa Café's wallets.)

Now, let's imagine James is an accomplished coder and that he knows how to override instructions in the software client that his computer uses to access the bitcoin network. He's also broke and sleepy and so gets that client to tap the same account information from which he paid the café to later buy a pillow from Overstock.com, effectively trying to pay with bitcoins he no longer had. After doing this, the blockchain's chronological ledger would reveal that the money had already been spent. *No,* the record-keepers would declare as they checked James's new transaction attempt against the permanent record, *he has spent those bitcoins before.*

Every transaction that's added to the ever-extending blockchain ledger is checked against the existing ledger before being given a stamp of legitimacy. Based on a consensus view among the miners as to which transactions are legitimate and which are not, the ledger provides irrefutable proof of who owns what and what has been spent and received.

For ease of explanation, we're going to focus on how bitcoin's blockchain, currency-creation, and transaction-confirmation systems work, though many blockchain variations exist across the cryptocurrency universe.

James's cup of coffee represented one transaction. The system must process many more.

The blockchain is managed, as we've mentioned, by bitcoin's core software protocol. Every user of the bitcoin network from Nakamoto to the present has in one form or another downloaded a set of programming instructions that tell their computer or smartphone how to interact, talk to, and work with others on that network. The blockchain doesn't live on a single computer or server but, as with our Yapese ledger-keepers, is shared around that community of computer owners, or *nodes*. Those nodes include machines that run bitcoin *wallets,* a form of software that gives consumers and businesses special passwords with which to propose changes to bitcoin balances (i.e., initiate payments) in those limited parts of the blockchain that are assigned to them. The nodes also include the individual PCs—or, more likely these days, specialized mining rigs—that are used by bitcoin *miners* to build the blockchain and earn bitcoin rewards. Working together according to the preordained system, these nodes collectively ensure the ledger's contents are legitimate and protected from abuse by rogue elements.

The blockchain is everything to bitcoin. In fact, this ever-shifting accounting of debits and credits constitutes the currency itself. Bitcoins don't exist per se, not in the sense that you can peer into some electronic vessel and isolate a set of self-contained coins. Bitcoins exist only insofar as they assign value to a bitcoin *address*, a mini, one-off account with which people and firms send and receive the currency to and from other people's and firms' addresses. Bitcoins do not constitute documents or other digital files. The balance you see in your wallet is simply a net value of spending power based on an accounting of the incoming and outgoing transactions. This model is extended across the blockchain, encapsulating all the debits, credits, and balances associated with each unique bitcoin address. This is an important distinction because it means there's no actual currency file or document that can be copied or lost. Your right to bitcoin is defined as the balance that the ledger recognizes as yours. You can lose your ability to exploit those balances and shift them to someone else—that is, if you lose the password needed to release them—but you can't literally lose bitcoins since they don't actually exist.

Also critical: the ever-lengthening blockchain of confirmed transactions is public. That distinguishes bitcoin from closed electronic-currency systems such as PayPal's, where the ledger is a tightly kept secret. Using specially designed software—most commonly, the free tool provided by the eponymous London-based company Blockchain—you can see the details of every bitcoin transaction ever conducted. You can only change, or request to change, those parts of it that are accessible via your special passwords, but at all times you have full view of every other transaction and bitcoin address.

When looking at these addresses on the blockchain, we see nothing to identify their owners. Instead, they appear as strings of letters and numbers of between twenty-six and thirty-four characters. Each of these addresses, brought into being when a past transaction occurred, represents what cryptographers call a *public key.* As the owner of such an address, you are free to share it with outsiders and invite them to make a deposit there. But only you have the power to make a withdrawal, which you can do with the aid of a *wallet.* Here's how you might carry that out: You could open a smartphone app that's linked to your online wallet and then use its built-in QR code-scanner to import a merchant's address into the "To" line of a transaction window. You would then type in the desired payment amount and hit "Send," thereby instructing the wallet software to find a sufficient bitcoin balance in one or more of your preexisting addresses and send that balance to the merchant.* To do this, the wallet program accesses an embedded passcode that's known as the *private key;* each private key is uniquely associated with one address. By mathematically combining the public and private keys—or, in cryptographic terms, by *signing* the former with the

---

* Sometimes, the structure of the bitcoin address network is such that the wallet often can't send the right amount in one go and so sends a larger amount than was ordered while deducting a smaller amount as "change" from the recipient and transferring it back to the sender.

latter—information is released, which in this case amounts to an instruction to transfer a bitcoin balance from one blockchain address to another.*

This public-key encryption system, which is akin to applying the secret password for your online bank account to your not-so-secret username, is used widely in Internet and financial applications, including online banking and e-mail; it allows people to share selected data without giving away access to all their information. An important feature of this system is that it's essentially impossible, using current computing technology, to do the public-private key calculation in reverse and discover the private passcode.† But that doesn't mean an outsider can't discover a private key if, for example, he or she gains access to a computer or smartphone on which it resides. That's why it's important for people and institutions to safeguard their wallets and protect their bitcoins. Failure to do so is what happened at Mt. Gox, at least according to its version of how it lost 650,000 bitcoins.

The traceability of this record of transactions helps build community trust in the monetary system. But this feature of bitcoin has also been exploited by law enforcement, most famously when the FBI seized bitcoins during its 2013 crackdown on the Silk Road online drug marketplace.‡

---

* For added protection, sophisticated new "multi-sig" wallets require more than one private key to be applied before bitcoins can be released, often with more than one party controlling different keys. But the mechanism as described here is otherwise the same.

† "Impossible" in this sense means it would currently take hundreds of years for a computer to use "brute force" to discover the private key through trial and error. If quantum computing is successfully implemented, however, that time frame could be significantly reduced, in which case the entire world of banking and information systems may have to come up with an alternative to public-key encryption.

‡ We don't know exactly how the FBI conducted its operations, but it likely picked up transactions on the Silk Road Web site and traced those payments to addresses in wallets that had been set up to accumulate the site's service fees. Then through other modes of investigation, the agency will likely claim, it linked those addresses to its prime suspect, Ross Ulbricht. Those events have shown that bitcoin isn't quite the anonymous haven that Nakamoto and some underground businesses thought it would be.

Unlike with credit-card transactions, which are linked to an individual's name and made known to that person's bank and to anyone else with access to the person's account records, a bitcoin address has no personal connection. It's one reason some people turn to bitcoin to conduct embarrassing transactions they'd rather not have others know about. On the other hand, if they publicize that such and such a bitcoin address is theirs, then anyone can see every transaction they make in or out of that address. Because only alphanumeric identifiers appear and not names, law enforcement agents cannot easily navigate this system. Yet the traceability presents opportunities to follow leads that would otherwise run dead with cash. Armed with subpoena powers, an investigator would in theory be able to force whatever institution provided a bitcoin wallet to divulge the owner's identity. This is why some people see bitcoin as a greater tool for prosecutors than as a cloak for criminals.

This raises important questions. Tension always exists between the goals of maintaining individual privacy and allowing government access to information to protect us. As elsewhere with the Internet, the challenge for bitcoin, if and when it goes mainstream, will be to find a balance. It needs to preserve the positive aspects of its anonymity—whether it's the ability of a female blogger in Afghanistan to receive payments for her contributions without interference from others or more generally the right of individuals to legally pursue happiness in whatever form they prefer—against the threat that nefarious actors will exploit it.

Back to how the blockchain works. James's wallet has performed the private-public key signature and instructed the bitcoin network that he wants to send BTC0.008 to an address controlled by Coupa Café, but at this stage it is still a *pending transaction*. Later, if all goes to plan and James's purchase isn't suspected of being a double-spend, it will be confirmed as a legitimate transaction and installed on the blockchain. Once that has happened, the funds transfer cannot be reversed or canceled. There are no chargebacks to the merchant of the kind that banks impose if a credit-card customer later disputes a charge, and neither party can forcibly undo the deal outside of a common agreement to conduct a second, refunding transaction. This is why bitcoin's system for verifying that double-spending hasn't occurred is so important, which brings us to those hardworking "miners."

Bitcoin *mining* is, to our mind, a misnomer. The essential work being done is more like bookkeeping.

Work is another prominent word in the vernacular of bitcoin mining, in this case conveying the sense that the currency's underlying value isn't based on nothingness but on labor, and hard labor at that. In fact, computational difficulty is its defining feature. The harder it gets, the more real-world resources get spent performing the task, mostly in the form of electricity. Some crypto-economists argue that these inputs are what give bitcoins real value. Just as important, the amount of work— the computing equivalent of man-hours—gives legitimacy to the ledger, in that it represents a significant collective investment in assuring its integrity.

Here's how miners "work."

Once James has instructed his wallet to send bitcoins to Coupa Café, it broadcasts that pending transaction to the network, along with a host of important pieces of information: the two parties' assigned wallet addresses; the date and time stamp; various other details such as a unique transaction code; and whatever other information—a greeting, perhaps— that the sender might attach.

Enter the miners. Each mining *node* or computer gathers this information and reduces it into an encrypted alphanumeric string of characters known as a *hash*. Just as with document files that can be "zipped," this process allows relatively large amounts of information to be summarized and reduced to a much smaller store of data. Hashes are an integral part of encryption and data-storage procedures throughout the computing world. You may have seen them without knowing what they are. Depending on which hash algorithm is being used, the process produces a hash of a fixed length. In bitcoin's case the algorithm is called SHA-256, which delivers a hash of sixty-four characters in length taken from the full range of numbers (0–9) and letters (*a–z*). To see what one looks like, you can visit any hash generator Web site and write something into the text field. Here's what quickhash.com came back with when we wrote, "The only thing we have to fear is fear itself":

f72680b97551fc5eda1b3a33dda55796ba9619b371fdd03f66409
f2c4958c2cb

And here's what happened when we cut and pasted all 168 words of the preceding paragraph of this chapter into the same field:

e52a16c11d5c45b768b1bc87f0c1494799e92c019101562bfb4359 50b36de17b

Whether it's one single character or the entire text of *War and Peace,* the hash comes out at the same sixty-four-character length. Yet the tiniest change in the underlying information—a single decimal point or a space, for example—will change the hash completely. This power to pack a lot of information into the same hash structure but with completely different results each time makes its encryption function powerful. Much information can be reduced and encoded. And while it's virtually impossible to decrypt that code and find out what it contains, it's relatively trivial if a computer has access to the underlying source data to verify that the hash accurately encapsulates that data.

Hash algorithms also allow you to build a kind of hash hierarchy, which is useful because it creates a structure within which the miners can group concurrently timed transactions together. Here's how that works: The miner's software client takes the hash of the first transaction—with the pool of underlying data contained within it—and combines it with the raw data of the next, unhashed transaction to form a new hash. A full record of *both* transactions has now been hashed. A similar action then occurs with the next transaction that the mining client picks up. It merges the second hash, the one containing two transactions worth of data, with the next transaction's information to form a third hash. This process goes on as new transactions get picked up, with the computers constantly packing all the incoming data into a single hash, a code whose underlying information can easily be verified at a later time by working back through the unbroken chain. This is how transactions are packaged into the blockchain's crucial building blocks—called, appropriately, *blocks.*

While all this is going on, the computers are also participating in a kind of competition/lottery to try to be the first to "seal off" one of these blocks—that is, prepare it for insertion in the blockchain ledger and take home the prize of the next issuance of bitcoins. Until that happens, the network can't begin to confirm the validity of the latest round of transactions. Each miner has been individually hashing and rehashing the underlying data in the manner described above, but their details aren't yet ready to be checked by the network. There's still no consensus on their validity. James's payment to Coupa Café remains unconfirmed. Finding the solution to the puzzle is thus an integral part of the vital business of validating transactions.

The machines enter the competition by simultaneously and rapidly coming up with new potential *block hashes* to encode and capture all the data in the new, fully packaged block and link it to the block hash of the previous block. The winning block hash must match one that bitcoin's core algorithm has decided will be the current block's winning number. The match is extremely difficult to make, so the computers keep coming up with new hashes until they get it right, tweaking the process each time to change the readout—over and over and over. Each of the countless new hashes produced by the computer is created by adding a unique, randomly generated number called a *nonce* to the other data contained in the block hash, which, as mentioned, includes the hashed underlying transaction information and the block hash of the previous block. Adding a new nonce each time completely alters the output hash. It's worth noting that the word *nonce* is derived from a passage by Lewis Carroll in which he deployed the word *frabjous*, and described it as a "nonce" word that's made up for one occasion and not likely to be used again. Such is the fate of the billions of nonces produced and discarded as the high-powered mining rigs look for the winning block hash. It is a hunt for a digital pin in a massive haystack of numbers.

At the end of this laborious trial-and-error work, one mining node will eventually come up with the block hash that the bitcoin algorithm was looking for, a number that must have just the right amount of zeros in it and various other conditions. Getting there requires brute computational force, which is why a mining rig with the fastest hashing power is going to have a better chance than a slower one of winning each block. That said, the hashing process is totally random, which means that while the most powerful rigs will win the competition more frequently than lesser rigs, they won't win *every* time. (One way to think of it is that investing in hashing power is like buying extra lottery tickets—there's no guarantee of winning but your chances rise with each additional ticket.)

In fact, if the total hashing power of the network remains constant, the math of the random number-generating function is such that over an extended period a single node can expect to earn bitcoins proportional to the amount of power it contributes to that network. The problem is, with so many mining rigs now in play and only so many block prizes handed out, it can be a long time before a low-powered rig's winning number comes up for a twenty-five-bitcoin prize. That's why all but the very biggest of mining operators these days join mining pools, which divvy up the aggregate intake according to each member's contributed computation power, with the smaller members typically receiving just fractions of a bitcoin each month.

Miners are set the task of solving the puzzle for two reasons. One, it imposes a cost on mining, since the computing power it demands is expensive, in terms of both the machinery and the electricity it uses. That helps to regulate mining and create a reciprocal relationship between what otherwise would be free bitcoins and the work required to obtain them. And two, it creates a competition with a payout at the end, which incentivizes the miners to do the work needed to confirm the transactions.

Once the puzzle is solved, the bitcoin software client that's running on the winning node's machine "seals off" a new block of transactions with the block hash and assigns to it a *block number* that sequentially follows the last block number on the ever-extending blockchain. (At the exact moment that these words were being written, the blockchain was working on block number 318,685—that's how many blocks had been completed since Nakamoto mined the Genesis Block, and if you converted that into time by multiplying that number by ten minutes, it would bring you more or less out at January 2009.) Because the previous block hash has been included in the new hash, the latest block is now mathematically linked to the blockchain, as if to form the latest in an ever growing line of trailer hitches. Because of that hypersensitive quality of hashes described above, where the slightest data change will completely alter its output, this structure means that, in theory, no one can mess with any of the data contained in the blockchain's history. Doing so would turn the whole thing into gobbledygook. This makes it tamperproof.

Once a newly sealed block of transactions has been created and added to the chain, important work remains to be done: other miners must now confirm the legitimacy of the underlying transactions contained within it. Without their affirmation, no shared consensus exists on the truth of what lies in the blockchain. There would be no way to say for sure that a rogue miner had incorporated bogus transactions into a block. It could send bitcoins that it doesn't have the right to spend—that is, counterfeit them—and the system would simply accept that fraud as if it were a legitimate transaction. The other miners thus verify what's known as the winning miner's *proof of work*, comparing data from the underlying transactions to the hashed data within it so as to verify its legitimacy and check it against the history in the blockchain. While that seems like a mammoth task, these are high-powered computers; it's not nearly as taxing as the nonce-creating game and can be done relatively quickly and easily. The other miners' confirmations are then broadcast to the network and out to wallet holders. Coupa Café can now be reasonably satisfied that James's payment is legitimate. Just as important, the confirmation gives miners the satisfaction that the last block on the chain is indeed a legitimate one, which means they are prepared to go ahead and attach the next block to it if they happen to be the winner. From there, the whole process starts over again.

An important aside here: while the block-completion and confirmation process implies at least a ten-minute wait until a transaction is fully cleared, merchants that use the services of a bitcoin payment processor such as Bitpay, Coinbase, or GoCoin will typically accept a customer's payment immediately. For all but the very largest transactions, the processor usually bears the risk of non-confirmation. They do this because non-confirmations—or the double-spending actions that lead to them—are very rare. Sophisticated "big data" analytical tools are also coming onto the market, including one from start-up BlockCypher, that allow merchants and processors to gauge within seconds the probability that a particular transaction will be accepted, all with close to 100 percent accuracy.

Notwithstanding these expediting tricks, the bitcoin algorithm establishes certain rules to build confidence in the ledger over time and to ensure that miners are properly incentivized to confirm only legitimate transactions. Although a miner is allocated a new batch of bitcoins once it seals off a block and ties it to the blockchain, the bitcoin protocol won't let it use those bitcoins in a payment until a total of ninety-nine additional blocks have been built on top of its block. That makes sure that over time, the network consensus on the legitimacy of the transactions contained in that original block becomes rock solid. It also motivates every miner to make sure that everyone else is doing the right thing.

Occasionally, two blocks are found virtually simultaneously, which ultimately means that one block becomes "orphaned" as the network can pick only one on which to build the longest chain. The bitcoins awarded to the orphaned block will be left as worthless, and whatever transactions that were contained within it but excluded from the legitimized block that's now inserted into the chain will have to be processed later as new blocks are created. This capacity to orphan an illegitimate block is important because it means the entire network can be satisfied that the unbroken chronological chain, simply by virtue of continuing, represents the true record as recognized by consensus. But it also means that some transactions have longer wait times before they are fully confirmed and installed in the blockchain.

Anyone can become a miner and is free to use whatever computing equipment he or she can come up with to participate. Nakamoto knew that as more miners entered the hunt, the incentive would be strong to ramp up computing power to beat the competition. So to keep everything in sync, he programmed the bitcoin algorithm to calculate the so-called hashrate of the overall network—effectively, the total computational capacity per second—and automatically adjust the mathematical puzzle's difficulty so that blocks would become harder to seal off. That way, the bitcoin reward program could more or less stick to an ingrained ten-minute-per-block schedule. The ten-minute gap is somewhat arbitrary, but by choosing an interval and programming the software to stick to that fixed schedule, he could arrange the currency-issuance schedule to be consistent over a 130-year period.

In monetary-theory terms, the payout is seigniorage, the profit that a currency issuer—be it a sovereign, a monetary authority, or in this case a winning bitcoin miner—derives from the privilege of minting the community's money. The corollary is, this cost is borne by the rest of the community, since fresh supply depletes the market value and purchasing power of the existing currency. Seigniorage is unavoidable; someone has to be the

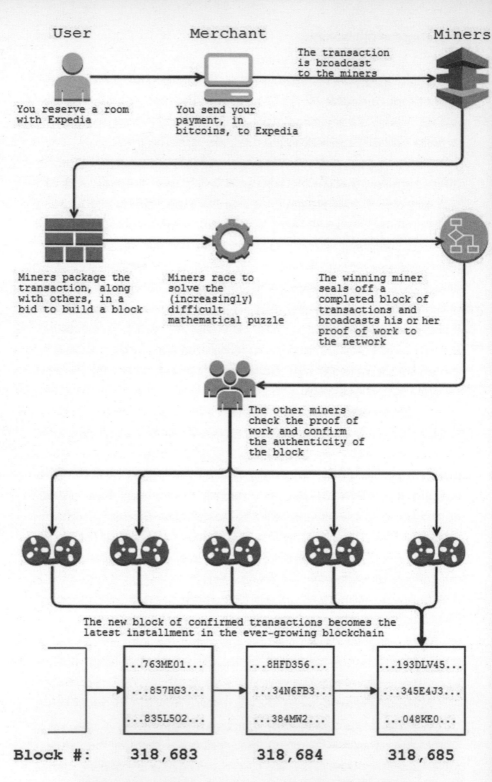

How Transactions Are Confirmed on the Blockchain

(Courtesy of Paul Vigna and Michael J. Casey)

first to own newly issued currency. The question is how to make it fair. Some cryptocurrency designers have created nonprofit foundations and charged them with distributing the coins based on certain criteria—to eligible charities, for example. But that requires the involvement of an identifiable and trusted founder to create the foundation. Even then, who's to say those distribution rules are fair? It is, of course, subjective. Some designers have given fixed allotments to people formally registered as belonging to a particular group, such as a national registry. But that creates the potential for fraud as people can set up more than one wallet per person, hiding behind the system's anonymity, and get higher allotments for themselves. Some have created the coins and sold portions of them to the public—garnering the seigniorage for themselves, much like a government.* Often this strategy requires some elaborate maneuvers to keep the faith with the community, occasionally employing a "proof of burn" strategy, where the founders periodically transfer some of their coin holdings to a verifiably unusable wallet to maintain scarcity and bolster the value of everyone else's coins.

The unidentified founder of bitcoin dealt with this fairness problem by resorting to the free-market principles of competition. That is one of the purposes of the relentless hashing competition, a process that, to the uninitiated, can seem pointless. It's a bit of a trick. Miners perform a task with the sole goal of winning a race to earn bitcoin, and almost as an unintended result, they end up confirming transactions along the way and keeping the blockchain up-to-date. This is the basis upon which bitcoin's protocol decides who should earn the seigniorage, a model founded on the idea that in return for this privilege the recipients must invest resources—equipment, electricity—and that their computer must do *work*. That in turn provides a foundation for putting a value on bitcoin.

To make sure his incentive system carried some real weight, Nakamoto devised a much more strictly prescribed monetary policy than the Federal Reserve's, a key element of which halves the bitcoin issuance every 210,000 blocks—roughly every four years. As of 2014, blocks were

---

* This approach has been followed by designers of special cryptocurrency projects intended to develop applications for decentralized commerce beyond merely currency payments. The coin sale proceeds are used to pay for the developers needed to build those systems. See chapter 9.

paying 25 bitcoins each, down from 50 before 2012. It will drop to 12.5 in 2016. This schedule means bitcoin is heavily front-loaded, with more than half of the 21 million lifetime supply of coins created in the system's first six years of existence. This creates a sense of scarcity over time, which, in theory, should support bitcoin's value if demand keeps up with it.

New bitcoins aren't the only way that miners get compensated. The core software also contains the ability to charge transaction fees, paid by the sender. As of now, some small fees are mandatory for only a few types of transactions. These include *dust* transactions, or tiny amounts—the idea being that antispam fees are needed to discourage denial-of-service attacks by nefarious actors who try to overwhelm a network with massive amounts of pointless transactions or messages—and transactions that contain excessive amounts of data, defined as more than ten thousand bytes. Users can also add fees to their transaction to increase the likelihood that miners will pick it up and include it in block, thereby reducing the potential wait time for final confirmation. (Not every transaction occurring with a ten-minute period ends up in a confirmed block within that time.)

As the issuance rate of new bitcoins slows further, the algorithm will almost certainly need to be tweaked to make transaction fees a more important part of miners' remuneration to keep them incentivized to do their job. (Once the issuance rates drops to zero in the year 2140, transaction fees will be the *only* form of compensation.) The core development team managed by the Bitcoin Foundation's Gavin Andresen has a plan in place to create a flexible scale of fees per confirmation wait times whose rates would be set by a market mechanism. This reminds us that while bitcoin is far more efficient as a payment system than the bank-centric, centralized system, it's not free. Both seigniorage and transaction fees represent a transfer of value to those running the network. Still, in the grand scheme of things, these costs are far lower than anything found in the old system.

With miners captivated by the spectacular price gains of 2012–13 and seemingly unfazed by the big price drop of 2014, the potential payoff continues to draw people and their computers to mining. Even amid signs that the costs involved, especially that of electricity, are making it harder to turn a buck, mining has gone through an absolutely astounding increase in computing power. There seems to be no shortage of people who think that bitcoin, as some in the community like to say, is headed "to the moon" and that mining is their ticket to those riches. Bitcoin mining is thus in the midst of an arms race or "hashrate war" as miners bring ever-more-efficient number crunchers to beat each other at solving the bitcoin puzzle.

Six

> Time is money.
> —*Benjamin Franklin*

Bitcoin mining, once performed by cryptography geeks in their basements, has become big business.

One U.K. researcher's rough estimate suggests miners collectively invested as much as $1 billion in new, superfast specialized "rigs" in the twelve months to April 2014. Anyone in this game has had to choose between forking out dough or accepting an increasingly lower bitcoin payout. There's still money to be made, but profit margins have shrunk, and the return on investment is vulnerable to an extremely volatile bitcoin price.

As we've discussed earlier, the race began when Laszlo Hanyecz realized that his graphics card, or GPU, was actually eight hundred times speedier than his computer's central processing unit for mining bitcoins. As his coins piled up, other existing miners soon copied him, converting to GPUs to regain what they'd lost. As techie discussion boards lit up with chatter about the new approach—as well about the pizzas that its inventor had spent his coins on—waves of newcomers joined the hunt for bitcoins from all corners of the globe.

One of those newcomers was Jason Whelan, a high school student in Belleville, Ontario, whose twin passions were computer gaming and computer networks. His interest in the latter drew him to online cryptography forums, and in the fall of 2010, he found that people were suddenly abuzz about bitcoin. He learned that a new exchange called Mt. Gox had come online earlier that year, which meant a growing number of people were not only mining bitcoins but buying them, and their price was rising—in the month of October its price had more than tripled, from six cents to over twenty cents. So, hoping to make a quick buck, Whelan made some adjustments to his personal computer, a unit he had custom-built for gaming with two superpowerful, parallel Nvidia graphics cards, and turned it into a bitcoin miner.

Right from the start, there were complications. A month in, he was confronted by his father, wondering why the hell the electricity bill had gone through the roof. Whelan had been running the mining software's intense hashing program 24-7. It was running so hot that Whelan had worried for the safety of his "pride and joy" and moved it to a cool corner of the basement where his dad wouldn't see it. But there was another problem: his beloved gaming computer was now completely occupied performing this mundane task. And it didn't seem to be making him rich.

"I was more interested in playing games with my new gaming computer than watching it sit there generating some magic money that I didn't really understand," Whelan recalls. So, he turned off the mining client when its tally of coins was at thirty. Back then, they were worth $6; when he spoke to us in late May 2014, they would have been worth $18,000. Sadly, he had overwritten the hard drive multiple times and had not written down the pass codes and keys for his wallet. Without knowledge of the private pass-code key he'd used or even the public key attached to the wallet itself, the coins are likely lost forever. "I'm sure others like me fantasize about their lost riches had they continued mining since the early days," he says.

Three years later, by then a sophomore studying networking and IT security at the University of Ontario Institute of Technology, in Oshawa, Ontario, Whelan was shocked to learn that bitcoin's price had risen to $120. He started reading up on the digital currency and, with his growing expertise in networking, soon grasped its social and technological importance, which had eluded him as a teenager. So he resolved to get back into mining.

This was easier said than done. In that three-year interregnum, GPUs had themselves become obsolete. Following the January 2013 breakthrough in which China-based Avalon shipped its first miners using ASICs (application-specific integrated circuits), the market had moved to fully dedicated "rigs" fitted with these superfast chips, each designed to do nothing but process hash calculations. With the price of bitcoin rising exponentially, the race was on to make ever-faster ASIC chips and more efficient rigs. At the time of writing, the newest machines, retailing for around $6,000, were promising three terahashes a second—3 trillion hash calculations every second, or 1,800 trillion within the ten minutes for block creation. That's roughly 3 million times faster than the fastest CPU could perform the same task when Nakamoto mined the first bitcoins in January of 2009.

But while the virtual world of mining has moved at lightning speed, the bricks-and-mortar world of factories and supply chains has struggled to keep up. By September 2013 the bitcoin press was full of stories about long delivery delays from the major manufacturers of super-high-end rigs. You can imagine the frustration of people plunking down $4,000 to "preorder" a Butterfly Labs Imperial Monarch miner, then waiting six months for it to be delivered, knowing that for every extra week, bitcoins were getting harder to mine, and ever-faster rigs were being released. The Missouri-based Butterfly Labs later had its operations suspended by the Federal Trade Commission. And it was not the only firm creating acrimonious relationships with its customers: Stockholm-based KnC Miner, Austin's CoinTerra, Alydian of Bainbridge Island in Washington State, and San Francisco–based Hashfast—they all had delivery problems, with the latter two falling into bankruptcy. Numerous lawsuits were filed alleging that companies had swindled their customers, taking in money for preorders that was then used to fund their own mining operations. For its part, the industry blamed it on ill-prepared parts suppliers. Avalon cofounder Ng Zhang said the ASIC makers in Taiwan didn't at first take the bitcoin-mining-rig-maker clients seriously. But as of mid-2014 delivery problems were still par for the course in this business.

For Whelan, the solution was to buy a secondhand rig. He picked up a Butterfly Labs Jalapeño mining rig in a local classified ad for $500, a little bit like buying a used Mercedes with one hundred thousand miles on the odometer. Even though its hashrate of five gigahashes per second was far behind the fastest machines on the market, it had the advantage of being immediately available. With the value of bitcoins steadily rising, the sooner he could start the better.

Whelan next did what virtually every small to medium-size miner does these days and joined a mining pool. That way he was assured of a steady flow of coins, albeit in small increments, rather than having to wait for that random moment, years away if ever, when his rig would win a full block of twenty-five coins. Yet the size of the payouts didn't bother him. Unlike his first foray into mining as a high school student, this one had a more philosophical underpinning. "In 2010, I saw that I was only making X amount of dollars," he says, "but now I had a new mind-set, that even if I was losing money in dollars, the bitcoin movement is so strong I'm betting on its future increase."

Whelan also had an ace up his sleeve: the university covered his electricity costs. (This is relatively common; colleges haven't yet cracked down on dorm-room bitcoin mining.) But he couldn't control the constant noise and heat emanating from the contraption in his tiny dorm room. So, in the fall months he kept the window open and used a fan to suck in the cooler air from outside. In the winter, he closed the window but turned the fan onto the machine on his desk, the combination making an almighty racket. Meanwhile, the price soared to an early-December peak above $1,150, a tenfold increase from when he'd started. So, with his belief in bitcoin's future affirmed, he reinvested a portion of his earnings into some additional miners, which in turn needed another fan to keep them cool. "I felt like a digital drug dealer," he says. "I had to tend to my crops, keeping them running cool, while avoiding residence staff who might object to the constantly running machines eating up their electricity."

This noisy, secretive business was profitable, but it didn't make for a comfortable existence. And right from the start Whelan faced the mathematical reality that his static hashrate was shrinking as a proportion of the ever-expanding network, whose computing power was by then almost doubling every month. That ensured that his already tiny share of the bitcoin payoff would systematically decline over time. In the early spring of 2014, Whelan contemplated buying a secondhand AntMinter S1 from Bitmain, which ran at a solid 180 gigahashes per second. But bitcoin's exchange rate was falling—it would lose two-thirds of its value in the first four months of the year—while the network hashrate was soaring. Those two factors had already rapidly depleted the value of a machine that was being outhashed by rigs running at more than a terahash per second. Back in December, the AntMinter had retailed for almost $3,000; but now Whelan was looking at a secondhand model for $800. Knowing that this rapid depreciation would continue, he changed plans.

Whelan knew that cloud hashing offered an alternative. These services would buy up rigs, set them up in data centers where they could be run cheaply, and then rent out portions of the hashing power. Clients would get a portion of the total bitcoin revenues proportional to how much of the overall hashing they were paying for. In Whelan's case, he opted for a five-year contract with pbcmining.com, putting down the full contract price of 1.1 bitcoin, or around $600. That way "I could get the damn machines out of my ear and not have to worry about their value depreciating," he says.

Whelan was never going to run off with millions this way, but he continued to make a modest profit. By late spring, he was bringing in about $200 a month in bitcoin, 50 percent of which he reinvested in additional hashing power at pbcmining.com, a necessity if he wanted to stay ahead of the ever-rising difficulty rate—the measure of how rare it becomes to win bitcoin as the system adjusts to the ever-increasing network hashing power. Some believe this equation means that many cloud-mining contracts are priced in a way that their customers won't ever break even. But Whelan remains convinced that he is doing the right thing. "I might not be able to buy a data center full of bitcoin-mining hardware, but I can generate enough BTC to become part of the revolution," he says.

Cloud hashing is made possible by the other big aggregating trend alongside pool mining: giant data farms, where hundreds or even thousands of rigs are stacked in warehouses designed to maximize hashing power and energy efficiency. These operations are often situated in cold climes to mitigate air-conditioning costs and take advantage of relatively cheap power. Popular locations include geothermal-powered Iceland, the areas fed by Washington State's hydropower plants, coal-rich Utah, and Sweden, whose extensive hydro, nuclear, and wind-power projects keep rates and carbon emissions low. Not all data centers are set up for cloud hashing. Some operate rigs for their own accounts. Others invite outsiders to locate their rigs on their property, charging for space and electricity. But they're all part of a phenomenon that has in five years turned bitcoin mining into a heavy-scale industrialized business.

•   •   •

Stacks of mining rigs

(Courtesy of CoinTerra)

At a data center on the outskirts of Salt Lake City, visitors must first pass through an unmanned cylindrical booth that's opened with an electronic badge and is equipped with sensors and a scale to gauge a person's weight, shape, and size, to prevent them from stealing the odd server. Upon entering, they shuffle past a monitoring center where security personnel train their eyes on a wall of screens, some showing live video feeds from cameras pointed at vulnerable points of the complex, others displaying computer simulations of the center's air and electricity flow. A second door down the corridor leads into the main facility.

Inside the cavernous building, twenty-foot-diameter fans installed on thirty-foot ceilings slowly circulate the ambient air sucked in from outside. Beneath them, the target of that superefficient, low-energy cooling solution can be found in racks filled with servers and other back-office equipment owned by financial firms and e-commerce sites selling everything from books to flowers online. Away in a separate area, an enclosed pen has been set up to accommodate the expansion plans of a new client:

CoinTerra, a bitcoin-mining-rig manufacturer that in 2014 decided to get in on mining. While the servers of the data center's traditional customers quietly hum away, their lights flickering red, green, and yellow as they diligently manage databases and update customer accounts, CoinTerra's machines make an enormous racket. Fifty columns are lined up side by side into which are stacked ten TerraMiner ASIC rigs, which, at 1.6 terahashes each per second, are 320 times faster than Whelan's Jalapeño. With three in-built, high-powered fans running at top speed to cool the rig while its internal chip races through calculations, each unit consumes two kilowatts per hour, enough power to run an ordinary laptop for a month. That makes for 20 kWh per tower, about ten times the electricity used for the same space by the neighboring servers of more orthodox e-commerce firms.

"Here alone we have eight hundred terahashes of mining power," says Ravi Iyengar, CEO of CoinTerra, shouting to be heard over the din as his slightly balding head of black hair blows in the wind that's rushing toward the mining rigs' whizzing fans. On a digital recording of our conversation it sounds as if he were standing in a hurricane. "In two weeks, we'll have a total of twenty-four hundred machines in this facility for just under four petahashes in total. And throughout North America, the goal is to reach ten petahashes."

Ten petahashes per second, or 10,000 trillion hashes per second, represented about a tenth of the entire bitcoin network's capacity when we met in June 2014. What CoinTerra planned to do with all that computing power was to diversify its exposure. Iyengar explained that demand for its stand-alone equipment would fall when the price of bitcoin fell, so it needed a hedging strategy. That came down to installing its own rigs to take charge of bitcoin mining on its own account. With some of the installed hashing power, CoinTerra would mine under its name; the rest of it would be rented out via cloud-hashing contracts to clients who ranged from small, individual hobbyists to an unnamed customer that had agreed to rent an entire petahash contract for a year at $1 million.

Iyengar, a former engineer at Samsung Corp.'s microchip plants in Austin, said he's not just betting that bitcoin will continue to expand as a payment system but that the blockchain network will grow to support a whole host of added value exchanges (the Bitcoin 2.0 concepts to be discussed in chapter 9). "For that reason there needs to be an ever-growing mining network," he said, explaining how he will make money by charging cloud-mining customers at cost but later increasing the profit margin on those contracts by banking on the ever-increasing hashing efficiency of this business.

A key consideration for Iyengar's mining operations is electricity. Salt Lake City is more expensive per kilowatt hour than Washington State (where he also has rigs), whose hydropower facilities deliver the cheapest power in the world. But Salt Lake City has its own advantages: an international airport and an established infrastructure and technical community, which makes it both relatively accessible from big cities such as Los Angeles and San Francisco and easier to draw a labor force to install new rigs to boost performance—something the hash war will compel him to do in short order. Because the site sits in a desert, ringed by searing, snow-capped mountains, and is perched at forty-two hundred feet above sea level, the air is dry, free of corrosive humidity, relatively cool, and low in static electricity. Utah also has abundant and reliable power from a mix of low-carbon coal, nuclear, and solar plants. In the large-scale, tight-margin business that bitcoin mining has become, these kinds of considerations can make the difference between a profit and a loss. The industry has come a long way from Jason Whelan's dorm room.

The mining arms race that led CoinTerra to Salt Lake City puts Moore's law, which foresaw that the computing capacity of a microprocessor would double every eighteen months, to shame. In the twelve months to June 2013, the hashing power of the bitcoin network increased eightfold. In the following twelve months, it grew another 845 times. By that time, the network, which was then producing 88,000 trillion hashes every second, had a computing power six thousand times the combined power of the world's top five hundred supercomputers. And just two and half months later, it had almost trebled to 252,000 trillion hashes. The world has seen nothing like this level of computational expansion. That's why some doomsayers are predicting that if bitcoin continues on its current path, the planet faces an environmental catastrophe.

There's no way to calculate the total energy used by the bitcoin mining network, but that hasn't stopped some from trying. Back in April 2013,

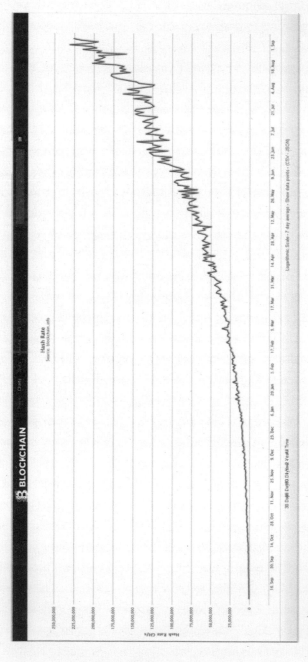

Bitcoin's Mining Hashrate over Time

(Source: Blockchain.info)

various press reports recounted that bitcoin was consuming 131,000 mega-watt hours a day, at a daily cost of $19.7 million. Months later, Guy Lane, an Australian environmental scientist, came up with his BitCarbon method for calculating the carbon footprint of bitcoin. Based on his assumption that a bitcoin miner will on average spend 90 percent of the value of the mined bitcoin on electricity, Lane calculated that a $1,000 bitcoin price would result in 8.2 million tons of carbon per year, about the size of Cyprus's emissions, and that a $100,000 bitcoin price would produce 825 megatons annually, or the equivalent of Germany's emissions. If the bitcoin's currency exchange rate ever got to $1 million, a number that some argue is feasible if bitcoin becomes a world-dominant payment system, its network would have a carbon footprint of 8.2 gigatons, or 20 percent of the planet's carbon output.

The problem with these alarming projections is that they were based on flawed data from Blockchain.info, which was still using outdated GPU-based assumptions about electricity usage. In the early summer of 2014, the new ASIC miners were running on as little as one watt per gigahash second, a rate that's 650 times more efficient than that of GPUs. If every miner used these rigs, the network would consume electricity equivalent to that of seven thousand average American homes—a manageable amount worldwide. Of course, people use a wide range of efficient and inefficient mining setups. Yet it's still profitable to do so. So although the total consumption is significantly higher than the seven-thousand-home estimate, we're a long way from bitcoin's adding an entire country's worth of power consumption to the world.

Innovative ideas are also being generated to offset this cost. One is to exploit mining's main output, heat, perhaps using it to warm homes in the winter and serve other energy needs. However, the ad hoc, dispersed nature of the network doesn't lend itself to a sound allocation of such a resource. Ideally, the mining network would go through a seasonal cycle, with the Southern Hemisphere taking over the lion's share of mining in the June-through-September months, while the Northern would crank up during its winter. That's not going to happen under the current laissez-faire, winner-take-all model. So instead, as we approached the Northern summer in 2014 with the mining network running at 845 times more computing power than twelve months earlier and thus being ill prepared for the change of season, data-center consultants were advising bitcoin miners to waterproof their rigs and store them in a special cooling liquid.

Is all this expenditure and resource use worth it? Adam Smith opined on a similar matter in the eighteenth century, arguing that to expend effort and real resources on mining gold for coins was wasteful when a currency is nothing but a symbol. But while Nobel Prize–winning economist and *New York Times* columnist Paul Krugman has used Smith's comments to mock bitcoin, the analogy overlooks a number of crucial factors. For one, power consumption must be measured against the value of validating transactions in a payment system, a social service that gold mining has never provided. Second, the costs must be weighed against the high energy costs of the alternative, traditional payment system, with its bank branches, armored cars, and security systems. And finally, there's the overriding incentive for efficiency that the profit motive delivers to innovators, which is why we've seen such giant reductions in power consumption for the new mining machines. If power costs make mining unprofitable, it will stop.

Bitcoin's environmental doomsday is not, therefore, just around the corner. Even so, it would be irresponsible to ignore energy usage as a concern. As BitCarbon's Lane points out, the improved energy efficiency of mining rigs simply increases profitability, which, when combined with a rising price, draws more miners into the race for bitcoins and increases total power consumption. It is one of the many flaws that leave bitcoin vulnerable to future threats and that are driving inventors to imagine ways to either improve bitcoin or come up with a better cryptocurrency.

One such vulnerability was thrust into prominence at 22:27 GMT, on March 11, 2013. Just before that moment, while the expansive global network of miners was busily confirming transactions and hunting for bitcoins, one alert miner noticed something odd. He'd seen a mining software client that was working on a block with a higher number than that currently registered on blockexplorer.com, a bare-bones version of Blockchain. info that was supposed to offer real-time information on the blockchain transaction ledger. This raised doubts about which block constituted the latest, confirmed extension of the chain. Was his machine making the right assumptions about which block to attach the next one to?

The bitcoin software is periodically updated by a small team of software developers who, by convention and with some funding from the nonprofit Bitcoin Foundation, are charged with running the open-source maintenance program. The miner thought the discrepancy might be the result of his efforts to reconcile his 0.7 version of the core bitcoin software with the newer 0.8 version that those developers had recently released and which other miners had already adopted. So, he went looking for answers in the IRC room for bitcoin developers on the Bitcoin Forum. Popping up in the commentary stream under his log-in as thermoman—a name shared by a British sitcom character, a superhero from the planet Ultron—he directed a message at Pieter Wuille (log-in: sipa), one of five lead developers working under Bitcoin Foundation chief scientist Gavin Andresen who have assumed responsibility for maintaining bitcoin's core software. Thermoman informed sipa of the block-count discrepancy. A discussion ensued that dragged in the entire brain trust behind bitcoin's open-source core software program.

Jouke Hofman (log-in: jouke) in the Netherlands chimed in that he, too, was finding discrepancies in block counts. So sipa suggested solutions, but none worked. Meanwhile, chat-room participants kept periodically checking on the block tallies at different locations. The discrepancies continued. Eventually, at 23:06 GMT, mining software inventor Luke Dashjr (log-in: Luke-jr) recognized what was going on:

23:06 **Luke-jr:** so??? yay accidental hardfork? :x
23:06 **Jouke:** Holy crap.

There is supposed to be a single blockchain, the idea being that the ledger's sequentially arranged hash-based linkages create an unbroken, monolithic record of all confirmed transactions. Short-lived forks will arise from time to time in the blockchain, sometimes when an orphaned block is created that is deemed incomplete or whose transactions are unconfirmed. That happens because other miners have sought to verify the block and aren't confident in attaching to it. But the genius of the consensus-building in the bitcoin system means such forks shouldn't be allowed to go on for long. That's because the mining community works on the assumption that the longest chain is the one that constitutes consensus. The majority of miners, by working together on a particular line of the chain, are conferring legitimacy on it, collectively having more total hashing power than any minority group that's mistakenly (or even fraudulently) following a separate line of the chain without consensus support. That greater amount of shared hashing power will mean that this majority group will win more block awards and so will increasingly build a longer chain (with higher block numbers) over time. This will immediately be noticed by the computers that were following the shorter chain with lower numbers and those wayward miners will then jump over to the longer chain. The majority view is deemed to be the legitimate one—which, as we'll learn, would be a problem only if one single miner ever garnered more than 50 percent of total hashing power.

This normal resolution process wasn't playing out here, however. The fork was continuing, block after block. That meant a common record of verified transactions no longer existed. It's as if half the families in our imaginary Yapese village were now working off a different set of assumptions about the community's *fei* balances. This is precisely the sort of thing that a fraudulent actor could exploit to double-spend bitcoins. For example, if the administrator of a mining pool that previously accounted for, say, 30 percent of the combined blockchain now had majority control of one of the new halves, it could make their wallet software re-send already spent bitcoins from one of their addresses to another one of theirs. The bet would be that other miners would recognize the second transaction as legitimate and so acknowledge a balance for the administrator that should have been marked down because of the prior spend. Ordinarily, the majority of other miners would catch them out and start working on a legitimate longer chain, but under this perpetuating fork, the mining pool would effectively have more than 50 percent of the hashing power with which to keep confirming those fraudulent transactions. If allowed to continue, it would eventually destroy the integrity of the entire bitcoin system.

Wuille realized early on that this particular fork was not caused by a greedy hacker—a violation of bitcoin itself, thought to be impossible—but by a glitch that had occurred when his colleagues on the core development team introduced the new version 0.8. Its reconstituted database was supposed to reconcile with the database records of version 0.7 but wasn't doing so. Lead developer Andresen soon stepped up. After consulting with Wuille and two other core developers, Jeff Garzik and Gregory Maxwell, and after checking in with Mt. Gox owner Mark Karpelès (log-in: MagicalTux), whose currency exchange was then the bitcoin network's most important financial institution, Andresen decided to abandon the new software and revert back to version 0.7.

One $10,000 case of double-spending was discovered, which suggests that one opportunistic rogue may have taken advantage of the snafu. But some miners had to forgo the bitcoins they thought they'd earned on the 0.8 fork, a total of six hundred coins worth $26,000. And this kerfuffle caused the price of bitcoin to briefly plunge 24 percent. The scary glitch got some play in bitcoin-focused press outlets, but didn't draw much attention elsewhere—in part because it was soon fixed and the price recovered fairly quickly.

The March 2013 fork had been an accident, but it brought new attention to a concern held by some in the bitcoin community, that industrialized mining operations might one day afford a nefarious actor the power to create a fork intentionally by seizing majority control of the total hashing power. That's come to be known as a 51 percent attack. Nakamoto's original paper stated that the bitcoin mining network could be guaranteed to treat everyone's transactions fairly and honestly so long as no single miner or mining group owned more than 50 percent of the hashing power. If malevolent actors secretly created an alternate chain of fraudulent transactions to spend bitcoins they didn't own, their efforts to have those transactions confirmed would fail if they didn't have majority hashing power. The probability of the dishonest miners winning enough of the mathematical puzzles to keep producing the longest chain and thus give their fraudulent transactions legitimacy would quickly tend toward zero. As each block progressed, the legitimate chain would get ever longer. They'd never attain the ninety-nine-block extension that, as we explained in the previous chapter, is needed to legitimize their block work. They would never be able spend the bitcoins they thought they'd earned. The bad guys can never catch up. That's the theory, at least.

But what if a powerful conglomerate took control of all that mining power? They could then fill a block with fraudulent transactions and then (equally fraudulently) confirm them. And since they'd be winning more than every second block, they could continue to build a viable, lengthy blockchain that other miners would assume to be the truthful one, all by virtue of its length.

According to coinometrics.com, in the summer of 2014 the cost of the mining equipment and electricity required for a 51 percent attack stood at $913 million. It's a costly proposition, but with a potential way around it: pooling. In fact, mining pools have already come close to the 50 percent threshold—in June 2014, the pool GHash.IO saw its share of total hashing power fluctuate between 40 percent and 50 percent throughout the month. Because such pools use software that combines their hashing power into a single formidable force, they can also confirm transactions as a group. That puts concentrated power into the hands of the administrators of the pool's software, which understandably causes some anxiety among bitcoiners. Bitcoin leaders such as Andresen are trying to encourage people to join new peer-to-peer mining pools that take the power of transaction confirmation away from the pool administrator and leave it up to individual miners through a decentralized network. But the largest pools have an established, first-mover presence that's hard to break down. What's more, GHash.IO's manager, CEX.IO, offers the appealing carrot of zero fees in a bid to steer business to its two side businesses: a cryptocurrency exchange and a cloud-mining service.

To make matters worse, Cornell University computer scientists Ittay Eyal and Emin Gün Sirer have since demonstrated that the threshold for an attack may actually be lower than 51 percent. In a controversial paper, they showed how a sufficiently large minority of colluding miners could successfully engage in "selfish mining," developing a secret alternative blockchain that's hidden from the majority but moving more quickly than the honest miners' fork. This way they would force everyone else to waste computer resources on what is mistakenly thought to be the correct chain and game for themselves a greater proportion of bitcoin distributions than their mining power warrants. The paper upset many in the bitcoin community—"the zealots who don't want to hear anything negative," as Sirer puts it. The noise died down, however, after one bitcoin fan, eager to prove the theory's fallibility, put it through a simulation and discovered that Eyal and Sirer were right. "People calmed down, and those who have an interest, as we do, in seeing bitcoin succeed, eventually saw it as an incredibly positive contribution. People now understand that with a decentralized system, you need to have some kind of good equilibrium point built into it," Sirer says. "The protocol can't have these kinds of vulnerabilities."

So, the open-source development community is now looking for added protections against selfish mining and 51 percent attacks. To be fair, nothing malevolent like this has so far happened or is likely to anytime soon—for good reason. As Nakamoto explained in his white paper, "If a greedy attacker is able to assemble more CPU power than all the honest nodes, he would have to choose between using it to defraud people by stealing back his payments, or using it to generate new coins. He ought to find it more profitable to play by the rules, such rules that favour him with more new coins than everyone else combined, than to undermine the system and the validity of his own wealth."

Self-interest, in other words, should prevent anyone with a stake in bitcoin from destroying it. In fact, bitcoin's short history shows that the same motivation extends to minority individuals who want to maintain a balance of power in the network. Mining pools that have closed in on 50 percent hashing power have in the past had members jump ship and join competing pools so as to keep the system honest. And to mollify concerns about its excessive size, CEX.IO has at times said it would decline to accept new entrants to the GHash.IO pool.

But what if bad actors have no interest in seeing bitcoin succeed? What if their whole motivation is to bring the system down, not to profit from bitcoin investments? Bitcoiners sometimes refer to this as a Dr. Evil attack and throw out hypothetical threats: a terrorist organization that wants to throw the Western world into chaos, a sovereign nation—Russia, perhaps, or China—whose monetary system is threatened by bitcoin, or a consortium of multinational banks seeking to protect their monopoly on the payment system. At close glance it seems unlikely. After all, these prospects become relevant only if bitcoin reaches enough penetration that its destruction would matter, and by that time attackers would need to part with much more than $1 billion, with every giant order for ASIC chips and mining equipment drawing attention to them. Nonetheless, the vulnerability exists. In essence, bitcoin is not watertight, and that's the kind of thing that might bother a hypercautious in-house lawyer for a company wondering whether to trade in it.

These extreme scenarios aren't the only ones breeding concern that concentrations of power and wealth can have undue influence over bitcoin. As of late August 2014, 44 percent of all bitcoins in circulation were assigned to just 1,528 addresses, each with balances of more than a thousand bitcoins ($507,000 at that time), according to bitcoinrichlist.com. That's less than 0.01 percent of the total 40.7 million addresses on the network at that time, suggesting a high and potentially distorting concentration of wealth.

First, some perspective. As a wealth-gap measure, this is a lousy one. For one, addresses are not wallets. The total number of wallets cannot be known, but they are by definition considerably fewer than the address tally, even though many people hold more than one. Wallet holders are randomly assigned addresses for different transactions and will typically generate multiple addresses. Many of the 39 million that occupy the bottom 96 percent of bitcoinrichlist.com's heap, those with balances of less than 0.001 bitcoin, are just "small change" accounts that the bitcoin protocol assigns to spenders in each transaction as part of its unique three-way reconciliation of balances. Even if many of these small balances are rolled into wallets with tiny aggregate balances, they're hardly likely to be their owners' only store of wealth. Most bitcoin users have a much richer financial existence in the fiat-currency world. This group of 96 percenters can never be viewed as an underclass of paupers.

Nonetheless, these numbers do reveal how much bitcoin's spectacular price rally has created a small, international cohort of wealthy "bitcoin barons," almost overnight. These elites have an outsize impact on the bitcoin economy. They have a great interest in seeing the currency succeed and are both willing and able to make payments that others might not, simply to encourage adoption. Hence the reports of ostentatious bitcoin-based purchases of villas in Bali, Lamborghinis in California, and Virgin Galactica tickets into outer space. Their intentions may be good, but if money is no object in their spending sprees, how can they apply the competitive discipline needed to drive prices lower for the rest of the bitcoin economy?

The wide wealth gap sits poorly with the image of cryptocurrencies as community-driven money and an escape from the dominance of Wall Street fat cats. Narrowly controlled wealth and power do not attract widespread trust. Of course, the dollar, euro, and yen economies already claim profound concentrations of both, with inequality having reached 1920s levels. But those fiat currencies don't need to win people over. For cryptocurrencies, these kinds of imbalances may need to be addressed if their future is to be assured.

On the positive side, many developers and businessmen are pursuing projects that try to tackle such concerns. Some are taking the existing infrastructure and finding ways to introduce it to a wider group, promoting bitcoin as a vehicle to empower the marginalized of the world. Solutions that help the "unbanked" of the developing world gain access to the global economy is one promising area, which we'll discuss in chapter 8. But just as important is the acknowledgment from many smart cryptocurrency enthusiasts that bitcoin as it stands is far from perfect and can be improved in many ways to get around some of the challenges and threats discussed above.

The 51 percent attack threat eats at a lot of bitcoin intellectuals. Why? Because it's the one irrefutable structural weakness in the bitcoin system. All the other dangers you hear about—hacked wallets, crime, and price volatility—aren't problems with bitcoin itself but with the ecosystem that has developed around it. Many are already being fixed: "multi-sig" wallets from innovators such as BitGo give almost impenetrable protection against hackers; high-tech, regulated exchanges like that of Atlas ATS couldn't possibly make the mistakes of Mt. Gox; closer government supervision will scare off drug dealers, to an extent. But it's hard to see any way to protect against a 51 percent attack. Even if the disincentives and cost of launching such an attack make it highly unlikely, some who've studied bitcoin's design are bothered that Nakamoto's brilliant, elegant solution for aligning the interests and incentives of individuals with those of the community has this one fundamental weakness.

Core bitcoin developer Jeff Garzik—one of the team of five who works with Gavin Andresen—has come up with a partial solution that takes advantage of ongoing advances in lower-cost private-space ventures: he's seeking to raise $2 million to launch a sizable fleet of tiny, low-cost satellites into space in a project aimed at making the mining network less concentrated. These ten-cubic-centimeter "bitsats" would provide low-cost, satellite-beamed Internet connectivity to nodes on the ground and would store a permanent record of the complete blockchain database on their internal hard drives. The benefits would, in theory, be twofold. First, it would make mining more accessible to a wider array of participants by lowering the cost of becoming a "full node," a vital role on the network that requires the storage of large amounts of data and which is these days typically performed by high-powered, expensive ASIC rigs. Second, because the satellites would be beyond the control of any person, state, or company, they could provide critical backup in the event of a shutdown by a large Internet service provider or a cluster of ISPs. Such an event, perhaps ordered by a government or an alliance of governments, could cut off many miners from the network and so raise the risk that a large group that's outside the affected geographic area could attain more than 50 percent control. An alternative, space-based source of bandwidth could thus lower the risk of such an unwelcome development.

A far less capital-intensive alternative to the concentration of network control, though, would be to change the rules that miners follow to earn bitcoin and so remove the motive to accumulate huge amounts of hashing power. The cryptocurrency computer engineers that are now thinking about such solutions could well play a core role in shaping the technology's future. Their ideas might one day even give bitcoin a run for its money in being the main driver of that future.

Much of this rethinking is happening via the development of altcoins. As we mentioned in chapter 3, hundreds of these bitcoin imitators now exist. Many are going nowhere, dismissed as get-rich-quick schemes or jokes. But a few have come up with sophisticated ways to change the rules of the game for the distribution of cryptocurrencies within their communities of users. Their founders are touting their coins as fairer and more sustainable models. They claim to take the good aspects of bitcoin's decentralized structure but to get rid of its negative elements, such as the hashing-power arms race, the excessive use of electricity, and the concentration of industrialized mining power. Bitcoin has a big first-mover advantage over these new players, which is why many developers think the best solution is to fix its flaws rather than come up with entirely new systems. Nevertheless, the best altcoins are bringing an edgy and potentially constructive force of competition to bear in the whole cryptocurrency arena.

Of these altcoins, litecoin, invented by Charlie Lee, is to date the most successful. Litecoin's secret sauce is its use of a different algorithm in the hashing process that miners use to package transactions into the blockchain. Lee's system still involves a competition among miners, but its hashing algorithm, known as scrypt, makes it easier for a miner to arrive at the sought-after block hash goal than does bitcoin's SHA-256. Without delving into the complicated details of how it works, scrypt essentially tweaks the targets so that miners don't simply gain an advantage by constantly building up brute computational power. The result is that mining power remains somewhat more evenly spread and more democratic with litecoin. Miners still have an incentive to chase coin rewards, but the arms race and the electricity usage aren't as intense. It also makes for faster turnarounds, with blocks completed within two and a half minutes, rather than bitcoin's ten minutes, which in turn means the system's wait for the final confirmation of transactions by customers and merchants isn't as long. Litecoin's main weakness is the corollary of its strength: because it's cheaper to mine litecoins and because scrypt-based rigs can be used to mine other scrypt-based altcoins such as dogecoin, miners are less heavily invested in permanently working its blockchain. In theory, that could raise the risk of a 51 percent attack if enough of them aren't online at any one time. Some also worry that scrypt-based mining is more insecure, with a less rigorous proof of work, in theory allowing false transactions to get through with incorrect confirmations. Thus far, however, litecoin has avoided major breakdowns. In time it could prove to be a more environmentally friendly, democratic contender to bitcoin.

Scrypt mining is not the only solution to bitcoin's concentrated mining and 51 percent attack threat. Some altcoins, including nextcoin and peercoin, use "proof of stake" as an alternative to the "proof of work" paradigm's wasteful and costly computing. This way, your computer's rights to rewards for confirming transactions increase the more you are invested in the coin's monetary supply. In the case of nextcoin, which is 100 percent proof-of-stake-based, the coins are not mined but "forged." A preexisting, fixed supply of coins circulate in the nextcoin economy, and each time they are used in a transaction, it generates a fee to be paid to the winning node that seals each block. As with bitcoin, the right hash to close off a block of transactions is found via a random lottery, but unlike with bitcoin, your chances of winning that lottery depend not on your hashing power but on how many proven coins you own. The idea is that this removes the incentive to build up environmentally destructive and wasteful computing power.

The existence of these alternatives underscores awareness of bitcoin's flaws. Nakamoto's invention faces other challenges, too. For one, the bitcoin network can currently process only about seven transactions per second, pitifully short of Visa's ten thousand. If bitcoin is to scale up, it must be upgraded so that nodes, currently limited to one megabyte of data per ten-minute block, are free to process a much larger set of information. That's not technically difficult; but it would require miners to hash much larger blocks of transactions without big improvements in their compensation. Developers are currently exploring a transaction-fee model that would provide fairer compensation for miners if the amount of data becomes excessive.

Bitcoin's fully open-source, collaborative approach to cryptocurrencies is its great strength. So far, the challenges that have arisen, from thefts at major exchanges, to forks in the blockchain, to the discovery of bugs in the underlying software, have been met by consensus-driven responses fashioned to be as fair as possible. Still, the challenges *are* complicated. Designers of cryptocurrency projects are working at the nexus of economics (which emphasizes the creation of incentives for individual behavior that benefits the group) and technology. Computer-system designers at firms such as SAP and IBM focus on similar problems in the behavior-technology balance, but they do so within the controlled environments of their centralized corporate clients. The laboratory used by cryptocurrency developers, by contrast, is potentially as big as the world itself, the breadth of humanity that their projects seek to encompass. No company rulebook or top-down set of managerial instructions keeps people's choices in line with a common corporate objective. Guiding people to optimal behavior in cryptocurrencies is entirely up to how the software is designed to affect human thinking, how effectively its incentive systems encourage that desired behavior.

The vulnerabilities and flaws enumerated in this chapter inevitably make it harder for many ordinary people to trust cryptocurrencies —ironically, for a program that's pitched as a way to bypass the need for trust. But one must also weigh these against the weaknesses of the existing system. Consider the amount of fraud and crime conducted in dollars, for example. And if you want to think about vulnerabilities in a financial system, focus the mind on the global financial-derivatives market that banks continue to manage despite the disaster wrought in 2008 by these "financial weapons of mass destruction," as Warren Buffett called them. That market has a notional—or face value—of $710 trillion.

The vital thing to remember is that the collective brainpower applied to all the challenges facing bitcoin and other cryptocurrencies is enormous. Under the open-source, decentralized model, these technologies are not hindered by the same constraints that bureaucracies and stodgy corporations face. The amount of innovation is tremendous, not only in making cryptocurrencies safer, but in figuring out how to make them even more useful for society. In the next chapter we meet the young inventors who are driving that effort.

Seven

> Men have a touch-stone whereby to trie gold, but gold
> is the touch-stone whereby to trie man.
>
> —*Thomas Fuller*

Bitcoin was born out of a crypto-anarchist vision of a decentralized, government-free society, a sort of encrypted, networked utopia. It got its early growth from a small band of young, tech-minded people who were repulsed by the excesses and abuses of the financial system. But the next stage, the bitcoin boom, has been driven by something far easier to understand.

The crypto-anarchists aren't driving bitcoin anymore. It probably happened sometime in 2013, when bitcoin went parabolic, and people started to understand that this digital money could mean real money, too. A new breed took the helm. If you want to understand who these people are, you have to go to San Francisco, the epicenter of this global, modern, digitized gold rush. Ensconced at the far end of America, the city's got an end-of-the-world feel to it and almost seems specially built to catch wandering wildcatters, entrepreneurs, indigents, and itinerants before they tumble into the ocean. The entire region has a go-for-broke, strike-it-rich vibe, and mixed with the high-tech bitcoin world, you get this odd crossbreed of people who want to change the world and become fabulously wealthy. They see no inconsistency in that.

This city and the people in it are drawn magnetically to each other, and this bitcoin boomlet is a direct descendant of previous booms, beginning with the famous discovery of gold at Sutter's Mill in 1848, a discovery that sparked a massive emigration of Americans out West that reshaped and remade the young nation. Some men made fortunes, some lost fortunes. John Sutter himself lost a fortune, as wildcatters overran the land he owned. Others, such as Levi Strauss and Leland Stanford, got rich by providing all the support services and infrastructure the miners would need.

Stanford would later donate land he owned for the establishment of a university, Stanford (named after his son, not himself). Decades later, two young students at that school, Bill Hewlett and Dave Packard, would strike up a friendship, and later a business venture that would go on to become a major global corporation. They would thus inadvertently launch San Francisco's next great boom: Silicon Valley. The Valley, as we've already explored, would attract and become home to Tim May's Cypherpunks, a group from which it's quite possible Nakamoto himself sprang. If that's true, it means you can draw a direct line from Sutter's Mill to, well, let's call it Satoshi's Mill, the latest in a series of prospecting waves to hit the Valley in its long history of booms and busts.

Other tech hubs around the world are also seeing heat and buzz around bitcoin innovation, which has cachet in and has captured the zeitgeist of the tech world. London, Toronto, Singapore, Hong Kong, Tel Aviv, Zug in Switzerland, and even Nairobi in Kenya, to name a few, are all home to a host of bitcoin-related start-ups. It all reflects the excitement that software developers and computer engineers everywhere—a group with an inordinately large number of libertarian-minded, individualistic thinkers—have for this vast new field that's now being probed and mined. But Silicon Valley's central role in the computer revolution that preceded all this gives it dibs on being the natural heartland of the cryptocurrency revolution. So it simply made sense to go out there and see it firsthand, to figure out what makes these bitcoin millionaires tick.

They don't represent the mainstream, these wandering, itinerant entrepreneurs who end up out there. They are compulsive builders, constantly constructing new things, tearing them down, reshaping them, taking risks, hoping to craft that billion-dollar business, going wherever the opportunity seems greatest. Failure is commonplace. They have an almost complete disregard for risk. Their energy and ideas simply propel them to the next thing, and with that energy and the myriad businesses that are arising from it, they are giving their all in the effort to make cryptocurrency the next defining phase in Silicon Valley's relentless reinvention.

Before we get too carried away, understand this is still early days. Even in this city, where people drive around in Segway gangs and drivers feed the meter via mobile apps, bitcoin is still a curiosity. We wandered into one specialty shop, Buyer's Best Friend, that accepted bitcoin, a sign in the window proclaimed it, and didn't find any rush of high-tech whiz kids gobbling up muffins. When the business had first started taking bitcoin in 2013, the girl behind the counter told us, there'd been a bit of excitement and a surge in traffic, but that died out. The bitcoin business these days isn't moving the needle.

So, bitcoin's more like a scene in a snow globe than a full-blown, dot-com-style bubble. But, as we said, it's early days. This is just the beginning.

If the Bay Area is the most important region from which bitcoin innovation is emanating, its ground zero may well lie inside a nondescript building in San Francisco's funky, crowded, mini-melting-pot Mission District. The sparks that led to some of the most exciting developments in bitcoin first arose from conversations and brainstorming sessions inside this ramshackle "hacker house." Sitting on the corner of Twentieth and Mission Streets, with its unassuming entrance behind an olive tree (the first missionaries brought the olive trees with them from Spain and they still dot the streets), the building now known as 20Mission was founded in February 2012 by Jered Kenna, the young bitcoin entrepreneur who'd previously founded Tradehill. It has become a working and living space for the smart, ambitious, tech-minded wildcatters driving the bitcoin boom. When Kenna first leased this place, it housed a shoe store on its ground floor and an abandoned residence hotel upstairs. He restored the upstairs quarters into small residences and cleaned the detritus out of the shoe store. The downstairs area would offer a common space for working, eating, and communing. Then he invited techies, hackers, and bitcoiners to take up residence. It was almost an instant success. Through bitcoin meetups, it quickly grew into a hotbed of ideas and entrepreneurship.

"There is a sense you're part of a movement," said Taariq Lewis at a

The entrance to 20Mission

(Courtesy of Paul Vigna)

Sunday meetup at 20Mission, "and part of something special." Lewis is a bitcoiner who now runs the hacker house's regular meetups. He came out to San Francisco from New York's Spanish Harlem, by way of Boston, another compulsive, restless entrepreneur. He'd got his MBA at MIT, but wanted to create things, to make his own businesses, so he headed out West. Lewis was initially a bitcoin skeptic, viewing it as little more than a tool for the drug trade. But after two start-up attempts failed ("Kill your babies quickly," he joked), he was looking for a new opportunity, and a chance meeting forced him to reconsider. "I had lunch with a really smart guy who said bitcoin was hot shit," Lewis said, "and that changed my life." These days, he operates a bitcoin-news Web site, *Bits of Coin*, and a start-up he founded, DigitalTangible.

This particular Sunday-morning group that Lewis had assembled didn't seem so revolutionary, but it was instructive. The small gathering, about a dozen people, were being introduced to a Bitcoin 2.0 company called MaidSafe, which had come up with a way for people to rent out the disk space on their own hard drives to a decentralized network of users. This meeting had been organized by Paige Peterson, a twenty-six-year-old, blond-hair-and-dreadlocked libertarian/anarchist who'd started working at MaidSafe a month prior. She'd arranged for the company's founder, a Scottish engineer named David Irvine, to "meet" the San Francisco group through a video chat. For a few hours, he answered whatever questions the group had. MaidSafe is trying to build a decentralized Internet network, and this meeting was part of the outreach effort. Meetups, which function almost like the church socials of the bitcoin religion and are now held in cities all over the world, offer a chance for all these decentralized, anonymous players to get together and break bread, as it were (or, perhaps we should say, bits).

Dan Held was twenty-five years old when he attended his first bitcoin meetup at 20Mission in January 2013. One sunny afternoon in the old beatnik bar Vesuvio, the blond-haired former linebacker on the Hebron High School football team from Carrollton, Texas, explained how he'd moved to San Francisco to take a job in a small investment bank. He was following in the footsteps of his hometown friend Kevin Johnson, who'd moved there four months earlier. In Texas, they were the only two people they knew who cared about bitcoin. In California, they found a group of people who shared their passion. Within a year of attending his first meetup at 20Mission, Held's life had changed dramatically.

"Kevin and I really became inspired" by the gatherings, Held said. "The energy there was tremendous." Those early meetings were small, he said, maybe fifteen or twenty people. But the people attending would go on to become big names in the bitcoin world: Among them were Brian Armstrong and Fred Ehrsam, the founders of Coinbase, which is second only to Blockchain as a leader in digital-wallet services and one of the biggest processors of bitcoin payments for businesses. Jed McCaleb, the Mt. Gox founder, was there, too. McCaleb was then busy working on the alternative payment system Ripple, which would go on to be something of a competitor to bitcoin. McCaleb had some of the Ripple development team there with him as well. Also at the meeting was Kenna himself, who had already started and lost Tradehill and despite his youth is something of a bitcoin graybeard.

Held and Johnson were determined to add their own contribution.

During a ski trip to Lake Tahoe, they sketched out on a napkin—yes, literally a napkin—the idea that would become their start-up, ZeroBlock, essentially a bitcoin pricing app. They launched it in the spring of 2013, a bare-bones product that provided bitcoin prices in dollars, a news feed, push notifications for price moves, and a price-conversion calculator. It filled a need in a rapidly growing market of bitcoin investors hungry for information about the market. The app also came out at roughly the same time bitcoin prices surged in response to the Cyprus fiscal crisis, and then dropped. Held and Johnson's app got a lot of notice, and by December of that year, they'd sold it to Blockchain for an undisclosed amount of bitcoins, making it the first M&A deal done entirely in a cryptocurrency. The acquisition was essentially an "acqui-hire"—acquiring talent in the bitcoin field is an ongoing, challenging task—that brought Held on board. He still has his fortune denominated entirely in the cryptocurrency. In little more than a year, Held had gone from a banker to a bitcoin baron, and these days he quenches his entrepreneurial thirst tinkering and building new products for Blockchain. The meetups had changed the course of his life. He wouldn't be the only one.

"It's a very specific type of brain that's obsessed with bitcoin," says Adam Draper, the fourth-generation venture capitalist whose Boost VC "accelerator" program has already pushed a number of bitcoin start-ups out in the world, including the Latin America–focused payment processor BitPagos and high-tech bitcoin exchange Vaurum. "They all know it's unpaved territory, and they get excited by that."

It's Kenna, 20Mission's founder, who best exemplifies the breed. He had a circuitous but not uncommon route, going from nothing to rich to broke and then to rich again. Long before his picture appeared atop that *Businessweek* article entitled "Bitcoin Millionaires," Kenna was nobody's idea of a world changer, having graduated dead last at his Oregon high school. He was not lacking for brains or ambition, as would later become apparent, but was decidedly lacking in focus. He drifted into the Marines, got sent to Afghanistan, and then wound up in Chile running a business importing graphics cards.

In Chile, in 2009, Kenna first saw a reference to bitcoin on an online forum. He had none of the head-scratching confusion that most people begin with when they first encounter the topic: "It hit me right away." He knew from his importing business how hard and expensive it was to move money internationally, so he saw bitcoin's potential there. But he wasn't convinced it would take off, believing it was too technical, too geeky, for most people to comprehend and adopt. "I honestly thought the chances are it would die in infancy," he recalled.

Nonetheless, he was hooked. "I'd never seen a project that I was so motivated to help see succeed," he said. He began to meet online with other enthusiasts, and this made him all the more resolved. Bitcoin would change the world, and he would be part of it. It was less about money and more about being part of a game-changing movement. "In the early days, there was no talk about 'this is going to make us rich.' I never heard that in the beginning." Kenna realized quickly one major problem with bitcoin, though. For mainstream adoption, people had to have ways to acquire bitcoin other than by mining it, which was a route for geeks and hard-core speculators. Yet in those early days, while many rudimentary exchanges had been set up online, only one truly functioning site existed where you could set up a trading account, wire dollars into it from a bank account, and easily swap those dollars for bitcoin—the perennially in-crisis Mt. Gox. Even there, *functioning* was a generous term. The site was inaccessible and had none of the customer-service features to which he and other Americans were accustomed. He'd tried to call Mt. Gox a few times to resolve service issues, but found to his frustration that he could never get through. This was a red flag, and a potential opportunity. To Kenna's mind, for a cryptocurrency to be dominated by one poorly run exchange, just one place to move money, defied the principle of decentralization on which the technology was founded.

His solution, naturally, was to start another. Tradehill would be different from Mt. Gox. Kenna didn't just hire a stable of computer engineers, he put financial professionals on the staff to try to mimic the way traditional exchanges work. He hired customer-service reps and responded to calls and e-mails quickly. He hired a CTO from Google and made account security a priority. He spread the word as most people did whenever they had a new service to sell to the small but growing bitcoin community: by posting information about the venture on forums such as Bitcointalk.org and Reddit bitcoin forums. Immediately the idea resonated with people. The first day of Tradehill's life, June 8, 2011, Kenna's new bitcoin exchange received $250,000 in deposits. In the first week, it took in $1 million. The surge, he figured, said a lot more about Mt. Gox than it did about Tradehill or him. "People were so disappointed with Mt. Gox," he said. "I didn't think I was going to make a penny."

He didn't. First, he had trouble with his payments processor, Dwolla, which he later sued for $2 million over what Tradehill claimed were undue chargebacks, those payment reversals on disputed transactions that merchants complain about with credit-cards. (The case was still unresolved at the time we went to print.) He also faced regulatory challenges as state agencies began eyeing with suspicion this unorthodox service for moving money around digitally. Meanwhile, other competitors began sprouting up in places less burdened by banking and regulatory demands, including Bitstamp in Slovenia and BTC-e in Bulgaria. The bitcoin pie was growing, and more and more people wanted a piece. Kenna expanded staff to help build a more competitive site. But Tradehill lost more than $100,000 due to the complications with Dwolla, and with legal bills mounting, the low trading fees that Tradehill was forced to charge to remain competitive weren't enough for it to turn a profit. By the summer of 2012 Kenna was unable to meet payroll and knew he had to shut the exchange down.

Kenna had to return all the money his customers had entrusted to Tradehill and shut down the exchange. The only other option was to "turn into a fractional-reserve bank," he said jokingly, referring to the bank model that allows banks to lend out deposits while holding only a fraction of those funds in reserve. "They call it a Ponzi scheme unless you have a banking license." He'd sunk everything he had into Tradehill. Now, he was broke, so broke that he couldn't afford rent. He figured the only way he could find shelter was to turn some place into a communal living space. If he could organize it, he figured, he could finagle the rent.

Kenna had always been intrigued by the idea of what's popularly called a hacker house, with people working together and pooling resources, "but until I got to San Francisco, I didn't realize you could actually do it." He soon found a warehouse in the SoMa district and moved in with ten friends, but after only six months they were kicked out because the building wasn't zoned residential. He hunted around for another place until a friend said he'd seen a building for rent in the Mission that might fit the bill. Only problem: "It's a complete shithole."

Kenna, though, perhaps as a result of necessity, or a good eye, or both, took one look at the building, twelve thousand square feet at the corner of Twentieth and Mission Streets, and saw just what he was looking for. The space upstairs, which was once a residential hotel, had been abandoned more than fifteen years earlier, so he didn't have to throw anybody out. The landlord, thrilled with Kenna's interest, agreed to forgive nine months of rent. In return, Kenna would fix the place up. He then brought in some friends, not all bitcoiners, charged them below-market rates, and used the rent money to fix the place up, with the promise that he'd keep their rent at the same level after the nine months.

He was still broke and lived off little more than a giant bag of rice and a giant bag of beans while he turned the place into habitable quarters. He sanded floors and painted the walls, doing all the work himself with help from a friend. Ten people moved in initially. Several months after he moved in, the shoe store moved out. Kenna now had the work space to go along with the living space. The news spread by word of mouth.

Today all forty-one rooms are rented, most for the long term. In a city with living expenses as high as San Francisco's, it didn't take long for the building to fill up. It's an eclectic mix. Yes, it's mainly young, white men, but some young women also live there, from as far away as Australia, and a few guys are even north of forty. They share kitchen space, a common room, and even the bathroom. It can best be described as a cross between a hostel and a dorm. The hall forms one big square. Tapestries are on the walls, and black-light fluorescent tubes on the ceiling. Each hallway has its own street sign, too: Litecoin Lane, for example. Dogecoin Drive. Most doors are covered in posters and pictures as if in a college dorm. A couple dozen bikes hang on the wall of the wide staircase running down to the street entrance.

They have movie-and-crepe nights and throw mad parties with hundreds of people descending on the house. And they work, incessantly, on their ideas. Even the most successful don't leave. Allan Grant is a cofounder of hired.com, a non-bitcoin-related recruitment site that in May 2014 raised $15 million in venture funding. Everybody assumed he'd leave, that rais-

A bitcoin meetup at 20Mission

(Courtesy of Paul Vigna)

ing that kind of money represented "making it." Instead Grant merely sank some money into improvements in his room at 20Mission.

The downstairs is a bright, open space, with a high ceiling, cream-colored walls filled with work from local artists, desks out on the open floor, conference rooms, and a little room in the back with "telephone booths," small, walled-off compartments for private conversations. The muffled sounds of the street, buses, cars, people talking and even yelling, add a constant background buzz. Handfuls of young, mainly white, techy guys are always quietly writing code for some project or other—typically in jeans and T-shirt, some barefoot, some bearded.

Kenna operates a small media hub out of the basement for his latest venture, a Web site called *Money & Tech,* staffed by a small group of editors and producers, freelancers mainly. He built a full studio down there, with a set for video, lights, cameras, a news desk and backdrop. In other corners of the basement are a couple of different ventures. One older artist uses a space to make his leather goods; another space is for a one-man bitcoin company called Piper.

Chris Cassano, a twenty-five-year-old from Florida with long, shaggy black hair, glasses, and a scraggly beard, had been working as a defense contractor in Mystic, Connecticut, when he first heard about bitcoin in 2011. After overcoming his initial skepticism, he realized that he had a bunch of computers that could be put to mining. Why not mine, convert the bitcoin into dollars, "and take their crazy, scam money"?

Living alone, away from family and friends, in the small Connecticut town, Cassano had a lot of time on his hands. Soon, most of that time was being spent in bitcoin chat rooms or thinking about how to improve his hashrate. He had a background in programming and file systems, and his work involved algorithms that were similar to the ones used in bitcoin. He mined, but says he blew most of his mined money on random things on the Internet, not thinking about how he could be storing its value for future growth. "It was cool at the time to be able to spend my fake Internet money on real-world things," he says with a laugh. But he was becoming consumed with a question: How best to protect a wallet?

The word *wallet* is thrown around a lot in bitcoin circles, and it's an evocative description, but it's just a user application that allows you to send and receive bitcoins over the bitcoin network. You can download software to create your own wallet—if you *really* want to be your own bank —but most people go through a wallet provider such as Coinbase or Blockchain, which melded them into user-friendly Web sites and smartphone apps. Either way, the "wallet," much like an account at a traditional bank, is little more than lines of code, and because of that, online security is an issue. In theory, so long as one of the most important components of that code—the all-important private key that unlocks a bitcoin address's ability to send money—resides somewhere online, it is vulnerable to hackers. New encryption-security solutions introduced in 2014, especially the multi-sig system that requires the coordination of multiple keys to access an address, should make such attacks virtually impossible outside of extortion or extreme negligence from two parties. Still, if you want to keep your bitcoins 100 percent safe, you can't leave the code online anywhere.

That's how Cassano hit upon a simple, nondigital solution: the paper wallet. With his program, the user would print out the code and store it off-line. It didn't take him long to create a prototype-dedicated printer based on a Raspberry Pi, a tiny, inexpensive motherboard that came with in-built security protections, which were necessary to avoid the problem of inadvertently registering your code on your hard drive whenever you communicated with a less well-protected printer. He posted a description of it on Kickstarter and immediately sold twenty-five. That netted him about $4,000. In September of 2013, he got a call from Kenna, inviting him out to 20Mission. The unusual deal was that Cassano could live and work at 20Mission in exchange for a small stake in his company; Kenna would essentially act as an angel investor for Cassano. So the Floridian moved to the hacker house in December. He had housing, office space, a product, and a backer. All he needed was a name.

"I kept saying, Raspberry Pi, paper wallet, Pi paper wallet Pi paper wallet," he said. Eventually, the words mashed into one: Piper.

"Money's great, too," Nathan Lands says, sitting in a booth in his wife's restaurant, Ramen Underground, which has become a hangout for bitcoiners in San Francisco, an alternative to 20Mission. "I'm excited about that, but this is change-the-world-type stuff."

The thirty-year-old high school dropout is the cofounder of Quick-Coin, the maker of a wallet that's aimed directly at finding the fastest, easiest route to mass adoption. The idea, which he dreamed up with fellow bitcoiner Marshall Hayner one night over a dinner at Ramen Underground, is to give nontechnical bitcoin newcomers access to an easy-to-use mobile wallet via familiar tools of social media. Users can sign up for QuickCoin's wallet through Facebook on their mobile devices and are then directed to a simple interface that dispenses with a lot of the imposing technical data shown on products such as Blockchain's. With cropped blond hair and an easy laugh, Lands still looks like the teenage gamer he was, though now he's a husband and a father who happens to have venture funds courting him like a prom queen. He has already built, sold, and lost a handful of businesses, made money and then lost it, and is now making it again.

At fifteen, Lands had made his first serious money—serious for a teenager, that is—running a large "guild" connected to the video game

EverQuest and selling virtual goods for real money. He was already an entrepreneur. He just didn't know it yet. "I didn't know anything about business," Lands said. "I didn't even know anybody who had a business. My spreadsheet was a notepad."

This was the time of the Columbine shooting, and a gamer with long hair who had a predilection for wearing black soon found himself the focus of authorities at his school, who worried he might have similar inclinations as the two young killers who orchestrated that massacre. Having money in his pocket gave him the courage to simply quit school rather than deal with the harassment. He traveled around the country, got into real estate in Florida, lost everything and more in the crash, got back into gaming, started gaming-related companies, and built himself up again. Those businesses brought him regularly to San Francisco. Eventually it just made sense to be there permanently.

His successes allowed Lands to raise $10 million for one company, Gamestreamer. He began to do stealth research on a competitor, which brought him into contact with one of its employees, Patrick Murck, now general counsel at the Bitcoin Foundation and a key figure in the bitcoin industry's complicated yet vital liaison efforts with government regulators and lawmakers. The two competitors struck up a friendship. Murck was the first to tell Lands about bitcoin.

Gamestreamer never took off, and in the summer of 2013, Lands quietly shut it down. As he killed time helping out his wife with the business end of her restaurant, he began to think about what he'd do next. He kept coming back to bitcoin, which increasingly seemed like a good bet. He started buying coins online, where he ran into his eventual business partner, Hayner (with whom he later had a falling-out, and whose stake he bought). They met in person, at Ramen Underground, and started sketching out ideas. One of those ideas became QuickCoin.

Lands is typical of most of the itinerant entrepreneurs we met. Bright and motivated, they possess, or at least believe they possess, internal divining rods that allow them to detect the next big thing and will go wherever the rod points. As we talked to Lands, he mentioned at least half a dozen businesses he'd built and lost or sold; he mentioned having $10 million, and being broke. At one point he quite unconsciously compared his small start-up to Apple and Google. The entrepreneurs also have an odd relationship with money. They all seem to treat money as if it doesn't matter in the least. It's not something to be concerned with. Sometimes they have it, sometimes they don't. However, they all seem to expect to become filthy rich someday, when they hit the big one.

"You almost have to be crazy," Lands says, "but you can't be *real* crazy. It does take being a little nutty, though."

Silicon Valley's venture capitalists didn't start getting into bitcoin in a serious way until well into 2013, more than four years after it was launched and after various ventures, such as Kenna's Tradehill, had already come and gone. But since then, the support has increased exponentially. The Valley is now putting money behind many young innovators like those we've met, providing them with a critical badge of legitimacy and vouching for cryptocurrency. VCs might not yet be dumping $100 million funding rounds into bitcoin start-ups, but a growing number of them have handed over significant amounts of money.

Of course, much VC money is thrown around as part of a scattershot strategy, the hope being that if just a few of the many bets make it big, investors can make their money back. Sensibly, many venture capitalists see their bitcoin bets in this context. Yet it is striking how many seem to be enthused by the technology; in the Valley, there's almost a sense that you *have* to be into bitcoin lest you miss out on a revolution. The tally of money coming in from venture capitalists has become something of an obsession with bitcoiners—and for good reason. It's a tangible measure of these influential players' interest in the cryptocurrency field and therefore of how far it has moved on the path to acceptance and legitimacy. According to surveys conducted by news site *CoinDesk*, venture capital invested in bitcoin companies jumped from $2 million in 2012 to $88 million in 2013. By the middle of 2014, more than $113 million had been raised in the first half alone. If it continued in the second half at that rate of a 30 percent expansion in six months, the full-year rise would have tripled from 2013. To be sure, the total amount dedicated to bitcoin is just a sliver of global VC money; Dow Jones VentureSource tallied $33 billion in venture-capital funding in 2013. But the growth rate is hard to ignore. It's not far off the money-raising that was swirling around Internet start-ups in the second half of the 1990s, and it suggests that claims of bitcoin's demise were premature.

Above all, it's the names of the investors that get people's attention. The list includes a selection of key players from the early e-commerce boom in the 1990s, including a man with as big a claim as any to having popularized the Internet: Marc Andreessen. The founder of Mosaic, the first mass-distributed browser, as well its better-known successor, Netscape, Andreessen is now a high-profile bitcoin bull. His firm, Andreessen Horowitz, has made major investments in the cryptocurrency sector, including in bitcoin processor Coinbase and in payments provider Ripple. He's not the only techie-turned-investor from that era now diving into crypto start-ups. Jerry Yang, who created the first successful search engine, Yahoo, put money from his AME Ventures into a $30 million funding round for processor BitPay and into one of two $20 million rounds raised by depository and wallet provider Xapo, which offers insurance to depositors and calls itself a "bitcoin vault." Stratton Sclavos, the former CEO of Verisign, the Web site security-rating firm that turned the promise of card-based e-commerce into a reality, took an important stake in high-tech wallet-security specialist BitGo via his Radar Capital firm. Other prominent bitcoin bulls from the Valley's investing establishment include Jim Breyer of Accel Partners, who took a lead role in Circle, the user-friendly bitcoin depository and brokerage service launched by Jeremy Allaire, the creator of the Brightcove online video player. Adam Draper's influential father, Tim, put money into Vaurum, a bitcoin exchange intended for banks and financial institutions. Jeremy Liew of Lightspeed Partners has steered money into BTC China and Ripple, and Reid Hoffman's firm Greylock Partners shared the lead on Xapo's second $20 million fund-raising, along with Index Partners of London.

Meanwhile, San Francisco–based hedge fund Pantera Capital has gone from investing in global bonds and currencies to converting itself into a fully dedicated bitcoin vehicle, managing money on behalf of New York–based mega-hedge-fund Fortress Capital. Also in New York, Union Square Partners has taken up a key East Coast bitcoin-booster role, most commonly via the person of cofounder Fred Wilson. Big-name individuals in business and entertainment are also popping up in bitcoin and other cryptocurrency investment pools: Virgin Group chairman Sir Richard Branson, actor Ashton Kutcher via his A-Grade Investments fund, and Hong Kong billionaire Li Ka-shing, who plowed money into BitPay via his Horizons Ventures firm. Then there are those investors who've become so involved that they're now part of the bitcoin community as mainstays on the bitcoin conference circuit: Matthew Roszak at Tally Capital in Chicago, Rik Willard of MintCombine in New York, and William Quigley of Santa Monica–based Clearstone Venture Partners, to name a few. On top of this, an active community of bitcoiners is putting its newfound wealth back into accelerator programs and angel investing projects, often with funds denominated in bitcoin and other cryptocurrencies. The most active of this crowd belong to the BitAngels group comprising people such as PR agent Michael Terpin, cryptocurrency developer David Johnston, and the digital currency impresario Brock Pierce.

Deals for $20 million and $30 million are becoming more common. BitPay, Blockchain, Coinbase, Xapo, mining-equipment maker BitFury, and Circle have come in around that, some on more than one fund-raising round, while decent multimillion-dollar amounts have gone to Ripple, BitGo, and San Francisco–based exchange Kraken.

In case this seems too America-centric, it's worth noting that London-based high-tech exchange Coinfloor was funded in part by that city's Passion Capital, Chinese exchange BTC China is backed by Lightspeed Ventures' Asian unit, and Nordic VC firm Creandum led a $14 million funding round for Stockholm-based rig-maker KnC Miner.

Not everyone seems to need—or want—this VC money, which, as we've mentioned, stirs suspicion among early-adopter bitcoin utopians who worry that "suits" are taking over. Until it landed $30 million in VC funds in October 2014, giant London-based wallet company Blockchain ran its entire operation in bitcoin. That requires paying staff in bitcoin and constantly tapping suppliers that accept the digital currency, such as CheapAir.com, which Blockchain's jet-setting CEO, Nicolas Cary, uses for flights. But it's also made easier because the wallet maker does not provide any fiat-currency exchange services. Bitstamp and Bulgaria's BTC-e must deal in dollars and euros, but the pair of highly successful Central European exchanges has never hooked into the venture-capital gravy flow. Some firms have been able to keep it all in the family, tapping the wealth of the bitcoin community by launching crowdfunding operations entirely denominated in digital currencies. This is the preferred route for the many "Bitcoin 2.0" ventures aiming to turn the blockchain into a multi-faceted platform for middleman-free exchanges of contracts and property and for creating decentralized applications and organizations.

Whether these start-ups are filling traditional bank accounts with investor dollars or accepting bitcoiners' grants in their digital wallets, the carousel of money is having a profound effect on the cryptocurrency land-scape. The surge in financing is rivaled only by the growing interest of government regulators as the major force shaping that landscape. In their ad hoc, boom-bust way, these cashed-up companies and their smart, young, wide-eyed founders are building and organizing the decentralized economy that will one day define how we all go about our lives.

Before the old guard of the Valley VC community took to bitcoin, they were led there by a major younger player in their field. Twenty-eight-year-old Adam Draper has been described as the bitcoin community's financing "prince," a reference to the powerful venture-capital dynasty from which he hails. Draper's father is the aforementioned Tim Draper, founder of Draper Fisher Jurvetson and another early and enthusiastic bitcoin believer. Adam's grandfather, Bill Draper, and great-grandfather, William H. Draper, were also both highly successful Silicon Valley VCs, the latter often referred to as the industry's founding father. The youngest Draper, who tells visitors to his personal Web site that his life's ambition is to assist in the creation of an iron-man suit, has clearly inherited his family's entrepreneurial drive. In 2009, while still in his senior year at UCLA, Draper founded Xpert Financial, a platform for trading shares in private companies that have not yet gone public. Functioning very much like SecondMarket, the five-years-older brainchild of prominent bitcoin booster Barry Silbert, Xpert has since earned SEC approval. A year later, the now-graduated Draper founded Enders Fund, a project designed to finance the development of mobile-phone games. In June 2012, after a meeting with Coinbase's Brian Armstrong opened his eyes to the enthusiasm of its community, Draper set up the venture that would launch him into the world of bitcoin: Boost, a special "accelerator" program for nurturing early start-ups.

Accelerators are tailor-made for Silicon Valley. Essentially, venture capitalists and so-called angel investors pool money together and designate it to help start-ups get going. But it's not just money. For a period of about three months, the financiers provide these budding companies with work space and living space and bring mentors in to advise them (the main difference between an accelerator and a hacker house, it appears, is the money). It's a crash course in how to turn their ideas into businesses, a boot camp for start-ups.

Draper's accelerator was the first to focus solely on bitcoin projects, but it didn't begin that way. "We were just trying to run a good accelerator program," he said. They took space in the basement of another accelerator, Hero City, a program that is part of Draper University—a business school that Adam's father started in 2012—on a tree-lined commercial street in prosperous San Mateo. From one batch of companies to the next, Draper was looking for a real breakthrough technology to get behind. He considered 3-D printing, and drones. Bitcoin kept popping up, and soon enough he became convinced of its potential, from both a technological standpoint and a business standpoint. "We ended up really diving deep on bitcoin," he said. "We see a lot of opportunity in the space." At the time, there were only a handful of bitcoin businesses. Draper thought he could double that.

He put word out that Boost would be taking between 5 and 7 bitcoin-related start-ups and quickly received 150 applications. He met all of them over a month and slowly pieced together the picture. "At the end of that month I was one of the foremost authorities on bitcoin," he said, only half-joking. Even other VCs, essentially his competitors, were approaching him, looking for information. He'd moved first, and he emerged as the leader in the field, which meant his start-ups could draw in money from the bigger guys when it came time for larger funding rounds. "You want to go where no one else is willing to go, so you can find the great things that are going to be built."

"We took a leap," he said; "we were the first ones to show there was any interest." Boost wasn't writing huge checks, but it was writing checks, and the businesses that were coming through were getting noticed. Before long the VC money started pouring into bitcoin. "It made us big fish in a small pond. And then it became a really big pond."

•   •   •

Scott Robinson is the marketing director at Plug and Play Tech Center, an incubator in Sunnyvale, between Palo Alto and San Jose at the southern end of San Francisco Bay. He is also the operation's resident bitcoin evangelist. He learned of the cryptocurrency in 2011, from a friend who'd used it to buy drugs online. He became intrigued as he noticed more and more mentions in the press. In late 2012, he started attending bitcoin meetups in Sunnyvale organized by Roger Ver, an early bitcoin investor and cofounder of the Bitcoin Foundation, who now also functions as a kind of motivational speaker on the bitcoin conference circuit. When Ver moved to Tokyo, he asked Robinson to take over the meetups. He did and eventually started holding them in the offices of Plug and Play.

Plug and Play is the brainchild of Saeed Amidi, a garrulous Iranian immigrant who started the accelerator in 2006 and has turned the successful idea into a global franchise that recruits start-ups worldwide. Plug and Play units are now in Canada, Spain, Singapore, Jordan, Dagestan, Russia, Poland, and Mexico, as well as at four other sites in the United States. A number of these kinds of programs exist around the world and in the Valley: Boost, Hero City, Y Combinator, 500 Startups, all with roughly the same idea. The difference between "incubator" and "accelerator" is somewhat vague, but the main idea behind the latter is to move fast. Billing itself as "Silicon Valley in a box," Plug and Play brings together start-ups, corporations, venture capital, and universities all in one place and bangs out companies. It's been a phenomenally successful, frenetic model. Hundreds of start-ups have cycled through the campus, some 325 being there in the summer of 2014, and several have gone on to become billion-dollar operations.

The Sunnyvale campus is massive. Its centerpiece is an open-floor-plan office space for the start-ups that's about the size of a football field. Many companies are clustered around corporate partners, such as Volkswagen and Panasonic. Others are clustered around industries and technologies; the bitcoiners, for instance, were all in the same big cubbyhole. The center has an auditorium, an expo space, and even a large patio with views of the Santa Clara Mountains.

Mentorships are arranged, bringing in people with experience in the same fields as the start-ups. The start-ups' founders are introduced to venture capitalists, corporate executives, and university representatives. In exchange for all this, Plug and Play gets an equity stake in each one, typically $25,000 for a 5 percent stake. At its best, it's a mutually beneficial arrangement. The companies get exposure and access to expertise and capital they never could otherwise, and the center gets to spud scores of wells, so to speak. If one pays off—PayPal, Dropbox, and Zoosk all came through this program—it pays off big.

In June 2014, Plug and Play hosted its quarterly one-day "expo," a networking event at the culmination of an accelerator program that brings investors and start-ups together for a series of presentations and seminars and that ends with a pitchfest, where each start-up sends one member from its team onstage in front of hundreds of interested investors from funds around the world. This manic day comes after months of late nights writing, testing, and rewriting software code and then drafting and redrafting business plans. At the end, these entrepreneurs get three minutes at the expo; three minutes to distill three months of effort, three minutes to go up on a stage and perform, to perform and sell their company, their idea, to a crowd with deep pockets, the deepest pockets, who are used to hearing all manner of fantastic pitches. It's a golden opportunity, which makes it all the more nerve-racking, particularly given that most tech guys are not natural pitchmen and lack the charisma of your average marketing manager. Three winners are chosen by a panel of judges. Robinson was especially proud because this expo included his special babies: five bitcoin-related start-ups among the two dozen pitching.

The whole thing has an *American Idol* feeling, and just as many of the most popular singers to emerge out of the *American Idol* factory are those who *don't* win—Daughtry, Katharine McPhee, Kellie Pickler—at Plug and Play's expo winning is great but not the only prize. Make a good pitch, and even if you don't win, people start paying attention to you, and the payday may come down the road.

The five bitcoin companies represented an impressive breadth of the kind of innovation currently being pursued in this field. CoinVox is a bitcoin-based political-donations service; 37Coins is a product for sending digital currency via SMS messages that's targeted for developing countries; CoinsFriendly is a bitcoin trading and market analytical tool; Purse provides a backdoor means of buying goods on Amazon with bitcoin; and

PeerPal is an online marketplace for people to trade bitcoin and dollars directly with each other online. Their teams came from Texas, California, and Maryland, and Ukraine, South Korea, and Germany. For the most part, these bitcoiners were young—with one exception—and despite their different backgrounds, they all had two common traits. They were all impressively intelligent, whether they came with an Ivy League sheepskin or had taught themselves to code, and they were all fantastically ambitious.

Purse's Andrew Lee, who has a background in payments at Merrill Lynch, had learned about bitcoin in 2011 and was interested enough to buy $5 worth online, which he promptly forgot about. More than a year had passed when he suddenly noticed that bitcoin's price was rising exponentially and remembered his $5 investment. "A cup of coffee," he explained by way of comparison, "had turned into a laptop."

Lee began attending bitcoin meetups and at one met Kent Liu, an IBM computer scientist. One day in February 2014, they got together at a coffeehouse around midday in the Mission District in San Francisco. By the time they finished their last cup of coffee—at 11:00 P.M.—they had hammered out a proposal that purported to solve two different groups of people's problems at once and would eventually land them at Plug and Play. First, it would allow those who want to spend bitcoins on goods at Amazon to do so even though the e-commerce site doesn't accept the digital currency—and at a negotiated discount price to boot. Second, it would let anyone who wants to buy bitcoin to do so with a credit-card, a convenience that most bitcoin exchanges and brokerages disallow because of the risk of chargebacks from credit-card-issuing banks. Lee and Liu's ingenious solution was to bring them together via an open marketplace, the credit-card holder buying the goods on the shopper's behalf and getting bitcoins as compensation. It was kind of like a mechanized, market-driven version of Laszlo Hanyecz's famous pizza deal. It would function as a simultaneous marketplace for bitcoin and goods, with bids for Amazon product discounts representing bitcoin price offerings with premiums imposed for the convenience of using a credit-card. And so Purse was born.

Both soon quit their jobs. "It was an easy decision," Liu says.

The team behind PeerPal was noticeably different from the others: they were the only group whose members were obviously on the far side of their twenties. Or thirties for that matter.

When they started meeting in August 2013, James Jones, Joshua Schechter, and Houston Frost were the only three bitcoiners in San Antonio, Texas. "We'd have meetups," Schechter explains, "and we were the only ones there." The three also fall into the entrepreneur mold. Frost is the CEO of Akimbo, which sells a prepaid debit card that allows users to set up a branch of several subcards, for family members. Schechter built and sold a payment-processing company, and Jones invented a product called CubeSpawn, a self-replicating printer. Schechter learned about bitcoin back in 2009, having read Nakamoto's white paper, but he was not cut from the Cypherpunk mold of the early bitcoin fanatics. "I'm not an anarchist or libertarian," Schechter says. "I'm a capitalist." In bitcoin, he saw his chance to strike it rich. A chance meeting with Robinson at a bitcoin conference in Las Vegas led to an offer to come to Sunnyvale. "How do you say no to an opportunity at a Silicon Valley accelerator?" he said rhetorically. So, the forty-eight-year-old put his wife, house, kids, fish, and dog on hold for three months and came out to California.

These guys have slightly different needs from most of their peers at the expo. While it's easy for a twenty-five-year-old whose only expenses are rent and beer not to worry about money, the men from PeerPal have families and mouths to feed. "We can't do it for free," Schechter explains. When we met, he was living off savings and his wife's job. In June 2014, he was staying at Circuit House, a hacker house like 20Mission, down in San Jose. "It's like being in college again," he joked. But if PeerPal didn't take off, he knew he'd have to pivot again, figure out his next move. Schechter represented the group onstage. A natural extrovert, he gave a good presentation, which got a good reaction. The crowd reactions all day weren't unlike those at a grammar-school play, with scattered family members cheering loudest when their child came onstage. Schechter ended his pitch somewhat unusually with a specific dollar request: $600,000. (He later told us he considered it a conservative figure.)

Schechter acknowledged that one of his goals was to be bought out. (They consciously chose their name, PeerPal, in hopes of attracting the attention of PayPal.) But in the end they didn't get any fresh investment or get bought out, and by the end of the summer the three were back in Texas, back to their old gigs, their dreams of bitcoin riches delayed, not destroyed. Frost had Akimbo. Schechter is helping Jones with

CubeSpawn, whose little self-replicating, decentralized machines are designed to encourage "distributed manufacturing." Naturally, their business takes bitcoin.

Virtually all the tech innovators and venture capitalists we spoke to say they are motivated by bitcoin's long-term prospects. By that they mean the moneymaking opportunities that they see coming from giving people decentralized cryptocurrency tools with which to change commercial practices, not the short-term gains from speculating on its price. Still, it's no coincidence that the pickup in VC money into the sector coincided with the surge in bitcoin's price in 2013, when the digital currency rose by 8,400 percent in eleven months to a peak of $1,151 in early December, a level sixteen hundred times higher than three years earlier. A rising market, especially one scaling new heights at a rate like that, can create buzz and attention around an asset. More than that, it also unleashes spending and investment power among those who own that asset.

A positive feedback loop is how Silicon Valley would describe it, with the higher prices begetting more interest in cryptocurrencies, more investment capital flowing into bitcoin, more innovation and more interest and benefits for the sector, which should push the price even higher. Skeptics could equally call it a bubble—and many sought to do so once the price retreated below $500 in the first half of 2014, using it to justify their depictions of "tulip mania" around bitcoin. But even at those newly lower levels, bitcoin was still higher than any level it had held in its entire history before mid-November 2013. That's left many miners, bitcoin entrepreneurs, and businesses that have earned the cryptocurrency for a year or more markedly wealthier. The choices they make in investing that wealth have encouraged still more innovation in the sector and have driven prices for bitcoin-related digital properties higher, much as the NASDAQ stock boom fueled the mania for IT start-ups and stocks in the late 1990s.

The meandering history of the domain name *bitcoin.com,* the cryptocurrency's most valuable piece of online real estate, illustrates this well. It was first registered in 2000 by a Swedish telecom company, which let the registration lapse. A South Korean tech company owned it from 2003 to 2005, then too let it lapse. In 2008, a Yale University student and entrepreneur named Jesse Heitler registered it, then sold it in 2010 for $2,000 to a Toronto businessman named David Lowy. Lowy flipped to the current owner, who remains anonymous. That owner has leased the name out to three different groups: one was Kenna, who paid $1 million in Tradehill equity in 2011 for the name. After Tradehill shut down, the man then leased it first to Coinbase, and then in 2014 to Blockchain. We don't know what the latter two paid, but if it was worth $1 million in 2011, it's a good bet it's worth a lot more than that now.

While it can feel as if everyone in the Valley is into bitcoin—just as it can feel as if everyone outside the Valley is against it or has little interest— the truth is that the clique of fervent believers is still relatively small. Some in the VC community have serious doubts—they just don't seem to express them often. In a post on the *StrictlyVC* blog by Connie Loizos titled "A Bitcoin Bear in Silicon Valley, It's True," Josh Stein, the managing director at Tim Draper's Menlo Park firm Draper Fisher Jurvetson, is quoted describing himself as a "bitcoin bear." Stein, whose firm has invested in Twitter, Skype, and Tesla, argued that transaction-cost savings on bitcoin weren't much more competitive than electronic wires or new dollar-based payment technologies, and that bitcoin, unlike gold, had no "intrinsic value." In a telling turn, however, Loizos wrote that Stein quickly cut his comments short, claiming that publicly revealing his views would "cue the trolls." He was probably referring to the bitcoin zealots who quickly take to Reddit or Twitter to discredit anyone who challenges the notion that cryptocurrency is the answer to the world's problems. But Stein's comment also makes it sound as if the VC community is trapped by its own groupthink on bitcoin, by a subtle kind of self-censorship that prevents any member from getting off message.

From our experience, VCs are a much more thoughtful, open-minded bunch than that. So, Stein can probably still happily lunch with his co-partner Tim Draper. But outside the narrow confines of the Bay Area, bitcoiners are very much in the minority. Stein's criticisms resonate there far more readily, especially his contestable point about the lack of any intrinsic value. However flawed that view—recall our discussion in chapter 1 about the myth of all currencies' intrinsic value—it's widely held by people living outside the Bay Area.

The picture that emerges is of a lopsided world divided between a small but well-financed clique that's convinced cryptocurrency is going to change the world and everybody else, who can't see what all the fuss is about. Without support from the second group, the vision of the first won't come true. That's as true for bitcoin as it is for any new technology. Silicon Valley needs to tread carefully. While Americans still generally see the region's start-ups and their risk-taking investors in a positive light—as young men and women furthering the American dream —discontent can potentially bubble up. With every facet of our economy now dependent on the kinds of software developed and funded in the Bay Area, and with the Valley's well-heeled communities becoming a vital fishing ground for political donations and patronage, we're witnessing a migration of the political and economic power base away from Wall Street to this region. Amid that shift, the omniscience of giant companies such as Google, Microsoft, Apple, and Facebook and revelations about the private information people cede to them makes many people, including some lawmakers, uncomfortable. Certainly, their all-encompassing power creates a far more negative impression than the romantic image of computer geeks making cool gadgets in garages. As new waves of highly disruptive technologies start to strip more Americans of their jobs—and as we'll see later, cryptocurrencies could well be included in those—resentment toward the "wisdom" of the Silicon Valley establishment could grow further. On the other hand, the products that come out of the Valley have made positive contributions to society, such as the ones that emerged from the advent of the Internet. In fact, it's their relatively recent experience with the Internet's development that helps many Silicon Valley types get excited about cryptocurrencies. They don't know what the future holds for bitcoin, but because of the unpredictable spin-off innovations that the Internet made way for, many sense that this new "platform" has similar, liberating prospects.

"If you went back to 1993 and you asked people what they thought they could do if they networked all the computers, a lot of people would have basically taken things they were already doing with computers and imagined doing them faster and to greater scale," says Chris Dixon, a partner at Andreessen Horowitz. "For example, people would say, 'At home, I currently copy files by sticking them in a disk and walking across the room, but now on the network I can do that instantly.' So, people imagined things like copying files and chatting on bulletin boards. But no one imagined Twitter or Wikipedia or YouTube or all these amazing inventions that have happened over the past ten to twenty years. It would be very hard to find anyone in 1993 who predicted all those things." Those unimaginable possibilities exist with bitcoin, Dixon says, because "extensible software platforms that allow anyone to build on top of them are incredibly powerful and have all these unexpected uses. The stuff about fixing the existing payment system is interesting, but what's superexciting is that you have this new platform on which you can move money and property and potentially build new areas of business."

If Dixon's right about bitcoin's being the Internet all over again—a vision shaped by the experience of his partner Netscape founder Marc Andreessen—then many of the start-ups that have dived into this field will have their dreams fulfilled and may well become the next PayPal, or at least get bought by PayPal. For the VCs, the hope is that their scattershot approach lands on just a couple of big winners. This inherently optimistic approach is founded on the idea that the opportunities lie in multiple, untapped places—we just don't always know which ones.

As we'll learn in the next chapter, some of the big opportunities —perhaps the biggest—are seen far beyond the well-kept neighborhoods of Palo Alto or the well-furnished apartments of New York or London. Cryptocurrency's great promise is not that the wealthy will rush into it and bid up its price, but that the poor will find it extremely useful. It's time to explore one of bitcoin's most exciting ideas: that it can liberate the "unbanked."

Eight

THE UNBANKED

> Money, it has been said, is the cause of good things to a good
> man and of evil things to a bad man.
>
> —*Philo*

Roughly 2.5 billion adults in the world don't have access to banks, which
means somewhere in the order of 5 billion people belong to households
that are cut off from a financial system that the rest of us take for granted.
They can't start savings accounts. They don't have checking accounts.
They can't get credit-cards. They live in places where banks don't want to
go, and because of this, they remain effectively walled off from the global
economy. They are called the unbanked. But they are not unreachable,
not by a long shot, and one of the biggest and most exciting prospects
bitcoiners talk about is using their cryptocurrency to bring these billions
of people roaring into the twenty-first century.

Money is neither good nor bad. It is simply a system of exchange and
accounting—a way for society to efficiently and effectively swap goods and
services and to keep track of it all on a large scale. People have, nonetheless, invested it with transcendent values. "Money" has become as much
a mental construct as "value" itself. Bitcoiners are no different in how they
describe their currency. In their minds, bitcoin is a force unto itself that
will reshape and improve people's lives everywhere it goes, which leads
them to this notion that they can both get rich and do tremendous good.
It's like capitalism with a radically altruistic bent. Nowhere is this more

evident than in how bitcoin is being offered as a solution for the world's poor—and in this case they do have a compelling case to make for a better, more widely accessible form of money.

To illustrate, let's go back briefly to one of the start-ups that debuted at Plug and Play's June expo day: 37Coins. The start-up is the combined work of its three founders, Songyi Lee, Johann Barbie, and Jonathan Zobro. Of the three, Lee seemed the most out of place in the Valley. Not a coder, nor a libertarian or crypto-anarchist, she was a social worker. Barbie, her boyfriend, was the techie and bitcoin enthusiast. But one day the two of them put their separate worlds together and realized they had a chance to do something big.

In September 2013, Lee was part of a film crew in Mali, working with the antipoverty nonprofit World Vision, on her first trip out in the field. Mali had just been through a brutal civil war, and people had emptied out of the north and fled for refugee camps in the south. There, Songyi met Fatima, a mother of five living in a "camp" that was more like a permanent residence. Her husband had immigrated to Ivory Coast for work, as so many Malians do, and would send money back when he could. How he did that made a huge impression on the young Lee.

Fatima's husband sent money back though people. Random people, people who were headed in the direction of his wife and family. Fatima's family didn't have any bank accounts, or even IDs. Sometimes the money arrived. Sometimes it didn't. To supplement that fragile income stream, Fatima worked as a housekeeper. If that wasn't enough, her older children would work as well.

She did, importantly, have a phone, a $5 feature phone. "I couldn't believe it," Lee said. This last point is critical. Without savings accounts, without access to banking services, people in emerging markets—as well as a good number in advanced markets such as the United States—have a difficult time building up lasting wealth. It's just one more challenge that leaves so many trapped in poverty. For them, the pursuit of other freedoms—of speech, for example—must be subordinated to the task of tackling these financial and economic challenges. The escape from all that, bitcoiners surmise, may lie in those $5 phones and a radical new mobile-money system.

Mali is one of the poorest nations on the planet. It ranked 175th out of 187 nations on the UN's Human Development Index. More than 70 percent of the population lives below the poverty line. It is largely dependent upon agriculture, and per capita income averages $500 a year. There are efforts to boost tourism, but the country's history of violence, including the coup in 2012 that drove people such as Fatima from their homes, makes that a hard sell.

After Lee returned to their home in Seoul, she showed Barbie the footage she'd taken, and a lightbulb went off in his head. Barbie was a software designer who'd worked for IBM and had become fascinated by bitcoin—"I didn't sleep for two days" is how he described his first reaction to discovering the cryptocurrency—and immediately saw a way that it could help solve Fatima's problem: mobile payments. Bitcoins, after all, are nothing more than lines of code. If somebody has a phone—it doesn't even have to be a smartphone, it can be a feature phone that can receive text messages—it can be hooked into a computer system to deliver bitcoin. Banks may not want to extend their cumbersome, Byzantine system into these pockets of the emerging markets because it just isn't profitable. But that isn't a problem for bitcoin.

"I figured that this is it," Lee said. "This is my lifetime chance to try and save the world and try and change the world." She quit her job at World Vision and, together with Barbie and Zobro, started building 37Coins. (The name is a reference to a comment from Satoshi Nakamoto, who opined once on a message board that bitcoin mining was "like trying to flip 37 coins at once and have them all come up heads.")

The service allows anybody with a plain-vanilla feature phone, including the low-end phones used by people in developing countries, to send money via SMS, i.e., text messages. All one needs to do is open a wallet with 37Coins. It's similar to a popular service called M-Pesa in Kenya, but where M-Pesa is run by a telecommunications company, Safaricom, and is built on top of the traditional banking infrastructure, 37Coins works off the decentralized bitcoin network. It uses people in the region lucky enough to afford Android smartphones as "gateways" to transmit the messages. In return, these gateways receive a small fee, which provides the corollary benefit of giving locals the opportunity to create a little business for themselves moving traffic. The business is still in the early stages, with tryouts in Asia and other countries where the populace is more tech-savvy, before being tried in places like Mali.

The founders of 37Coins have energy and passion, but they face major hurdles. Notwithstanding the remarkable penetration of cell phones into the world's slums, technology tends to move slowest in the poorest places. Other hurdles are cultural, social, and political, such as civil wars, or the remoteness of some potential customers, or their resistance to new ways of doing things. Moreover, 37Coins faces competitive pressures. More and more cryptocurrency start-ups are aiming their services at emerging markets, including BitPesa in Kenya, BitPagos in South America, and Volabit in Mexico. Some of them—37Coins, BitPagos, and Volabit, for instance—have gone through the Silicon Valley accelerator programs. Others, such as BitPesa, are well connected and financed. All share the belief that they can make good money *and* make money good.

People in developed countries often don't realize the hidden costs and privacy issues of credits cards. To them, credit-cards work just fine—merchants get hit with the transaction fees and chargebacks, not customers, and they don't have to bother fumbling with cash. So unless they have been burned by the unexpected cost of using their credit-card in a foreign country, they tend to view cryptocurrencies as a solution in search of a problem. But in the developing world, where the costs of an ineffectual financial system and the burdens of transferring funds are all too clear, cryptocurrencies have a much more compelling pitch to make. Bitcoin evangelists tend to focus on two areas there: remittances of money from developed countries to developing countries, and internal payments and transfers.

The World Bank estimates that the global remittance business is worth somewhere around $500 billion annually in cross-border flows. Countries such as the Philippines and those of Central America, which have large groups of citizens working in richer countries, depend heavily on these homecoming funds to drive their economies. Yet our inefficient international financial system ensures that only part of the money gets to where it's supposed to go. Depending on the receiving country, fees for money sent from the United States often hit 10 percent; from the United Kingdom and other countries it can be double that. With exchange-rate costs, the total "friction" in the transaction can run as high as 30 percent.

Within developing countries, equally great challenges can exist in conducting day-to-day commerce. For a merchant whose customers don't have access to credit, just carrying around all that cash can be dangerous. For a customer without a bank account, building up any kind of savings is virtually impossible. The problem isn't limited to the emerging markets. In Canada, the United Kingdom, Germany, and Australia, the proportion of people above the age of fifteen with a bank account ranges from 96 percent to 99 percent. But head to the United States, and the figure slips to 88 percent. Add in a separate "underbanked" category—that is, those who may have a bank account, but also are driven to "nontraditional" banking sources such as check cashers or payday loans—and the percentage of the American population with insufficient access to the financial system exceeds 30 percent. Whereas China has delivered bank accounts to 64 percent of its people, in Argentina, despite Buenos Aires' large, educated, and internationally savvy middle-class population, just 33 percent of the country is banked, a figure less even than India's 35 percent. In the Philippines, where remittances are so valued that returning OFWs (Overseas Filipino Workers) are exempted from airport taxes and given fast-track passport-processing at Manila Airport, only 27 percent of the population have bank accounts. In Pakistan, the figure is 10 percent.

Banks won't service these people for various reasons. It's partly because the poor don't offer as fat profits as the rich, and it's partly because they live in places where there isn't the infrastructure and security needed for banks to build physical branches. But mostly it's because of weak legal institutions and underdeveloped titling laws. Without documentation to prove their identity, to put up collateral and to create credit histories, the world's poor lack the basic foundations for participating in the world's banking system. This limits them to cash transactions. A whole tier of shadow banking has arisen to meet their needs, but it typically involves exorbitant money transmitters or, as in the case of migrant workers in Mali, putting themselves at the mercy of strangers.

Bitcoin, as we know, doesn't care who you are. It doesn't care how much money you are willing to save, send, or spend. You, your identity, and your credit history are irrelevant. You do need an electronic platform with which to connect to the Internet. But if you are able to get that, bitcoin allows you to send or receive money from anywhere. If you are living on $50 a week, the $5 you will save will matter a great deal.

Financially integrating a third of humanity could create vast new opportunities for world trade and for attacking poverty. We've already seen the sweeping impact that globalization and digitization have had on people's lives even without reforming the financial system. It has meant that young people in India with a command of English and an understanding of a desktop computer can now get jobs servicing American and European computers without leaving their homes. It has allowed multinational companies to source their goods from anywhere in the world, creating manufacturing jobs in regions that never had them. While many have been losers in rich countries that have seen factory and other outsourced jobs disappear, on a macro level the benefits of globalization are hard to ignore—even if its critics often do so. Between 1990 and 2010, the percentage of the world's population living on less than $1.25 a day dropped from 43.1 percent to 20.6 percent, which actually puts the world ahead of the UN's Millennium Development Goal to halve extreme poverty by 2015. Life expectancies rose by seven years over the same period, and infant mortality rates were almost halved.

This unprecedented improvement in the developing world's prosperity does not reflect some sudden outpouring of philanthropy from rich countries. It is directly associated with the post-Cold War growth of trade with and between emerging markets from Asia, Latin America, and Africa. This is clearly shown in the correlations between the advance of trade in the world's most populous region, Asia, and the rapid rise of a middle class there. But it's even evident in the poorest of those regions, in Africa, which has piggybacked on China's globalization-led economic advance to become a supplier of its insatiable appetite for commodities and a magnet for its investments, all of which is fostering small but growing hubs of prosperity across the continent. The more the world trades and the deeper and broader its economic integration, the greater the creation of aggregate wealth. Global financial integration could kick that process into overdrive.

Of course, bitcoin isn't the only tool for economic integration, and skeptics will often emphasize two points—neither of them particularly convincing. First, they make an argument that poor populations, with varying degrees of literacy, aren't capable of handling complicated new technologies such as bitcoin. Their second claim is that they don't have sufficiently sophisticated telecommunications systems to enable its use. In reality, these areas are arguably now what make these regions ripe for bitcoin's adoption.

With regard to literacy, the developing world as a whole is significantly more literate than it was just a decade and a half ago. Between 1999 and 2012, low-income-country literacy as measured by the World Bank leaped to 71 percent from 50 percent, middle-income-country literacy went to 96 percent from 83 percent, and for the entire world it rose to 92 percent from 81 percent. The key point is that despite those advances, the vast majority of those in poor countries and a large portion in middle-income countries are unbanked. They lack access to banks not because they are uneducated, but because of the persistent structural and systemic obstacles confronting people of limited means there: undeveloped systems of documentation and property titling, excessive bureaucracy, cultural snobbery, and corruption. The banking system makes demands that poor people simply can't meet.

One more point on illiteracy: the illiterate are predominantly older. In the developing regions of Eastern Europe, East Asia, Latin America, and the Caribbean, completion of primary education is now more or less universal. Huge waves of school-educated people are entering the workforces in these regions, where the demographics are the opposite of the aging societies of the West. This massive influx of schooled young will be more than qualified to handle the increasingly simple task of sending and receiving digital currency.

In fact, people in developing countries may be better prepared mentally than people in the West for digital money, by virtue of having made do with jerry-rigged financial arrangements. People who have suffered waves of financial crises are used to volatility. People who have spent years trusting expensive middlemen and flipping back and forth between dollars and their home currency are probably more likely to understand bitcoin's advantages and weather its flaws. "I remember I was in the Caribbean once when an old lady surprised me by negotiating a price in three different currencies," says Pelle Braendgaard, whose firm Kipochi has developed a mobile bitcoin wallet aimed squarely at developing countries. "Regular people in these markets are able to do things that we here in the United States, Europe, or Canada find to be quite difficult."

Another feature of developing economies that makes them open to this kind of change is that they have a much greater proportion of self-employed people, i.e., a much-larger hustling entrepreneurial class. From food-stall operators to rickshaw drivers, small-business owners are a mainstay of emerging-market economies, and for these people the ability to save costs on financial transactions could make a big difference to their profitability. Just as important, it creates opportunities for expansion. A seamstress serving local markets in Dhaka, Bangladesh, can widen her product line if she can now send money to a fabric producer in Chittagong, 160 miles away. And if she can find foreign buyers willing to pay her in bitcoin, all of a sudden she has a means for taking in export revenues.

While roads and other forms of infrastructure need to develop, too, bitcoin, in addressing the payment system, promises to tackle at least one flawed area of infrastructure. That could in turn drive change in the other areas by freeing up wealth to deal with them. Most important, communication technologies have come a long way in the developing world. Go to an Internet café in a dusty altiplano town in Bolivia, the poorest country in South America, and you may well find the connection is faster than in most American or European homes. In many cases, these countries virtually skip over legacy technology, going straight to high-tech fiber-optic cables. An explosion of wireless telephony has brought telecommunication capacity to rural areas and shantytowns that would otherwise be excluded from the installation of those cables. Ericsson ConsumerLab estimates that sub-Saharan Africa alone had 635 million mobile-phone subscriptions as of the end of 2014, or two-thirds of the population. By comparison, just 20 percent of African adults have bank accounts. As demonstrated by 37Coins' project—and others we'll explore below—even basic versions of these phones offer a rudimentary platform with which to enter a global cryptocurrency network. And the technology is getting more accessible all the time: bitcoin wallets are becoming easier to use and smartphones cheaper. Mozilla, the company behind the Firefox browser, is now selling very basic smartphones in developing countries with prices as low as $25.

So there's a lot of promise here, but as in developed countries, big barriers remain in developing countries to the rollout of cryptocurrencies. Some have to do with bitcoin's flaws and risks; some reflect social and cultural practices that are difficult to change. People without a lot of money are naturally wary of a risky new form of payment in a currency that not everyone accepts and many have never heard of. Many people favor tried and practiced methods for avoiding financial instability—cash under mattresses, gold jewelry, dollars. Paying Western Union up to 11 percent to transmit money to relatives overseas may be annoying, but it has always worked. And there are regulatory challenges. As in developed countries, officials could create licensing obstacles for digital-currency exchanges and other services needed for a more smooth integration of cryptocurrencies. Corruption and the lobbying power of crony interests could make that process unpredictable.

All of that fosters the same chicken-and-egg problem that cryptocurrencies face in developed countries: if too few people are willing to use bitcoin, everyone else will be less willing to receive it. At least to start with, people will need infrastructure in place to make it easy and cheap to convert digital currencies into local currencies or dollars, which means low-cost exchanges, brokerages, and bitcoin ATMs. A number of people in the bitcoin community are working on just these issues. Nowhere, however, are the promises and pitfalls of cryptocurrencies more starkly rendered than in the world's most populous nation: China.

China is a tantalizing market to bitcoiners, as it is to nearly all businessmen. On paper, the appeal of independent cryptocurrencies to Chinese citizens is compelling. They promise an escape route for their $12 trillion hoard of savings trapped in Chinese banks, where they earn interest rates too low to cover inflation. Chinese laws curtail their ability to buy or sell foreign currency and offer them only limited alternative investment vehicles. China's trapped savers subsidize property speculators and corrupt state-owned enterprises, facilitating a gravy train of artificially cheap bank loans that's raising the specter of a Chinese debt crisis to rival those of the United States and Europe. With bitcoin, the theory goes, people could bypass that unjust banking system and get their money out of China at low cost.

While China has a big, enthusiastic community of bitcoin investors and miners, demand for bitcoin as a practical tool for commerce or for transferring funds simply hasn't materialized. The few merchants that accept it are concentrated among businesses servicing the bitcoin community, such as Beijing's Cheku Café, which hosts bitcoin meetups, and some Shenzhen-based makers of bitcoin-mining equipment. Bitcoin in China is purely a speculator's game, a way to gamble on its price, either through one of a number of mainland exchanges or by mining it. It is popular—Chinese trading volumes outstrip those seen anywhere else in the world. Demand from China was the main factor behind bitcoin's vertical climb to a peak above $1,100 in December 2013, and mining activity in China has been estimated to account for 30 percent of all hashing power. (That could change if subsidies for coal power plants are removed, driving up the cost of electricity.) But again, this is all about speculating. While plenty of venture capitalists are looking at China, and a few are investing in local bitcoin exchanges and mining operations, almost no VC or angel money is being invested in merchant businesses or payment processing.

Ambiguous government rules don't help. Bitcoin isn't prohibited in China, but it isn't afforded the legitimacy of regulation, either, and media outlets have been discouraged from writing about it through a centralized censorship regime. When combined with the central bank's restrictions on financial companies, that creates a catch-22 for bitcoin companies, says Bobby Lee, CEO of BTC China, which became the world's longest-running bitcoin exchange after Mt. Gox's collapse. "They put payment companies in the category of financial companies that aren't allowed to touch bitcoin," Lee says. "We're allowed to touch bitcoin, but by definition we're not allowed to apply for a payments license." Should he just go ahead and create an unlicensed bitcoin payments processor? "That's not clear," he says.

But it's not just rules stopping Chinese from conducting payments in bitcoin. There are also few financial incentives. The government-controlled UnionPay payment-card network is deliberately designed to incur low transaction fees, so card payments are more financially attractive for both consumers and vendors than bitcoin, which carries the added cost of volatility risk. What's more, a vibrant, convenient digital-money system already exists around renminbi-based e-commerce providers.

Tencent Holdings' ubiquitous WeChat messaging app, which has around 400 million smartphone subscribers and which, it seems, every Chinese person you meet is constantly consulting, has its own easy-to-use digital-payments tool. With WeChat you can instantly send money to friends, pay taxidrivers, or buy things from vending machines. This service, as well as e-marketplace Alibaba's competing Alipay offering, is helping turn China into the world's most dynamic e-commerce economy. How is bitcoin to compete with that?

But what about the potential to get around the controls the government puts on cross-border fund transfers? Well, a more convenient alternative than bitcoin exists for that, too, personified by a man who introduced himself to us as "Mr. Fei," a black-market money changer in Shanghai's Gubei district. Mr. Fei spends his days with a colleague camped on a sidewalk right in front of branches of the Industrial and Commercial Bank of China and the Bank of China. In full view of security guards and staff from those state-owned commercial banks, Mr. Fei openly plies his illegal trade, changing currencies for cash in the street. He quoted us 6.16 renminbi per dollar to change $200 for local currency, a better rate than the 6.12 figure being charged at the airport. He said that for a renminbi purchase of $150,000, the rate would be 6.18. In that case we would wire the money to his associate in Hong Kong, and he would personally deliver the equivalent in Chinese currency in whatever form we preferred in Shanghai. He could also do the reverse, if we desired, accepting renminbi in Shanghai to release dollars in Hong Kong. While we talked, Mr. Fei's partner completed a deal with a well-groomed woman who purchased 720,000 South Korean won with about 4,000 renminbi. A contact of ours in Shanghai said he uses Mr. Fei's services frequently and has absolute confidence in him.

The value Mr. Fei provides for his customers comes not only from the better exchange rate, but also from the convenience. The government limits each Chinese citizen to purchases of $50,000 in foreign currency per year. That might seem a decent amount, but to tens of millions of newly wealthy Chinese residents who want to invest in property in Singapore or send children to college in the United States, it's an onerous restriction. What's more, every time they want to change money, they must hand over piles of paperwork to prove their identity, nationality, right to work, tax receipts, and source of income, all so that the government can keep tabs on their foreign-exchange activity. Mr. Fei makes all that go away. Well-known loopholes such as this one—others include using a UnionPay card to buy dollar-denominated chips at casinos in Macao—appear to be tolerated by the government. Thousands of Mr. Feis are all over China's coastal cities. With alternatives like that, bitcoin in China starts to look like a solution in search of a problem.

One scenario that could foster Chinese acceptance of the cryptocurrency would be a banking crisis, a threat that economists take seriously and which some see as the greatest risk facing the global economy. Exploiting the controlled interest-rate model that penalizes savers, banks have recklessly built up trillions of renminbi worth of debts to municipalities and developers that are certain to go bad. When that happens, the government will likely bail out the country's biggest banks as it did when their debts became too unwieldy in 2003, but this time chances are it will let some small- and medium-size banks and trust companies fail. After all, the People's Bank of China has declared plans to liberalize interest rates and open banks up to foreign competition. It has flagged plans for a modern deposit-insurance scheme to facilitate that reform at minimal cost to depositors. This shift to a more market-led model is necessary for China to achieve its international aspirations for the renminbi to one day rival the dollar, but it also means banks' profitability can't be assured and they will have to pay a price for bad investments. The question is, if a bank is allowed to fail, what signal will that send to Chinese savers about their country's renminbi-based financial system? Might they then warm to bitcoin?

"Many people in the U.S. don't trust banks because of the 2008 crisis. They know a bank can go under. But in China it's a different atmosphere," says Eric Gu, who runs a bitcoin meetup in Shanghai. "If there's anyone who's experienced a bank failure, he's probably in his seventies. But people like those of my father's generation, they've never seen a bank failure. And this is why Chinese people trust banks. They think money in the bank is the safest." Gu knows that when bank failures come "it is going to be painful" and wonders whether this might change people's attitudes toward the banking system and generate more interest in bitcoin. He notes that those who are interested in bitcoin for more than a speculative investment are people like him who've lived overseas—Gu lived for seven years in Toronto—or who at least have a college degree. "They get it," he says.

The Caribbean is another area of the emerging-market world where a strong case can be made for locals to use bitcoin to get around a restrictive financial system. But as with China, cryptocurrencies face specific, but very different, challenges there. Whether they can break through those barriers makes the region a useful test case.

"I tried everything," Jamal Ifill says, sitting at the desk that doubles as his office and work space in his small glass-blowing studio in Bridgetown, Barbados. "Credit-cards, PayPal, Western Union. They're too expensive."

Ifill, a young, soft-spoken artist with a head full of dreadlocked hair and a warm smile, has been blowing glass in Barbados for eleven years and has had his own one-room studio/showroom for five years. He does absolutely amazing things with glass; he can blow a perfect, marble-size pendant with a blue flower inside it with a red pistil. One of his latest pieces is a two-foot-high, rectangular, latticework lamp that to our New York eyes looked like one of the Twin Towers. Ifill calls its Imperfect Perfection and says if you look carefully, you can spot the imperfections (we couldn't) in an outer layer and an inner layer. He sells his artwork locally and has attracted some attention; a piece he made was presented to Princess Anne when she visited the island in 2011. He wants to expand internationally, into the U.S. market, but the logistics and costs of moving money from there to here are prohibitively high, so most of his business remains local.

Barbados is relatively well-off. At $25,000, the island's per capita GDP is higher than that of Greece and not far below Spain's. Barbadian literacy is at 99 percent, and its poverty rate, at 14 percent, is one point lower than that of the United States. It shares much in common with Jamaica, Trinidad, Bermuda, and other island nations of the British West Indies. They speak the same language and share a colonial past whose volatile history is replete with naval battles, pirates, slavery, the rum trade, and rebellion. The West Indies even band together to form one international cricket team when they play England, Australia, and other members of the Commonwealth. What they don't have, however, is a common currency that could improve interisland commerce.

Virtually every nation in the British West Indies has its own, separately printed currency—each called the dollar, each fluctuating in value against the others and against the better-known U.S. dollar. And the former Spanish, Dutch, and French colonies all have their own pesos, guilders, and gourdes. The governments of the region have long talked about creating a monetary union to deepen the region's free-trade arrangement, the Caricom common market. But as with the development of that free-trade area, progress toward building a single monetary authority and the other institutions needed for a common currency has been fitful. A Caribbean dollar remains a pipe dream.

Because of this, shifting money around the region's island nations requires constant and costly currency exchanges, which further undermines trade relationships that are already constrained because their tourism-, finance-, and commodity-heavy economies compete with rather than complement each other. To make matters worse, a number of central banks impose capital controls on their citizens. Barbadians such as Ifill, for instance, are limited in the amount of foreign currency they can buy. That Barbados, the Cayman Islands, the Bahamas, and other Caribbean nations serve as tax havens for hedge funds and other foreign financial institutions is an irony not lost on the region's tightly controlled residents. This mix of monetary systems and financial regulations, and the frustration that it breeds, make the sunny islands of the Caribbean ripe for bitcoin—or so says Gabriel Abed.

Friends call him Mr. Bit, and it's not clear if the nickname is meant seriously or as playful ribbing. Educated in the United States, Abed is an itinerant entrepreneur, a young man with boundless energy who runs three different companies while making plans for others and discarding plans for still others and who's intently focused on one revolutionary idea: to bring bitcoin to the Caribbean.

Abed, twenty-seven, comes from a prominent Barbadian family of Syrian descent. Most members of his extended family have gone into prosperous enterprises; it is not uncommon to see shoppers walking along Swan Street in Bridgetown with bags hanging off their arms printed with ABED, the eponymous retail store owned by a relation. It would've been easy for him to follow in those footsteps. But he studied IT in college, with a focus on cryptography. He wasn't interested in settling in a tech foothold such as the Silicon Valley or Portland, although he worked in the latter for a short time. He wants to be in his beloved Barbados, and he wants to bring his island into the digital age.

Abed turned to cryptocurrencies as the answer to a problem: how to expand e-commerce. He is the CEO of Web Designs, a local business that sells Internet domain registrations, Web site designs, maintenance, and e-commerce platforms. The last has been a particularly tough sell. Because of the costs of foreign exchange and credit-cards and PayPal, which can add up to 8 or 9 percent, he said, most merchants simply avoid selling abroad.

Abed learned of bitcoin early on and saw its potential to solve this problem. He began with the idea for a Caribbean cryptocurrency, which he dubbed CaribCoin, but realized quickly it was a bigger project than he wanted to take on. He pivoted to the idea of a bitcoin exchange, and a merchant service that he could bundle with his Web-design and hosting service, and began building Bitt (the URL is actually bi.tt, the .tt being the domain for neighboring Trinidad and Tobago). He also began mining his own bitcoins—in Trinidad, taking advantage of relatively low electricity costs there, and using the profits from that and from Web Designs to fund Bitt.

Bitt is designed as a Caribbean-focused online exchange and merchant service, providing trading between different cryptocurrencies and fiat currencies, as well as a module for helping local business adopt digital currencies for payment. His appeal to businesses is simple: What if I can give you a payment option that costs only 1 percent?

It's easy in Bridgetown or Mantego Bay or Port of Spain to pick some fruit off a tree—coconuts or ackee, perhaps—set up a roadside stand, and sell your produce. It's much harder to set up a legitimate, customer-facing business, or even business-facing business, and offer everything a modern business should. In developed countries, banks typically offer these services, from payment processing to credit lines to fraud management. But in Barbados, says Dr. Leroy McClain, managing director of the government-run Barbados Investment Development Corp., the banks will "sell us a credit-card so we can spend money, but they won't give us merchant services so we can sell products." He took a meeting with Abed to explore ways to help the young company, and, he hoped, the island more broadly. From McClain's vantage point, the big international banks are happy to provide merchant-banking services to companies in the United States and Canada, but they make island businesses jump through far more hoops for the same services.

Jamal Ifill, the glassblower, understands the problem all too well. In fact, he has all the problems of an international business. The particular glass he uses must be imported from Ukraine. His customers are not only on the island, but overseas. He is competing with foreign artists who aren't hamstrung by the costs that tie him up. He tried e-commerce— through Abed's Web Designs company—but gave up on it because not enough customers were using it, which meant he wasn't getting any business out of it. A vicious circle. "I even tried Etsy," he says, the online arts-and-craft site. Again, he couldn't compete on costs with U.S. artists.

Ifill is eager to expand his business overseas. He has big ideas about marketing and how to get some press for his brand. But his ambition is blocked. So when Abed went into his bitcoins spiel, Ifill's eyes lit up: a 1 percent fee for conducting business? As opposed to 5 percent, or 8 percent or 9 percent?

The catch is that the 1 percent fee comes with bitcoins, which as of this writing can't buy you much in Barbados. To say that cryptocurrencies are not big in Barbados would be an understatement. They effectively don't exist on the island, and neither does mobile commerce. While virtually everybody has a cell phone, the proverbial badge of a digital citizen, people use them only for texting and talking. E-commerce is barely getting started, as is online banking.

The way to get over the chicken-and-egg problem and encourage adoption, Abed believes, is to focus on the merchants. He believes that if he can offer them a dramatically cheaper payment method, they can be talked into accepting that method at their shops. But he has his work cut out for him.

David Simpson, managing director of Prestige Accounting, a regional trade school, and a client of Web Designs, sees a steep curve toward widespread adoption for bitcoin. "In my opinion, Bajans haven't really taken to using technology to make their lives easier," he says. "Even transferring money online, they'd prefer to go to a bank, to stand in line." He recounts a story of one local bank that tried to promote online banking; it installed ATMs and cut back on tellers in an attempt to move its customers off lines and online. It backfired. The customers revolted; they didn't want to go online for their banking, they actually wanted to wait in a physical line, to talk to a physical teller. Barbadians are simply not interested in new technologies. Such attitudes will change, says Simpson, whose own company has embraced e-commerce, using e-books and offering classes online. "The question is how long it takes." As for his own view of bitcoin, he's pragmatic: "Once the customers are willing to use bitcoin and embrace it, I'm flexible." Chicken-and-egg.

The chicken-and-egg dilemma will require incentives. The promise of saving money is certainly one of them. But there are others. As in the developed world, one hope is that if big firms or institutions whose relationships run deep in the economy start using bitcoin, they can create incentives for their suppliers and customers to use it.

Patrick Byrne, the CEO of Salt Lake City–based online retailer Overstock.com, which began accepting bitcoin in early 2014 to become what was then the biggest revenue-earning merchant to do so, believes his firm can play such a catalytic role creating a bitcoin "ecosystem" in the developing world. Byrne's belief in bitcoin was forged during the financial crisis, when hedge funds began short-selling Overstock's shares, a practice in which borrowed securities are dumped on the market so as to profit when they fall to a lower price. The hedge funds said they didn't trust the company's accounting; Byrne saw it as purely manipulative speculation, all facilitated and encouraged by Wall Street's centralized systems for buying, selling, lending, and borrowing securities. Cryptocurrency, he believes, is a weapon to combat this because it brings willing buyers and sellers of assets together, without the brokers and investment banks acting as fee-grabbing middlemen. It's an instrument, he believes, to reform a world that has become too dependent on such centralized institutions and which has therefore become prone to the "authoritarianism" of privileged elites in the worlds of government and finance. Overstock works with vendors in eighty different countries, and among his suppliers are hundreds of small, low-income entrepreneurs who contribute to Worldstock, Overstock's offshoot site for artisanal "fair trade" products. It comprises artisans, people just like the glassblower Jamal Ifill, living in fifty-four developing countries, who are hungry for a fairer financial system than the outdated, costly payment model to which they are currently beholden.

When we met in June 2014 in Utah, Byrne explained that he viewed bitcoin as a way to widen economic opportunity, if only he could get people to accept it. He was still figuring out the carrots he would use, but he had some ideas. He spoke animatedly; a dharma-wheel pendant that he'd obtained from Tibetan monks near the Dalai Lama's residence in northern India swung back and forth from a leather strap around his neck. "If we can get vendors to accept it, maybe we give them an extra two percent if we pay them in bitcoin, or an extra one percent, or maybe we pay them in net ten days or net fifteen days instead of thirty. That would cost us fifteen days, but bitcoin allows for that fast settlement. And you know in the world of payments and dealing with vendors, there's all this sensitivity around the terms of payment. Vendors will sometimes give you a two percent discount for shaving off twenty days, because to them that's like a thirty-six percent cost of money over the year. That affects all kinds of things. The very fact that vendors offer those terms means there's an enormous opportunity for bitcoin to step up in this area." A few weeks later, Byrne announced he would not only be paying bitcoin-accepting vendors one week early, but that he'd also pay his employee bonuses in bitcoin.

What companies such as Overstock are trying to do with digital-currency payments has parallels with what Walmart achieved by pioneering communications technology to revolutionize supply-chain management in the 1990s and early 2000s. The Arkansas-based retailer famously developed a sophisticated network with which to tie all of its suppliers worldwide into a single, integrated database for managing the goods and services flowing in and out of Walmart's warehouses. Along with big improvements in shipping logistics, this allowed the company to optimize its just-in-time inventory management, which drastically cut its costs. Walmart parlayed those cost savings into the cheapest prices anywhere in the United States, which turned it into the iconic and, to some, infamous behemoth that now dominates American suburbia. Just as important, its high-tech network had a feedback effect on suppliers, contributing to the concentration of manufacturing in hubs such as China's Pearl River Delta. As Walmart became an increasingly powerful but relentless

hunter of the cheapest manufacturing sources, and as other Western buyers caught on to its high-tech lead, factories paying low wages in the developing world would congregate in locales where it was most efficient to
tap into Walmart's network. Byrne now sees similar opportunities for
firms like his to build influence by leveraging bitcoin in its international
payment relationships and thus creating a tipping point from which change
starts rippling over the world economy. As a group of businesses in one
region begins adopting the currency, it will become more appealing to
others with whom they do business. Once such a network of intertwined
businesses builds up, no one wants to be excluded from it. Or so the
theory goes.

"Just as American retail collapsed into Walmart, who knows how
much can collapse into us? And I don't mean Overstock. I mean bitcoin,"
Byrne said. "You start getting network effects. You are incentivizing
everyone—it's like we have the first fax machine but nobody else has a
fax machine, so it doesn't do you any good. But you start adding other
nodes and making incentives to add nodes and eventually get a critical
mass. Now people aren't just faxing us, they are faxing each other."

"I have no compassion for these women in Afghanistan," Francesco Rulli
says from behind the bar at which he entertains visitors to his company's
whitewashed loft in a downtown Manhattan building. "I just have a mathematical approach about it." It's not true what he says about compassion,
at least not in the usual sense of the word. Rulli appears to care deeply
about the welfare of the young women in this war-torn Middle Eastern
country now being educated in computing and media via the foundation
he set up in conjunction with his media company. But with this emphatic
statement, Rulli is making a philosophical point about the empowering
qualities of bitcoin. Like Overstock's Byrne, he's playing an activist role,
exploiting his control over the purse strings to alter people's behavior, encouraging them to use cryptocurrency to liberate themselves.

The Afghanistan-based Women's Annex is a not-for-profit offshoot
of Rulli's for-profit firm the Film Annex—now going by the trade name
Bitlanders—an online video-content site that shares its ad revenue with a
worldwide army of low-budget moviemakers. Rulli was inspired to create the foundation after seeing a NATO-produced video on his site about

Roya Mahboob, the CEO of the Afghan Citadel Software Company. He approached her about setting up a school, and now the diminutive businesswoman, who in 2013 was included in *Time* magazine's list of the world's hundred most influential people, heads up the Women's Annex foundation. With cofounder Fereshteh Forough, who, like Mahboob, was born in Iran as an Afghan refugee, she manages a budding student body of more than fifty thousand teenage girls in eleven schools across Afghanistan with a program that is now going global.

Many of the women in the program would never have seen a computer before joining the school; now they are learning how to post blogs, produce movies, write computer code, and develop social-media strategies. Their education is on the Women's Annex dime, but many students —more than six thousand of them—also earn incomes from content they provide to the for-profit Bitlanders. There, their work is judged, like that of every contributor, by editors and analyzed in terms of how widely it is viewed and shared. These criteria form their "Buzz" score, which determines how much income they can earn. Those earnings, as with every other Bitlanders contributor's, are paid in bitcoin. We met one of these contributors, Parisa Ahmadi, in the opening of this book.

The decision to pay movie contributors in a digital currency inevitably stirred some grumbling around the world among the old hands of the Film Annex. But it had a logic. The company makes millions of dollars of payments in frequent transfers of small denomination. With its capacity for micropayments and low transaction fees, bitcoin could save the company money on its multiple bank wires and exchange-rate costs, which in turn left more to share with Film Annex's three hundred thousand filmmaking contributors. But another, more profound benefit was that this method of payment had a profound empowering effect for the service's female Afghan clients, who could use it to circumvent the strictures of their patriarchal society.

"We thought that perhaps every student should have a bank account so we could transfer money out of the [Women's Annex] bank account to them, but the problem was that female students couldn't have a bank account until they were eighteen, and most of their families preferred that the girls don't have a bank account at all," Mahboob said. What's more, trips to bank branches and remittance outlets such as Western Union were

fraught with danger and discrimination. Mahboob herself was not im-
mune from this. "It was very difficult in Afghanistan when you had cash,
and especially when the money had to go to your bank account. People
would always find out that your bank account had money going in and
out—the people who are at the banks would tell the people who are outside the banks. I always had to go to the bank with some of my colleagues,
with four or five men to take the money and give the money to the students." For the Afghan girls of the Women's Annex schools, bitcoin solved
those problems—even if it created other ones.

Rulli first got interested in bitcoin in mid-2013 when he learned about
the massive investment in the digital currency by Tyler and Cameron
Winklevoss. Cryptocurrency quickly became an abiding passion, a vehicle through which Rulli could pursue the philosophy of personal empowerment that had emerged from his experiences as a black-belt judo
master. The salt-and-pepper-haired Rulli is fond of referencing the Renaissance and the Medici bankers of his native Florence and humorously cites
a Spider-Man quote—"with great power, comes great responsibility"—as a
motif to live by. From this perspective, he sees bitcoin as a force for building "digital citizenship," a new society dedicated to the personal pursuit of
excellence, where everyone is valued for what he or she creates. Bitcoin
allowed the Film Annex to fine-tune its Buzz score concept with such pre-
cision, Rulli says, that it could be used as an ongoing motivator of personal
improvement. With bitcoin, "you can clearly break down the value of every single stroke on the keyboard," he says. "So, even if you think you can
for a moment produce content of low quality, you're going to disappoint
the moderators, your Buzz score will go down, and you're going to damage
your long-term reputation and consequently your long-term income."

The basic problem, however, is if the choices for spending bitcoin are
limited in the United States, Afghanistan is a challenge of another order
of magnitude. One solution that the Film Annex is now pursuing in conjunction with bitcoin-trading platform Atlas ATS is a Pakistan-based exchange for swapping bitcoins into traditional currencies. But Rulli only
reluctantly went along with this; it was too soft an option, he felt. He wanted
the exchange to be solely in bitcoin for other digital currencies, with no
option to buy rupees or dollars: "The belief I have is that if you lock these
people into this new economy, they will make that new economy as efficient

as possible. If you start giving people opportunities to get out of the economy, they will just cut it down, whereas if the only way for you to enrich yourself is by trading bitcoins for litecoins and dogecoins, you are going to become an expert in that . . . you will become the best trader in Pakistan."

Rulli prefers to focus on another route that the Film Annex has pursued to give his contributors spending options. Using his personal American Express card—thus leveraging a credit history that Afghan girls could never have—he buys gift cards from Amazon, prepaid cell-phone minutes, and various other easily delivered products and then offers them for sale via the Film Annex Web site. Each contributor's account not only shows the balance earned but also a selection of products that they have sufficient bitcoins to buy. He wants the Afghan girls to spend it on technology such as Mozilla's forthcoming $25 smartphone, which they can convert into a camera and a tool for producing better video and blog content. He is trying to turn the Film Annex Web site into its own self-enclosed bitcoin economy.

The image many have of girls in Afghanistan comes from a single, famous photo: *Afghan Girl*. Taken in 1985 by *National Geographic* photographer Steve McCurry, it shows a twelve-year-old girl in a tattered red scarf at a refugee camp in Pakistan, her green eyes locked in an expression of defiance. The plight of most Afghan women is perhaps no longer quite as desperate as that refugee girl's was, but even with the ouster of the misogynist, medieval Taliban and the new social structure introduced under U.S. occupation, Afghanistan remains a male-dominated society. Women are second-class citizens. Most have no money of their own and aren't allowed to travel outside without a male family member accompanying them. Can Francesco Rulli, the Film Annex, and bitcoin liberate them?

"I am against welfare," Rulli says. "We're teaching them to be their own businesspeople." He adds, "My logic is, how can I make sure the girls are safe? . . . [If she's making money,] she is more likely to be protected by her brothers because she's an asset to the family instead of a second-class citizen. . . . Then eventually the family's priority is not only to protect her but also to invest in her."

According to Mahboob, Women's Annex family members are coming around to this way of thinking: "At the beginning, most of the families didn't want the girls to learn the Internet; they were in disagreement because they thought the Internet was a very bad thing. But when they started to earn money, then the families supported them. And then other families supported their daughters. So we don't only have the girls in school, but we have the community behind them."

In the United States, bitcoin-payment processors such as BitPay and Coinbase generally find merchants want them to convert their incoming bitcoins into dollars, a service they provide free of charge. In Argentina, the exact opposite occurs. Firms such as San Francisco–based BitPagos will take the dollars received by hotels and other tourism-industry clients in Buenos Aires and deliver them bitcoins in return. In almost every speech bitcoiners make about the potential for cryptocurrencies in the developing world, Argentina receives top billing. The hope is not only that bitcoin succeeds there; it's that the South American country demonstrates how cryptocurrencies can provide an escape route for people who are trapped by capital controls into using untrusted and unwanted national currencies.

BitPagos's service is so attractive to many businessmen in Argentina because it gets them a much more favorable exchange rate. In mid-June 2014, every dollar received from credit-card purchases had to be processed through the Argentine banking system, where it would pay out 8.15 pesos, an official rate that values the Argentine currency at roughly twelve cents. By contrast, a cash payment could be converted at twelve pesos per dollar at a clandestine *cueva*, or cave, the thriving businesses that run Argentina's underground currency in Buenos Aires and other cities. In this black market, the peso was worth a markedly lower eight cents; you could get more of them with the dollars you get from tourists. The problem is that most travelers these days pay hotel bills with a credit-card. So bitcoin offers merchants a middle way. On the person-to-person trading site Local Bitcoins Argentina, the going rate for selling bitcoins was around 6,400 pesos in late June 2014. Based on the going bitcoin-dollar exchange rate of around $560, that translated into a round-trip of 11.42 pesos per dollar, a 40 percent better deal than the official rate.

Over the past eight years, as Argentina entered the latest in a cycle of financial crises that repeats every ten years or so, its people have sought dollars as a hedge against rampant inflation. As the situation deteriorated and the government struggled to obtain the dollars it needed to pay foreign bondholders and energy suppliers, President Cristina Fernández de Kirchner doubled down. Her government made it increasingly difficult for Argentines to gain access to foreign currency, often shifting the rules day to day to protect its reserves. That made life exceedingly difficult for anyone whose business regularly dealt in foreign exchange. It's also why an underground market with a sharply lower rate for the peso came into existence.

To Mike Abridello, a U.S. expatriate who runs the Prodeo Hotel & Lounge in Buenos Aires' hipster neighborhood of Palermo Soho, the bitcoins he receives from BitPagos provide a way to deal with these confusing regulations and bifurcated currency markets. "Right now if you're working in Argentina, bitcoin just operationally offers you a cash-flow solution that's much more efficient," he said. Some of BitPagos's clients also view bitcoins as a superior store of value over the peso. That might seem crazy, given the volatility of bitcoin's exchange rate. But with Argentine inflation holding around 30 percent in recent years—according to unofficial statistics that gained far more credence than the government's manipulated numbers—the peso has been a far bigger losing bet for the past decade. Argentines don't need to be that old, either, to remember the over 10,000 percent rates that occurred during the hyperinflation of the late 1980s. For such people, "bitcoin is a way to hedge against inflation," says BitPagos CEO Sebastian Serrano.

There's no sure way to measure the uptake of bitcoins in any country, but the evidence suggests Argentina is outpacing most. The number of traders listed on Local Bitcoins Buenos Aires was for much of 2014 running at three times that of Manhattan, and the Fundación Bitcoin Argentina is known to run the largest bitcoin meetup in the world. BitPagos has been a direct beneficiary of this. As of mid-2014, the company had signed up more than six hundred merchants across Latin America, though not all were very active. And after having doubled its transaction volumes in three months from March of that year, the start-up had nabbed a $600,000 financing round with contributions from Pantera Capital Management, SecondMarket CEO Barry Silbert, and venture capitalist Tim Draper. Others have also sensed opportunity: Atlanta-based processor

BitPay has opened an office in Buenos Aires, and a new bitcoin exchange, Bitex.la, was launched in May 2014.

To be sure, most crisis-wary Argentines have yet to take up this strange digital unit, preferring instead their long-favored safe haven: cold, hard greenbacks. Although the government had by mid-2014 taken no explicit regulatory action against bitcoin, the central bank's Web site carried a stern warning about its dangers, noting that "so-called virtual currencies" aren't issued by "this central bank nor by any of the other international monetary authorities and so they carry no legal recourse and have no backing." The risk of a crackdown was always there. As with backlashes seen in China and elsewhere, authorities could do this by impeding connections to the traditional banking system—by making it hard for people to link their bank accounts to peso-for-bitcoin exchanges, for example. Still, as with everything about cryptocurrencies, the barriers to adoption can be weighed against the costs of not adopting them. In Argentina, that affords bitcoiners such as Serrano an even more compelling pitch than that which Abed makes about transaction fees to Barbadians: Are you sure you want to stick with those Argentine pesos?

The remittance business, where emigrants and expats living abroad send money home, seems as if it should be ripe for disruption by low-cost cryptocurrencies. The current business model relies on electronic transfers over the old banking rails, and its practitioners charge high fees for that privilege. Globally, it's a huge business.

More than $500 billion is expected to be sent back to home countries by emigrants in 2016, according to the World Bank. "Those are only the official flows," says Dilip Ratha, an expert on the subject who tracks it for the World Bank. Another $200 billion is sent that isn't tracked by the bank, it estimates. Those numbers dwarf the roughly $125 billion the developed world sends annually in aid. For many countries, more money comes in through remittances than through exports. Moreover, the totals are net of the charges and fees emigrants pay to transfer agents such as Western Union; on average those costs are about 8.5 percent globally, but in many countries, it's around 10 percent or more. In countries where annual salaries can be counted in hundreds of dollars, those costs are a serious burden.

Kenyans living abroad who want to send money home can choose between, say, Western Union and MoneyGram, but both charge high fees. Although at 42 percent the proportion of Kenyan adults with a formal banking relationship exceeds that of many countries, a majority in the country are still unbanked. But Kenya's experience with microfinance and telecommunications has inspired people's imaginations over how to address some of these problems. In particular, the excitement revolves around one key product: M-Pesa.

M-Pesa (the *M* is for "mobile," and *"pesa"* is Swahili for "money") started out as an experiment by Kenya's biggest telecom company, Safaricom. Because many more Kenyans had phones than bank accounts, microfinance experts realized during the 2000s that they could use those phones to deliver loans to borrowers and receive repayments from them. So in 2007, Safaricom began a pilot program that allowed users to send money via their phones—effectively converting the standard units of prepaid calling minutes into a form of currency. The system proved wildly popular. Today two-thirds of Kenyans use it, and about 25 percent of Kenya's GDP flows through it. And Vodafone, which owns 40 percent of Safaricom, has rolled out the product in Tanzania, South Africa, Mozambique, Egypt, Fiji, India, and even Romania.

To use M-Pesa, people sign up for an account and get an e-wallet on their phone. To add money to it, they go to their local Safaricom agent —more than fifteen thousand are spread across Kenya—and give the agent cash for an equivalent amount of "e-float." This money isn't actually held in the form of Kenyan shillings but as a separate claim on the overall M-Pesa e-float, all of which is backed by deposits in the banks with which Safaricom has accounts. Users can then send money to other M-Pesa account holders, buy airtime, or pay bills. To withdraw money, users go to the agent and put in for a withdrawal. As long as they have an equivalent amount of e-float in their account, the agent will hand them over the cash right there and then.

M-Pesa had a few things going for it. For one thing, Safaricom already had a massive infrastructure in place, not just the telecommunications equipment, but those thousands of agents. M-Pesa was also lucky enough to escape government regulation early on. Lastly, a different form of politics may have played a part. After the country's hotly contested

An M-Pesa stand

(© Tom Spender)

December 2007 election, violence burst out across Kenya. Scores were killed, and the entire country was thrust into a crisis. With the nation's institutions essentially frozen, people realized there was one way to move money effectively: M-Pesa. For example, one relief group, Concern Worldwide, prevented by violence and cost from getting aid to the region's remote Kerio Valley, found a solution in M-Pesa. They sent representatives into the valley and set people up with accounts, giving some families phones and solar chargers. Since the nearest agent was some eighty kilometers away, they also set up an agent at a local police station. The gambit worked; the group was able to get aid to an isolated community, and the cost of Safaricom's transaction fees was far less than the cost of transporting food and material. Not only that, Concern Worldwide brought these remote villages technology that would prove useful beyond the crisis, and the crisis itself showed M-Pesa's true worth to its customers, who've been steadfastly loyal ever since.

M-Pesa has proven to be a lifesaver in other unusual ways, too. On its Web site, Vodafone notes that in Tanzania, where some citizens don't live near a hospital and can't afford to travel to one, an organization called

Comprehensive Community Based Rehabilitation sent patients money via M-Pesa to cover their travel expenses.

But here's the rub: M-Pesa is not a frictionless system, and in some ways its drawbacks mirror those we've outlined in chapter 4: what appears automatic to the user has a massive, unwieldy, and expensive infrastructure behind it. Safaricom's agents must deal with huge amounts of cash daily. This is not only cumbersome, but can also be dangerous. When agents run out of money, they have to either stop what they're doing, close the shop, and go to a bank, or stop what they're doing and send somebody on their behalf. Agents in rural areas, where the customers are more likely to be withdrawing money rather than depositing it, face a special challenge: not only is their liquidity—their literal cash pile—drained faster, but the odds are higher that they are farther away from a bank branch, meaning a trip there takes longer and leaves less time to do actual business.

Then there's the question of how to import funds into the M-Pesa system from overseas. It is not borderless. Its mobile, phone-linked system offers an easier "on-ramp" for remittances than other countries' more traditional financial systems, but it's still going through traditional pipelines. Vodafone has partnerships with MoneyGram, Western Union, and other payment networks—with all their routine fees and banking-system-dependent costs. With bitcoin, it is possible to send money via a mobile phone, directly between two parties, to bypass that entire cumbersome, expensive system for international transfers.

Perhaps inevitably, then, someone like Duncan Goldie-Scot, a veteran of microfinance, would come to see Kenya as the right place to start a full-scale remittance business. He approached fellow microfinance expert Elizabeth Rossiello, a native of Queens, New York, who was then working as a consultant in Kenya, with an idea: How about combining M-Pesa with a digital currency? It would offer all the advantages of M-Pesa, but would make the costs to users even cheaper for those who import money into that system from abroad, because those remittances from relatives in London or New York would arrive via bitcoin rather than the traditional banking system. Call it BitPesa.

They would begin with a simple and achievable goal: take a single "corridor" in the remittance business—between the United Kingdom and

Kenya—and build a bitcoin-based money-transfer business around it. They hired a development team to build the initial prototype, then a coder to revamp it. Next, they sent a staff member to London, to go into the cafés in the Kenyan neighborhoods and recruit beta testers for the initial trials. They began their beta test in the summer of 2014 with about two dozen emigrants.

The idea didn't just appeal to Kenyans looking to send money home more cheaply. Rossiello quickly raised $700,000 from investors, including SecondMarket's Barry Silbert, who also invested in BitPagos, the Argentine start-up, and whose company is building its own bitcoin-trading platform. She could have raised more. "We took thirty meetings in two weeks, talking about linking bitcoin and M-Pesa, and we saw eyes light up," she said. Investors understood this was a simple and potentially powerful way to undercut and take market share from a handful of companies, the Western Unions of the world that had a stranglehold on a huge global business. After the company was profiled in a Bloomberg article in November 2013, before it had launched a single product, Rossiello started getting calls from "high-net-worth" subscribers to Bloomberg's financial-information platform and firms in California wanting a piece of the action. But she wasn't prepared to give control of the company away. "I said no to a lot of big guys," she said.

Rossiello hadn't even heard of bitcoin until Goldie-Scot mentioned it to her. But she quickly caught on to the possibilities and now has ambitions for BitPesa that go beyond bitcoin, or digital currencies. For all the good it has done, the microfinance industry pioneered by Nobel Peace Prize–winning Muhammad Yunus's Grameen Bank still operates within what she described as "a busted financial system." An alternative based on cryptocurrency could bypass a lot of the costs of the existing system, and it offered the promise of doing more than just allowing cheap remittances.

Rossiello sees bitcoin as a way to spark not just a financial revolution in Kenya, but a technological one as well. The idea is that cryptocurrency fosters innovation, as we've seen in San Francisco and other places. She has started a meetup culture and teaches coding to schoolchildren. Five people were at her first meetup; six months later, there were forty, and they were doing coding and coming up with their own apps. "People are responding, people are excited about it," she says.

M-Pesa, now combined with a nascent bitcoin community, is proving to be Kenya's on-ramp to a broader technology revolution, as mobile money and the Internet spark a wave of creativity and entrepreneurship. Nairobi has become one of Africa's most important tech hubs, if not the biggest. It is sometimes called Silicon Savannah. The city even has its own version of 20Mission, a hacker house called iHub that's not far from the University of Nairobi's science center. It occupies a spacious, modern space on the fourth floor of an office building that would be right at home in Silicon Valley, with lots of light, room for talks and presentations, couches and lounge space (including a foosball table), and a coffee bar. It also has work space for the people creating things, those who are driving the growth of Silicon Savannah. The place is wired, literally and figuratively, and filled with young, energetic, bright kids. They have meetups, and "fireside" chats, and attract heavy talent: Joi Ito, the director of the MIT Media Lab in Massachusetts, spoke at iHub in May 2014. Google's Eric Schmidt also visited.

The center's goals are similar to those in Silicon Valley: to foster entrepreneurship, to build a network and get young people and young minds engaged and creating—one can almost hear Steve Jobs saying "magical"—things. But whereas in the United States techies are often coming up with gee-whiz devices to fulfill needs we didn't know we had—do you *really* need a robot to sweep your floor?—in Nairobi, the goals tend toward more immediate needs, e.g., toward products that improve governance or make the health-care system more effective or the water supply safer and better allocated. A group called Geeks in Gumboots, for example, is trying to focus the tech community on environmental issues.

As is the case with all efforts of outsiders attempting to better the lives of distant people, an uneasy awareness exists of the legacy of colonialism and the fine line between assistance and paternalism. Rossiello is all too aware of these issues and bristles at the notion, sometimes heard at bitcoin conferences, that BitPesa is "saving Africa." She wants nothing of the subconscious colonial paternalism that the idea implies. "There are actually a lot of African people here doing things," she says.

It's important to resist the impulse to view cryptocurrencies' technology, or any technology, as a panacea. For all the promise that technology holds—this idea that developing nations are going to "leapfrog" decades of development thanks to cheap, distributed, decentralized technology—the reality on the ground resists easy solutions. What M-Pesa has achieved, and what BitPesa promises, matter because they are effective tools for promoting economic activity, and thus development. This is why the stories coming out of Silicon Savannah are important—not only for Kenya but for the developing world as a whole. "There's a much bigger story here," Rossiello says. "We're just getting started."

The root causes of financial isolation in poor countries go beyond people's lack of bank accounts and how much it costs to send money. They start with the underprivileged being typically cut off from what Peruvian economist Hernando de Soto calls the "mystery of capital," the idea that economic growth and the creation of wealth depend on clearly defined and documented property rights. De Soto has done as much as anyone else to further the idea that economic development should focus on documenting poor people's assets—the homes that slum dwellers rightfully own but for which they have no title; the unlicensed businesses they operate; the under-the-table jobs for which they are paid. In the West, the documents attached to these assets can be presented as collateral to a bank to borrow money or used to convince an investor to put money into a worthwhile project. But without that documentation, the poor are often condemned to a hand-to-mouth existence. It's why de Soto and others from his Lima-based Institute for Liberal Democracy spend time in the slums of Peru, Haiti, Egypt, and other places surveying and documenting people's property and handing out mortgage deeds. But with this work, they are merely scratching the surface. In aggregate, this global informal economy, or System D as the journalist Robert Neuwirth has chosen to call it, is worth $10 trillion by his estimates. If it were its own country—Neuwirth suggests the names Bazaaristan or the USSR, the United Street Sellers Republic—this economy of the undocumented would be second only to that of the United States.

As BitPesa's Rossiello suggests, the biggest opportunities may lie not with the digital currencies per se but with the technology behind them.

The potential is great for people in the informal economy to exploit the blockchain's middleman-free way to exchange assets and information and its irrefutable public record that's free from the control of any one central institution. These features create unique opportunities for such people to overcome legal and institutional barriers to advancement. Lowering payment costs is only the beginning. As we've mentioned, weak and corrupt institutions are the root cause of poor people's exclusion from the banking system because they deny people the chance to prove their integrity and net worth to bankers. Well, the blockchain, if taken to the extent that a new wave of bitcoin innovators believe possible, could replace many of those institutions with a decentralized authority for proving people's legal obligations and status. In doing so, it could dramatically widen the net of inclusion.

We'll discuss the myriad of new ideas in the following chapter's examination of these so-called Bitcoin 2.0 inventions. In theory, the blockchain's groundbreaking model for authenticating information could liberate the poor from the incompetence and corruption of bureaucrats and judges. Digitized registers of real-estate deeds, all fully administered by a cryptocurrency computer network without the engagement of a central government agency, could be created to cheaply and reliably manage people's rights to property, administering digital documents that could be used to obtain loans in digital or fiat currency. Whereas judicial corruption means that low-income people in a developing country can't rely on watertight contracts to shore up their businesses and unlock de Soto's mystery of capital, subjecting such agreements to the infallibility of the blockchain could end all that.

Jonathan Mohan, who works at Ethereum, the new Bitcoin 2.0 platform that's seeking to disrupt all sorts of legal and contractual arrangements, offers a compelling explanation for how these "smart contracts," each designed to be executed on the blockchain via an automated piece of software, would benefit the informal economy. "As long as you render collateral for a contract and the blockchain recognizes the contract, then you know there's no fraud and you know there's no need to have to trust a third party," he said at an Inside Bitcoins conference in New York. "So the contract is simple and all these other things sort themselves out. If you are in places like Africa, in China—hell, even in America—you know that justice will be rendered because the entity will execute the contract exactly how it was programmed to execute."

While it may not be so simple as "all these other things" sorting themselves out, real potential is here. To understand how it could work, we must return to the blockchain and explore the great variety of ways it can be used.

Nine

THE EVERYTHING BLOCKCHAIN

Every man takes the limits of his own field of vision for the limits of the world.

—Arthur Schopenhauer

We've taken you into the Cypherpunk movement and the proto-coins that preceded bitcoin, and into the mechanics of the blockchain. We've taken you inside the formation of the community, and to the high-tech scene in San Francisco. We've shown you miners in Utah, and bitcoin in the Caribbean. We've shown you how the currency can empower women in Afghanistan. Now it's time to take our deepest plunge into the crypto waters, to look into bitcoin's future, into things that are on the cutting edge of the cutting edge. It's time to talk about the potential to build things *on top of* bitcoin. These could range from projects as mundane as gambling sites to those as transcendent as the foundation of entirely automated, self-owned corporations. The common tie is that all of them are taking the crucial underpinning of bitcoin, a decentralized system that uses the incontrovertible blockchain for its legitimacy and verification. Like everything else in the cryptocurrency world, the goal is to decentralize, to take power out of the hands of the middlemen. As we'll see, though, innovators seeking to encourage the growth of profitable businesses via these decentralized systems can find that cryptocurrency purists will sometimes accuse them, often unfairly, of acting as "centralizers." "Every man takes the limits of his own field of vision for the limits of the world," the philosopher Arthur Schopenhauer wrote. For the people we are about to meet, though, the limits of their field of vision are their *starting* points.

Casino gamblers have historically been at the mercy of the establishments they frequent. Before the advent of regulation, one couldn't check that the one-armed bandits weren't unreasonably programmed in the house's favor. Who was to say the roulette wheel's ball wasn't guided by magnets or that the blackjack card-shuffling machine hadn't stacked the deck? In most countries, casinos are now tightly regulated and those laws are for the most part enforced, but there's still no guarantee. Now that online gaming has taken off, it's arguably even harder. The cards in your average online blackjack game are dealt by what is supposed to be a completely random number generator, but because it resides on the gambling site's server, it could easily be manipulated.

One bitcoin enthusiast saw this dilemma as an opportunity, got rich solving it, and unwittingly demonstrated the power of the bitcoin blockchain to create an inviolable realm of transparency—one that turned out to be extremely marketable. While a story of a guy who made a quick few million with an online casino mightn't be quite as inspiring as a project to liberate the world's unbanked, his venture revealed key elements of cryptocurrency's far-reaching potential.

Joseph Gleason, better known as Fireduck on the Bitcointalk.org and Reddit social forums, figured he could use bitcoin's blockchain to create a "provably fair" system for online betting. Gleason's was a no-frills concept: people would place short-standing bets whose outcome depended on a random number derived from the hashes appearing in transactions sent over the blockchain—i.e., a provably independent source. Gamblers would send bitcoin to one of a selection of special addresses associated with bets that a certain five-digit "lucky number" of up to 65,535 would come in below a chosen threshold. The lower the upper limit chosen, the lower the odds of a win and the higher the possible payout. Gleason's program would then use a basic encryption process to come up with a lucky number. It would take the transaction code that the bitcoin core algorithm assigned to the gambler's payment and combine it with a separate secret daily key known only to his program, thus creating a new stand-alone alphanumeric hash code. The lucky number would be created by converting the first four characters of that hash—which appears as a mix of letters and numerals—into a regular number. Because of the mathematical conventions of this particular type of hash, this number would always come out at 65,535 or less.* The fair part of the proposition was that after twenty-four hours, the system would divulge the secret key, which allowed users to go back and unpack the numbers by doing all the calculations backward.

For providing this service, Gleason's bitcoin-based casino awarded itself a fully declared 1.9 percent edge over all bets. A winning ten-bitcoin bet that the lucky number would fall below 32,758—more or less even odds—would pay the winner 19.6 bitcoins, with Gleason holding back 0.4 of a bitcoin, or about $2 at the time he first conceived of the project.

After little more than a week, Gleason realized he was sitting on something explosive. He had invested 45 bitcoins (about $225 at the time) and had already made 146 bitcoins in profit. But he could already see the legal complications—only a few states had legalized online gambling, and those states had adopted strict licensing laws. So, on April 17, 2012, he put a notice on Reddit saying he would hand his creation over to anyone prepared to take on legal challenges by the state and hire him as a consultant. Erik Voorhees, an emerging libertarian voice among bitcoin enthusiasts, soon took up the offer. Christening the service SatoshiDice, Voorhees turned it into a gold mine. SatoshiDice transactions would soon account for half of all bitcoin transfers on the digital currency's network. (Most bets were tiny and therefore together represented a much smaller portion of the overall transaction volume in value terms.)

Over the next year, Voorhees sold shares in the service in return for bitcoins, listing the securities on MPEx, a Romanian equity exchange where digital assets are quoted and traded in digital currencies. Then, a few months after those share offerings, he announced that he had sold

---

* Under standard encryption models, hashes are hexadecimal, which means they contain sixteen possible characters in a range from 0 to 9 and from a to f. That represents a base-16 number system, with a through f representing 10 through 15. When you convert that back to the base-10 structure of our standard decimal system, it produces 65,535 possible numbers, where 0000 equates to zero and ffff equates to 65,535.

SatoshiDice to an undisclosed buyer for 126,315 bitcoins, then worth $11.5 million. While that meant his investors enjoyed a big gain, as majority shareholder Voorhees ended up with most of it. Not bad for a year of ownership.

SatoshiDice provided an early indication of the potential for what the industry calls Bitcoin 2.0, or, our preference, Blockchain 2.0 applications—products, services, and even full-blown companies that are run autonomously by a decentralized cryptocurrency network.

Gleason and Voorhees were not the first people to envision alternative uses for the blockchain. If, some adventurous minds thought, two parties could now securely exchange funds without a trusted third party creaming fees from them, then perhaps this new tamperproof record of verified information could also be used for other "trustless" exchanges. Contracts could be drawn up and executed without lawyers or courts getting involved; digitized property deeds could be transferred and verified by the blockchain sans real estate agents; financial securities could be traded directly between investors, bypassing a central exchange or clearinghouse.

Mike Hearn, who worked for three years on security software at Google before quitting to devote himself to cryptocurrency development, offers perhaps the most far-reaching forecast of such potential in blockchain technology. In a speech at the August 2013 Turing Festival in Edinburgh, Hearn envisioned an economy composed of autonomous economic agents. He used the example of a driverless taxi, one guided only by sensors and GPS technology. The one-car taxi service would be run by a smart software program plugged into an automated, electronic marketplace Hearn dubbed the Tradenet. There, prospective passengers could post ride requests and receive competing bids from multiple driverless cars. They would choose their preferred taxi based on fare, travel time, and model of car and could negotiate the route based on durations and fares that the service derived by bidding in a separate Tradenet "load space" market, where variations in traffic conditions would offer differing market-based toll-road prices for each route.

If all that sounds futuristic but feasible, try this additional feature of Hearn's imaginary taxi: it has no owner. The car owns itself—or, more precisely, the operating computer program owns it. This program would pay the car's running costs and take in its own revenue; all of this would be made possible by cryptocurrency and the invention of the blockchain.

"I suspect if I tried to go to the bank and open a bank account that's owned by a computer program, they'd tell me to get lost or they'd think I'm crazy and report me to the police," Hearn said. "But bitcoin has no intermediaries. Therefore, there's really nothing to stop a computer from connecting to the Internet and taking part [in the bitcoin network] all by itself. All you need to do to generate a bitcoin wallet is to generate a large random number, and pretty much anything can do that."

Right now you are probably wondering why we'd give a machine such rights. Because we could program it to provide the cheapest and most efficient service possible, Hearn's car would be focused on maximizing productivity and surviving, not building up a fat pile of retained earnings to spend on McMansions and trips to the Bahamas. It could keep its profit margins superthin and its prices low. That said, if it brought in more revenue than expenses, the car could be programmed to "have children," as Hearn puts it, investing its excess bitcoins in new driverless cars that would "inherit" a clone of its software program. To stay ahead of the game the car could also spend its surplus by hiring a human to write it a superior code—after seeking bids for these services via the Tradenet—and then apply special testing protocols to ensure the human isn't scamming it out of its competitiveness. If economic conditions in its area deteriorate too much, the car could "go to sleep" in a long-term parking lot for six months, Hearn says, or it could drive itself to another city where Tradenet data indicated stronger demand for taxi services.

There's a genesis problem here, though: Who will put up the initial capital to create this not-for-profit entity if its founder can't earn a return from investing in it? Clearly, the assets of these autonomous agents need to be thought of as public goods. The societal profit we all share from having more services abundantly available at low prices should be self-evident, but what incentive is there for profit-motivated individuals to invest in providing them? One option is to have governments direct this effort, applying taxpayer money. Another is to hope that philanthropists pick up the challenge. Ideally, though, the investment would come as a community effort. Perhaps residents of a particular neighborhood could invest in a driverless car and be rewarded with free or discounted rides for a prescribed period, and to achieve that kind of broad-based funding objective, Hearn offers up another solution: cryptocurrency assurance contracts, a blockchain-based version of the popular crowdfunding model in which organizers pledge a certain amount when others' donations reach target levels. Rather than organizers having to chase down pledgers and set up expensive, lawyer-managed escrow accounts to protect pledged funds, the blockchain and special software attached to it would just run the whole thing automatically. When a target funding level is reached in a designated, tamperproof wallet that only the software can control, a separate such wallet containing the organizer's funds would be tapped to merge the funds. If the target isn't reached, the money would automatically be sent back to everyone's personal wallets. Funding problem solved. Self-owned driverless taxis, here we come.

Of course, a world of driverless taxis is a world of no jobs for human taxidrivers. If many of these Blockchain 2.0 ideas come to fruition, they're not the only people who will worry about obsolescence—lawyers, investment bankers, stockbrokers, and a host of other "trust-based" services could be in lesser demand in a blockchain-run world. Later, in chapter 11, we'll explore how society may have to handle the painful process this entails. But for now we'll just delve into the mechanics of the technology itself and explore the many disruptive ways in which its inventors see it changing our economy.

Assurance contracts are just one form of one of the most prevalent Blockchain 2.0 ideas: "smart contracts," an idea first floated by Nick Szabo, who some researchers believe to be Satoshi Nakamoto. At its crux, this idea contends that the blockchain can replace the legal system, the ultimate trusted third party. Instead of having a law firm draft a written agreement to be enforced by a judge, if one party fails to meet its obligations —with all the costs and uncertainty that go along with those institutions' involvement—the execution of those obligations is automated by software, with the criteria for doing so verified by the decentralized blockchain. Think of a standard escrow agreement where an indebted homeowner puts away a monthly amount guaranteeing that home insurance and taxes will be paid. Well, in this case, those payments would be made with cryptocurrency and deposited into a neutral wallet, all automatically triggered once the tax and insurance payments fall due. The blockchain keeps everyone honest, and a whole layer of banking bureaucracy is removed, lowering costs.

Financial markets are especially ripe for Blockchain 2.0 innovation. Many modern securities contracts are already codified, digitized, and automated. Yet they are run by Wall Street banks and are written and litigated by high-powered lawyers pulling down six- or seven-figure retainers. One can imagine credit-default swaps, a class of derivative that gained notoriety during the financial crisis, established on a blockchainlike decentralized infrastructure. CDS contracts, which function as insurance, require one party, usually an investment bank or an insurance company, to make a payment to the other party, typically a creditor that has lent money to a third-party debtor, if and when that debtor is deemed to be in default. Disputes often occur over what constitutes a "credit event" to trigger the payment, sometimes requiring rulings by banker-dominated bodies such as the International Derivatives and Swaps Association (ISDA) and frequently involving lawyers and court cases. If the CDS contract were lodged with the blockchain, however, these third-party intermediaries could, in theory, be removed from that arbitration process. Any nonpayment from the debtor's wallet would trigger a corresponding bitcoin payment from the insuring party's wallet to the CDS-insured investor. No ambiguity, no legal challenges, all of it easily and cheaply installed with some standardized software.

But "smart contracts" need not be limited to finance. When paired with "smart property"—where deeds, titles, and other certifications of ownership are put in digital form to be acted upon by software—these contracts allow the automatic transfer of ownership of a physical asset such as a house or a car, or an intangible asset, such as a patent. Similarly, the software initiates the transfer when contractual obligations are met. With companies now busily putting bar codes, QR codes, microchips, and Bluetooth antennae on just about every gadget and piece of merchandise, the emerging "Internet of Things" should make it possible to transfer ownership in many kinds of physical property in this manner.

One creative solution applies to cars purchased on credit. Right now, if an automobile owner misses his or her payments, it's laborious and costly for the finance company to reclaim both the title to and physical possession of the car, involving lawyers, collection agencies, and, in worst cases, repo men. But under a smart contract, if the payments are not met, the digitized title would automatically revert to the finance company's digital wallet. What's more, the ignition could wirelessly be paired to an online encryption system requiring the presence of special remote digital "key" for the car to start. In the event of a default, the system would remove that key and deny the borrower access to the car. No doubt, this sounds intrusive and Big Brother–like, but it would have real, widespread benefits. By removing inefficiencies, bureaucracy, and costs from the system, such an automated approach to asset seizure could drive down the cost of financing. In theory, it would open up affordable financing to millions of people with bad credit who are currently denied by finance companies that don't feel confident that their loans are properly secured. And the contracts need not be entirely constrictive: they could be written in such a way that allowed for off-line negotiation and/or court intervention.

Another application for smart property: if government auto-licensing agencies could get their heads around codifying car registries and making them viable for blockchain-approved transfers, great efficiencies could be achieved. What's not to like about the disappearance of the Department of Motor Vehicles? Unless you're a DMV employee, of course.

Formidable technical, legal, financial, and cultural obstacles exist to the widespread adoption of many of these Blockchain 2.0 solutions. Hundreds are under way right now, and many seem half-baked and will likely never get off the ground. But the energy and innovative brainpower being invested in them is significant and is manifest in a string of serious start-ups and development projects.

The pioneer in the field was the Colored Coins project, which launched in the second half of 2012; its purpose: to allow people to exchange digitized securities and fiat currencies directly over the bitcoin blockchain. (Two people could set up a contract to directly exchange a digital claim on euros for a digital claim on gold, for example.) Since then the field has become crowded with Blockchain 2.0 start-ups and projects, including Next, Ripple, Mastercoin, Ethereum, BitShares, Counterparty, and Stellar. Each provides a specially designed blockchain-based platform that allows other entities to create peer-to-peer contracts, to issue and permit trading of digital and digitized assets, or to install special software-driven applications, all of them with decentralized functioning. Each also issues a unique coin or digital token—nextcoin, mastercoin, ether, bitshares, and Counterparty's XCP—that facilitates the many transaction-like exchanges that have to occur between parties that use these protocols to implement the back-and-forth functions of their decentralized applications. These are tradable for bitcoins and other cryptocurrencies on special altcoin exchanges such as Cryptsy, where their value is expected to rise and fall according to the success or failure of the protocol to which they belong. However, such Blockchain 2.0 "coins" are probably better thought of as digital vessels in which embedded information can be passed around the blockchain rather than as currencies. They are the vehicles through which smart contracts are implemented, digital assets are exchanged, and all sorts of other decentralized actions can occur.

Techies have a soft spot for killer apps, the ultimate disruptive technologies, and when taken to their extreme, the ideas driving each of these companies are about as disruptive as one can imagine. David Johnston is a senior board member at the Mastercoin Foundation, the body that coordinates the funding for the Mastercoin project, which offers a special software platform for developers to design special decentralized applications that can run on top of the bitcoin blockchain. He says blockchain technology "will supercharge the sharing economy," that emerging trend in which apartment owners use Airbnb.com to rent out quasi hotel rooms and car owners sign up as self-employed taxidrivers for smartphone-based Uber and Lyft. The idea is that if we can decentralize the economy and foster multiple forms of peer-to-peer exchanges, people will figure out profitable ways to turn much of what they own or control into a marketable service. Johnston is known for having coined the term *DApp*, for "decentralized autonomous application," to describe the kind of specialized software programs that could thrive in blockchain-based settings. He excitedly reels off various examples of such DApps: a completely decentralized stock exchange; a network of interlinked computers that contribute to and draw from a collective pool of hard-disk space, all paid for with cryptocurrency; a "meshnet," where users are paid to contribute bandwidth to a low-cost network of Wi-Fi–connected users who get to bypass the cable and telephone companies that currently function as centralized Internet service providers.

The start-ups and nonprofit projects that are seeking to carry out this massive disruption come in essentially two different forms. Some directly use the bitcoin blockchain for their activities, including Colored Coins, Counterparty, and Mastercoin. Just as bitcoin has its own core protocol —which, as we discussed in previous chapters, is the software program that lays out the basic rules for bitcoin's network of computers—so, too, do these projects come with their own foundational protocols. That makes them a second-layer platform, one that a third layer of services and applications can be built upon. These Blockchain 2.0 providers' platforms allow their customers to access the power of the underlying, decentralized bitcoin blockchain to do quite different things from merely trading bitcoins—smart contracts, smart property deals, digital asset exchanges, etc. Under their model, the underlying bitcoin transactions are usually of small value—as low as a "Satoshi" (BTC0.00000001). That's because the bitcoin value is essentially irrelevant versus the more important purpose of conveying the decentralized application's critical metadata across the network, even though some value exchange is needed to make the communication of information happen. These providers have decided to throw their lot in with bitcoin, betting that its first-mover advantage, which has made it by far the most heavily traded, mined, and liquid cryptocurrency, with a global network of prodigious computing power, assures their users of a robust, reliable network to authenticate the integrity of their operations.

Other Blockchain 2.0 projects have adopted a different philosophy. They didn't want to force the bitcoin protocol to do things it wasn't designed to do. Why would miners commit resources to support the installment of a digitized property-deed claim, for example, when their entire incentive system is based on rewards for confirming transactions in bitcoin currency? Although some developers are looking to modify bitcoin's core software to make it more versatile, these people felt that the core blockchain's capacity to handle this new and different workload had structural limitations. They felt it was better to go off and build an entirely new network, a whole new blockchain. That allowed them to rethink the network's incentive system, tweaking it so that computer nodes would be encouraged to confirm transactions that are designed to have vast amounts of additional information embedded in them. The Next project, whose "proof of stake" concept we discussed in chapter 6, was a leader in this push. But brasher, bolder new blockchain projects have also come forward. One of them believes its technology can reinvent the very idea of a company.

For Daniel Larimer, one basic conceptual obstacle to expanding Blockchain 2.0 ideas stems from nomenclature. People have a hard time labeling cryptocurrencies—are they digitized securities, virtual currencies, or some kind of token or software that's used in an application? For his part, the founder of BitShares believes that if Satoshi Nakamoto had described bitcoin as a kind of a company that runs a payment system and whose ownership shares also function as that system's currency, people would better comprehend both the original project and the Blockchain 2.0 projects coming in its wake. Instead they wrongly fixate on bitcoin as money, he says, rather than simply as a form of money. "It's really difficult to explain what bitcoin is because people don't understand money. Even the experts don't agree," Larimer says. "But the fact is bitcoins don't cease being a share in a company just because they are used as money. Gold doesn't cease to be a hard, durable metal just because it's used as a currency. Money is defined by the way it is used, not what it is." Bitcoin, as he defines it, is a "company [that] earns its revenues from transactions fees." It has to pay for securing the system, "and for that it employs subcontractors, who are the miners . . . paid for with newly issued bitcoin shares in itself." Once Larimer began thinking of bitcoin this way, he started seeing myriad possibilities to create other companies that issue their own digital "currency" as shares and run their businesses on top of a blockchain.

Whereas David Johnston and others are focused on designing DApps, Larimer and BitShares are all about DACs, "decentralized autonomous corporations." (Others use the acronym DAO, decentralized autonomous organization.) These are entities owned by multiple shareholders for which routine financial decisions—when to release funds to pay for expenses, how big a dividend to pay—are automated by the firm's guiding software and entrusted to a tamperproof system that's verified by the blockchain.

Any change in strategy that requires an alteration to the software is put to a shareholder vote, all done verifiably over the incontrovertible blockchain. But the rest of the time this corporate entity runs on autopilot—no need for trusted employees such as a treasurer or payroll clerk to handle cash, no need for a board of directors to keep management in check. Mike Hearn's driverless taxi could function like this; it's just that the car would not own itself but would be owned by the taxi service's crypto-shareholders.

Larimer gets animated as he spells out idea after idea for DACs built on BitShares' platform. The spindly developer from Blacksburg, Virginia, talks about musicians founding DACs that issue shares in their songs. Fans rather than record companies become the financiers of studio work. When a song becomes a hit, the fans' digital bitshares in that song will rise in value. "It turns the concept of copyright upside down," Larimer says. He's also excited about automated "contracts for difference," which allow people to speculate on the difference between two assets' prices and receive an automated payout if that "spread" crosses a predetermined threshold according to a market-data feed that's talking to a blockchain-installed software program. He even sees blockchain-based reputation markets arising, where everyone from restaurateurs to contractors to freelance journalists can market themselves based on mathematical metrics and market forces. Not only would the irrefutable blockchain's record of recommendations create a much more honest system than that of Facebook "likes" or TripAdvisor reviews, it could eventually allow businesses and freelancers to create securities based on those reputations—a way to automatically monetize what accountants call goodwill.

A pet idea of Larimer's is corruption-proof, blockchain-based voting. Under this model, each voter would use an encrypted private key to send a tiny, essentially worthless amount of cryptocurrency to a designated polling wallet, creating a permanent, irrefutable vote that's time-stamped on the blockchain to prevent fraud. "We aim to enhance democracy," Larimer says matter-of-factly. Ideas similar to his are already entering into practice, many motivated by the rise of computerized voting, which, while promising efficiency and—if extended into online voting—wider participation, also raise the specter of voter fraud by those with access to vote-counting systems' proprietary software. The municipality of Takoma Park, Maryland, has for the past five years been using different versions of an encrypted remote voting system that allow voters to check that their votes were correctly counted without losing their anonymity. In recent years, the legendary cryptographer and DigiCash founder David Chaum has worked on such projects.

In mid-2013, journalist Vitalik Buterin also got to thinking about how bitcoin was set up. In his view, its core protocol was too clunky for software developers to create robust yet user-friendly application programming interfaces (APIs). All the secondary protocols being built upon it were similarly narrow. He was essentially saying it was like DOS, before Windows was created.

What if he built an entirely independent protocol and blockchain that could sustain any kind of application written in any programming language, one that was, as developers say, "Turing complete"? What if it could support any decentralized service—currency-trading systems, smart contracts, shareholder registrations, voting systems, DApps, DACs, DAOs, whatever—and let developers construct as pretty an interface as they felt their market needed? The solution he came up with quickly took the cryptocurrency world by storm: a completely redesigned, fully versatile, decentralized blockchain that could function as an open platform on which all manner of contracts and decentralized applications could be installed. He called it Ethereum.

"We are hoping to be like the Android of cryptocurrency," Buterin says, referring to the Google-designed mobile operating system that's used by multiple models of smartphones and which had by 2014 inspired more than a million apps. "On Android you can install Google Maps, you can install Gmail, you can install whatever you want. That's where we want cryptocurrency to go. Ethereum provides the base layer, and if you want to install a wallet, there's an app for that; if you want to install a block explorer, you can design one; or a merchant payments solution or whatever."

A self-taught computer geek and hacker with no formal cryptography background, Buterin first laid out his vision in a white paper. In November 2013, he posted it on GitHub, a key repository for open-source coding projects where coders float ideas and collaborate on software development. "I was seriously expecting five or so cryptographers to either immediately dismiss it as worthless and explain the reasons why this can't work in any form, or to say, 'Here are the ten projects that are doing this already,'" he says. But it had quite the opposite effect, setting off a spark of imagination among cryptographers and software engineers. By January 2014, when we caught up with Buterin on the sidelines of a bitcoin conference in Miami, Ethereum, which had been conceived only a few months earlier, already boasted a team of fifteen full-time developers led by Gavin Wood, a noted British programmer schooled in C++ programming language, and had almost a hundred part-time developers adding their input. They established themselves in Zug, Switzerland, and set about building a brand-new, versatile blockchain platform.

The team also planned a fund-raiser. Described as a "presale" of ether, Ethereum's special internal currency—which in compliance with Swiss law was described in the fund-raiser not as a currency or a security but as a piece of software needed to run future applications—the offering raised more than twenty-nine thousand bitcoins, worth more than $14.5 million in late August. By that measure, and considering the relatively short six-week period, it's fair to say it was the most successful crowdfunding exercise in history—beating anything else that's even been done over platforms such as Kickstarter.

Needless to say, Buterin, a Canadian of Russian birth, was not your average teenager. Still not twenty when we met in Miami, he explained how he first became interested in bitcoins in March 2011, and how in September that year, still in high school, he was hired by Swiss bitcoin entrepreneur Mihai Alisie (later an early cofounder of the Ethereum project) to be the lead writer for *Bitcoin Magazine*. He was paid solely in bitcoin. The next year Buterin entered the University of Waterloo in Ontario to study computer science. But while at school he was constantly distracted by cryptocurrency ventures: he read and wrote about the topic voraciously, and he earned bounties doing freelance development work for Alex Mizrahi's Colored Coins project, the early Blockchain 2.0 scheme for embedding information about assets and contracts into bitcoin transactions. With the price of bitcoin soaring and interest in the topic expanding, the Canadian teenager dropped out of college to dedicate his time to cryptocurrencies. (When Buterin told us this, bitcoin evangelist Roger Ver, listening in from the sidelines, piped up, "Good call!")

Buterin went on a listening tour of bitcoin communities around the world, paid for with the bitcoin he was receiving for his continued contributions to *Bitcoin Magazine,* articles that were fast becoming vital reading for cryptocurrency newcomers and old hands alike. He visited the Free State project in New Hampshire, dedicated to libertarian ideals, attended bitcoin meetups across Europe, hooked up with an underground hactivist group led by the legendary London coder Amir Taaki, and hung out for a couple of months in what he described as an "anarcho-leftist" commune in Spain. All the while he picked up thoughts and concepts that would help him flesh out his master idea.

Sounding every bit the MBA-qualified financial engineer, Buterin rattles off concepts for apps that could run on Ethereum and help reinvent Wall Street: digital-currency-denominated derivative contracts through which traditional currencies and commodities trade as digital IOU tokens; Ethereum-based security offerings that function without a need for the underwriting and book-running services of an investment bank; decentralized algorithms to challenge the sinister "dark pool" investment vehicles and high-frequency trading machines with which hedge funds, investment banks, and Wall Street high rollers get an edge on the market. But he admits he's just tossing out ideas.

For now, Ethereum is an unproven project. The ether-based compensation model for miners and the system of proof by which they would obtain their compensation was still a work in progress at the time of writing. No one could say for sure whether the network will be stable, whether it will ensure a broad enough base of committed miners to avert the threat of concentrated hashing power that we discussed in chapter 6. Still, Ethereum's large, talented staff and its solid war chest exist precisely to tackle these challenges, to get the architecture right. A lot of brainpower is being dedicated to creating the ultimate decentralized platform.

Sometime before Buterin set his sights on an entirely new blockchain, another school of Blockchain 2.0 developers started taking decentralized cryptocurrency ledgers in another direction. They believed you didn't have to completely overhaul the traditional economy of fiat currencies to slash the costs of transferring funds in those currencies. You just had to simplify the financial system's back office.

Here, once again at the vanguard, was Jed McCaleb, the mercurial, reclusive innovator who founded the Mt. Gox exchange and so almost single-handedly created a means for people to pass to and from the fiat and bitcoin economies. McCaleb's new project, which he cofounded with Internet entrepreneur Arthur Britto and Chris Larsen, a founder of various peer-to-peer finance projects, was called Ripple. It boldly aimed to supplant many parts of the intermediating infrastructure through which financial institutions sent money to each other.

Like the other Blockchain 2.0 projects, Ripple has its own internal currency, XRP—often colloquially called ripples—which functions as a vessel for transferring information and as a store of value for participants and investors in the network, be they users who want to cheaply trade euros for yen or speculators betting on Ripple itself. But the system differs from just about every other cryptocurrency in that its network for confirming transactions does not depend upon currency rewards or transaction fees as incentives. No basement-dwelling home miners are running their computers 24-7 in an obsessive hunt for ripples. Rather, the ledger of transactions is typically confirmed by the same institutions that use it, the "gateways" as Ripple Labs, the network's managing company, calls them, and the creators of digital assests and contracts that trade over the Ripple network. The gateways are banks, remittance services, money transmitters, and exchange houses and are expected to freely contribute computing resources to the network. The digital asset traders are designers of altcoin backed by gold or of contracts denominated in fiat currencies. They confirm transactions by a system of consensus that, unlike bitcoin's ten-minute blocks, is virtually instantaneous and consumes minimal energy. They are motivated to do so purely by a common interest in having the system function well.

Outside customers can go to one of the gateway institutions and request to send money—or any other asset that can be given a digitized representation within an XRP transaction—to someone else, who receives the payment in his or her currency of choice from a reciprocal gateway anywhere else. The gateways do not deliver physical currency to each other. Rather, they build up a ledger of tradable IOUs, where one gateway's payout to a customer can be claimed by the holder of that IOU in satisfaction of another customer's claims elsewhere. If the two corresponding gateways in an exchange trust each other, there's no need to use the "trustless," decentralized network over which XRP is traded; instead it's a straightforward contractual exchange. In some respects, then, it mimics the Muslim world's *hawala* system—the centuries-old global network of money dealers that uses long-standing, cross-border relationships of trust to send customers' money around the world under an accord that debts will be reciprocated—while being partly modeled on bitcoin.

Once the Ripple network is fully built out, it will be able to trade fiat-currency-denominated IOU tokens against one another, creating de facto exchange rates. Ripple Labs hopes it will attract enough currency-trading gateways for its decentralized global exchange to be liquid enough to offer more attractive rates than those of the current centralized system of currency exchange, which runs through trading desks at big international banks. Its decentralized structure will hopefully give buyers and sellers access to a much wider and fairer selection of prices, narrowing the gap between buy and sell prices, the so-called spread that creates the profit for banks. To give you a sense of the opportunity, that bank-centric global currency market was worth more than $5 trillion in daily turnover in 2013. It's the world's biggest financial market.

But Ripple is as much about cutting out middlemen as narrowing foreign-exchange spreads. It removes the need for payment processors, settlement agents, foreign-exchange banks, custodial services, and the ACH (Automated Clearing House) network. Like bitcoin, it has its sights on the trillions of dollars in middlemen fees that currently get attached annually to both international and domestic money transfers, particularly on the correspondent banking services that Wall Street banks provide at steep costs to small or regional banks. Not for nothing, Ripple is aggressively marketing to these smaller banks. David Andolfatto, the chief economist at the Federal Reserve Bank of St. Louis, has sung Ripple's praises for cutting waste in the financial system. By mid-2014, the concept was just starting to resonate with a few early adopters. U.K.-based AstroPay, which claimed to manage the largest cross-border payments network in Latin America, signed on as a gateway for its six hundred thousand business clients in the region, and Fidor Bank of Germany, already a pioneer in providing services to bitcoin businesses, said it planned to use Ripple to offer supercheap international transfers, as did CBW

Bank and Cross River Bank in the United States. Meanwhile, Ripple Labs had by then attracted $6.5 million in investments from important Silicon Valley firms such Andreessen Horowitz, the venture-capital vehicle of Netscape pioneer Marc Andreessen, Google Ventures, and Lightspeed Venture Partners. Enticingly, the start-up claimed to be engaged in intensive discussions with the biggest international banks, offering them a chance to cut the costs of their global money transfers and gain a competitive edge. It's a potentially appealing prospect for any bank that isn't heavily invested in the intermediary functions of the payment infrastructure that Ripple would make redundant. It's much less appealing for those that constitute that infrastructure.

Still, as of mid-2014, it seemed Ripple had generated more enthusiasm among techies and individuals than it had among bankers. The project had a fanatical following—nothing on the order of bitcoin, but a distinctive, impassioned community nonetheless. At times, these fans have been dragged into clashes with bitcoiners, some of whom have decried Ripple for working with, rather than against, the financial system. In part because the Ripple network is run by a private, for-profit company, rather than taking on an ownerless and *decentralized* structure like bitcoin's, it draws suspicion from cryptocurrency purists, who often wrongly define it as a *centralized* system. Despite the company's elaborate efforts to create transparent, arm's-length rules for issuing and disseminating its XRP currency, it inevitably comes in for flak on Reddit and other forums favored by the crypto mob.

The issue of Ripple's profit motives came to a head in May 2014, when McCaleb made the stunning announcement that he would sell all of his XRP holdings. In a short message posted on Reddit, the cofounder said that after giving away some of his 9 billion XRP to charity, he now planned to sell the remainder over two weeks. That represented about 9 percent of the initial 100 billion XRP money supply, which unlike the drawn-out, 130-year issuance of bitcoins, was created in one batch in 2012. McCaleb's comments alluded in passing to the decision that he and cofounders Larsen and Britto had made to allocate 20 percent of that initial issuance to themselves. (The remaining 80 percent was given to Ripple's OpenCoin foundation, which was to coordinate the gradual release of the currency over time to optimize its value and utility as a transactions vehicle.) But no real explanation was given for his actions in an otherwise matter-of-fact note: "Because I have immense respect for the community members and want to be transparent, I'm publicly announcing this before I start. So just fyi . . . XRP sales incoming."

Inevitably, with such a large number of coins expected to come to market, the price of XRP tanked, losing 45 percent of its value in bitcoins, the currency against which it trades on altcoin markets, in two days. The Reddit thread that McCaleb had initiated lit up. Some commentators applauded McCaleb for being so open about his sales; others decried him for generating FUD (fear, uncertainty, and doubt) around Ripple. Ripple Labs stated that the sale was of no consequence since the price of XRP would have no impact on the cryptocurrency's ability to convey payments over the network. But then things got nasty when Jesse Powell, the CEO of cryptocurrency exchange Kraken, announced on Ripple's own open forum that he was resigning from Ripple Labs' board because CEO Chris Larsen had rejected Powell's request that the founders transfer their personal XRP allocations to the company. (That such a request would be made speaks to the awkward relationship that cryptocurrency founders have with the people who hold the new currency they create. Whereas investors in regular start-ups happily let the founders get wealthy, the expectation is that those who issue a cryptocurrency won't exploit the unique power of that role, that they won't engage in the same seigniorage practices as traditional central banks and make money for themselves simply by making currency.) Ripple's management responded by accusing Powell of lying and sent him a cease-and-desist letter, which also demanded a retraction. Powell then posted the letter, which had been marked "confidential," online, along with annotations defending his statements as true. The happy community of Ripplers was suddenly consumed with bad blood. Some wag called it Jedmageddon.

Fences were mended three months later when Ripple's management struck a deal with McCaleb to spread out his sale of XRP over a seven-year period. Larsen, meanwhile, agreed to make a 7 billion XRP donation (worth $33 million at the time) to an independent foundation committed to the financially underserved. The XRP price stabilized.

Larsen doesn't downplay that Ripple Labs is out to make money. Whereas "the crypto world" is sometimes suspicious of for-profit ownership structures, "when we meet with the banks to talk about our service, they don't care," he says. "They want to hear about what it can do, and they see the benefits." Still, as with a number of altcoin launches that soared in price at their outset only to subsequently plunge when investors began suspecting the founders of running a "pump and dump" scam, it's difficult to dispel a sense of conflicted interests whenever new cryptocurrencies are created. It gets back to the seigniorage problem we discussed in chapter 5 and which Nakamoto chose to tackle through the competition for bitcoins.

Jed McCaleb would use an entirely new project to make a point about the importance of avoiding these perceptions of self-interest. Called Stellar and launched in July 2014 with the backing and money of some key investors, including Khosla Ventures' Keith Rabois, an early founder of PayPal, and Stripe, a maker of cutting-edge software for payment processors, the project was mostly a carbon copy of Ripple with a couple of key differences. Of the 100 billion initial issue of coins, known as stellar, 95 percent would simply be given away, half of those to early applicants who sign up via Facebook and half to charitable causes that focus on poverty alleviation and economic development and/or are early adopters of cryptocurrencies. While 5 percent was still being reserved for founders and early investors, the otherwise giant giveaway seemed necessary to win the trust of the powerful hordes of crypto enthusiasts who dominate Reddit, Bitcointalk, and Twitter.

The experiences of one of Mastercoin's most important clients, MaidSafe, further highlights the pitfalls that Blockchain 2.0 projects face in raising money via their internal currencies. As a product that facilitates the pooling of disk storage and computing resources, MaidSafe is simply ingenious. As a fund-raiser, it has proven to be much less savvy. MaidSafe's experiences raising money demonstrated the challenges of issuing newly minted cryptocurrencies in an arm's-length way—in particular, the challenges that founders face in assuring their investors that they are not granting unwarranted seigniorage to themselves or their business partners.

MaidSafe is founded on the notion that many people, including most home-computer users, are "long" on storage—they have excess unused disk space on their computers and external drives—and could lend it to those who are "short" on storage. Matching those two groups via a network could make computing resources available cheaply to the programmers who will write the code for all the cool stuff of our decentralized future. Meanwhile, the rest of us can turn our unused disk space into a money earner. The math works out if you compare a terabyte external hard drive at $100 with the premium rates on cloud storage from Dropbox, Google Drive, and Amazon Cloud, which in 2014 ranged from $120 to $500 a year for the same amount of storage.

MaidSafe, whose name stands for Massive Array of Internet Disks, Secure Access for Everyone, purports to avoid the "ecological disaster" that's brewing under the current, data-center-based paradigm for outsourced storage, said David Irvine, the Scottish engineer who founded MaidSafe. Data centers, he says, are an enormous waste of electricity because they store vast amounts of underutilized computing power in huge warehouses that need air-conditioning and expensive maintenance. It's a highly inefficient way to allocate resources around the network. To learn how to truly optimize networked resources, Irvine studied ant colonies and other elements of the natural ecosystem. The natural world, he says, is in essence a giant decentralized system of coexistence within and across species. It has no central organization. He discovered that ants, for example, are constantly changing the role they provide to the colony, shifting jobs depending on what the group most needs at any time. He aimed to design a computer network to do the same thing, so that each node could switch between consuming and offering storage space on the network's giant pool.

For an internal currency that MaidSafe participants could use to pay for and earn funds for shared computing resources, Irvine turned to Mastercoin, the bitcoin-based platform for decentralized applications. Mastercoin was to design a decentralized fund-raiser, transparently run without a middleman over the Mastercoin platform and bitcoin blockchain, that would simultaneously bring the new currency—safecoins—into existence and raise money to pay for MaidSafe's ongoing development. The offering was designed to permit investors to buy safecoins either with bitcoins or with Mastercoin's own internal currency—naturally called mastercoins. The good news is that the offering drew in a whopping $7 million in five hours, at least based on exchange rates at the time. The bad news is that this surge in demand led to a major breakdown in the delivery of safecoins, in part because the organizers had created favorable pricing for mastercoin holders two weeks before the offering was launched. This meant that for a short time the amount of safecoins you could buy with mastercoins was greater than the amount you could buy with the market-derived equivalent in bitcoins. In effect, it implied a price for mastercoin twice as high as its market rate on Cryptsy. Savvy investors saw that as a classic arbitrage opportunity and embarked on a strategy to profit from it. Knowing that many developers and longer-term investors in MaidSafe's project would buy mastercoins as a route to getting safecoins, these speculators cornered the market and bid up the price until the arbitrage gap disappeared. But this left too few mastercoins available for those who wanted safecoins. Inevitably, once the offering was over, the artificially supported price of mastercoins plunged, leaving a horde of angry investors holding stakes in a highly illiquid altcoin and no safecoins. MaidSafe and Mastercoin tried to make amends by buying back some of the new safecoins and reselling them at a discount for bitcoins, but the whole affair left a bad impression, with some jaded investors predictably bad-mouthing it as a pump-and-dump scheme on bitcoin message boards. It was more likely just a case of poor planning. After all, MaidSafe itself was holding the short end of the stick, too, as the mastercoin price plunge forced it to downgrade its fund-raising tally to $5.5 million. Not only that, but an otherwise ingenious new product would now, sadly, be associated with a disastrous fund-raiser.

This MaidSafe problem has no doubt influenced other Blockchain 2.0 innovators' thinking on how to issue a new currency, raise money for themselves, and keep the faith with the community. But they also had to figure out how to stay on the right side of the law. This concern was highlighted in 2014 when the Securities and Exchange Commission imposed a $35,000 fine on former SatoshiDice owner Erik Voorhees and forced him to forgo $15,000 in profits for having sold shares in that project via an unregistered offering. Big projects such as Ethereum have not only attracted solid developer talent, but they've also signed on some experienced lawyers and financial engineers who are trying to draft rules of engagement to keep everybody happy.

Still, "everybody" in this sense includes one constituency that's especially difficult to please: regulators. The lawyers who are currently acting as liaisons between cryptocurrency innovators and government regulators are struggling to get the latter to shape rules around a concept that the existing legal system never contemplated. "You think it's hard to figure out what bitcoin is from a regulatory standpoint, well, now we're talking about figuring out what an autonomous corporation is," says Jacob Farber, senior counsel at Perkins Coie in Washington. "To them it's like something from *The Matrix.*"

The developers might also be getting ahead of themselves technologically. If bitcoin's blockchain ends up as the default protocol for these new applications, it's going to need some serious upgrading before it can live up to all these sweeping, life-altering promises. Bitcoin can handle only seven transactions a second (against Visa's ten thousand), for instance, all because of an explicit hard limit on the amount of data that can go into a transaction block. That limit will need to be raised significantly if the system is to be expanded to include all these other value exchanges in addition to bitcoin payments. Some also worry that miners will be disincentivized to confirm transactions if they are embedded with contracts for high-valued property, the idea being that the miners' compensation won't be commensurate with the value contained in the block. There are also problems with fees that bitcoin imposes on the smallest transaction—a policy, like the data limit, designed to discourage spam and make it prohibitively expensive for a nefarious actor to launch a massive distributed denial of service, or DDOS, attack. The problem is these fees also make it prohibitively expensive to develop certain Blockchain 2.0 applications that entail large amounts of individual data exchanges of low or no monetary value such as blockchain-based voting or encrypted messaging. The good news is that among the disparately spread global community of developers working on bitcoin, many are addressing these problems and are seeking to either modify the core protocol or find work-arounds for the new applications.

But even beyond fixing the technicals, some serious marketing challenges lie ahead if these projects are to achieve mainstream adoption. Consider the idea of smart contracts. Traditional contracts often need to be adjudicated by lawyers because life is more complicated than what can be described on a contract or a piece of software code. If someone defaults on a loan, it may be in the long-run interests of the creditor to cut a debtor some slack. Can an automated, machine-run contract figure that out? Having recourse to a court in which human beings can sort through all the nuances and competing interests is of value to society broadly. We know that bankruptcy, for instance, a time-honored institution for encouraging renewal and for offering second chances, has helped the U.S. economy recover more successfully from crises than places that are less kind to debtors. People might balk at giving up these options; they might feel uncomfortable with the finality of an automated smart contract. Yet the efficiencies of blockchain-based solutions promise to dramatically cut prices if they can become entrenched. So, perhaps there's a need for hybrid models, with a judicial avenue attached to a blockchain smart contract, or some other means of off-line arbitration.

Hybrids, compromises, pragmatic solutions. There must be room for this kind of thinking if Blockchain 2.0 ideas are to break out of the hypothetical realm and into the real world. Some of the rigid ideological positions will have to be tempered. That's already happening. Some new projects are piggybacking on bitcoin's distributed, decentralized structure but are also using the power and efficiency of an in-house, centralized system to create value for users.

One that came to light in the summer of 2014 is called Realcoin, founded by prolific bitcoin investor Brock Pierce and former ad executive Reeve Collins. Realcoin is a new cryptocurrency that promises the holder the right to redeem it for the equivalent in dollars at any time. The digital tokens can be traded over the bitcoin blockchain, allowing people, in effect, to cheaply and easily send an asset that is, in theory, as good as a dollar to anyone anywhere in the world. The problem with this seemingly simple idea is that for the digital coin to retain its value, it requires trust in Realcoin to make good on its commitment. It reintroduces trust and central counterparty risk into what is supposed to be a trustless, decentralized environment. Realcoin gets around that rather cleverly by promising to carry a permanent reserve of dollar-based assets and to publicize its holdings in real time and, as best as possible, to use the blockchain to prove the accuracy of its accounting. It is centralized, which many bitcoiners can't abide, but it is transparent.

An even more centralized version of a similar concept is Bitreserve. This start-up, launched by Halsey Minor, the founder of tech-news-and-reviews service CNET, allows people to import bitcoins from a digital wallet into a unique Bitreserve account where they can then use the service's internalized system to instantaneously convert it into a dollar-, euro-, or yen-based account at going exchange rates. Once inside that in-house system, they can also make cheap, transparent, and instantaneous transfers within and across the accounts of other Bitreserve users anywhere in the world. As with Ripple, Bitreserve holdings expressed in these fiat currencies are, in effect, tradable IOUs rather than actual rights to dollars. But unlike Ripple, and like Realcoin, they are backed by reserves of real fiat currencies that are held by the company itself and whose balances are updated and published in real time. The advantage is that with Bitreserve's server-centralized system backing up all that value, users get a guaranteed store of value denominated in their currency of choice. Centralization here offers a solution to the volatility of holding bitcoins in the decentralized blockchain but retains the ability to quickly and cheaply transfer funds digitally.

Bitreserve's viability is yet to be proven, but Minor's idea is worth contemplating as a general lesson in how traditional approaches such as fiat-currency reserves and centralized servers can give the revolutionary aspects of cryptocurrency a practical application. It's a departure from the decentralize-at-all-costs principles behind most big cryptocurrency ideas, but it would not be a surprise to see more start-ups like Bitreserve launched.

"It's like we're Henry Ford and we're working with this incredible new invention, the automobile, but we haven't even gotten around to starting production of the Model T and now we're saying, 'Hey, let's go out and build a rocket ship,'" says Nicolas Cary, CEO of Blockchain.info. He wants the developer community, whose services are in limited supply, to focus on getting bitcoin right before it moves on to all these new applications.

But it's impossible to stop the dreamers from dreaming. The creation of the blockchain, with its attendant opportunities to reorganize how human beings interact and do commerce, has unleashed an outpouring of imagination among computer geeks. They sense a revolution and are already setting their targets on it, regardless of whether we're ready.

Not only are start-ups such as Ethereum and MaidSafe launching much-hyped cryptocurrency-denominated fund-raisers, but special incubators such as Swarm are now creating cryptocurrency-denominated investment vehicles to foster the development of *other* cryptocurrency-financed decentralizing start-ups. With layers upon layers and platforms upon platforms, this stuff can get confusing, but the key idea is that new software applications can convert extensible platforms such as bitcoin into powerful agents of change.

New start-ups are trying to deal with the influx of innovations in this field and make sense of it. A company called Chain provides highly specialized software and network-management services to firms that want to create decentralized applications on top of bitcoin or any of the other blockchains and protocols. Coinist has established itself as a rating agency for the influx of digital assets and cryptocurrencies coming to market on Blockchain 2.0 platforms such as Next and Ripple. Founder John Whelan is positioning the firm as the Moody's Investors Service of cryptocurrencies. If there's a market for his services, it will be recognition that, quite apart from decentralized blockchain transactions themselves, the issuers of those new assets are inherently centralized institutions that require trust and, therefore, demand objective assessments of their trustworthiness. Meanwhile, Tel Aviv–based venture capital firm Aleph is incubating Blockchain 2.0 projects by offering $50,000 bounties—a kind of investment award—for start-ups that devise solutions to some of the obstacles to these projects' development. At least one consultancy, Humint, is advising firms and even people on how create their own corporate and personalized digital coins.

To top this all off, Zurich-based Open Transactions is vying for the meta-project to end all meta-projects. It is developing a software program that instructs servers to connect all these competing blockchains, protocols, and coins within a decentralized, interlocking structure. To oversimplify a highly complex idea, it seeks to create gateways between distinct platforms without entrusting the gatekeepers with valuable information or paying them any fees. If successful, the project would create a single, seamless, self-functioning, decentralized exchange, a giant Internet bazaar in which just about anything can be traded, transferred, and priced in real time. Open Transactions founder Chris Odom wants to reverse the trend where the paths for connecting bitcoin with other platforms, be that with alternative cryptocurrencies or with the fiat-currency economy, have run through trusted third-party entities, failed bitcoin exchange Mt. Gox being the case that highlights the dangers of this approach. "This is not Satoshi's dream," Odom says.

We don't know whether Satoshi's dream included all the Blockchain 2.0 applications now being built atop his more narrowly defined currency and payment system. But in opening the door to all these new ways of organizing businesses and society, he perhaps inevitably unleashed the kind of tension that's implied by Odom's comment. Satoshi set off a decentralization movement that's now clashing with a preexisting system of businesses and law that it seeks to disrupt, giving rise to tension within wider society but also within cryptocurrency communities themselves. This battlefront is the subject of the next chapter.*

---

* During the late stages of this book's production, some of the most influential software developers in the cryptocurrency community caused a stir with the launch of a bold proposal that has the potential to accelerate Blockchain 2.0 innovation and integrate every different cryptocurrency project. Called "Sidechains" and outlined in a white paper by a group that includes Adam Back, whose early work on hashing algorithms provided the foundation for bitcoin's software, and two members of the bitcoin core developer team, it would permit people to shift digital currency in and out of different blockchains in a transparent, decentralized way. The goal is to allow inventors to leverage the power of bitcoin's mining infrastructure as they develop new, innovative cryptocurrency ideas without jeopardizing bitcoin's core code.

Ten

SQUARE PEG MEETS ROUND HOLE

> The insolence of authority is endeavoring to substitute money
> for ideas.
>
> —*Frank Lloyd Wright*

Gavin Andresen opened the door to his threadbare sublet office, located
in a nondescript building above a Dunkin' Donuts in the college town of
Amherst, Massachusetts. The room contained little more than a make-
shift plastic desk and his computer, an Apple iMac. A week earlier he had
cleared out his office at the home he shares with his wife, Michele—a ge-
ology professor at the University of Massachusetts—and two kids. He'd
decided that a man essentially if not titularly in charge of running an $8
billion economy needed something more than a home office. If the new
office was sparsely furnished, it had the virtue of uninterrupted privacy.
Today, he would need it.

It was February 10, 2014. When he had checked his e-mail that morning, he found his in-box overflowing with panicked messages from around
the world. Overnight, the struggling digital currency exchange Mt. Gox,
this time truly on its deathbed, had warned of a dangerous bug in bitcoin's underlying software that was allowing hackers to create fake transaction codes and demand unwarranted payments. Now, people with all
manner of stake in the currency were looking to Andresen for help. The
versatility afforded by bitcoin's unregulated and leaderless structure had

been one of its great strengths, but now the flaws in that lack of oversight were becoming apparent.

While bitcoin's open-source core code allowed anyone to peruse it and suggest additions and improvements, only a handful of people, essentially five men assigned to the core development team, had password access to the live code inside the core protocol. Of those, the one who had the most responsibility for overseeing the program was Andresen, the forty-seven-year-old chief scientist of the main bitcoin representative group, the Bitcoin Foundation. The foundation pays him to coordinate the input of the hundreds of far-flung techies who tinker away at the open-licensed software. Right now, the bitcoin community needed answers, and in the absence of a CEO, a CTO, or any central authority to turn to, Andresen was their best hope. What was this "transaction malleability" bug that Mt. Gox was talking about? How bad was it? Was the blockchain compromised? Was people's money safe?

After arriving at his office, Andresen spent some time reading through the messages, trying to determine the nature of the problem. To him the "transaction malleability" line in Mt. Gox's statement was suspicious. This issue had been identified way back in 2011 and much discussed on developer forums. It referred to a feature of the supplementary wallet software that was created along with the original core protocol code and which within a short window after a transaction allowed someone to alter a transaction ID so as to batch more than one together. In theory, this meant a fraudster could trick an exchange such as Mt. Gox into believing an intended payment had never happened—essentially making it look as if the transaction had never landed in the fraudster's wallet—and ask for it to be resent. But this "quirk," as Andresen liked to call it—the malleability of transaction codes was a deliberate, if questionable, feature, not necessarily a glitch or a bug—was easily resolved if a currency exchange used basic accounting procedures to check against its internal records of outgoing bitcoins. Andresen was surprised to hear that Mt. Gox CEO Mark Karpelès, an active participant in bitcoin developer forums in which the transaction malleability had been discussed at length, didn't know about it or have precautions in place.

Andresen concluded that Mt. Gox had misinterpreted and/or

willfully misstated its internal problems and had unfairly and inaccurately blamed bitcoin for those problems. He whipped up a post for the Bitcoin Foundation's blog that said as much. It carried the title "Contrary to Mt. Gox's statement, Bitcoin is not at fault" and declared the protocol to be sound and simply reminded businesses to use "best practices" in managing their wallets.

The topic encouraged Andresen to work once and for all on a solution to end the transaction malleability feature, which had been put off for some time in favor of more pressing tasks. By broad agreement it was a nuisance, but removing it entailed some complicated engineering. Still, as far as he could tell, nothing in the core code was immediately threatened. Using an IRC room, he discussed the matter with some of his colleagues—two of whom are in Europe, two in the United States—as well as some other developers, but there was no sense of urgency. That is, until a new message arrived, from Gregory Maxwell, a Mountain View, California–based volunteer bitcoin coder.

Maxwell had spoken to Karpelès overnight, done some digging, and realized that there was indeed a problem, a potentially big one, in the underlying code for the standard wallet software. He believed it could allow a rogue actor to hack into the transaction records and cause mischief. Essentially, a hacker could turn the transaction malleability quirk into a kind of DDOS (distributed denial of service) attack and flood the network with false transaction codes. It was, Andresen would later say, one of those things that was "just hiding in plain sight." The integrity of the blockchain itself was not compromised, since both the transaction malleability feature and the bug resided on the supplemental wallet software, not on the core protocol that dictated the critical mining and blockchain management functions. However, exchanges and other entities that make frequent transactions were vulnerable to multiple fraudulent requests for payment. The bitcoin network was safe but the bitcoin ecosystem around it was in distress—all from a bug that was lurking in the original software introduced by Satoshi Nakamoto. The founder, Andresen told us, was a brilliant "lone wolf" coder, but a bit of a sloppy operator who would never subject his code to the kind of testing that's routine in most development work.

Nakamoto himself—or whomever the anonymous chat room user represented—had chosen the bespectacled, boyish Andresen for his current job. In bitcoin's early days, the Australian-born software developer had had a back-and-forth with bitcoin's incognito founder about a far bigger problem than this one. In 2010, someone quietly told the two of them that a bug in the software would let people spend other people's bitcoin. Keeping the problem secret, Nakamoto simply fixed it and announced to the fledgling community that they should use a new version of the code. Not long after that, Nakamoto, in consultation with another core coder, Jeff Garzik, decided that Andresen should be the leader in coordinating the small team of core developers with access to the code. Nakamoto told him he was chosen, Andresen says, because of his calm demeanor.

Now, the computer engineer found his stress level rising. He was worried that with all the attention that Mt. Gox had drawn to the transaction malleability issue, someone would step in and exploit the bug that Maxwell had identified. But the deeply rooted problem would not easily be written out of the program; it would take significant new coding and testing. Meanwhile, the global bitcoin community was on edge; not only was the Gox claim about the bug confusing, but coupled with its having frozen customers' access to their bitcoins, it panicked some. Andresen worked late into the evening consulting with fellow developers in the chat room on how to protect the network. At 2:00 A.M., he dispatched marching orders for the next day's repair job to the other four members of his team—one each in Mountain View, Atlanta, Zurich, and Eindhoven in the Netherlands. At last, he could sleep.

But the morning did not restore calm. Overnight, as word got out about the vulnerability, people had already busied themselves trying to exploit it. He awoke to find that the exchanges Bitstamp and BTC-e, along with other bitcoin brokerages and services, had been forced to halt operations as they buckled under a barrage of false claims exploiting the transaction malleability bug. These heavy, commercial users of the generic bitcoin wallet software had come under the very DDOS-like event the developers feared. The price of bitcoin, at $703 just twenty-four hours earlier, had fallen to a low of $535 overnight.

Andresen went back to the core developers. Now they not only had to address the bug but also had to help get the exchanges back up and running. Garzik, who is paid by payment processor BitPay in Atlanta but is deemed to be a permanent member of the bitcoin development team, would focus intently on writing "patches," work-around solutions that Bit-stamp, BTC-e, and other affected operators could install while a perma-nent fix was designed. Amsterdam-based Wladimir van der Laan, who is also on the Bitcoin Foundation payroll, would work with Andresen on a more lasting fix. They would do a deep dive into the bitcoin software code, identify the bugs, and go through the laborious process of writing them away and then testing the whole system. The two volunteer devel-opers, Maxwell, who's employed by the XIPH Foundation for keeping the Internet free of special interests, and Pieter Wuille, who works for Google in Zurich, would do what they could with whatever time they could spare from their day jobs. All the while, the demands kept coming in from software developers, miners, bitcoin investors, and traders. Was bitcoin safe? Why was this happening?

We spoke to Andresen one evening in the middle of the crisis. "I got to get to bed," he said. "I have to maintain my sanity. I have to tell myself, 'It's not all on me.' You know, part of the open-source philosophy is sup-posed to be that if you have problems, don't expect someone to fix it for you, fix it yourself. Maybe we've done too good a job and people have be-come complacent and expect that the core development team will fix any-thing lickety-split. That's an unreasonable expectation. We are five people and only three of those are full-time."

Imagine a currency crisis of the same magnitude for a government—a quarter of the national wealth, as gauged in dollar terms, wiped out in two weeks. It's the kind of thing that happens from time to time in emerg-ing markets. Imagine the army of staff that the national finance ministry and central bank would command into action to stabilize the economy; imagine also the reinforcements of technical and financial support that would come from SWAT teams at the International Monetary Fund. Compare that to what these five men, two of them volunteers, were up against, and you get a sense of how very differently bitcoin's economy is structured, as well as the particular challenges of maintaining an open-source model such as this.

The minimalist arrangement for bitcoin's core team, right down to the bare, exposed walls and Andresen's flimsy desk in the twelve-by-twelve-foot office he sublets from a New England investment firm, reflects an organizational structure that's fundamentally decentralized. The state-

run institutions that run our monetary systems and the public corporations that effectively manage our capitalist economies are hierarchical; the
buck is supposed to stop with the CEO. So what does this mean for bitcoin, where nobody is really in charge? Andresen is a stand-in for something that doesn't exist.

It would take Andresen's team almost a month to properly fix the
bug, though Garzik's patch solution ensured that most exchanges—other
than the doomed Mt. Gox—were back up and running by the end of the
week. At its worst moment in this crisis, the price of the digital currency
would drop 32 percent, destroying $3 billion in wealth, before recover-
ing some ground in the latter part of February.

But something positive had emerged as well. Despite the chief coder's
lament over having the weight of the world on his shoulders that evening, in the end the open-source setup served bitcoin's software well in
the aftermath of the Mt. Gox meltdown, because it put many minds to
work, all with a vested interest in fixing the problem. The five core developers did most of the heavy lifting, but legions of talented coders in the community contributed thoughts and coding solutions, and they stress-tested
the core team's work. So while bitcoin's lack of centralized leadership creates the problem of having no one with whom the buck is supposed to
stop, its deep, global bench of talent often means it comes out of crises
such as this one with markedly improved software.

"Probably ten thousand of the best developers in the world are working on this project," says Chris Dixon, a partner at venture capital firm
Andreessen Horowitz. "Because they are not sitting in a building called
Bitcoin Incorporated, people seem to miss that point." Dixon says his
team "bets on computer science innovation, and since [open-source
collaboration] is how computer science innovation happens today, this is
the kind of stuff we bet on. I certainly wouldn't want to bet against the
ten thousand smartest people." This giant brain trust is a key reason why
he's not worried about the various bugs yet to be found in bitcoin's software and why he thinks the greatest innovations to be built still lie ahead.
"You read these criticisms that 'bitcoin has this flaw and bitcoin has that
flaw,' and we're like 'Well, great. Bitcoin has ten thousand people working hard on that.'"

It's not a smooth process, but this vast, worldwide community of software developers ultimately muddles its way to a consensus solution. It's not exactly democratic, either, as the five core members must ultimately decide what to do. But the core team itself uses a consultative process and pays a great deal of attention to the suggestions of the wider community with whom it communicates frequently with broadcast messages. In this way, bitcoin's open-source program, a collaborative development model that's used by countless other software projects these days, elegantly exploits the inherent wisdom of a crowd. It's why the Mt. Gox collapse actually fostered, and rapidly, some of the most brilliant cryptographic solutions for bitcoin security—if not for financial security as a whole. The decentralized, open-source arrangement means that chaos will descend upon the project from time to time, but it also means that progress and improvement can happen quickly.

The Mt. Gox collapse and the Silk Road drug bust before it helped galvanize a movement within bitcoin, one led by a growing faction of entrepreneurs and businessmen, to take a more welcoming view of regulation in what had been a lawless domain. It was time, a few quipped, for this rebellious adolescent to grow up. Going against the views of some of the early, libertarian-minded adopters, who saw government as a meddling presence that would destroy this laissez-faire project, these newcomers with less investment in bitcoin's philosophical mission now saw regulation as the route to bitcoin's salvation. Without it, they believed, the cryptocurrency would continue to be perceived by the general public as a risky fringe product and so never fulfill its potential as a disruptive technology. Naturally, such views stoked division within bitcoin's ranks, with the ideologically driven early adopters on one side and a new wave of more pragmatic "suits" on the other.

Meanwhile, law enforcement had real concerns about criminals drawn to the up-front anonymity of cryptocurrency, and financial regulators worried that investors in bitcoin and bitcoin products were vulnerable to fraud. But regulating cryptocurrencies was easier said than done because of what might be called the starfish challenge.

In their 2006 book, *The Starfish and the Spider: The Unstoppable Power of Leaderless Organizations*, Ori Brafman and Rod Beckstrom developed a metaphor to explain the power of the kind of open-source collaboration and *decentralized* decision-making that defines bitcoin. If you cut off a spider's leg, it is crippled, and if you cut off its head, it dies, the authors tell us. But if you cut off a starfish's leg, it grows a new one, and the dislodged leg can grow into an entirely new starfish. As for a head or brain, it has none. Similarly, a decentralized organization has no central point of vulnerability and is thus virtually impossible to shut down or destroy. Brafman and Beckstrom explore some contemporary Internet organizations that thrived under the starfishlike advantages of decentralization: Wikipedia, Craigslist, and Skype, for example. They also cite cases from outside the Net: the leaderless Alcoholics Anonymous, the Apache tribe, and the ultimate decentralized institution of our era, al-Qaeda.

The experiences of Napster and BitTorrent are also instructive. While the former's groundbreaking file-sharing service posed a challenge to record companies' control of the music business, its network was *centralized*, controlled on an identifiable server. Thus, government agents, armed with copyright-infringement judgments, were ultimately able to shut it down. BitTorrent, by contrast, resides nowhere in particular. It's impossible to shut down, which is why its file-sharing service has survived.

What makes this possible for BitTorrent, as it does for bitcoin, is a *distributed* network—the ultimate form of decentralization—as per a schema on network structure laid out by computing pioneer Paul Baran in an influential 1964 paper. With bitcoin, so long as no single miner garners control of 51 percent of the hashing power, the mining network that administers the monetary system has a fully distributed power structure. No single entity anywhere has control over the system, which means it has no vulnerable point of attack. This is not to say there aren't vulnerabilities in the ecosystem that has been built *around* that network—in flawed exchanges such as Mt. Gox, whose problems of recentralized control we'll explore later, or in bugs attached to software that interacts with that ecosystem as the one described above. But the distributed network itself, the ad hoc group of computers that collectively decides on what bitcoin is and how it should function, is virtually impossible to shut down.

How were regulators to confront this dilemma? Without a CEO in charge of the currency or anyone to subpoena, how do you control the bitcoin economy? The law is designed to deal with centralized institutions in which identifiable managers are deemed responsible for an organization's conduct.

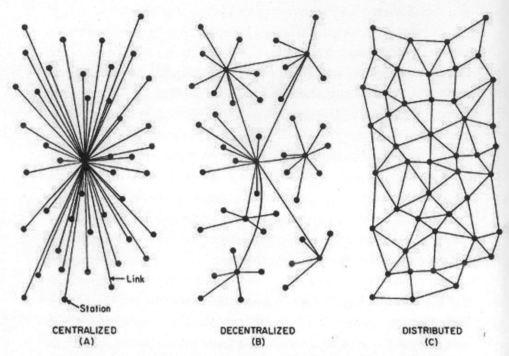

Paul Baran's Degrees of Network Centralization/Decentralization
*(As seen in Paul Baran's 1964 article "On Distributed
Communications Networks" at Computer HistoryMuseum.com;
image courtesy of Computer History Museum)*

One incident whose recounting tends to elicit smug laughs from audiences at bitcoin conferences illustrates the problem. In June 2013, the California Division of Financial Institutions served a cease-and-desist letter on the Bitcoin Foundation saying it needed a proper money-transmission license from the state. But the foundation doesn't actually do any business; its mission is to promote bitcoin adoption, liaise with governments on regulatory matters, and fund development work to safeguard the cryptocurrency's open-source protocol. But if not them, who?

It's still often hard for many lawmakers to get their heads around the nature of the challenge they face. In February 2014, West Virginia Democratic senator Joe Manchin called for bitcoin to be banned. But what would this involve? You could make it illegal, but that would come up for immediate constitutional challenges. What exactly are you banning people from owning? Digital code? At its core it's a form of communication.

That implies First Amendment rights. Or is it a commodity, something to be traded in return for something else? If so, that would raise issues with commercial and property rights. It's hard to see how bitcoin could be captured under a legal definition of controlled goods such as child pornography or illegal drugs. Still, the biggest point of all: How do you police it? It's the BitTorrent problem again. There's no central server for the Feds to shut down.

Yet, notwithstanding bitcoiners' belief in the invincibility of their cryptocurrency domain, governments are equipped with immense legal power. They have all sorts of ways to make life difficult for cryptocurrency. As Gareth Murphy, the director of markets supervision at the Central Bank of Ireland, said at a bitcoin conference in Dublin, the audience "shouldn't be surprised if Moses came down from the mountain with the law."

In the United States, the first descent from the mountaintop was the FBI's 2013 bust of Silk Road. While this marked a serious reputational hit for bitcoin and left a negative impression in the minds of both government officials and the general public, it arguably paved the way for regulators to engage with the bitcoin community in a more constructive way. Since the FBI had seized bitcoins and planned to hold them for auction, it implicitly acknowledged that these strings of digital code had some real value. In a backhanded way it was a stamp of legitimacy. What's more, the operation's apparent success made bitcoin less daunting for U.S. law enforcement. Officials learned they could use the blockchain as a tool to trace transactions and keep tabs on users, if not easily identify them.

One month after the bust, the Treasury Department's Financial Crimes Enforcement Network, or FinCEN, took a surprisingly accommodating approach to cryptocurrency. FinCEN issued guidelines treating bitcoin payment processors and exchanges as legal entities that would need to register with it and would have to comply with state-by-state rules on money-transmitter licenses. This set the stage for a much-anticipated Senate hearing in November 2013, where FinCEN director Jennifer Shasky Calvery uttered words that overjoyed all but the most doctrinaire of bitcoiners: "The decision to bring virtual currency within the scope of our regulatory framework should be viewed by those who respect and obey the basic rule of law as a positive development for this sector. It recognizes the innovation virtual currencies provide, and the benefits they might offer society."

The government had spoken. Not only was it not too worried about cryptocurrency, it saw advantages in it. And if bitcoiners were not big fans of government regulation, the FinCEN rules were simply an extension of those that had long applied to dollar-based remittance providers, payment processors, and foreign-exchange services. It was, on paper at least, equal treatment. Bitcoin businesses had been given legitimacy.

But this was just the beginning. Legitimacy needed more than a federal agency's blessing, especially in the United States, where the business of transmitting money is a state concern as a well as a federal one. Bitcoin businesses still had to be licensed by these states, which in turn required them to explain their unfamiliar activities to each state's agency and to prove they had compliance procedures in place to prevent money laundering and other nefarious uses of money-transfer systems. Getting licensed was laborious, unpredictable, bureaucratic, and lengthy.

Some states, such as Texas, took a deliberately accommodating stance, deciding that cryptocurrencies didn't fall within the bounds of their rules and so could be allowed to function without a license. That led a bunch of storefronts in tech-friendly Texan locales such as Austin to set up bitcoin ATMs to allow people to convert in or out of bitcoin and cash on the spot. Meanwhile, many businesses kept operating elsewhere on the assumption they would eventually get licensed in the states that mattered. Even so, much of the customer outreach for bitcoin start-ups stalled—even if those firms continued to undertake innovation and development at a breakneck pace—because without licenses from most states their management teams weren't sure if they'd be prosecuted. These bureaucratic delays meant that U.S.-based bitcoin exchanges such as Kraken and CoinMKT struggled to compete with far less regulated competitors in Europe such as Bitstamp and BTC-e.

Around the time of Shasky Calvery's Senate appearance, New York's Department of Financial Services' ambitious superintendent, Benjamin Lawsky, said he was exploring the idea of a special "BitLicense" to lay down rules tailor-made for the digital-currency industry. Given New York's prominence in the world of finance, many in the bitcoin community expected this would become a template for other states to follow. Lawsky took a proactive approach. In February the following year, he held hearings on bitcoin regulation, at which some of the more well-heeled and better-connected newcomers to bitcoin entrepreneurship got to testify, including Tyler and Cameron Winklevoss, SecondMarket CEO Barry Silbert, and Jeremy Allaire of Circle Financial. After the hearings, Lawsky took to Reddit to conduct one of that social forum's AMA (Ask Me Anything) sessions. This was a bold but strategically astute move. Reddit's bitcoin community can be a tough, unruly bunch, and they aren't known for deference to authority.

Lawsky fared pretty well in that forum. He broke the ice by admitting he was a Reddit neophyte. The bitcoiners were mostly polite in response, asking tough but practical questions. One person cited the U.K. bank HSBC, which had just agreed to a no-guilt $1.9 billion settlement with the U.S. government over charges it did business with Mexican drug cartels, and asked, "Why does Bitcoin get the hammer when everything else just slides under the radar when it comes to money laundering?" But most asked questions about what kinds of bitcoin transactions would come under money-transmitter rules and Lawsky's definitions of "virtual currency." His responses suggested he'd be open to a constructive dialogue with the community on these matters.

As bitcoin businesses awaited the new licensing rules in New York, they continued to face obstacles to gaining legitimacy, among them the caution bordering on paranoia of bankers. Ever since the post-9/11 Patriot Act and other initiatives launched to starve terrorists and other bad guys of funds (with limited success), banks had beefed up their compliance teams, whose officers were charged with implementing tough new anti-money-laundering (AML) and know-your-customer (KYC) rules. Their power was ramped up further in the wake of the financial crisis as the Dodd-Frank Act's multifaceted overhaul of the U.S. financial system made banks even more concerned about falling afoul of their government overseers. Compliance officers' first responses to a customer whose business model was slightly outside the ordinary were to say no and then perhaps try to figure things out later. In this environment, the word *bitcoin* was like a *leper* label. Many in the cryptocurrency industry had to set up banking relationships overseas and find other ways to jury-rig their operations.

It was hard to get around not having a bank account. Not everyone could be like Blockchain, the wallet-and-bitcoin-analytics firm that paid staff and suppliers in bitcoin and had no regular bank account. The London-based company stood for the bank-free ideal that bitcoiners dreamed of, but for now most firms found it extremely difficult to replicate. How would they interact with suppliers and customers who expected to pay or be paid in fiat currency? It was especially difficult for bitcoin exchanges, which without a bank account were reduced to taking, storing, and paying out hard cash in return for bitcoin trading. This was hardly a way to scale up operations.

The problem couldn't be entirely blamed on overzealous bank compliance officers, either. The signals banks received from government were ambiguous and contradictory. FinCEN was accommodating toward bitcoin, and the Federal Reserve was ambivalent—Fed chairwoman Janet Yellen pointed out during one hearing on Capitol Hill that the Fed had no authority to supervise bitcoin, kicking the issue back to lawmakers to resolve. However, bitcoiners would report that agents from the Federal Deposit Insurance Corporation, the body charged with cleaning up failed banks so that insured depositors can be kept whole, were pressuring bank compliance officers not to work with bitcoiners. It's hard to verify this claim. The FDIC had long communicated its concerns to bankers over supposedly high-risk categories of merchants, and bitcoin businesses were told by bank compliance officers they were included in those groups. But there's no blanket policy; FDIC supervisors use their discretion in each case. However, in the wake of Mt. Gox's $500 million bankruptcy—whose relevance to this debate we'll come to later—it wouldn't have been surprising if bitcoin seemed high risk to the FDIC. Unlike Mt. Gox's creditors, its Japanese bank, Mizuho, avoided big losses, but its involvement in that mess would have reminded FDIC officials of the risks when banks engaged with bitcoin businesses.

The U.S. Department of Justice, too, sent banks messages that contradicted FinCEN's accommodating message. In 2013, the DOJ launched an initiative known as Operation Choke Point, in which it investigated banks dealing with merchants in businesses that weren't necessarily illegal but were considered high fraud risks. Miami-based lawyer Andrew Ittleman, who has become something of an accidental expert on the subject, told us that Operation Choke Point now occupied most of his time and that primarily his clients were legal providers of bitcoin services and medical marijuana, along with a few pornographers and gun dealers. The law was having a chilling effect: banks might not be breaking the law by servicing such businesses, but the risk of an audit from the DOJ was enough to dissuade them from doing so. Ittleman fought hard for his clients, who were denied a vital instrument of financial access, but it was an uphill battle. The matter, he said, should be taken up to the Supreme Court by civil rights activists such as the American Civil Liberties Union.

Around the same time that the U.S. regulatory debated heated up, the same began to happen in other countries. The People's Bank of China also began using banks to keep bitcoin under control, though in a more blunt fashion. Eventually, a formal ruling came down in April 2014 explicitly barring Chinese banks from dealing with bitcoin business. After that, the European Banking Authority, the continental supervisory body created in the aftermath of the euro crisis, weighed in; in July it advised each member nation's bank supervisory agency to "discourage credit institutions, payment institutions, and e-money institutions from buying, holding, or selling virtual currencies" until a "substantial body of regulation" had been drawn up to address risks associated with them. The Bitcoin Foundation's chief government-liaison officer, Jim Harper, said the EBA had gone beyond its own pledge to "identify risks arising from financial activities, prioritise them, and take mitigating action, if required." Instead of mitigation, he said, it had taken preemptive action that emphasized "stopping the integration of digital currency into Europe's financial services system."

Harper, a D.C.-based fellow at the libertarian think tank the Cato Institute, had been hired by the foundation in March 2014; he would soon be very busy. Beyond the actions taken in the United States, Beijing, and Brussels, various emerging-market countries issued stern statements. Bolivia said it would ban bitcoin outright; Bangladesh warned bitcoin traders they could be jailed under anti-money-laundering laws; Russian regulators released a damning statement that declared the ruble to be the only legal currency in Russia; and while Ecuador opened the door to digital money, it said it could be issued only by its central bank.

Back in the United States, on March 25, just in time for the April 15 tax-filing deadline, the Internal Revenue Service came out with hotly anticipated guidance, declaring that bitcoin was not a currency in the legal sense. Nor was it a commodity. Rather, it was "property," like real estate or stocks, and was subject to the same capital-gains taxes if its value changed. It was the first bid at clarifying how bitcoin transactions should be counted for tax purposes.

In a sense, this move codified bitcoin within the legal framework. Some, especially those who were trying to create an investment vehicle out of bitcoin, were happy that it would be treated like any other investment and would not be subject to income taxes, which are typically higher than capital-gains taxes. But the overall community's stated goal was not to make bitcoin a speculative vehicle but rather a medium of payment. Capital-gains tax rules could make using bitcoin as a currency a logistical nightmare. It meant that when U.S. citizens filed taxes, they had to account for every single bitcoin acquired, sold, or used for purchases, and the prices and dates at which those transactions happened. If you purchased 0.5 bitcoins at $360 in April 2014 and sold them for $645 on June 9, you'd have to declare that gain as a taxable event in 2015. Fair enough. But did you have to account for swings in the value if you used your bitcoin to purchase a vacation on Expedia or to order a pizza? The IRS's move seemed to undermine bitcoin's potential for use as a currency.

On the positive side, the IRS had at least removed uncertainty as to how digital currencies would be treated for tax purposes, and there was reason to believe that after a review it would come up with exemptions to ease the compliance burden. What's more, ever-inventive bitcoin technologists did what many do when regulations arrive: they saw it as a new opportunity for innovation. Techies began to dream up apps that would permanently track a person's bitcoin transactions and spit out a net gain or loss for the year and a permanent record come tax time.

A few months later, in July, Lawsky at the NYDFS finally came out with his BitLicense proposal. Any entity in the business of storing, exchanging, or sending "virtual currency" in New York would require a license, the outline said, and would need to meet various criteria designed to protect against money laundering, terrorist financing, and other illicit activities. These included compliance officers to assess customers' profiles for both digital-currency and fiat-currency operations, maintaining an as-yet-unspecified amount of backup capital, updates with the department every time the company changed its business model (which was sometimes monthly for small, rapidly changing start-ups), and—most challeng-ingly—a store of "virtual currency" equivalent to whatever amount the firm held on behalf of customers. It was a heavy load.

Some of bitcoin's bigger fish initially lauded the announcement —perhaps prematurely. "We are pleased that Superintendent Lawsky and the Department of Financial Services have embraced bitcoin and digital assets and created a regulatory framework that protects consum-ers," Cameron Winklevoss said in an e-mail. Indeed, these rules weren't a big problem for well-capitalized firms that already maintained a com-pliance infrastructure—the Winklevoss twins' bitcoin trust fund, for example—and might even give them a competitive advantage. But most bitcoiners were alarmed by what they saw. The draft seemed to cast a net far beyond exchanges and payment processors, suggesting that any little start-up in a San Francisco garage could suddenly be stifled with red tape. Many felt its burdens were far more onerous than those with which banks had to comply—banks needed just one set of compliance officers, not two, and could get away with simply segregating proprietor and cus-tomer accounts instead of also having to hold one-to-one capital against their clients' holdings. Meanwhile, Perianne Boring, the founder of the newly formed Digital Chamber of Commerce, argued that the absence of a distinction between digital assets and digital currency in the pro-posed rules could stifle new blockchain applications. What this meant for all the Bitcoin 2.0 projects simply wasn't clear. Many bitcoiners felt the BitLicense proposal was deliberately discriminatory because it had breached a long-standing regulatory principle of not making laws "tech-nology specific"—i.e., that authorities should regulate the particular business activity, not the technology handling that activity.

The bitcoin community's response was swift, demonstrating how well organized this ad hoc, global group had become. A petition quickly cir-culated and was signed by hundreds, including a who's who of bitcoin. It called for an extension of the forty-five-day comment period that Lawsky had set, arguing that this was an inordinately short period for poorly funded tech firms with limited experience on Wall Street. Some suggested more drastic action and started lobbying New York State lawmakers in Albany to rein in Lawsky, framing him as a killer of innovation and new job creation in New York. Most dramatically, Circle CEO Jeremy

Allaire, perhaps the bitcoiner with the best connections to the political establishment,* wrote a powerful blog post arguing that his high-profile and well-funded retail bitcoin service might have to shut out people with New York ISP addresses. Allaire posited that it would be "devastating" for bitcoin if the New York BitLicense became a template for other states.

The pressure clearly had some effect. Lawsky agreed to another forty-five-day extension and said the proposal was not intended to trap little tech outfits. Conceding that the NYDFS didn't have "a monopoly on the truth," he said the agency was "seriously" considering some of the counterproposals coming in. At the time of writing, the process was still ongoing, and it wasn't clear what the result would be, but it's worth pondering whether some of the sweeping implications that bitcoiners laid out had sunk in. The idea of "geofencing" ISPs, hinted at by Allaire, captured the extent of the geographic fragmentation that these rules might generate. So, too, did another notion discussed on bitcoin chat rooms: that bitcoins processed by firms unlicensed in New York would be viewed as inferior to those that were licensed, creating a bifurcated marketplace where suspect, "dirty" coins would be quoted at a discounted price compared to "clean" ones. That would be counterproductive to the idea of a fluid, global standard price for a digital currency. As Harper of the Bitcoin Foundation points out, it would also be counterproductive for regulators seeking to control the flow of money, as it would push bitcoin business into unregulated areas outside these U.S. agencies' regulatory purview. Indeed, as the elation generated by the FinCEN hearings in November gave way to dismay at New York's initially ham-fisted handling of the BitLicense, some U.S.-initiated bitcoin businesses started making this happen. They moved.

It's an axiom of finance that in a globalized economy, businesses will respond to regulation and tax burdens by moving operations to where they are less inhibiting. The phenomenon is known as regulatory arbitrage, because it allows businesses to leverage one location's lax posture to extract an easier stance from another. In 2014, the problem became a political lightning rod in the United States as company after company engineered

---

* Allaire represents the digital-currency industry as a member of the Treasury's Bank Secrecy Act Advisory Group.

"inversion" mergers, acquiring competitors overseas and then co-opting their corporate headquarters to lower their U.S. corporate tax bill. Island nations in the Caribbean and autonomous British territories in the English Channel have built entire economic models around such ideas, with somewhere between $5 trillion and $32 trillion said to be held offshore in such tax havens.

The same opportunistic reactions to regulation are already occurring in the cryptocurrency world. With their decentralized, distributed networks, cryptocurrencies epitomize the untethered institutions of our digital, global age. So, not surprisingly, as the world's regulatory landscape takes shape, the cryptocurrency equivalents of the Cayman Islands are being founded.

Certain Eastern and Central European countries have adopted an accommodating stance toward digital currency and have become home to bitcoin exchanges as a result. BTC-e, one of the biggest bitcoin exchanges, is based in Bulgaria, whose tax agency formally recognized digital currency and set a low 10 percent tax rate on bitcoin income gains. Its rival Bitstamp resides in Slovenia, while the digital-currency-denominated stock exchange MPEx has set up shop in Romania. But businesses are also taking advantage of more open-door policies in much larger, more established economies.

One is Switzerland, situated conveniently outside the reach of the European Union's new regulatory bodies but with all the trappings of an advanced Western European economy and highly sophisticated financial and technology industries. The Swiss Financial Market Supervisory Authority announced in June that it didn't intend to draft special rules for bitcoin because for now existing rules imposed on financial firms would suffice. This hands-off approach has turned the country into a mecca for financial cryptography projects, according to Chris Odom, who runs the decentralized-networks project Open Transactions out of the Alpine town of Zug. Among Open Transactions' neighbors in what Odom calls Crypto Valley are Ethereum, the high-profile Blockchain 2.0 operator, bitcoin ATM provider Bitcoin Suisse, and various nonfinancial cryptography projects such as ProtonMail and Silent Circle, which provide securely encrypted e-mail and telephone services.

Even in the United Kingdom, which is within the European Union but often goes its own way on tax and regulatory rules, the prospect is for an easier hand for cryptocurrency. In August 2014, Chancellor of the Exchequer George Osborne said the United Kingdom would launch a comprehensive study to figure out how to take advantage of cryptocurrency technology and devise rules to turn Britain into "the global center for financial innovation." Though some worried about a repeat of New York's BitLicense disappointment, Osborne's words certainly sounded encouraging. He said digital-currency-based "alternative payment systems are popular as they are quick, cheap, and convenient" and that he wants to "see if we can make more use of them for the benefit of the U.K. economy." Even before then, various bitcoin firms had chosen to make London their home, including Blockchain and Coinfloor, a high-tech, fully regulated bitcoin exchange. What's more, a number of the U.K. tax-haven islands are competing to become the world's most cryptocurrency-friendly locales. The first fully regulated bitcoin investment fund was launched in the Channel Island of Jersey, and the Isle of Man announced that bitcoin exchanges were free to operate there without a license.

In the same way that Switzerland and the Channel Islands present alternatives to the heavier hand of the rest of Europe, Mexico and Canada can woo cryptocurrency business from the United States. The Canadian government broke its silence on bitcoin regulation in June 2014, albeit vaguely, as it included a reference to "virtual currencies" in a sweeping bill designed to update laws on money transmission and money-laundering protections. While that implied that an era of laissez-faire opportunity in Canada could be closing for bitcoin companies, many saw it as an encouraging sign, one that legitimized their industry and gave it the same treatment as existing financial services. Already, Canada's biggest cities were becoming mini digital-currency hubs. Toronto boasts an aggressive accelerator known as Bitcoin Decentral and is home to digital-wallet provider KryptoKit. Meanwhile, VirtEx, which operates a digital-currency exchange and makes bitcoin debit cards, is based in Calgary, and the world's first bitcoin ATM was installed in a café in downtown Vancouver. As for Mexico, in July its government announced it would study the prospect of creating a blockchain-based digital peso and explore how the country might leverage the benefits of decentralized cryptocurrency networks to attack corruption. Though it was thin on details, this was an unprecedented statement, suggesting a forward-looking view of the block-chain's potential to keep officials and their business associates accountable.

After the People's Bank of China's antibitcoin directives to its banks, a number of the nation's cryptocurrency businesses relocated to Hong Kong, where the charter left over from the United Kingdom's 1997 hand-over to China and its status as a financial hub all but guarantee an open-market, laissez-faire stance. ANX and Bitfinex, two of the most high-tech bitcoin exchanges in the world, are based there. The only problem is that Hong Kong's banks, which do a great deal of business with counterparts in the United States and China, are often wary of new bitcoin businesses. "All the banks are crazy scared about this compliance stuff," says Aurélien Menant, cofounder and CEO of bitcoin exchange Gatecoin, who also runs a program for bitcoin-based charities around Asia. "You can really easily open and register a company. You can easily get a license. But then . . . as soon as you are registered as a money-service business, you are going to be blacklisted" by banks, he told us during a visit to the territory. It's a reminder of the vast, indirect influence that both Washington and New York have over the financial world.

With Hong Kong banks concerned about keeping both Beijing and New York happy, Singapore, with its rather contradictory mix of author-itarian government and free-market economic principles, represents a friendlier territory for running bitcoin businesses out of Asia. Interna-tional bitcoin-payments processor GoCoin, which includes bitcoin's self-proclaimed "serial dealmaker" Brock Pierce as a founder, is headquartered in the city-state. Like any reputable cryptocurrency hub, Singapore has some established bitcoin exchanges, including FYB-SG and First Meta, though the latter has come under some scrutiny following the untimely death of its twenty-eight-year-old American CEO, Autumn Radtke, in March 2014. After explicitly stating in 2013 that it would not intervene in businesses that choose to trade in bitcoin, the Monetary Authority of Singapore said in March the following year that bitcoin exchanges would have to fulfill regular anti-money-laundering compliance requirements. But generally, Singapore's government has shown itself cautiously inter-ested in encouraging cryptocurrency innovation. According to one re-port, giant, state-owned conglomerate Temasek Holdings, a pillar of

Singapore's financial establishment, has been experimenting with bitcoin investments in its $300 billion portfolio of investment assets.

Singapore's March 2014 move to regulate bitcoin came in the wake of a difficult period for the cryptocurrency. The bad-news headlines came thickly in the late Northern winter, giving skeptics and outsiders what they saw as "proof" that bitcoin was an anything-goes world of drug dealers, hackers, and underregulated online exchanges that could run off with your money at a moment's notice. To those who'd bet big on building out this technology, the businessmen plowing money into it, the developments amounted to an existential crisis for their beloved cryptocurrency, one that they felt demanded a more orderly infrastructure of regulation.

It began in late January with the arrest of Charlie Shrem, the twenty-four-year-old head of the New York–based bitcoin brokerage BitInstant and vice chairman of the Bitcoin Foundation, on charges—later reduced in a plea deal—that he had conspired with a customer of Silk Road to launder drug money. But even more important were the subsequent developments at Mt. Gox, which just spiraled out of control. It halted customer withdrawals and blamed its problems on a universal bitcoin-software glitch, inviting the DDOS-like attack that denied Gavin Andresen a decent night's sleep, all before collapsing into total bankruptcy on February 28 with an announcement that it had "lost" 850,000 coins worth $500 million. Two hundred thousand of those coins were later "found" after some members of the bitcoin community said they had traced blockchain transactions back to Mt. Gox–owned wallets that the exchange had, mysteriously, failed to include in its bankruptcy filing. As of the time of writing, the remainder had yet to be accounted for.

It's hard to imagine a bigger abuse of investors than that of the 127,000 who were left high and dry when Mt. Gox collapsed. Their experience captures the inherent problems in melding the unregulated, decentralized, and laissez-faire world of bitcoin with the ordered, centralized world of traditional currencies and commercial law. For investors, Mt. Gox represented the worst of both worlds. On one hand, it was unregulated, with neither Japan's nor the United States' financial and securities trading laws able at that time to properly place bitcoin businesses in their framework for regulation. After the exchange collapsed and a Japanese bankruptcy court began to process the multitude of claims from all around the world, it faced a fundamental dilemma: What, from the perspective of Japanese law, is a bitcoin? And on that basis, what is it actually worth? Other un-regulated exchanges such as Bitstamp and BTC-e might have been saying that one bitcoin was worth $600, but if we can't legally define a bitcoin, how can we trust those prices? Were all these creditors' claims worth any-thing at all?

On the other hand—although it might seem odd to say so—Mt. Gox was an old-world, traditional institution in the sense that it assumed cen-tralized control of people's funds. By allowing people to exchange dol-lars and other traditional currencies for bitcoin, it gave people an "on-ramp" into the "trustless," transparent, and decentralized environment of the blockchain, yet to get them there it carried them through the kind of trust-dependent, centralized environment that bitcoin was designed to upend. There were no ways around this, given that one-half of every bitcoin pur-chase or sale involved a noncryptocurrency such as the dollar or yen and these did not reside on a decentralized blockchain. But the upshot was that you had to trust Mt. Gox with your money. Even after you had com-pleted a trade to buy bitcoin, you still had no blockchain-based control over those coins until Mt. Gox complied with a request to transfer them to your personal wallet. It wasn't much different from having an account at a Wall Street brokerage. If it went under, you had no automatic, direct control over your assets; you simply had a claim on the bankrupt institu-tion, one that you hoped a court would enforce.

Many cryptocurrency developers have become uncomfortable with this reversion to centralized models. Some, such as Odom at Open Trans-actions, are now working on software solutions based on decentralizing principles that would allow people to move in and out of these different cryptocurrency and fiat-currency realms without having to invest trust in centralized servers. Whether such a crypto-technological fix is needed, or whether stricter regulation of these centralized exchanges is the way to go, is open to debate. Either way, it's hard to imagine a more egregious abuse of centralized trust than that of Mt. Gox. That's not because its owner stole the coins—there are no well-founded claims to that effect—but because the whole operation was set up with none of the fiduciary duties of care typically required of regulated finance businesses. When former New Jersey governor John Corzine's MF Global collapsed in 2011, its investors discovered with dismay that the brokerage had dipped into the segregated accounts that were supposed to protect their funds from being used for the firm's own account. But if that was bad, it appears Mt. Gox had no segregation of accounts whatsoever. All the bitcoins were controlled by the exchange in its own wallets.

So Mt. Gox was centralized *and* unregulated. In this environment, virtually all decision-making responsibility at this company of some three dozen employees resided with CEO Mark Karpelès. Reuters reported that only Karpelès knew the passwords to the Mt. Gox wallets and that he refused a 2012 request from employees to expand access in the event that he became incapacitated. On top of that, at least to some, he doesn't come across as the kind of person you want running the world's biggest digital-currency exchange with such concentrated authority.

During the hacking attack of June 2011, when the price dropped to near zero and the exchange had to cancel, or reverse, mountains of outstanding orders, Roger Ver and his high school buddy Jesse Powell gleaned insights into this. They set themselves up in Mt. Gox's Tokyo offices to try to sort out the mess and revive the exchange, then a crucial part of the bitcoin economy. Working through and reconciling ten thousand canceled or stalled tickets, they slogged away with other Mt. Gox employees over the weekend, only to find that Karpelès took those two days off. "It was sort of perplexing," recalls Powell, now the CEO of San Francisco–based bitcoin exchange Kraken, who also says that Karpelès acknowledged to him then that Mt. Gox had lost four thousand bitcoins in the hacking attack. "In hindsight," Powell says, "I can't help but wonder if he discovered he lost a lot more than that and had to take the weekend off to collect himself."

To be fair, while Ver and Powell were busy getting Mt. Gox back on its feet, Karpelès was doing his part to restore confidence in the exchange, albeit in a way that would seem bizarre for modern financial institutions with normal auditing procedures. Interacting on bitcoin forums with other bitcoiners via his MagicalTux username, Karpelès pulled off a stunt to prove Mt. Gox's solvency. He told his online correspondents to keep their eyes on two particular bitcoin addresses via a live, online blockchain monitor and that he would transfer 424,242.424242* bitcoins between them. It was the cryptocurrency equivalent of the old "wall of money" that bank managers of years past would put behind their tellers to dissuade panicked depositors from engaging in a bank run. After he moved such a large amount of coins, the maneuver had its desired effect. Such a massive handover of bitcoins suggested Mt. Gox was more flush than everyone feared. Three years later the blockchain-embedded history of this exercise, in which Karpelès effectively identified those addresses as belonging to Mt. Gox wallets, provided the starting point from which a posse of bitcoiners would trace the blockchain to discover two hundred thousand coins that were still present in Mt. Gox's accounts.

Many theories would later develop tying those events to the disappearance of the remaining 650,000 bitcoins in 2014. One of the more elaborate holds that Mt. Gox lost far more bitcoins than it let on during the 2011 hack, and that Karpelès relied on an ever-rising bitcoin price after that to make it seem as if all were normal. If so, it was like a Ponzi scheme to undo losses rather than make personal profit. It would mean that as the value of Mt. Gox's unsegregated bitcoin holdings rose as more and more investors signed on, Karpelès traded for Mt. Gox's account with those remaining holdings, then booked profits to meet redemptions from investors who were none the wiser to what had happened. But when things got tough in 2013—when the U.S. government froze Mt. Gox's U.S. accounts, for example—moving funds around became difficult, and it became harder and harder to stay on that Ponzi treadmill. Finally the 2014 price collapse made the whole game impossible—or so the theory holds. Another theory holds that Karpelès, with his complete control over the private keys to the wallets, simply lost them, making the bitcoins irretrievable. A third theory is the one Mt. Gox stands by: that it lost its coins as a result of the transaction malleability glitch, that its system just repeatedly

---

* This appears to be a play on a popular meme from Douglas Adams's comical science-fiction novel *Life, the Universe and Everything* in which the answer to the meaning of life is discovered to be the number 42, the problem being that the question to which it is an answer is unknown. The meme enjoys a cult following among coders.

and mistakenly responded to rogue operators' fraudulent requests to re-send money. But to many, it just seemed implausible that Mt. Gox could not have noticed a scam of such proportions. Adam Levine, a bitcoin talk-show host and developer who was in the hunt to find the missing Mt. Gox coins, said it was as if "brick by brick somebody comes and steals your entire house from under you while you're doing business in it and you never notice."

We may never know what happened. Our repeated attempts to get Karpelès to respond to the various accusations and theories elicited a few, limited e-mail responses whose contents were insufficient to permit a clear characterization of his position. He would sometimes explain that the in-vestigation undertaken by the bankruptcy court limited his ability to re-spond. But clearly, the management structure of Mt. Gox was unworkable for a financial institution of this size. Karpelès was effectively CEO, CTO, CFO, and chief compliance officer rolled into one. His 2011 wallet trans-fer might have had the impressive effect of a George Bailey–like stunt in Jimmy Stewart's classic portrayal of a bank run in *It's a Wonderful Life,* but that was no way to run a modern financial exchange. Clients had zero protection, their trust lodged entirely in this man. Marrying bitcoin's de-centralized Wild West to an excessively centralized model of trust was a disaster waiting to happen. When it did, the pressure to regulate bitcoin became unstoppable and created tensions within the bitcoin community.

Bitcoin's "suits" started getting serious—regulation, security, compliance, and engaging Wall Street's know-how suddenly made sense. BitGo's highly secure multi-sig wallet came out at this time, offering a digital version of the dual-key system used by Swiss bankers to give customers access to their valuables in deposit boxes. Firms such as Circle and Xapo rolled out their insured depository services to give customers peace of mind.

Meanwhile, the Winklevoss twins progressed with a request at the U.S. Securities and Exchange Commission to have their Winklevoss Bit-coin Trust properly authorized as the first bitcoin-focused exchange-traded fund, a move that would allow people to invest in bitcoin without having to own the coins directly. Later, Atlas ATS launched a network of glob-ally interlinked exchanges with technology from Perseus Telecom that ac-commodated the heavy-bandwidth demands of the high-frequency trading firms and provided sophisticated, computer-driven compliance to manage sensitive customer relations. Bitcoin enthusiast Barry Silbert launched his own bitcoin fund, which claimed a backdoor route to federal regulatory approval that supposedly beat the "Winklevii" in the race to offer a regulated bitcoin fund to ordinary, lower-income Americans. Silbert also started building his own exchange, one designed to have traditional clearinghouse capabilities, brokerage-owned seats, and the same self-regulatory structure that's fundamental to how Wall Street now functions. It would, he said, "look like the New York Stock Exchange" and "nothing like Mt. Gox."

However, a clearinghouse-based stock exchange—which has a communal fund to make sure all trades are settled within a specified, short time—implies the hubs-and-spokes structure of a centralized institution. These kinds of solutions, all aimed at building investors' trust, aren't a departure at all from the Mt. Gox problem. Users are still compelled to trust a single counterparty. The question is whether such institutions are needed to win over ordinary people and keep regulators at bay.

That the emerging bitcoin business community was making a case for this was deeply disturbing to puritan anarchist types that unflinchingly embraced the mind-set of a second scenario. With a large number of brainy techies in their midst, this rebellious faction went in search of new cryptographic tools to make it even harder for regulators to influence and control a decentralized bitcoin network. Their most radical solution was called Dark Wallet. The brainchild of an American crypto-anarchist named Cody Wilson and his Iranian British hacker colleague Amir Taaki, Dark Wallet is a "mixing" service. It takes transactions, breaks them into smaller pieces, and runs them through multiple wallets and addresses to create an indecipherable array of dense data. For Wilson, this meant being true to a philosophy of protecting privacy and reflected a deep desire to return bitcoin to what he saw as its core reason for being: an instrument of personal freedom.

Wilson believes that people who'd once believed in bitcoin's liberty-seeking qualities have been seduced by money and power. "A bunch of start-ups are coming in—ostensibly libertarian—and saying [to government], 'Look, we can do this for you,'" he told us. "It's the easy money. And that's creating a narrative about bitcoin, a conversation that's easy to have, one that says, 'Actually, bitcoin in the end is your partner. It's your friend. Look, it will help the banking system; it will help the regulatory system.' . . . People who three years ago were pretty radical are now putting on a suit and tie and just throwing in the towel and saying, 'Even if bitcoin can't be a thing that will change the world, I can make a lot of money. I can enter the kingdom.' "

Dark Wallet was a response to that. Elsewhere, Wilson was quoted describing it as a way to "mock every attempt to sprinkle [bitcoin] with regulation," and to say to government, " 'You've set yourself up to regulate bitcoin. Regulate this.' " Wilson, who'd previously made a name for himself by designing the first 3-D-printed gun, had no qualms, he said, about his project becoming a vehicle for money laundering, drug dealing, kiddie porn, or terrorism. His response: "Liberty is a dangerous thing." This was hardly a way to take bitcoin into the mainstream, but that wasn't his objective. If Dark Wallet achieved freedom for only those at the fringes of society, so be it.

The response in the bitcoin community to Dark Wallet was divided. The hard-core libertarians loved it. Some techies were impressed—Gavin Andresen, the Bitcoin Foundation's chief scientist, called the technology "fantastic" and said that more "privacy is better," though he also expected regulations to catch up. Andresen's praise was somewhat ironic given that Wilson and his cofounder, Amir Taaki, had repeatedly mocked the foundation as a vehicle for bitcoin business interests to ingratiate themselves with the Washington establishment. However, the freelance journalist, commentator, and bitcoin entrepreneur Ryan Selkis articulated what must have worried many of those businessmen. Dark Wallet opened up "a regulatory nightmare" for bitcoin. "Telling the most powerful government in the world to go screw itself while you're in your infancy certainly makes for excellent theater, but it also burns everyone else in the bitcoin community in the process," wrote Selkis, whose blog carries the moniker *TwoBitIdiot*. "The big issue is whether dark wallets and dark markets will make all bitcoiners look guilty by association."

Thus the tensions between centralizing interests of bitcoin businessmen and the pure vision of a decentralized utopia were again thrust into the noisy public arena in which this community discusses and debates its ideas. A similar division arises when Blockchain 2.0

entrepreneurs launch smart new applications that exploit bitcoin's decentralized infrastructure only to have them labeled by fanatics on Reddit as pump-and-dump schemes run by centralizing profiteers. Much is at stake in this debate, for it will dictate the approach that cryptocurrency takes in its bid to become broadly relevant. Will it seek to achieve that goal as a rebellious guerrilla outfit openly defying the establishment? Or will it play the role of compromiser, a negotiator that incorporates some of the existing system into its model yet still brings something new and valuable to the market? The latter offers a far more frictionless route to a meaningful assertion in society, but the question is whether doing so would sap bitcoin of its meaning and its true capacity to disrupt the current political economy. If this middle-ground approach succeeds, perhaps services like Dark Wallet would merely become underground domains where illicit activity continues and the bitcoins in its circulation remain cut off from a wider mainstream cryptocurrency economy—which is more or less what government money-laundering laws seek to achieve with drug and terrorist dollars. But clearly some fear that if bitcoin is watered down and regulated too far, it loses its power, its purpose, and its value to society.

This is not a debate that the bitcoin community can or will resolve on its own. These issues will be addressed by the wider society in which they are playing out. And society itself is already undergoing profound change, the result of sweeping technological, demographic, and global economic shifts. In this evolving environment, cryptocurrencies are poised to play a highly disruptive role. It will be up to us, the citizens, voters, and economic agents of this future society, to figure out how much of a role we want this technology to take and thus which of the two cryptocurrency models ends up dominant.

Eleven

A NEW NEW ECONOMY

> Progress is a comfortable disease.
>
> *—E. E. Cummings*

Until now, we've largely focused on how cryptocurrencies have developed and the benefits and challenges they pose to society. But these new forms of money and ways of organizing commercial activity are not landing in a static, dormant society, as if human beings were just waiting to be woken by a new monetary idea. Society itself is changing, rapidly. Digital technology and online computing are at the center of this change, shifting how we form communities, social relationships, and business ties as every aspect of our lives becomes increasingly subject to the power of computing and network connections. Other factors are at work, too—the demographic shifts of an aging West, the unprecedented growth of a middle class in developing nations, the rise of terrorism in place of international conflict as the biggest security concern of our time, and the legacy of the 2008 financial crisis with its damage to people's confidence in the traditional financial system. All of these create both opportunities and challenges for cryptocurrencies as they seek to impose some arguably even bigger changes on the societies to which they are being marketed.

In this confusing period there's no shortage of people who claim to have figured it all out. Countless books have appeared about the digital age and what it means, about the "end of work," or the impact of debt left over from the financial crisis. This book fits right into that genre. But it's important to recognize that the linear thinking that has people recognizing one trend or another can often prevent them from recognizing a simultaneous contradictory trend. Below, we'll explore some of these contradictions and look at what they mean for how societies grapple with the introduction of disruptive technologies such as cryptocurrency. We examine the tension it creates and the demands that the tensions be resolved through compromise and negotiation—typically through the intervention of government.

One of the biggest of these contradictions occurs along the continuum described in the previous chapter: that of decentralization versus centralization. Conflicting forces at either end of it are evident not only within the realm of cryptocurrencies but across society.

It can seem we live in an age of übercentralization. The concentration of power and control that contributed to the financial meltdown of 2008, most importantly in the form of overly powerful too-big-to-fail banks, has by many measures only got more intense since that crisis. Although new regulations sought to curtail banks' power, the solution preferred by policymakers to the economic and financial maelstrom was to double down on the old system of concentrated power. Central banks became even more important, pumping trillions of dollars' worth of fiat currency into the global economy via their age-old partners, the banks. This may have staved off disaster by preventing all-out collapse in the financial system, but it played into the hands of big institutions and those who run them and left the little guy behind. Big public companies were able to borrow cheaply via the corporate bond market in this era of zero interest rates and so grew even bigger, as it created incentives for corporate mergers. However, small- and medium-size businesses found that their main source of finance—commercial banks—had become much tighter with credit, constraining their ability to grow and hire. Meanwhile, underlying demand continued to sag, which meant that the bigger companies also had no incentive to invest in new hires, not when they could exploit lower financial costs to maintain profit margins and turn to outsourcing and robots to take the place of local workers.

This big-is-better solution favored the few and held back the many.

While the wealth of hedge fund managers and other elites surged thanks to the relentless stock market gains after the financial crisis subsided in 2009, the incomes of most households in Western societies stagnated, creating the widest wealth gap since the Great Depression. It's a story of big banks, big companies, and big homes for the 1 percent, with close to nothing left for the rest. That's one of the features of our twenty-first-century economy, and it speaks to a trend of centralization, not decentralization.

Yet, at the same time, signs of decentralization are clear, mostly on account of new technologies that have given people both the tools and the motivation to extract themselves from dependence on those big, centralized institutions. For example, take energy. The modern utility, with its power plants and transmission lines, has a state-mandated license to operate; it is subject to state controls on pricing; it is a private enterprise that serves a public need. But it's increasingly possible for homeowners to configure their properties with enough solar- and wind-power capacity to significantly reduce reliance on utilities or take themselves off the grid entirely. As former U.S. vice president Al Gore put it in an essay published by *Rolling Stone* in the summer of 2014, "We are witnessing the beginning of a massive shift to a new energy-distribution model—from the 'central station' utility-grid model that goes back to the 1880s to a 'widely distributed' model with rooftop solar cells, on-site and grid battery storage, and microgrids."

Beyond energy, many other industries are experiencing shifts toward decentralized models that bypass middlemen gatekeepers: tourist accommodation without hotels, driver-owned taxi services without central dispatch services, e-marketplaces for neighborly tool rentals that take business away from hardware stores. This is happening even *without* the use of cryptocurrencies or blockchains. People have figured out that if they have idle assets, they can lend them to people who need them, while those people have in turn equally realized that they don't need to go through expensive central distribution points to find those assets. This new system is called several things: the sharing economy, the mesh economy, the collaborative economy. Got some extra computing power sitting on your desktop? Share it with those who need it. Got a car sitting idle in your driveway? Share that. Got a big idea? Share it online and raise the money online to fund it. Business symbols of this era so far include the personal-apartment rental site Airbnb, the crowdfunding site Kickstarter, the peer-to-peer lending network Lending Club, and the taxi services controlled by individual car owners Uber and Lyft.

In some respects these new business models are extensions of a process that began far earlier with the advent of the Internet. While no self-respecting bitcoiner would ever describe Google or Facebook as decentralized institutions, not with their corporate-controlled servers and vast databases of customers' personal information, these giant Internet firms of our day got there by encouraging peer-to-peer and middleman-free activities. GoogleAds allowed small businesses to bypass big media organizations and to market more directly to prospective customers; Facebook allowed people to organically form groups, communities, and associations that weren't tied down by geography or social and national structures; Twitter meant people could design their own news feeds.

The importance of decentralization goes beyond the emergence of new business models or even that people are finding ways to save a few bucks here or make a few there. By unleashing this DIY approach to commerce, changes in technology and culture are leading to new methods of interacting, both socially and economically. Profit and nonprofit organizations alike are now eschewing vertical hierarchies in favor of more horizontal, democratic lines of command. (For a visual representation of how this plays out, compare the open-planned office layouts in the contemporaneous TV show *Silicon Valley* with the closed offices of the sixties-era *Mad Men*.) Much like the open-source-software development teams that look after bitcoin and countless other computing projects, communities are being formed—mostly online—with no titular head and no central hub. They are held together by the commonly recognized convention that the consensus of the crowd trumps everything else.

Is a clash building between these two movements, the corporate world's concentration of wealth and power, and Silicon Valley's reempowerment of the individual? Perhaps these trends can continue to coexist if the decentralizing movement remains limited to areas of the economy that don't bleed into the larger sectors that Big Business dominates. But that's not what the proponents of this technology foresee—especially those in the cryptocurrency sector. They believe that decentralization is just getting

started and that the centralized economic and political establishments
—even governments and nation-states, those ultimate centralized loci of
power—will be disrupted by it. If so, cryptocurrencies and blockchain
technology could ride that wave triumphantly. A phrase from Mastercoin's David Johnston that some in the cryptocurrency community call
Johnston's law could come true: "Everything that can be decentralized
will be decentralized."

This especially optimistic view of cryptocurrency technology's
potential runs up against the many obstacles that it faces. But if we set aside
cryptocurrencies for a moment, it's hard not to believe that the decentralizing trend has momentum. When we stand that up against the en-
trenchment of Wall Street's and Washington's concentrated power in the
postcrisis period, these twin trends start to look less like parallel movements and more like two trains on a collision course. We may well be on
the verge of a profound societal upheaval, perhaps the most significant
since the sixteenth century, when, in the second half of the Renaissance,
banking and the nation-state established themselves as the central forces
of power around which the world's monetary and economic systems
would revolve.

When faced with these kinds of disruptive challenges from new technology and new ways of organizing society, businesses and institutions that
occupy the center—those that represent the economic and political
establishment—have three choices. One is to just ignore the new idea, to
dismiss the new idea and carry on as normal. A second is to fight it,
perhaps through political lobbying, or by using advertising campaigns
or smear campaigns to destroy the nascent threat through negative associations in the public eye. A third is to try to adapt to it, to incorporate,
co-opt, or otherwise work with the new technology or concept.

Silicon Valley innovators will frequently warn against the perils of
the first approach, but history suggests it's often not a bad idea to let a
new technology fall victim to its own hype. The dot-com bubble of the
late 1990s, in which the exuberance behind higher stock prices reflected
an abiding belief that the first Web site retailers in every sector would win
just by carving out a niche and marketing to it, makes the case. Neighborhood pet stores weren't killed by Pets.com, no more than wedding plan-

ners were made redundant by OurBeginning.com, whose representatives joined Pets.com's talking sock puppet among a host of overhyped Super Bowl XXXIV ads in 2000, but whose domain name has since passed to a Seattle day-care center. Remember also the Y2K threat, which reached its anticlimax weeks before that Super Bowl. We'll never know whether it amounted to nothing because computer consulting firms successfully convinced everyone to upgrade their mainframes or whether they just brilliantly hyped a nonevent. Well before then history was littered with other failed tech ideas: the Apple Newton, digital audiotapes, and the Betamax video format, to name a few that our generation might remember. Still, ignoring change is risky, for which Eastman Kodak provides a cautionary tale. The century-old, Rochester, New York–based maker of film for analog cameras failed to pick up on the digital-imaging invention of one of its own engineers in the 1970s, only to be overwhelmed in the 2000s by the arrival of mass-marketed digital cameras.

The stand-and-fight option typically requires money, bravado, and political connections. Wall Street, which has all three, is the most effective practitioner of this. One would have thought that the backlash to the disaster of 2008 would have guaranteed that banks would be forced to list the nontransparent derivative securities that helped blow up the financial system on new online exchanges designed to allow transparent pricing and information about products such as credit default swaps. But Wall Street lobbyists fought the various reform-mind lawmakers that tried to make that happen and succeeded in watering down their bills such that many derivatives continued to trade in opaque "over-the-counter markets," leaving us in the dark about the financial risks they contain. Still, the stand-and-fight strategy is expensive and not guaranteed to win. Indeed, even Wall Street banks have failed to entirely hold back the winds of change in their industry since the crisis, including regulations that require them to carry much higher risk-absorbing capital on their books.

Sticking with Wall Street, we can also see the merits of the co-opting strategy. Electronic trading systems emerged in the late 1990s as a major threat to the Street's traditional business of trading bonds and other off-exchange securities by quoting prices over the telephone. By broadcasting prices widely, the new systems empowered investors and made it harder for banks to make money by quoting wide bid/ask spreads on those investments. But the technology never seriously dented Wall Street's power in any of these markets, in part because the banks figured that in this case the best approach was not to fight their rivals but to join them. Various bank consortia were formed to offer online markets in bonds, foreign exchange, and other asset classes, and although the profit margins on each trade shrank as the light of transparency was shone on their business, this was more than offset by the revenues that came from new business steered their way.

Now, with the sharing economy and the power of the "crowd" threatening to upend traditional business models again, other old-school companies are looking to co-opt some of these new ideas and adapt to them. U-Haul, the venerable truck-rental company, about as old-economy as you get, is taking this tack. Embracing a cryptocurrency-like view of finance, it has started an investment program that allows people to invest directly in the company, buying notes backed by specific hard assets, such as individual stores, trucks, even mattress pads. No investment bank is involved, no intermediary. Investors are simply lending U-Haul money, peer-to-peer, and in return getting a promissory note with fixed interest payments, underwritten by the company's assets. Unlike a blockchain model, the lending is done in a centralized way in which the investor must trust the company itself, but the middleman-less mechanism has some of the same effects as projects touted by cryptocurrency advocates.

Other big companies are also looking to figure out an adaptive response to the onset of new crowd- and sharing-based business models such as those employed by Uber, Airbnb, and Lyft. Silicon Valley–based Crowd Companies, which advises old-world companies on how to survive in this new economy, boasts an impressive list of clients, among them Visa, Home Depot, Hyatt, General Electric, Walmart, Coca-Cola, and FedEx. All are trying to figure out how to adapt their businesses to a centerless economy.

What about the payments industry? Well, it looks to be dabbling in all three strategies in response to the challenge from cryptocurrencies. Employing the ignore-and-dismiss posture in an early 2014 interview with *Wall Street Journal* editors and reporters, MasterCard CEO Ajay Banga said about bitcoin, "The world is not short of currencies, so what is this currency solving for?" But in reality, MasterCard, with Banga at the helm, is one of the payments industry's most dynamic engagers with digital technology. The company is also adopting the stand-and-fight strategy, having hired five employees from D.C. lobbying firm Peck Madigan Jones to lobby Congress on bitcoin and virtual currencies. But MasterCard's most powerful response to bitcoin lies in its own engagement with new technologies. Its heavy investment in its MasterPass program for smartphone payments has paid off to the point that the company, along with American Express, was a key partner in Apple's move to incorporate digital payments into the iPhone 6.

Jason Oxman, the CEO of the Electronic Transactions Association, whose members include some of the heavyweights in payments, e-commerce, and mobile telecommunications—companies such as MasterCard, PayPal, Amazon, Google, and AT&T—likes to distinguish his industry from the music industry. Whereas record producers "did everything they could to kill" Napster and file-sharing technology, the payments industry is "embracing new technology," he says. Indeed, the stuff that is happening there—even setting aside cryptocurrency—is dizzying. As Oxman says, the industry is going through "the single most important period of innovation since the invention of the magnetic strip [fifty years ago]. It is truly a revolutionary time for payments." This poses a real challenge for the cryptocurrency industry's efforts to gain a foothold in payments. Even if cryptocurrencies seem tailor-made for the current age, with the sweeping decentralizing shifts discussed above, their prime competitors in the payments industry are coming up with alternatives that might just keep the general public from shifting to the crypto model.

Indeed, in the era of the Internet of Things, technologies that leverage the old sovereign money system are finding various ways to impress customers with improvements to the payment experience. The smartphone, the preferred tool of mobile bitcoin exchange, is also being harnessed by a host of finance tech companies seeking to revolutionize how we make payments. PayPal, which was the first firm in the 1990s to figure out how to send money digitally before Web sites began accepting credit-cards directly, is now aggressively repackaging itself as a mobile-payments firm with an app that supports payments at retail outlets via QR codes and other wireless technologies such as Bluetooth and near-field communication, or NFC. With the same app, users who preload their

PayPal account with dollars can send money to other PayPal users via the network. Similar smartphone-based products include the Google Wallet and Softcard, a joint venture of U.S. carriers AT&T, Verizon, and T-Mobile that bore the name ISIS until September 2014, when it moved to dissociate itself from the extremist Islamic group of the same name. Facebook is widely believed to be working on something similar, having applied for an e-money license in what could be the experimental locale of Ireland. And as mentioned, Apple's iPhone 6, with its built-in digital wallet, could finally open up the United States to this new way of paying.

In many places outside the United States, smartphone payments are already well established, with technology-leapfrogging emerging-market countries often taking the lead. Chinese citizens make mobile payments over the ubiquitous WeChat messaging service and with Alipay, a service from giant e-marketplace Alibaba. And let's not forget that the phone-as-money idea had its genesis in Kenya, with the wildly successful M-Pesa, now branching out into Eastern European markets.

Then there are the dramatic changes seen in the old technology of card payments. Square's portable card swipe has allowed millions of small-business owners such as taxidrivers and food vendors to turn their smartphones and tablets into mobile payment processors. As much as bitcoiners rightfully complain about the security risks that come with credit- and debit cards, whose system depends upon transmitting information about the identity of the user, the security in the networks that use them has dramatically improved. In particular, that's come with the advent of the EMV (Europay, MasterCard, and Visa) standard for card-embedded microchips, a technology that's only now coming to the United States, more than a year after it was introduced pretty much everywhere else. The use of biometrics such as fingerprint scanners and facial-recognition technology should also make the system more secure, so long as privacy concerns can be addressed.

All these technologies promise to make the shopping experience virtually seamless. While they might not be eliminating the fee-charging banks and payment processors, which will still coordinate the back-office infrastructure of the monetary system, these technologies could put cashiers out of a job. One idea is that after you've filled up your shopping cart at the supermarket, you walk through a scanner that reads signals

from each of the items in your cart and automatically debits the debit card
or phone in your pocket. These systems make the use of money ever more
automated. These new ways to exploit the very old sovereign-money system will help to enhance that system and will make it harder for bitcoin
and other cryptocurrencies to make inroads into mainstream commerce—at least at the retail level.

But here's the rub: because they are tapped into that legacy system,
these new technologies carry all the costs of transferring money within
it. The providers of the technology have no choice but to pay banks and
other players in that system for processing and taking on credit risk. Merchants using PayPal, for example, are hit with a 2.7 percent fee for those
costs. And for all its rapid-fire growth, back-end fees are making it difficult for Square, which posted a $100 million loss in 2013, to turn a profit.
The burden of those fees raises questions about the widespread product's
long-term viability. By comparison, bitcoin processors such as BitPay,
Coinbase, and GoCoin say they've been profitable more or less from day
one, given their low overheads and the comparatively tiny fees charged
by miners on the blockchain. Even if consumers don't feel those costs, businesses that must incur them may start to insist that the back end of their
transactions be handled by some sort of cryptocurrency-based processing.
The capability is there to make this happen with consumers and merchants
still happily seeing their payments and receipts denominated in fiat currencies.

Things are different in China, the one place where both consumers
and merchants pay close to zero fees on mobile payments. There, the issue is that it takes the excessive influence of the state to achieve that. State-
owned banks, clearly under instructions from Beijing, levy close to zero
fees on payment processing. That de facto subsidy leaves bitcoin with no
competitive edge over WeChat and Alipay or the national credit-card
network, UnionPay, but it also means that the renminbi-based system is
dependent on the largesse of the state, which can be taken away at any
time or used as a form of official extortion.

These new payment mechanisms, while technologically advanced,
are still trapped in the five-hundred-year-old model of centralized financial management. That may not matter one iota to the average person using them, whose ambivalence could be enough to ensure that sovereign

money survives, even as the collaborative economy of the future continues its drive toward individual empowerment in all other realms of the
economy. But its survival would be inherently inconsistent with all the
other sweeping, decentralizing shifts under way. It's hard to get away from
the idea that these trends point inevitably to an age of cryptocurrency, if
not immediately, then a decade or so in the future.

That leads us to one important question: What happens to banks as
credit providers if that age arrives? Any threat to this role could be a
negotiating chip for banks in their marketing battle with the new technology. They could argue that a cryptocurrency system that replaces
sovereign paper money would leave banks unable to generate credit and
thus fulfill their singularly sanctioned role as creators of private money.
(We refer here to the critical concept of fractional reserve banking,
discussed in chapter 1.) Too bad, many bitcoiners would say. To the libertarian factions within the cryptocurrency community, who tend to see
their monetary model as a zero-sum transactional system in which a
finite supply of currency is simply shared back and forth, endless bank
credit is just a recipe for currency debasement and financial crisis. But
what would all the businesses that rely on bank lending to pay their employees or to run their operations or to expand into new markets do?
Credit might not be so readily created in a cryptocurrency-based economy. You can't just create bitcoin money out of thin air in the way that
bank credit does in the fiat-currency system. Yes, that removes inflationary risks and means central banks no longer need to manage the money
supply with imperfect policy tools such as interest rates, but bitcoin's
critics will counter, with some merit, that shackling credit would starve
economies of growth.

Still, it might not have to be so stark. If we consider that banks simply act as middlemen aggregating the funds of those seeking to lend their
excess savings and delivering them to those who are short of money and
need to borrow, there's nothing to say such matching of lenders and borrowers can't occur in a disintermediated fashion with cryptocurrencies.
The new trend of peer-to-peer loans, exemplified by the Lending Club,
offers one model that easily scales to cryptocurrency systems, with the
checks and balances of the blockchain potentially helping to enhance a
system of credit checks and credit reputations. Either way, the flow of credit

and money in a cryptocurrency-led financial system would take on a very different form if banks were removed from those flows.

What of the nation-state itself? How will it respond? Ignore, fight, or co-opt? The sovereign-money system, and especially the fiat money that gives the state unchecked power to print currency as it sees fit, has arguably been the most powerful weapon in the nation-state's arsenal. More than just generating seigniorage—the seductive idea that every dollar printed is an interest-free loan flowing from the people to the state—controlling the nation's money has allowed governments to control the apparatus of power. With paper money they can purchase arms, launch wars, raise debt to finance those conflicts, and then demand tax payments in that same currency to repay those debts. A functioning democracy should, in theory, put limits on all that. But in reality this monetary system permits the extension of power. It funds bureaucracies and agencies whose employees put their own survival above all else. In the worst nation-states (think North Korea), it finances the instruments of terror and repression that destroy people's dignity.

If that system were to go away, the nation-state, whose interests lie like all of ours in survival, would have to figure out how to respond. The nation-state has proven adaptable over the past five hundred years, so we don't doubt that it could again find ways to adapt and survive. As we'll discuss in the conclusion, one co-option approach might be to start issuing sovereign cryptocurrency itself. Another could be for nation-states to band together and strengthen their international cooperation in money. We have no idea how this all will wash out. It may all amount to nothing. But for the first time in centuries these questions must now at least be asked.

As we've highlighted before, it depends on what people do, how they vote with their feet. From Silicon Valley, the impression is that human society is now ready to throw out the centralized system altogether and embrace a decentralized model run by "the crowd."

"Now the crowd has their own business model," says Jeremiah Owyang, the founder of the consulting service Crowd Companies. Offering a broad definition of the collaborative economy that encompasses everything from barter to lending to gifting, Owyang suggests that the entire human populace is now taking charge of the means of production and changing the rules of the game. "They're making their own freaking currencies, for God's sake," Owyang adds emphatically.

But beyond these catchphrases, the picture is more nuanced. The Valley's language about these new technologies makes it seem as if people now have a utopia at their fingertips, if only they could let go of the old ways, reach for that app on the smartphone, and bring the power of the crowd to bear. But even the millennial generation, a group routinely described as drivers of these new apps and the most engaged in the new ways of socializing and doing business, seems apprehensive about ditching a centuries-old social structure. A comprehensive 2011 study of U.S. society by the Pew Research Center found that millennials—typically defined as those born after 1981—were the only generation out of four in which a majority wanted government to provide more services, not less. Other Pew studies have shown this cohort more likely to define government as an "efficient" provider of services than older generations. This is not to say that this group, which in job prospects and earning power has arguably been more damaged than any other by the flawed policies that led to the financial crisis, expects the government to be there for them. Separate Pew data from the same study also show at least 50 percent of millennials doubting they will ever receive a single benefit payment from their Social Security account. It could be that millennials are simply realistic: they'd like more government; they just don't expect it.

If all this new technology disrupts jobs as expected, society will inevitably call on government to soften the blow. This could especially be so if cryptocurrency technologies become properly embedded, not only in payments but in the disruptive, decentralizing ways foreseen in chapter 9's examination of Blockchain 2.0 technologies. Gil Luria, an analyst at Wedbush Securities who has done some of the most in-depth analysis of cryptocurrency's potential, argues that 21 percent of U.S. GDP is based in "trust" industries, those that perform middlemen tasks that blockchains can digitize and automate. Lifted from the Commerce Department's national accounts, Luria's estimate encapsulates commercial banking, securities industry firms, funds and trusts, insurance providers, real estate agents, and legal services, a group that employed 10 million people in mid-2014, according to the Bureau of Labor Statistics. No one expects these industries to disappear overnight, but even a gradual slide into partial obsolescence will be painful for anyone working within them.

Glorivee Caban knows a thing or two about what it's like to work in a financial services industry and get disrupted by new technology. Between 2009 and 2013 she saw her hours as a bank teller for Banco Popular in New York City dwindle from a full-time job at thirty-five hours a week down to twenty-four hours, all paid at $11 an hour, a rate that never rose. Although losses sustained during the financial crisis contributed to Banco Popular's need to reduce payroll costs, the real enabler of these cutbacks was more advanced ATMs, which allowed deposits and online banking services. "When I first started at Banco, we would see maybe two hundred and fifty people a day come through the branch. By the time I left it was down to one hundred and twenty," she says. This undermined her ability to achieve one of her job's main performance goals, which was to make ten to fifteen referrals of new business per day. "If the customers are not physically coming to the bank, how are we are going to make referrals?" she would ask. With her take-home pay shrinking, Caban did not have enough income to cover the $1,380-per-month rent on her Brooklyn apartment and raise her infant daughter, even with the help of a monthly contribution from the Department of Veterans Affairs that stemmed from her three-time deployment with the U.S. Navy in the Middle East. She had no choice but to apply to the New York City government for welfare. Consider it a sign of the times: an employee of a bank in the world's financial capital in need of government financial aid.

A teller's position was once a safe, decent job, which often laid out a path to more lucrative positions in bank management. These days it's a symbol of how much the business has changed. While the job's disruption by ATMs and other banking technology is not new, it's worth contemplating what it portends for other jobs in the financial services and legal sectors if cryptocurrency technology achieves the disruption its advocates are looking for—people working in payment processing, in escrow services, in real estate advocacy, in money-transmission firms, could all be affected. Visa, MasterCard, and Western Union combined—to name just three players whose businesses could be significantly reformed—had twenty-seven thousand employees in 2013.

It's unlikely that Western Union, for one, will sit on its hands, Kodak-style, in the face of the cryptocurrency challenge to its international remittance business. The 163-year-old company is already promoting online tools to lower costs, and its executives are well versed on the prospects of digital currencies. Indeed, many companies in this arena will ultimately choose to incorporate blockchain-based processing to save costs. But that won't protect all those data-input and customer-service jobs for which this technology has no use.

Once they reach a big enough scale, those job losses will arouse political tensions. Whereas the benefits to society from technological advancement are often shared broadly, the losers will be concentrated in geographic areas or in specific, easily identified industries. As the old adage goes, all politics is local. So expect a backlash once banks start shutting back-office administrative centers in midtown Manhattan or London's Canary Wharf when their merchant customers start booking more customer sales via cryptocurrency systems to avoid the 3 percent transaction fees.

The challenge for technologists and their venture-capitalist backers is to frame the disruption within a politically digestible narrative of overall progress, says Andreessen Horowitz venture capitalist Chris Dixon. "On the one hand you have the bank person who loses their job, and everyone feels bad about that person, and on the other hand, everyone else saves three percent, which economically can have a huge impact because it means small businesses widen their profit margins. But from a narrative perspective it doesn't feel as good. There are individual losses and socialized gains."

Asked to describe the job market if and when the kinds of decentralized autonomous companies envisaged by his firm become prevalent, BitShares CEO Daniel Larimer confidently predicts that these projects "can create millions of information-based jobs." What's more, he says, blockchain-based prediction markets, where people buy and sell contracts that pay out depending on how accurately they predict an event, will create new moneymaking opportunities in the intermediary industries destined for disruption. "If you're a middleman in the lending industry or a middleman in commodities, or have medical knowledge, you know that industry better than anyone else, which means you can take the knowledge you have and turn it into value," Larimer says. "At the same time that you are making money, you're providing information to the market, which makes everyone more productive." These, he insists, are not "make-work jobs" in which people "dig holes and fill them in"; they are "high-end value-producing jobs."

Larimer's jobs-for-everyone utopianism—the pervading ethos of Silicon Valley, shared by many bitcoiners—glosses over how many, if not most, people find change difficult. Not all, and perhaps not many, laid-off workers can easily pick themselves up and parlay their knowledge into making an income from speculative trading on a BitShares prediction market. To many it will seem like a form of gambling. To subject their lives to such uncertainty is anathema to people who've expected a salaried job to last a lifetime and to provide security and permanence.

People will have to figure out how to apply their particular skills to this Brave New World and, if they can't apply them, how to rapidly acquire the right skills. As Tyler Cowen noted in his book *Average Is Over,* "The key questions will be: Are you good at working with intelligent machines or not? Are your skills a complement to the skills of the computer, or is the computer doing better without you? Worst of all, are you competing against the computer?" Cowen's thesis, which drew in part from the "work is over" theory, wasn't a rosy one for Middle America. It attributed much of that social sector's recent economic stagnation to the ever-increasing speed of technological change, which for the first time appears to be displacing jobs faster than the economy can draw upon the growth unleashed by that technology to create new jobs.

These questions will be especially relevant in the age of cryptocurrency—certainly for all those working in "trust" industries challenged by blockchain automation. They could blindly hope that this strange new way of handling finance will never amount to anything, much as Eastman Kodak mistakenly did about the digital camera. But you've probably gathered by now that we think that's a dangerously naïve viewpoint. While it's true that quite a few prominent economists see bitcoin as a passing fad—Yale's Robert Shiller and New York University's Nouriel Roubini were still in that camp in mid-2014—the longer that digital currency defies these expectations and the further along the innovation curve bitcoin businesses go, the more out of touch such views will seem. Former U.S. treasury secretary Larry Summers, one of the most influential economic minds on the planet, recognizes the risks of ignoring this technology for a financial sector that's "ripe for disruption." As he put it in an interview, "The people who rejected the Internet as a curiosity for scientists were on the wrong side of history, the people who rejected digital photography as really an artificial thing were on the wrong side of history, and the people who felt that nongimmicky tennis racquets were made with wood were on the wrong side of history. So it seems to me that the people who confidently reject all the innovation here [in blockchain-based payment and monetary systems] are on the wrong side of history."

Given what that portends, it's incumbent on society to figure out the right mix of safety-net provisions and transitional support to soften the blow for the millions who could be out of work. In contrast to the idea of a quasi-anarchic world in which government is reduced to a weakling in the face of a resurgent "crowd," and where nation-states have their relevance challenged by stateless cryptocurrencies, the people whom we choose to run society will have a big, important job ahead of them. Public education plans need to be developed so that people can be properly trained for the jobs of the future. Kids should be taught to code, but also to use their creative talents to conceive of new, exciting ways in which decentralized systems can be used to improve people's lives. Meanwhile, adults should get the kind of vocational retraining needed to prepare them for a very different work environment. For those that don't make it—because, contrary to Larimer's forecasts, the evidence suggests there simply won't be enough jobs to go around—a stronger, fairer welfare state is needed. Cutting welfare might have been in vogue in the era of small government that emerged with Reagan, but as the ranks of unemployed and underemployed grow, their political clout will, too. No matter what cryptocurrency technology can do to bypass governments, it's the interests of people like these that will determine the laws and policies of the future.

In the United States, all this will take place within Washington's highly fraught money politics, an arena the cryptocurrency industry is just starting to enter as a lobbying force. While their rivals in the traditional financial-services industry have long made hefty political donations, always useful for shaping favorable legislation, bitcoiners have recently earned an entrée into this world. In 2014, the U.S. Federal Election Commission unanimously agreed to allow bitcoin contributions to politicians and political organizations up to $100 in value, the same maximum allowed for cash donations in dollars. More important, the six-member FEC repeatedly split down party lines, with Republicans on the pro-bitcoin side, over whether significantly bigger donations should be allowed under the existing terms for noncash contributions via check and credit-card. This led the FEC's Republican chairman, Lee Goodman, who'd supported the more generous approach, to controversially argue that digital-currency donors effectively had a green light to go all the way since the three Democrats couldn't muster a majority to stop them. No one in the bitcoin community was going to argue with that. So the donations started flowing in. According to Make Your Laws, a not-for-profit PAC that focuses on campaign finance reform, dozens of candidates were accepting bitcoin donations as of September 2014, including Texas Republican congressman Steve Stockman and his Colorado Democratic counterpart Jared Polis, along with various Libertarian Party organizations and a number of PACs.

As bitcoin slowly gains a financial voice in Washington and begins to compete at the margins with the behemoths in the traditional financial sector, it will have some influence on the regulatory process laid out in the previous chapter. But, ironically, if the cryptocurrency industry is as successful as it wants to be, it might find itself facing an even more formidable opponent from groups representing people facing job displacement. For society to arrive at a happy medium where the great, liberating benefits of community empowerment are achieved through decentralized cryptocurrency applications but at minimal cost to those human beings who are displaced, all these parties will need to come together to find a negotiated solution.

This is not a moment for government to be sidelined and made irrelevant by this technology. For all the utopian dreams of a self-help society that has no need for a centralized authority, it's difficult to imagine how all these conflicts and diverging interests can be negotiated without a central arbiter.

It's not just about protecting displaced workers. Bitcoin businesses, too, can benefit from the support of a government that seeks to keep the playing field level. In the age of cryptocurrency it will be just as important to insist that antitrust laws, transparency rules, and consumer-protection agencies are upheld as it will be to ensure that overly onerous regulations don't quash innovation. This is not to say that the current government model for containing monopolies and trusts and for promoting competition has not been abused in multiple ways. But to throw government out entirely could be to invite new monopolizing—another way to say "centralizing"—forces to take control of the economy of the future, even if its underlying infrastructure is built upon decentralized cryptocurrency technology.

Whereas cryptocurrency enthusiasts tend to think now of Google, Facebook, Twitter, Apple, Microsoft, etc., as the centralized establishment —the enemy—it's worth remembering that they, too, once only existed as radical, disruptive ideas from unheard-of start-ups. Because the legal system was structured such that those start-ups were allowed to flourish and seek profits, the world has changed—and for the better, we would say. If it weren't for a political and regulatory framework that's deliberately designed to encourage innovation and competition, these entities would have had no chance against the established media and communications industries whose markets they were targeting.

Contrary to the crypto-anarchists' mind-set, there is still liberty and progress in the halfway compromises that are made both with government and with VC-funded businesses that are looking to profit on top of cryptocurrencies. The libertarian ideal behind cryptocurrencies may be noble in spirit, and we must embrace key elements of that battle for liberty. But, to borrow an idea from an editor of ours, such utopian projects often end up like Ultimate Frisbee competitions, which by design have no referees—only "observers" who arbitrate calls—and where disputes over rule violations often devolve into shouting matches that are won by whichever player yells the loudest, takes the most uncompromising stance, and persuades the observer.

One day the new crypto start-ups that currently hold the baton in society's ongoing fight for liberty will become part of the establishment themselves, much as Google and Facebook now are. We should hope that at that time both our cryptocurrency networks are sufficiently decentralized and that our governments have written accommodative laws that make it possible for the next wave of innovators to disrupt those future Googles and Facebooks. Let's also hope for a sufficiently supportive and constructive social safety net so that everyone can benefit from the profound improvements these newcomers can bring to our way of life.

Conclusion

Reality is a historical process.

—Georg Hegel

For everything we've just set out, for all the promise and potential of cryptocurrency, it's still very much a niche product. Say there are 12 million wallets, and even one hundred thousand merchants accepting it, and even $500 million in VC money now invested in cryptocurrency projects. Those numbers pale next to the 6 billion people in the world, or the 23 million businesses in the United States alone. Nobody's fully studied how much business merchants are doing with bitcoin and cryptocurrencies, but actual and anecdotal reports tend to peg it at a low number, about 1 percent of total sales for the few that accept them.

That's far below what the hype might suggest. If bitcoin is going to be this revolutionary, global force for change that its proponents fervently believe it is, some evolutionary things are going to have to happen first. For one thing, the stain of association that cryptocurrencies have with the Silk Road site and Mt. Gox is still visible; most people simply assume the whole thing is some kind of scam. At a bare minimum people have to feel as if cryptocurrencies are safe and not liable to suddenly lose value. They're nowhere near that right now. A mid-2014 survey found that only about half of U.S. citizens were aware of bitcoin, only about 3 percent had used it, and 65 percent said they were unlikely ever to use it (and those numbers were an *improvement* from a survey several months earlier).

Cryptocurrencies, as Ricky Ricardo used to say to Lucy, have got some 'splaining to do before people adopt them.

A second problem is that, were bitcoin to actually become a dominant monetary power, it could create economic forces that would shock most global citizens. With the creation of new bitcoins capped at 21 million, bitcoin is a *deflationary* currency. Our global economy as currently constructed is predicated on inflationary currencies. Bitcoiners rightly point out that this can have a destructive effect for anyone with decent savings, as it means those dollars and euros lose value over time. But at least in times of economic crisis, these unlimited fiat currencies allow central banks to issue as many as needed to stop people from hoarding money and to free up credit so that jobs can be created. Bitcoin, by comparison, would be like a big spoonful of castor oil. Some bitcoin advocates argue that we wouldn't have to take the medicine because self-interested financial institutions and unaccountable central banks would no longer be able to precipitate the kinds of financial crises as they have in the past. But there's no way to prove that. For a global economy that runs on credit and is no longer accustomed to the rigor of monetary control, such a system could do great harm if it's not properly introduced. Economists such as Boston University's Mark T. Williams and *New York Times* columnist Paul Krugman warn that in times of financial panic and economic disruption, people would hoard the limited-supply and highly sought-after digital currency. This would restrict the flow of money to everyone else and exacerbate the downturn. Without a central bank acting as a lender of last resort, we would all starve for currency. It would, in effect, be a repeat of the Great Depression, these people say.

A third concern is competition, and forget the obvious competitors such as Visa and MasterCard. What if, say, there's a payment system that offers all of the convenience of digital payments, without any of the real or perceived downsides of bitcoin? What if that system was already installed within another system that people trust? What if that was all packaged and sold by a company whose name and logo are . . . a fruit? Apple will have a far easier time finding converts to its mobile payment system than bitcoin will with its payment system, no matter its qualities.

The security/volatility issue can and should be overcome with the cryptocurrency innovation unleashed by its open-source model. Already, bitcoin security has made great strides since the Mt. Gox debacle; it's now virtually impossible to imagine such a massive loss occurring again. Volatility in bitcoin's price will also eventually decline as more traders enter the market and exchanges become more sophisticated. What's more, the deflation/inflation problem is likely a nonissue. As we note below in a discussion of what the future might hold, most serious analysts of cryptocurrency do not have bitcoin world dominance as a base case. Governments will almost certainly maintain their power to issue fiat currencies, which have no issuance limits and would offer an escape valve for economies that find themselves short of money. What's more, a number of altcoins coming to market are more open-ended, with flexible issuance schemes. These could one day pose an alternative to a deflationary bitcoin monetary system. (That might scare off bitcoin's libertarian supporters, who see deflation as a strength, not a weakness, but it can make for a practical currency.)

As for competition, that's a harder one to deal with, and not because cryptocurrencies will be inferior. The kind of payment products that Apple and others are toying with are built upon the old bank-centric system and so are fraught with the same underlying costs and inefficiencies, whereas bitcoin is free of them. But the question is, what do people want? That brings us to the ultimate measure of whether cryptocurrency can succeed: whether, when it is weighed against the competition, people can be convinced of cryptocurrency's benefits, dissuaded from fearing its pitfalls, and made willing to abandon the government-issued currencies with which they were raised. That's no simple task.

Even so, we will go out on a limb here and argue that encryption-based, decentralized digital currencies *do* have a future. It could be bitcoin or some other cryptocurrency, or one that hasn't yet been created, but this groundbreaking technology has a momentum behind it that will be hard to stop. Far more important, it solves some big problems that are impossible to address within the underlying payment infrastructure. Cryptocurrencies promise to dispel much of the enormous cost that a bank-centric model of payments imposes on our global economy; they could bring billions of people excluded from that system into the global economy; and via multiple blockchain-based applications, they promise to hold whole classes of middlemen, centralized institutions, and government agencies accountable as never before.

Exactly how cryptocurrency technology gets to become a major part of the global financial infrastructure is the next big unknown we'll tackle. However, a few routes are obvious. One or several may play a role, or this could be led by some factor that nobody's even thinking about.

The most obvious way cryptocurrencies become mainstreamed is through ongoing adoption, and nothing would ramp that up faster than a major player's adopting them and becoming an effective advocate. A number of big names jumped on the bitcoin bandwagon in 2014: Overstock, Expedia, Dish Network, Dell, PayPal through its Braintree subsidiary, as well as a host of smaller names. That all helped build the network, but if a big player, a really big player, were to get on board, you could see cryptocurrency reach the general public far more rapidly. Here we are talking not about a company accepting bitcoin from its retail customers per se but about using cryptocurrency in business-to-business transactions to cut out financial middlemen, reduce operational costs, and boost the bottom line. Imagine how much wider the use of cryptocurrency would be if a major retailer such as Walmart switched to a blockchain-based payment network in order to cut tens of billions of dollars in transaction costs off the $350 billion it sends annually to tens of thousands of suppliers worldwide. What if, further, such a player really got religion, as Overstock CEO Patrick Byrne did with his plan to incentivize suppliers to accept bitcoin? That way it would foment changes that go far beyond its direct payment relationships. With networking effects like that in mind, it's not hard to imagine a Walmart-like player feeding the spread of adoption until a critical mass of self-reinforcement is reached. (For the record, we have no idea of Walmart's current thinking on cryptocurrency.)

The major catalyst for adoption might be a government seeking to reduce procurement costs or bring greater transparency to governance. We already know that Canada explored the idea of a digital Canadian dollar with its MintChip, and Ecuador is planning to introduce a centrally issued digital currency. What if Mexico's government goes through with the even more ambitious plan that it has floated? (Recall that it said it was studying both the prospect of creating a cryptocurrency of its own and how to use blockchain technology to improve governance.) If Mexico became the first crypto-focused government, it could turn itself into a crypto-tech hub, encouraging governments of the many other developing nations that it trades with to follow. Since nearly all bitcoiners obsess about bitcoin's promise to fix developing nations' problems such as remittances and unbanked populations, a Mexico-led mushrooming effect across emerging markets could have far-reaching effects.

Or might the driver be the discovery of the proverbial "killer app"? In the 1990s, the Internet boom was kicked off by the creation of the Web browser Netscape, which had user-friendly features lacked by its predecessor, Mosaic, and could thus take off as a consumer product. A cryptocurrency equivalent could be a wallet that meshes seamlessly with e-commerce platforms and is so secure that people aren't afraid of its being hacked. The equivalent could be a service that makes it ridiculously simple for people in emerging markets to send and receive cryptocurrencies and convert them in and out of their local currencies. It would need to be something that everyone viewed as a must-have.

Lastly, nothing forges character like a crisis. When the Panic of 2008 hit, bitcoin did not exist. Instead, investors flooded into that age-old safe haven, gold, which tripled in price in two years. But now bitcoin offers an alternative, one that is significantly more useful than gold. It has similar finite-supply qualities, which supports its value, and central banks can't mess with it. But you can much more easily use bitcoin to buy things than you can use gold. The idea of another financial crisis is hardly inconceivable. In a world awash with debt and subject to central-bank interventions, overstretched asset prices, and market interconnections whose fault lines were revealed six years ago but never fixed, many analysts assume another is inevitable. There's also a payments-technology precedent: M-Pesa in Kenya, which you will recall got its big break during that country's 2007 political crisis, when people found they could use it to transfer funds when the traditional financial system broke down. It's not hard to imagine bitcoin's enjoying a similar right-place-at-the-worst-time situation. If cryptocurrencies get a chance to prove their worth in a world on financial fire, they may find a legion of converts.

With those potential catalysts for change in mind, we can now contemplate the ways in which this technology could develop and what impact that might have. We'll engage in a kind of thought experiment to explore the many scenarios for how this process might play out. Yes, this is entirely speculative, but as with the exercise we just went through, we believe it's useful. Clear lines of logic unfold as one thinks through the cause-and-effect relationships. Nobody knows which direction cryptocurrencies will travel, but smart people, smarter people than us, make it their business to try to figure out which path these things will take.

We feel it's fairer to lay out a range of scenarios rather than make bold predictions. As we said at the outset of this book, we're journalists, not futurists. As we explore those scenarios, we will deliberately go beyond the question that most people ask: Will bitcoin itself succeed or fail? We have stressed all along that the underlying technology presented by bitcoin's blockchain matters far more than the specific currency that bears its name. Having said that, let's start with the two scenarios alluded to in that same question—whether bitcoin gets to dominate the world or joins Betamax on the trash heap of history. From there we'll go on to look at possibilities in between those two contradictory conclusions as well as some completely different tangents on which cryptocurrency could take society.

The "No" Case

Money has three broad characteristics: it's a unit of account, a medium of exchange, and a store of value. For bitcoin, or any cryptocurrency, to achieve all three, that whole concept is going to need broad-based support—if not from consumers then from businesses that will use the technology to cut costs. It may fail to earn that support even if the product is technically solid. To this day, you can find people who will explain why the Betamax videocassette recorder was technically a better product than the VHS. But most people now don't even know what Betamax was. Cryptocurrency, for all its purported glories, could similarly lose out to a "just good enough" competitor, one that works through the traditional, bank-centric system but which adds sufficient cost savings and convenience to give it an edge.

While business adopters could be the most powerful catalysts for change, they will watch how consumers and the general public view bitcoin and other cryptocurrencies before jumping. Most consumers may never show sufficient support. Consumer-focused digital-wallet, payment-processing, and bitcoin-depository services such as Coinbase, Bitreserve, Circle Internet Financial, and Xapo are making it easier to use cryptocurrencies and safer for the general public, trying to erase the lingering memory of Mt. Gox. But little evidence suggests that they've managed to reach people beyond the small groups of tech-minded early adopters and cryptocurrency enthusiasts currently using it. Perhaps cryptocurrency's reputation has been forever ruined by bad press. Add to that public image the headache of capital-gains-tax tracking now required in the United States, as well as the regulatory burdens that make it hard for cryptocurrency providers to seamlessly reach ordinary consumers, and it's possible that this new form of money will never gain appeal. In this scenario, cryptocurrencies get stuck, forever, in the perpetual chicken-and-egg cycle: not enough users, not enough places to use them, not enough reason to own them. The critical mass is never reached and the whole idea withers and dies.

The "Yes" Case

(Note: Whereas the "no" case referred to a scenario in which no cryptocurrency makes it big, here in the "yes" case we're talking purely about bitcoin. As we'll discuss below, cryptocurrencies could in other imaginable scenarios become entrenched without bitcoin's becoming dominant.)

The case for bitcoin's becoming the king of currencies might seem far-fetched given the adoption stats we cited above, but all big things had to begin somewhere. Back in 2009, few expected bitcoin to get as far as it has. What's more, as we've discussed, the low-cost, high-speed decentralized network on which bitcoin's blockchain is based has a genuine benefit. Given that bitcoin is by far the most entrenched of all cryptocoins, with a clear first-mover advantage, if any new currency is to capitalize on those benefits, it might as well be bitcoin.

This is a digital age, and bitcoin is digital money. In a world where people live on their phones, in a world where so much commerce is done online, simplicity and cost savings are in its favor. All that's needed is for one of those catalysts described above, and then another, and another, and another. Eventually, it becomes so popular that all three characteristics of money are met and bitcoin is as big as the dollar.

Despite its public-image problem and regulatory constraints, the environment isn't entirely unaccommodating for bitcoin to flourish. Some of the more cryptocurrency-friendly states such as Switzerland, Singapore, the United Kingdom, and Canada could foster hubs of innovation that give the technology an unstoppable momentum. Even in the United States, despite the rancor over New York Department of Financial Services superintendent Ben Lawsky's BitLicense idea, thoughtful regulators are leaving space for innovation. While developing nations have been slow to catch on, many have noticed the appeal of bitcoin there. If bitcoin were to take off as the main vehicle for international remittances and financial transfers within developing countries as quickly as, say, WeChat took off in China, it could rapidly become the chosen currency of the 2.5 billion unbanked. They're not superrich, but they represent a new market that frontier investors and salesmen now want to tap. To be in it, you need bitcoin. This is the kind of giant global conflagration around which it's possible to imagine bitcoin's becoming a dominant global force.

How would this world look? It's not just a cosmetic matter. It's not just about people tapping their phones to unload bitcoin payments at checkouts. As you'll know from having read this book, a bitcoin-dominant world would have far more sweeping implications: for one, both banks and governments would have less power. And if all the other decentralized applications that we've talked about come along with it, this would be a world in which people lived largely on their own, in their solar-powered homes with their driverless, community-owned cars, exchanging money and value directly, peer-to-peer. It starts to sound like science fiction. Of course, if you had described the world today, just as it is, to somebody a hundred years ago, they'd have thought it sounded like something out of an H. G. Wells story, too.

People like to talk about bitcoin in the extreme terms laid out in the two scenarios above—yes or no, domination or dustbin—but it's not a simple black-and-white question. What's likely is that bitcoin will continue to grow, not alongside the "real" world, but attached to it, the underlying technology adopted by a variety of institutions and businesses to suit their needs. The whole process resembles something you'd see in biology, evolution among and between species. This is what we expect to happen. The trick is to try to guess where that evolutionary track goes. Once again, rather than make outright guesses, we'd prefer to offer another set of scenarios.

A Vital, If Unseen, Cog

One scenario that Silicon Valley visionaries frequently articulate is that cryptocurrencies end up playing a vital role inside the infrastructure of our financial systems but in the background, with fiat currencies continuing as the economies' main units of account and mediums of exchange. In that case, cryptocurrency protocols and blockchain-based systems for confirming transactions would replace the cumbersome payment system that's currently run by banks, credit-card companies, payment processors, and foreign-exchange traders. Some of those intermediaries would disappear; others would simply use cryptocurrency technology for their own institution-to-institution transactions. Because of instantaneous conversion into fiat currencies after each transaction, the end-user consumers and businesses would go about their lives quoting prices and handing over money in the same currencies they've always used.

If the bitcoin blockchain becomes the preferred choice in this scenario, its value as a currency—or perhaps better conceived here as equity in the entire "ecosystem"—would still rise considerably, as bitcoins would constantly be in demand. If you believe this hidden role is bitcoin's future, go ahead and invest in it. You don't need buy-in from Mom and Pop to realize some impressive gains.

But we can equally imagine various altcoin alternatives becoming the preferred payment infrastructure. Ripple Labs' system, for example, is deliberately designed to facilitate international transfers in fiat currencies and other units of value while cutting out all of the intermediary steps that make money transmission expensive. Ripple is also actively marketing to banks and other financial institutions. It offers them a sweet plum: a digitized financial network that's far less disruptive to the banking system than a scenario in which everyone closes his or her bank account for a bitcoin wallet. If any of these "gateway" institutions are suspicious—as some bitcoiners are—of Ripple's profit motives, they could try Stellar, the clone that Ripple's estranged cofounder Jed McCaleb set up with a deliberately charitable agenda. Alternatively, projects such as

Realcoin, an altcoin built upon the bitcoin blockchain that's transparently backed by an auditable reserve of dollar-based assets, turn altcoins into a proxy for the dollar and an instrument with which people can cheaply send money to each other without incurring bitcoin's exchanges' risks. Or there's Bitreserve, Halsey Minor's in-house system in which account holders can send digital dollars, yen, or euros to each other at no cost. Any or all of these could form the components of a cryptocurrency-based financial system.

Still, bitcoin is the clear frontrunner to become the cryptocurrency platform of the world's transactional system. Its market capitalization dwarfs all other altcoins combined. Wences Casares, the CEO of bitcoin wallet and custodial firm Xapo, sees bitcoin's future as the "native currency of the Internet," where it would become the preferred unit of exchange for online commerce. But he sees no reason why governments would unilaterally give up the power to issue sovereign currencies, which would remain as key pillars in the financial system and coexist with bitcoin. It's another reason to believe that concerns about a bitcoin-induced deflation crisis are overblown.

The Multicoin World

There's no guarantee that bitcoin remains the dominant cryptocurrency. If cryptocurrencies do survive, more than one, or many, could end up playing an important role in commerce. Given that the blockchain will allow anybody to attach a digital value to anything, it's conceivable that you could end up with a world in which everything is its own currency. In that economy, digitized claims to assets would be created via the technology behind the blockchain. It works off the "smart property" idea we discussed in chapter 9, where all manner of property is assigned a digital ownership token, a tradable title. Each can be divided into whatever coin denominations are needed to allow for easy exchange with other digitized asset claims. These digital coins, or tokens, would trade against each other via interlinked blockchain-based exchanges that would fairly and transparently set universally recognized prices. This dynamic, multi-asset, giant digital exchange would do away with the need for a common currency altogether. It becomes, in effect, a form of barter, but a form whose divisibility and flexibility overcome the original limitations of that ancient form of exchange, because now, quite literally, you could sell half a horse in exchange for a flight to Acapulco.

In this world, where almost anything has a coin, currency as we know it becomes far less important. Many forms of goods and services can be traded without needing a medium of exchange such as a dollar or a bitcoin. By extension, we end up with less need for central banks and certainly no need for centralized interest rates, as everything's price would float against that of everything else, which—if the market is allowed to function—would mean all things ultimately find some equilibrium.

Zurich-based investment manager and high-tech financial innovator Richard Olsen has talked up the prospect of this "digital barter society" with bankers, hedge fund managers, and anyone else who'll listen. He says that as foreign as it sounds, it resonates with lots of people on Wall Street. Why? "Because it's the only way out of the mess we've gotten ourselves into," he says. Olsen argues that because prices, especially wages, have not been allowed to find their natural level, economic distortions have arisen, leading to crises like those of 2008 and the euro crisis after it. That in turn led central banks to meddle with interest rates to try to find a desired economic balance, ultimately introducing new distortions that lead to new crises. Free-market economists have often dreamed of a world in which all these prices become unstuck and finance becomes far less crisis-prone. A world of cryptocurrency-based digital barter is the way to get there, Olsen says.

A lot of factors could prevent this from happening. One is the logistical complexity of a global exchange system to deliver market-based valuations for an infinite number of digitized assets. How we get from here to there is almost incomprehensible. Then there are the political barriers. A world of entirely free-floating prices could put an end to sticky wages, which are rarely allowed to fall in most economies. While such wage flexibility should help solve unemployment, it's hard to see how workers, the real losers in the latest round of crises, will give up such protections. Still, if digitized assets and blockchain exchanges become the norm, some form of this digital barter economy may well start to emerge.

The Digital Dollar

If a multi-cryptocurrency world is a free marketer's dream, at first blush the scenario we lay out below would seem its antithesis. It goes like this:

deciding to live by the maxim of "if you can't beat them, join them," governments everywhere start launching their own cryptocurrencies. The technology is there. It has been shown to have many advantages. Why wouldn't governments adopt it?

People could trade these state-run digital currencies peer-to-peer without middlemen. Yet they would exist within an overall centralized structure—indeed, the ultimate centralized system, with the state operating as the central titular counterparty. People would simply receive a digital version of the same currencies in which they currently get paid, acceptable wherever those paper currencies are accepted. That would give fiat cryptocurrencies a natural advantage over their upstart independent competitors—again, with the important caveat that some crisis doesn't drive millions into the same camp as the anti-fiat-currency lobby.

Things really get interesting when the U.S. government issues a digital dollar. The dollar is already the world's primary reserve and commercial currency, but this would give it an even bigger edge. That's because people in countries whose currencies aren't trusted or who are barred or restricted from buying foreign currencies—think China, Argentina, Russia—could now easily obtain the one currency that has long symbolized international stability. Whereas the international movement of paper dollars can be (somewhat) controlled with physical checks at border crossings and regulation of bank transfers, digital dollars would be far more footloose. They would invade other jurisdictions' currency zones. If citizens of other countries can easily acquire dollars—by far the most sought-after currency in the world—and use them to buy almost anything, why would they need renminbi or pesos or rubles? In this scenario, other currencies become less sought after, the dollar more powerful. It is the ultimate expression of U.S. hegemony, and, for other governments, undermines their nation-state sovereignty.

If and when the dollar goes digital, "national borders are not going to have much meaning anymore," says Cornell professor and former IMF economist Eswar Prasad, who has written extensively on the dollar-based global financial system. "The walls that countries try to put up around capital inflows and outflows, those are going to disappear very, very quickly."

A monetary system based entirely on digital fiat currency would empower governments in various other ways. Central banks could, for example, set negative interest rates on bank deposits, since savers would no longer be able to flee into cash to avoid the penalty. That would create a powerful incentive for people to spend their money rather than save it, a way to induce economic stimulus. To anyone suspicious of excess central-bank power, this sounds like a nightmare. It's the antithesis of a cryptocurrency utopia.

But here's the rub: none of this is a zero-sum game. In a world in which anyone can create a cryptocurrency, government issuers of fiat digital currencies will face competition like never before. The Fed will be held accountable in a way that's far more powerful than any congressional rule that the Fed chairman must trudge up to Capitol Hill from time to time. The digital dollar will be held to account by a global marketplace of competing currencies. If the market perceives the management of digital dollars as confiscatory or otherwise destructive of people's livelihoods, other currencies will gain at the dollar's cost. If, on the other hand, trust grows in policymakers' stewardship of the dollar economy, the greenback will advance. So even if governments do co-opt cryptocurrency technology for their own ends, a powerful force will constrain what they can and can't do. Even in this scenario, people are empowered.

Bretton Woods II

As you may have sensed, this speculative exercise can take you a long way. When you start contemplating ideas such as a digital dollar, secondary effects and other far-reaching implications arise. The most profound of these is what it means for the nation-state, that ultimate arbiter of power that defines the global economic and political order. Without a doubt, if a digital dollar or any other cryptocurrency were to rise to such global dominance that it poured across borders and challenged national currencies, states would see it as a threat. The greater the extent of capital controls already in existence, the greater the perceived danger to the government, which means China, India, South Korea, Taiwan, Argentina, Venezuela, and various other emerging-market countries would be among those to react most aggressively. But all nations, even those in the West with internationalized currency markets, would to some degree be unsettled by such a fluid monetary situation.

How might they react? The first response could be to censor the Internet with firewalls that restricted access to outside cryptocurrencies. But not only do encryption tools already make it easy for people to get around such controls, the unintended consequences would be to curb innovation, gum up commerce, and drive economic activity to more laissez-faire settings. It's not hard to imagine, then, that governments might band together. Cryptocurrency controls and common solutions would become matters of international importance, discussed in heated debates at the Group of 20's annual meetings or the semiannual gatherings of the IMF. We nation-states are all in this together, the refrain would go. We need to jointly figure out a solution.

What would that solution be? Well, keeping our imagination hats on, we could foresee a set of international standards to define what governments can and can't do with digital money, maybe some sort of international board of cryptocurrency regulators to align rules and regulations that pertain to independent cryptocurrencies such as bitcoin. But given that nation-states have trouble keeping control of decentralized, leaderless cryptocurrencies, it's fair to say international law would be even harder to impose. After all, there is no fully endorsed international criminal court; the one in The Hague isn't recognized by Washington. The international realm exists in a state of quasi anarchy—a perfect fit for borderless cryptocurrencies.

Some international agreements do stick, such as the Bretton Woods system of pegged currencies established in 1944 amid the crisis of World War II (and ended when President Nixon squelched the gold standard in 1971). Might a cryptocurrency crisis goad governments into another such sweeping agreement? A Bretton Woods II? Those who've dreamed of the IMF's playing an intermediary role in international commerce, who've wanted to free the world of its unhealthy dependence on the dollar and to reduce the excessive influence of the Fed and U.S. Treasury, might suddenly feel empowered. The Chinese and the French, who've pushed to have the IMF's Special Drawing Rights elevated from their current role as mere units of accounting to becoming an international reserve currency for storing central bank deposits, might have themselves a new cause. We doubt officials in Paris or Beijing are conceiving of such things right now, but if cryptocurrency technology lives up to its potential, they may have to think about it.

Under this imagined Bretton Woods II, perhaps the IMF would create its own cryptocurrency, with nodes for managing the blockchain situated in proportionate numbers within all the member countries, where none could ever have veto power, to avoid a state-run 51 percent attack. Maybe the cryptocurrency would be limited to use only by central banks for investing their reserves. Or maybe such a digital currency could act as a payment intermediary for international trade, a kind of government-sanctioned Ripple network. That way the international community could sponsor a giant reduction in the cost of international transfers and so promote business, commerce, exports, and innovation.

After decades in which countries have struggled to reach international agreements, let alone enforce them, you'd be right to see all this as far-fetched. But cryptocurrency's future has a binary aspect: if it fails, nothing happens; if it succeeds, it's a game-changer. If and when the game changes, so much else about the structure of the world changes as well.

That's a lot of scenarios to throw out there. Who knows if any of them will come even close to realization. One thing we are relatively sure of, however, is that the next few years will be critical. Most of the people we talk to seem to think of cryptocurrencies and related projects in terms of two to three years, or five to ten years. We seriously doubt that there could be a world of multicoins, a digital dollar, or an IMF cryptocurrency within two, three, or even five years. But ten years? Twenty years? Maybe. A lot will depend upon what happens with bitcoin and its imitators in this interim period, and in particular on the actions of those who've invested their dreams in it, those who see it as a vehicle to change the world.

Bitcoin is just six years old. It has gone from what was ostensibly one lonely coder's pet project to a global phenomenon that has sparked the imagination and activism of libertarians, anticorporatists, crypto-anarchists, utopians, entrepreneurs, and VCs. Bitcoin has gone from being essentially worthless to dearly valuable, only to crash and rise again, a wild trading pattern that has few analogues in capital markets. It's certainly gone from nowhere to somewhere, and where it goes from here may be as messy and chaotic as where it's been.

One way to think about bitcoin is as a movement, yet a movement that's made of different, sometimes competing parts. The crypto-anarchists and libertarian techies built bitcoin up and made the intellectual case for it, and they will continue to play a role in furthering its development as a currency and a cause. But the VCs and entrepreneurs who are taking it out of the dark Web and putting it in front of the masses will also play a critical role in its development. This dichotomy reflects that while bitcoin's expansion is at least partly based on a political response to the financial crisis, it is also founded on technology, which by definition separates it from ideology. That makes it very different from any other political movement and creates crosscurrents that shape its development in unpredictable ways.

Society at large will play a role, too, partly because of the disruptive impact that technology is having on people's lives. Cryptocurrency is a potentially powerful new disruptive element. Interconnected computing gadgets give people far greater control over their daily lives, creating opportunities to discover new ideas, new markets for their products and labor, and new tools for organizing politically. But the technology also fuels anxiety. Some fear the surveillance that it permits; others feel overwhelmed by the relentless barrage of information; a good many will have their jobs replaced by new machines and software. Technology has always fueled a backlash, and cryptocurrencies will be no different.

These conflicting forces can't bang on each other forever. The passionate believers and the threatened masses are already rubbing up against each other in the public square. They are going to meet and mix and mingle and test out each other's ideas and hash out where this whole thing goes. This is how change actually happens, a constant, slow-moving evolution by which human society alters and adapts. It's why we see neither extreme of the bitcoin-domination/bitcoin-failure dichotomy playing out and instead expect the middle ground to win out.

Cryptocurrency enthusiasts inevitably throw out the word *revolution,* one of the most overused in the English language. But real revolutions, those moments in which the existing order is totally overturned, are rare—notwithstanding their prominence in history books. These violent, caustic events are the occasional result of the plate tectonics of human relations, but more often change happens via a more orderly negotiation. This evolutionary process is what brought us to this moment, this age of cryptocurrencies. It's the same process that will determine how that age will develop. The cultural movement that stands behind bitcoin and cryptocurrencies can be viewed as an extension of a long, multicentury line of evolutionary thought on how people should best live together. That's what sets up the real-world tests that will determine cryptocurrency's future. If aspects of cryptocurrency and the new social order that comes with it improve people's lives, they will be adopted. Those that don't will be discarded. Compromises will be devised. "Reality," as Hegel said, "is a historical process."

This is not to deny the extent to which bitcoin has filled people's imaginations about the prospects for a better future. The idea that bitcoin is going to change the world has become an article of faith among its adherents. They believe this is their chance to be part of a historic shift. "If suddenly the entire world starts using a money where governments can't just print extra money because they feel like it," Roger Ver said at a Miami bitcoin conference, "they'll no longer be able to fund these giant war machines that are killing people around the world. So I see bitcoin as a lever that I can use to move the world in a more peaceful direction."

Curious parallels of altruism, greed, and utopianism drive the bitcoin phenomenon. Those nineteen words that Satoshi Nakamoto used to introduce bitcoin in 2009 have been stretched to encompass the dreams and schemes of libertarians, technophiles, anarchists, and ordinary folks looking for something better. Something about these digital currencies and their backers is almost desperately utopian, this idea that people can conduct business, any business, among themselves, without the need for a middleman. This idea is as outlandish to the modern mind as the idea of self-governance must have been to many in 1776. "We hold these truths to be self-evident, that all men are created equal," Thomas Jefferson wrote, fourteen words that did, in fact, change the world.

But Jeffersonian notions of democracy and equal rights didn't spring full born out of the minds of a handful of British subjects living in the New World. They were the products of several hundred years of human development, a period that encompassed both scientific discovery and an

ongoing struggle for individual freedom. It dates back to 1215, the year
in which King John signed the Magna Carta with English nobles, the first
document to set limits on a monarch's power. It later got a boost from
Gutenberg's printing press, the ultimate disruptive technology, which
would make scribes and their quills redundant, exponentially expand the
spread of knowledge, and spur the development of modern education.
Those advances would eventually give rise to the Enlightenment, to the
new ideas of liberty and individual rights expounded by Francis Bacon,
John Locke, and Voltaire. The long interim period also entailed the great
voyages of Columbus, Vasco da Gama, James Cook, and others who
opened the seas, while Galileo, Leonardo da Vinci, Copernicus, and
Newton opened up the heavens and our understanding of our universe.
Together, these explorers expanded the world for Europeans. Once their
discoveries were complete, once the true nature and breadth of the
world were clear, it was impossible to go back to the old conception of
how things were. Our point isn't to compare Satoshi Nakamoto to those
giants. It's that, once again, our worldview has been expanded. There is
no way of going back to the old ways of thinking.

These days more than ever, technology is driving the twin processes
of human discovery and the struggle for freedom. True to the spirit of
Gutenberg's invention, information technology now fully occupies the engine room. For information truly is power. The telegraph, telephone, and
later television all helped spread ideas and shift power away from those
who'd previously monopolized information. Then came the Internet,
which has amplified this effect to new extremes, giving people more power
than they've ever had. Whatever you want to call this new economy—
the sharing economy, the collaborative economy—it is upending centuries of accepted social norms.

Cryptocurrency, a pure form of information technology, a deliberately, explicitly disruptive form of information technology, promises to
take things to a new level altogether. The decentralized bitcoin network and
its public ledger, the blockchain, are at their essence a radical new way of
dealing with information. In this case, it takes information about monetary transactions and economic exchanges out of the hands of monopolist
institutions and creates a decentralized mechanism for society to judge the
validity of that information. Thus cryptocurrency can claim to be the lat-

est in a long line of technological developments that have shifted power out of the hands of centralized elites and handed it over to the people.

Just don't expect revolution. The libertarians are still there in the bitcoin movement, as are the crypto-anarchists. And there's Dark Wallet, and the dark Web, and that entire online black market for bitcoins. Those won't go away, but if cryptocurrencies are going to make a difference, these radical elements will become a minor part of what makes them tick, perhaps relegated to a sideline role as agitators or as the idealists whose standards keep the middle from compromising too much. The bigger part of cryptocurrency's cultural makeup will be found in the parts of the wider economy into which it meshes, both the traditional economy and the new-age sharing economy. Eventually, we believe, this transformation will happen, and all will be changed. Bitcoin will end up something less than the stateless, third-party-less utopian dream of its most passionate supporters. But the creaking, crashing banking state will have some much-needed competition and discipline forced upon it. Costs will come down, commerce and economic activity will grow along digital lines that transcend the lines on a map, and the world will seem even smaller than it already does.

Acknowledgments

Writing a book is a juggling exercise, with multiple odd-shaped balls and objects in the air at any given time. It's not just about juggling the research, writing, and editing; it's also about juggling people's lives, balancing work with family, dealing with ever-shifting priorities and demands. In our case, with the manuscript submission date and production schedule set to a deliberately tight deadline, that juggling exercise was especially complicated. We would never have completed it without a small army of helpers egging us on and picking up the pieces when they fell. Through their hard work and generous provision of information, advice, and moral support, they made this book happen. This army is too numerous to name in full here. But we hope that those who go unmentioned understand the gratitude we feel.

Among those who deserve thanks are the many who acted as primary sources for our material, most of whom come from a vibrant community of bitcoiners. When it boils down to it, this community *is* bitcoin. For all the talk of a desire for secrecy, privacy, and anonymity in cryptocurrency projects, we found so many of these people willing to share their stories. Most provided their full names, with a very few opting for their online forum pseudonyms. To all, we express our thanks. We would also add that we alone are responsible for the content of this book, including any inadvertent errors it may contain.

We need first to single out our agent, Gillian McKenzie, who immediately grasped the value of this book project when we brought it up and was from then on an enthusiastic and unflagging advocate. She made sure this book got in front of the right editor, and even came up with the title.

Tim Bartlett, our editor at St. Martin's Press, was a tough taskmaster who kept us on the straight and narrow, whipped our meandering prose into shape, and helped find the right balance of awe and caution that this contentious subject demands. It's hard to imagine anybody else being able to get us over the finish line. Claire Lampen was a calm but hardworking assistant editor, who provided sharp insights into how to improve the manuscript and kept the production machine running to its hectic schedule. Thanks to the rest of the team at St. Martin's, too, for their energetic embrace of this book and willingness to bend to that tight schedule.

Parts of the manuscript were reviewed by people with far more knowledge of the topics they covered than we have, including Jonathan Mohan, Emin Gün Sirer, Gil Luria, and Felix Martin. Their generous advice is greatly appreciated.

Many at *The Wall Street Journal* provided invaluable support for this book and for our ongoing coverage of cryptocurrencies in the paper, on the *MoneyBeat* blog, and for *WSJ Live*. Some were and remain skeptical of the future of cryptocurrencies, but they kept an open mind and continually offered their encouragement. We are grateful to editor in chief Gerry Baker and ethics editor Neal Lipschutz for blessing this project early on. Within the *Journal*'s Money & Investing section, we must mention the support of the section's managing editor, Francesco Guerrera, and his deputies Emma Moody and Larry Edelman. *MoneyBeat* editor Stephen Grocer suffered our enthusiasms as the main editor of our "BitBeat" column. His skeptical but sharp questioning has made all our work better. Special thanks also go to Stephen's deputy, Erik Holm, as well as *WSJ* markets editor Colin Barr and banking editors Rob Hunter and Aaron Lucchetti. Robin Sidel, a trailblazing reporter in bitcoin coverage, was generous with contacts, time, support, and good humor. And Steven Russolillo, Maureen Farrell, and Simon Constable were great sources of news tips and all-around advice. Meanwhile, various staffers in the *Journal*'s San Francisco, Washington, and London bureaus pitched in with coverage of bitcoin through 2014. From *WSJ Live*, producers Joanne Po and

J. R. Whalen provided our bitcoin coverage with a valuable video platform. From the *Journal*'s China team, Beijing bureau chief Charles Hutzler and researcher Kersten Zhang helped smooth out Michael's visa needs while Shanghai reporter Chao Deng introduced him to contacts and shared her insights during his visit. Elsewhere within the *WSJ*, Vanessa O'Connell and Reed Albergotti provided critical advice on how to coordinate as paired authors, sharing lessons learned from writing their brilliant book on Lance Armstrong, *Wheelmen*. Two more colleagues to thank: Gabriella Stein for, as always, being a fount of enthusiasm, support, and advice and, finally, David Benoit, whose casual remark one day in the newsroom that bitcoin sounded like "something Michael Lewis would write a book about" was the lightning bolt that inspired this one.

We need to highlight a few names from a long list of bitcoin community members who helped us. At the Bitcoin Foundation, chief scientist Gavin Andresen never seemed to tire of our demands for explanations on this or that aspect of bitcoin's software, and press representative Jinyoung Englund would go to great lengths to make introductions and provide information. We are especially grateful to Fran Finney, who went out of her way to obtain information for us during what must have been an extremely difficult period. In San Francisco, Jered Kenna opened up 20Mission to Paul and was generous with his time in the midst of a housing move; Erik Innocent, also of 20Mission, helped him navigate San Francisco's public transit system; Dan Held, the founder of ZeroBlock, provided valuable data; and Scott Robinson at Plug and Play hosted him on expo day. In Barbados, Gabriel Abed spent much more time than he had showing Paul around town. In Shanghai, Bobby Lee opened many doors for Michael, and Zennon Kapron helped put everything in perspective. And in Utah, Ravi Iyengar hosted Michael on an eye-opening tour of CoinTerra's bitcoin mining operation.

Paul: I want to thank my immediate and extended family, all of whom have meant so much to me all these years: my mother, Michele Vigna, and mother-in-law, Sara Krischer, and my aunt, JoAnn Kulpeksa; my sister, Jeanne-Michele Vigna, and brother-in-law, Matt Anderson; as well as cousins David Kulpeksa and Christine Kulpeksa. Space precludes mentioning all the Vignas in my family, but thank you for your friendship and support. Thanks as well to Rob Copeck, a great photographer and better friend who might as well be family. I certainly would not forget my late father, Joseph Vigna, who taught me early, important lessons about the value of money, and so much more.

Then there's my son, Robert. Having Robert in my life inspired me to work harder than I'd ever worked before. I especially want to thank my wife, Elizabeth, who quite literally got my writing career started back in high school when she dragged me by the hand into a meeting of the school's literary magazine. She saw something in me that I didn't know was there, and she's been my biggest and best supporter ever since. There are so many ways in which this book would not have happened without her.

Michael: I want to thank various friends for their support and advice, including Cameron Wilson, Phillip Chambers, Michael Ginn, and Scott Robbins. To my beloved family in Australia—mother, father, and four sisters, as well as their partners and kids—I am grateful for their patience whenever I would disappear with my laptop during a midyear reunion back home. The same goes for Isabel and my other in-laws in Long Island and New York, who let that laptop occupy a dining-room table during an emotionally tough period for the family. Pete will always be remembered as a loving and ever-supportive father-in-law.

I also give special thanks to and for my daughters, Zoe and Analia, who have now lived through three books by their sometimes absentee dad and yet rarely complain and always sustain an upbeat, positive outlook on life. For Alicia, my loving wife of eighteen years, thank you—for everything.

Lastly, from both of us, a special thanks to Satoshi Nakamoto, whoever you are.

Notes

Introduction: Digital Cash for a Digital Age

1 *"Here in Afghanistan a woman's life is limited by"*: Parisa Ahmadi, interviewed by Paul Vigna via e-mail, July 4 and 11, 2014.

2 *Francesco Rulli, aware of the difficulty faced by women like Ahmadi*: Francesco Rulli, interviewed by Michael J. Casey and Paul Vigna, June 19, 2014.

8 *"If you think about what a modern economy is all about"*: Lawrence Summers, phone interview by Michael J. Casey, April 30, 2014.

8 *the "unbanked," the Parisa Ahmadis of the world*: Asli Demirguc-Kunt and Leora Klapper, "Measuring Financial Inclusion," World Bank Policy Research Working Paper 6025, April 2012.

11 *"Every time I give a talk, I emphasize"*: Gavin Andresen, interviewed by Michael J. Casey, February 11, 2014.

11 *"a terrible store of value"*: Jamie Dimon, interviewed on CNBC, January 23, 2014.

11 *investor Warren Buffett, who called it simply a "mirage"*: Warren Buffett, interviewed on CNBC, March 14, 2014.

1. From Babylon to Bitcoin

22 *In his recent and provocative book*: Felix Martin, *Money: The Unauthorized Biography* (The Bodley Head, 2013).

22 *he declares that "currency is not itself"*: Ibid., 14, 27.

22 *Martin takes us to the Micronesian island of Yap*: Ibid., 3–8.

26 *This "metallism" viewpoint*: Distinctions between metallism and chartalism informed by Stephanie Bell, "The Hierarchy of Money" (Jerome Levy Economics Institute of Bard College, April 1998).

27 *Aristotle, who wrote, "When the inhabitants"*: B. J. Gordon, "Aristotle, Schumpeter, and the Metallist Tradition," *Quarterly Journal of Economics* 75 (4) (1961): 608–14.

27   *Adam Smith in* The Wealth of Nations: See Martin, *Money,* 8–10.

28   *The anthropologist David Graeber hypothesizes*: David Graeber, "On the Invention of Money—Notes on Sex, Adventure, Monomaniacal Sociopathy and the True Function of Economics," http://www.nakedcapitalism.com/2011/09/david-graeber-on-the-invention-of-money-%E2%80%93-notes-on-sex-adventure-monomaniacal-sociopathy-and-the-true-function-of-economics.html.

29   *Money, then, made human settlements less vulnerable*: See Martin, *Money,* 50–64.

29   *worsened by Emperor Diocletian's flawed attempts at price controls*: Robert L. Schuettinger and Eamonn F. Butler, *Forty Centuries of Wage and Price Controls,* chap. 2, excerpted by the Ludwig von Mises Institute's blog, http://mises.org/daily/3498.

29   *As the historian Niall Ferguson reminds us*: See Niall Ferguson, *The Ascent of Money* (Penguin, 2008), 42–49.

30   Staters, *the gold-and-silver-alloy coins*: Robert J. O'Hara, "Ancient Greek Coins of Miletus," posted on the *Rjohara.net* blog, http://rjohara.net/coins/lydia-electrum/.

31   *Chinese emperors were taking money into its next phase*: See Martin, *Money,* 76–81.

31   *They described it as a means "to preserve wealth"*: Richard von Glahn, *Fountain of Fortune: Money and Monetary Policy in China, 1000–1700* (University of California Press, 1996), p 29.

32   *The most impressive of these was the* écu de marc: Marie-Thérèse Boyer-Xambeau, Ghislain Deleplace, and Lucien Gillard, *Private Money & Public Currencies : The 16th Century Challenge* (M. E. Sharpe, 1994).

32   *This negotiation between the sovereign*: Martin, *Money,* 115–21.

34   *Based on the ideas of liberal thinkers*: Ibid., 122 36.

34   *Spearheaded by Walter Bagehot*: Ibid., 196–204.

35   *But in the end, the United States, as the only major power*: See Ben Steil, *The Battle of Bretton Woods: John Maynard Keynes, Harry Dexter White, and the Making of a New World Order* (Princeton University Press, 2013).

2. Genesis

41   *"I've been working on a new electronic cash system"*: Satoshi Nakamoto, "Bitcoin P2P e-Cash Paper," cryptography mailing list, October 31, 2008.

41   *"We define an electronic coin as a chain of digital signatures"*: Ibid.

43   *"People will not hold assets in this highly inflationary currency"*: Ray Dillinger, "Bitcoin P2P e-Cash Paper," cryptography mailing list, November 6, 2008, http://www.metzdowd.com/pipermail/cryptography/2008-November/014822.html.

43   *to achieve the "old Cypherpunk dream"*: James A. Donald, "Secrets and Cell Phones," cryptography mailing list, November 5, 2008, https://www.mail-archive.com/cryptography@metzdowd.com/msg09969.html.

43   *hackers would ultimately be the "killer" of Nakamoto's system*: John Levine, "Bitcoin P2P e-Cash Paper," cryptography mailing list, November 3, 2008, https://www.mail-archive.com/cryptography@metzdowd.com/msg09966.html.

44   *Come the New Year, he turned on*: The first block, Block #0, referred to as the Genesis
       Block, was mined on January 3, 2008. https://www.biteasy.com/blockchain/blocks/
       000000000019d6689c085ae165831e934ff763ae46a2a6c172b3f1b60a8ce26f.

45   *"Announcing the first release of bitcoin"*: Satoshi Nakamoto, "Bitcoin V0.1 Released,"
       cryptography mailing list, January 9, 2009, http://www.metzdowd.com/pipermail/
       cryptography/2009-January/014994.html.

45   *Jonathan Thornburg, an astronomy professor at Indiana*: Ibid.

45   *"We were all saying, 'Uh-huh, yeah'"*: John Levine, interviewed by Paul Vigna,
       March 8, 2014.

46   *"He was just a name on a mailing list"*: Russ Nelson, interviewed by Paul Vigna,
       March 7, 2014.

47   *the essence of cryptography—which takes its name from*: Alfred Menezes, Paul
       van Oorschot, and Scott Vanstone, *Handbook of Applied Cryptography* (CRC
       Press, 1996), http://cacr.uwaterloo.ca/hac/about/chap1.pdf.

47   *Thus perhaps naturally, Finney was intrigued*: Hal Finney, interviewed by Paul
       Vigna, March 18, 21, and 27, 2014.

48   *The early e-mail exchanges between this pair*: Hal Finney and Satoshi Nakamoto
       e-mails provided to the authors by Hal and Fran Finney, March 21, 2014.

48   *"In retrospect, I wish I had kept it up longer"*: Hal Finney, "Bitcoin and Me (Hal
       Finney)," *Bitcoin Forum*, March 19, 2013, https://bitcointalk.org/index.php?
       topic=155054.0.

49   *The movement was founded in September 1992*: Details of early Cypherpunk
       meetings and correspondence taken from a phone interview with Tim May by
       Michael J. Casey, April 21, 2104; from archives of the Cypherpunk mailing list cor-
       respondence managed by cypherpunks@MHonArc.venona; and from accounts
       in Andy Greenberg, *This Machine Kills Secrets* (Dutton, 2012), 49–137.

50   *"A specter is haunting the modern world, the specter of crypto-anarchy"*: Tim
       May, "The Crypto Anarchist Manifesto," http://www.activism.net/cypherpunk/
       crypto-anarchy.html.

51   *A few products were downright scary*: Jim Bell, "Assassination Politics," April 3,
       1997, http://www.jrbooksonline.com/PDF_Books/AP.pdf.

51   *a new, encrypted Web-site-based assassination market*: Andy Greenberg, "Meet the
       'Assassination Market' Creator Who's Crowdfunding Murder with Bitcoins," *Forbes*,
       November 18, 2013, http://www.forbes.com/sites/andygreenberg/2013/11/18/meet-
       the-assassination-market-creator-whos-crowdfunding-murder-with-bitcoins/.

51   *Six years after that first meeting of the Cypherpunks*: Wei Dai, "B-Money," posted
       at Wei Dai's personal archives and http://www.weidai.com/bmoney.txt.

52   *Around the same time, Adam Back, another Cypherpunk*: First announced on the
       Cypherpunk mailing list by Adam Back on March 28, 1997, http://www.hashcash.
       org/papers/announce.txt.

52   *Szabo's wide-ranging interests are laid out*: *Unenumerated* blog and papers of Nick
       Szabo, http://unenumerated.blogspot.com/.

52 *But although Wei says he told Nakamoto*: Per e-mails between Nakamoto and Wei
    Dai posted by Gwern Branwen, a pseudonym used by a researcher on cryptogra-
    phy and other matters who posts to www.gwern.net, http://www.gwern.net/docs/
    2008-nakamoto.

53 *David Chaum, the highly innovative and influential cryptographer*: Details of
    Chaum's early biography posted by David Chaum at Chaum.com.

53 *Chaum explained to us the great promise*: Details of DigiCash's conception, devel-
    opment, implementation, and wind-down partially provided in two phone inter-
    views with Michael J. Casey on August 18 and 23, 2014.

56 *Another view, conveyed in a 1999 report in the Dutch magazine* Next!: Translated
    version posted by Ian Grigg to the dbs@philodox.com mailing list, http://cryp
    tome.org/jya/digicrash.htm.

58 *The man who drove this project was Sholom Rosen*: Details of Citibank's e-cash
    project from interview with Sholom Rosen by Michael J. Casey, April 23, 2014; and
    follow-up interviews with other sources familiar with the project.

61 *This "historic legislation," Clinton said*: William J. Clinton, "Statement on Signing
    the Gramm-Leach-Bliley Act," November 12, 1999, http://www.presidency.ucsb.
    edu/ws/?pid=56922.

62 *Mohamed El-Erian, then co-CEO of the massive asset manager*: "When Wall
    Street Nearly Collapsed," *Fortune*, September 14, 2009, http://archive.fortune.
    com/galleries/2009/fortune/0909/gallery.witnesses_meltdown.fortune/.

63 *In one forum post, Nakamoto said*: Satoshi Nakamoto, "Re: Transactions and
    Scripts: DUP HASH160 . . . EQUALVERIFY CHECKSIG," *Bitcoin Forum*, June
    18, 2010, https://bitcointalk.org/index.php?topic=195.msg1617#msg1617.

63 *In a February 11, 2009, post on a forum*: Satoshi Nakamoto, "Bitcoin Open Source
    Implementation of P2P Currency," *P2P Foundation Forum*, February 11, 2009,
    http://p2pfoundation.ning.com/forum/topics/bitcoin-open-source.

63 *Another clue is embedded in the code*: Text of message visible on the blockchain
    monitor provided by Biteasy, https://www.biteasy.com/blockchain/blocks/00000
    0000019d6689c085ae165831e934ff763ae46a2a6c172b3f1b60a8ce26f.

67 *By October, a new coder-focused IRC room*: Taken from "History of Bitcoin" time-
    line, http://historyofbitcoin.org/.

67 *So, by October of 2009, some in the community*: Historical exchange rates posted on
    New Liberty Standard's Web site, http://newlibertystandard.wikifoundry.com/
    page/2009+Exchange+Rate.

67 *This would change in the New Year as Laszlo Hanyecz*: Laszlo Hanyecz, inter-
    viewed by Paul Vigna, April 22, 2014.

3. Community

69 *On December 12, 2010, the following post*: Satoshi Nakamoto, "Added Some DoS
    Limits, Removed Safe Mode (0.3.19)," *Bitcoin Forum*, December 12, 2010, https://
    bitcointalk.org/index.php?topic=2228.

69   *As far as we know, the last one went to Gavin Andresen*: Gavin Andresen, interviewed by Michael J. Casey, February 11, 2014.

70   *although community members have debated*: Nermin Hajdarbegovic, "Bitcoin
Foundation Forms Committee to Create Bitcoin Unicode Symbol," *CoinDesk,*
June 19, 2014, http://www.coindesk.com/bitcoin-foundation-forms-committee-
create-bitcoin-unicode-symbol/.

71   *"In business, creation stories reinforce the role"*: Paul Vigna and Michael J. Casey,
"BitBeat: Bitcoin's Creation Myth Is Different, Too," *Wall Street Journal, Money-
Beat* blog, March 3, 2014, http://blogs.wsj.com/moneybeat/2014/03/10/bitbeat-bit
coins-creation-myth-is-different-too/.

73   *"Mysterious in the case of money"*: Tamara Audi, Robin Sidel, and Michael
J. Casey, "Bitcoin Report Rattles Currency's World," *Wall Street Journal,* March 7,
2014.

73   *That's the estimate that cryptographer Sergio Lerner*: Sergio Lerner, "The Well Deserved Fortune of Satoshi Nakamoto, Bitcoin Creator, Visionary and Genius,"
Words on Bitcoin Design, Privacy, Security and Crypto blog, April 17, 2013, http://bit
slog.wordpress.com/2013/04/17/the-well-deserved-fortune-of-satoshi-nakamoto/.

73   *SecondMarket's CEO, Barry Silbert, describes*: Comments made at media round-
table sponsored by Circle Internet Financial, New York, December 10, 2013.

74   *Nick Szabo, whose writings, the forensics linguists tell us*: Paul Vigna, "Bitcoin
Creator 'Satoshi Nakamoto' Unmasked—Again?," *Wall Street Journal, MoneyBeat*
blog, April 16, 2014, http://blogs.wsj.com/moneybeat/2014/04/16/bitcoin-creator
-satoshi-nakamoto-unmasked-again/.

74   *Writing for* The New Yorker: Joshua Davis, "The Crypto-Currency: Bitcoin and
Its Mysterious Inventor," *New Yorker,* October 10, 2011.

74   *New York University journalism professor Adam Penenberg*: Adam L. Penenberg,
"The Bitcoin Crypto-currency Mystery Reopened," *Fast Company,* October 11, 2011,
http://www.fastcompany.com/1785445/bitcoin-crypto-currency-mystery-
reopened.

74   *Next came Ted Nelson*: Ted Nelson, "I Think I Know Who Satoshi Is," YouTube,
May 17, 2013, https://www.youtube.com/watch?v=emDJTGTrEm0.

75   *Then, on March 6, 2014, the weekly magazine* Newsweek: Leah McGrath Goodman, "The Face Behind Bitcoin," *Newsweek,* March 6, 2014.

77   *"It piqued my interest," says Andresen*: Gavin Andresen, interviewed by Michael
J. Casey, February 11, 2014.

78   *Andresen started a project he called Bitcoin Faucet*: Ibid.

78   *On May 21, 2010, Hanyecz ate a cheese pizza*: Details of Laszlo Hanyecz's pizza offer come from Paul Vigna's phone interview with Hanyecz on April 22, 2014, as well
as follow-up correspondence on September 1, 2014. Also, Lazlo Hanyecz, "Pizza for
Bitcoins?," *Bitcoin Forum,* May 18, 2010, https://bitcointalk.org/index.
php?topic=137.0.

79   *"I had a lot," he says, so many*: Hanyecz, interviewed by Vigna.

79   *"I'll pay 10,000 bitcoins for a couple of pizzas"*: Hanyecz, "Pizza for Bitcoins?"

79   *"Fresh pizza," he said, "from London"*: Hanyecz, interviewed by Vigna.

79   *In March of 2010, for example*: Post by SmokeTooMuch, "Bitcoin Auction: 10,000
      BTC—Starting Bid 50.00 USD," *Bitcoin Forum,* March 30, 2010, https://bitcoin
      talk.org/index.php?topic=92.0.

79   *"So, I finally got my client to start generating"*: Post by AgoraMutual, "Is My Second
      Transaction Working Correctly?," *Bitcoin Forum,* January 1, 2010, https://bitcoin-
      talk.org/index.php?topic=17.0;wap2.

80   *"Back then, it was a lot of people helping"*: Hanyecz, interviewed by Vigna.

80   *"sounded like a vacuum cleaner when they were busy"*: Laszlo Hanyecz, inter-
      viewed by Paul Vigna, September 1, 2014.

81   *"In one week, the difficulty shot up so high"*: Hanyecz, interviewed by Vigna, April
      22, 2014.

81   *Over five days, bitcoin's exchange rate*: Via the bitcoin wiki "History," https://en.
      bitcoin.it/wiki/History.

81   *"Hi everyone," he wrote*: Jed McCaleb, posting as mtgox, "New Bitcoin Exchange
      (mtgox.com)," *Bitcoin Forum,* July 18, 2010, https://bitcointalk.org/index.php?
      topic=444.msg3866#msg3866.

82   *In 2007, McCaleb had started an online platform*: Jed McCaleb, interviewed about
      Mt. Gox history and early days via e-mail by Gwern Branwen, February 16, 17,
      and 24, 2014, http://www.gwern.net/docs/2014-mccaleb.

82   *In March 2011, he told the forum*: Jed McCaleb, posting as mtgox, "Mt. Gox Is
      Changing Owners," *Bitcoin Forum,* March 6, 2011, https://bitcointalk.org/index.
      php?topic=4187.msg60610#msg60610.

82   *A lover of Japanese manga and cosplay*: Sophie Knight, "At Mt. Gox Bitcoin Hub,
      'Geek' CEO Sought Both Control and Escape," Reuters, April 21, 2014, http://in.
      reuters.com/article/2014/04/21/uk-bitcoin-mtgox-karpeles-idINKBN0D
      700J20140421.

82   *Whereas the Bitcoin Forum had added new members*: Taken from statistics page
      at *Bitcoin Forum,* https://bitcointalk.org/index.php?action=stats.

83   *Mt. Gox rose from six thousand to sixty thousand*: Mark Karpelès, posting as
      MagicalTux, "Mt. Gox: If Your Coins Were Stolen, Please Write Here," *Bitcoin
      Forum,* June 18, 2011, https://bitcointalk.org/index.php?topic=18858.0;all.

83   *reports put the amount at anywhere from two thousand to half a million coins*: For
      the low-end two thousand: Marc Bevand, "Major Attack on the World's Largest
      Bitcoin Exchange," *Zorinaq,* June 19, 2011, http://blog.zorinaq.com/?e=55; for the
      high-end half a million: Jason Mick, "Inside the Mega-Hack of Bitcoin: The Full
      Story," *DailyTech,* June 19, 2011, http://www.dailytech.com/Inside+the+MegaHa
      ck+of+Bitcoin+the+Full+Story/article21942.htm.

83   *Bitcoin's prices plunged to meet it*: Jack Hough, "Bitcoin's Flash Crash," *Market-
      Watch,* June 22, 2011, http://blogs.marketwatch.com/paydirt/2011/06/22/bitcoin
      %E2%80%99s-flash-crash/; also, Tyler Cowan, "The Bitcoin Crash," *Marginal
      Revolution,* http://marginalrevolution.com/marginalrevolution/2011/06/the-bit
      coin-crash.html. The fraudulent trades would later be unwound and do not show

up in historical price charts, although a chart at Bitcoin Charts, http://bitco incharts.com/charts/mtgoxUSD#tgCzm1g10zm2g25zv, does show a "double float" of 1.7e+308 in the price columns, for six days after the nineteenth, the time the trades were being unwound.

83 *In July 2011, Mt. Gox was handling 80 percent*: This figure was reported by the exchange itself and widely cited; see Paul Vigna and Michael J. Casey, "BitBeat: Mt. Gox Halts Withdrawals, Bitcoin Price Drops," *Wall Street Journal, MoneyBeat* blog, February 7, 2014, http://blogs.wsj.com/moneybeat/2014/02/07/bitbeat-mt-gox-halts-withdrawals-bitcoin-price-drops/.

84 *The most extreme manifestations of that idea*: Post by silkroad, "Silk Road: Anonymous Marketplace. Feedback Requested," *Bitcoin Forum,* March 1, 2011, https://bitcointalk.org/index.php?topic=3984.msg57086#msg57086.

84 *With the Bitcointalk forum now*: Taken from statistics page at *Bitcoin Forum,* https://bitcointalk.org/index.php?action=stats.

84 *The Web site* Gawker, *in June 2011*: Adrien Chen, "The Underground Website Where You Can Buy Any Drug Imaginable," *Gawker,* June 1, 2011, http://gawker.com/the-underground-website-where-you-can-buy-any-drug-imag-30818160.

84 *"The site went mainstream way"*: Post by silkroad, "Silk Road: Anonymous Marketplace. Feedback Requested," *Bitcoin Forum,* June 9, 2011, https://bitcointalk.org/index.php?topic=3984.msg189007#msg189007.

86 *New York State senator Chuck Schumer*: "Schumer Pushes to Shut Down Online Drug Marketplace," *NBC New York,* June 5, 2011, http://www.nbcnewyork.com/news/local/Schumer-Calls-on-Feds-to-Shut-Down-Online-Drug-Marketplace-123187958.html.

86 *The response on the Bitcoin Forum was mixed*: Post by FatherMcGruder and others, "Silk Road: Anonymous Marketplace. Feedback Requested," *Bitcoin Forum,* https://bitcointalk.org/index.php?topic=3984.260.

86 *In August 2012,* Forbes's *Andy Greenberg*: Andy Greenberg, "Black Market Drug Site 'Silk Road' Booming: $22 Million in Annual Sales," *Forbes,* August 6, 2012.

86 *The FBI estimated that between February 6, 2011*: From the FBI complaint against Ross Ulbricht, September 27, 2013, http://www.scribd.com/doc/172773561/Criminal-Complaint-Against-Silk-Road-and-Dread-Pirate-Roberts.

87 *Trading platforms for bitcoin started appearing*: Various developments in 2011–12 taken from the timeline at http://historyofbitcoin.org/.

87 *Charlie Shrem, a Brooklyn-based twenty-one-year-old*: Adrianne Jeffries, "Bored with Bitcoin? BitInstant Is About to Goose the Market by Making Trading Faster," *BetaBeat,* August 23, 2011, http://betabeat.com/2011/08/bored-with-bitcoin-bitinstant-is-about-to-goose-the-market-by-making-trading-faster.

88 *By mid-2012, SatoshiDice*: Megan Geuss, "Firm Says Online Gambling Accounts for Almost Half of All Bitcoin Transactions," *ArsTechnica,* August 24, 2013, http://arstechnica.com/business/2013/08/firm-says-online-gambling-accounts-for-almost-half-of-all-bitcoin-transactions/.

88   *One of the first was Peter Vessenes*: Blog post, "Bitcoin Startup Incubator, Coin-Lab, Launches in WA," *Bitcoin News Network*, September 25, 2011, http://www.btcnn.com/2011/09/bitcoin-startup-incubator-coinlab.html.

88   Bitcoin Magazine, *founded by Mihai Alisie*: According to *Bitcoin Magazine* "About Us" page, http://bitcoinmagazine.com/about-us/.

88   *In September 2012, the Bitcoin Foundation was founded*: Jon Matonis, "Bitcoin Foundation Launches to Drive Bitcoin's Advancement," September 9, 2012, http://www.forbes.com/sites/jonmatonis/2012/09/27/bitcoin-foundation-launches-to-drive-bitcoins-advancement/.

88   *At that time, the Bitcoin Forum had about sixty-eight thousand members*: Taken from statistics page at *Bitcoin Forum*, https://bitcointalk.org/index.php?action=stats.

89   *Beginning in March 2012, thefts totaling*: "Bitcoinica, Twice Hacked in 2012, Is Being Sued," *Infosecurity Magazine*, August 15, 2012, http://www.infosecurity-magazine.com/news/bitcoinica-twice-hacked-in-2012-is-being-sued/.

89   *Kenna's Tradehill exchange*: Timothy B. Lee, "Major Bitcoin Exchange Shuts Down, Blaming Regulation and Loss of Funds," *ArsTechnica*, February 15, 2012, http://arstechnica.com/tech-policy/2012/02/major-bitcoin-exchange-shuts-down-blaming-regulation-and-loss-of-funds/.

89   *Yet all the while, the bitcoin price went up, up, and up*: Prices taken from *CoinDesk*'s Bitcoin Price Index chart, http://www.coindesk.com/price/.

89   *Litecoin, the oldest and largest of the altcoins*: Market-capitalization data taken from CoinMarketCap Web site, http://coinmarketcap.com/.

90   *altcoin that started out as a joke by Billy Markus and Jackson Palmer*: Patrick McGuire, "Such Weird: The Founders of Dogecoin See the Meme Currency's Tipping Point," *Motherboard*, December 23, 2013, http://motherboard.vice.com/blog/dogecoins-founders-believe-in-the-power-of-meme-currencies.

90   *Through campaigns launched on Reddit*: For an overview of dogecoin fund-raising efforts, *The Dogesonian* has an overview at http://thedogesonian.weebly.com/the-early-dogecoin-projects.html. Also see Roop Gill, "Manchester Co-op Gets a Hand from Dogecoin to Smash Fundraising Targets," *CoinDesk*, April 22, 2014, http://www.coindesk.com/manchester-co-op-gets-hand-dogecoin-smash-fundraising-target/.

91   *Our favorite dogecoin endeavor*: Paul Vigna, "BitBeat: Dogecoin Makes Its NAS-CAR Debut; Ripple Signs a Bank," *Wall Street Journal*, *MoneyBeat* blog, May 5, 2014, http://blogs.wsj.com/moneybeat/2014/05/05/bitbeat-dogecoin-makes-its-nascar-debut-ripple-signs-a-bank/.

91   *When GoCoin decided that it would*: Michael J. Casey, "BitBeat: Much Good, Dogecoin; So Hip," *Wall Street Journal*, *MoneyBeat* blog, March 13, 2014, http://blogs.wsj.com/moneybeat/2014/03/13/bitbeat-much-good-dogecoin-so-hip/.

91   *though with bitcoin's market capitalization more than ten times*: as per the market capitalizations of the top 100 cryptocurrencies quoted at coinmarketcap.com.

92   *Andreas Antonopoulos, chief security officer at wallet provider Blockchain.info*: Paul

Vigna, "BitBeat: Dorian Nakamoto Writes a Letter," *Wall Street Journal, MoneyBeat* blog, March 17, 2014, http://blogs.wsj.com/moneybeat/2014/03/17/bitbeat-dorian-nakamoto-writes-a-letter/.

92 Forbes *writer Andy Greenberg started an effort*: Andy Greenberg, "Nakamoto's Neighbor: My Hunt for Bitcoin's Creator Led to a Paralyzed Crypto Genius," *Forbes*, March 25, 2013, http://www.forbes.com/sites/andygreenberg/2014/03/25/satoshi-nakamotos-neighbor-the-bitcoin-ghostwriter-who-wasnt/.

92 *"Oh, bitcoin, I know you're gonna reign, gonna reign"*: John Barrett, "Ode to Satoshi (The Official Bitcoin Song)," YouTube, February 13, 2014, https://www.youtube.com/watch?v=zEQ2nPSL5-0.

92 *"10,000 Bitcoins"*: Laura Saggers, "10,000 Bitcoins," YouTube, March 5, 2014, https://www.youtube.com/watch?v=RIsZyg8OXlI.

93 *"Bitcoin Barons"*: YTCracker, "Bitcoin Barons," YouTube, August 4, 2013, https://www.youtube.com/watch?v=RIsZyg8OXlI.

93 *Meanwhile, the German artist Kuno Goda*: "BitBeat: China's Central Bank Means Business," *Wall Street Journal, MoneyBeat* blog, April 1, 2014, http://blogs.wsj.com/moneybeat/2014/04/01/bitbeat-chinas-central-bank-means-business/.

93 *L.A. photographer Megan Miller*: Paul Vigna, "BitBeat: Doing Math on Mining," *Wall Street Journal, MoneyBeat* blog, April 16, 2014, http://blogs.wsj.com/moneybeat/2014/04/16/bitbeat-doing-math-on-mining/.

94 *The Craigs were unlikely proselytizers*: Austin and Beccy Craig, interviewed by Paul Vigna on October 20, 2013, and April 28, 2014.

4. Roller Coaster

97 *You're in a Starbucks in New York*: Prices of grande lattes at Starbucks in New York and Oslo taken from "More or Less Brew for Your Buck," *Wall Street Journal*, March 8, 2013.

100 *the whopping $11 trillion in payments that Visa and MasterCard*: Annual reports, 2013, MasterCard Inc. and Visa Inc.

100 *about 87 percent of the global market*: "Market Shares of Purchase Transactions Worldwide 2013," *Nilson Report*, March 2014.

100 *Benefiting from a global explosion in e-commerce*: Will Craig, "Opportunities Abound as the Web Extends Its Reach Around the World," 2nd Quarter Report, 2014, Capital Group, http://capitalgrouppcs.com/opportunities-abound-as-the-web-extends-its-reach-around-the-world.html.

101 *In letting the existing system develop, we've allowed*: Gil Luria, phone interview by Michael J. Casey, April 15, 2014.

101 *the top ten credit-card issuers in the world*: "World's Top 10 Credit-card Issuers," CNBC.com, April 13, 2013, http://www.cnbc.com/id/36471668.

102 *this netting process is coordinated by the Fed's Fedwire service*: Up-to-date statistics available from the Federal Reserve Bank Services, http://www.frbservices.org/operations/fedwire/fedwire_funds_services_statistics.html.

102   *Securing and distributing all this cash*: Ajay Banga, "Reflections on FI2020—Part 1," *Center for Financial Inclusion* blog, October 30, 2013, http://cfi-blog.org/2013/10/30/ajay-banga-reflections-on-fi2020-part-1/.

103   *a list of merchants accepting bitcoin that, by CoinDesk's count*: "State of Bitcoin Q2 2014 Report Reveals Expanding Bitcoin Economy," July 10, 2014, http://www.coindesk.com/state-of-bitcoin-q2-2014-report-expanding-bitcoin-economy/.

103   *Blockchain cofounder Peter Smith says*: Peter Smith, interviewed by Michael J. Casey, August 11, 2014.

103   *processed daily by Visa and MasterCard in 2013*: Annual reports, 2013, MasterCard Inc. and Visa Inc.

106   *a hacker hijacked an Internet service provider's computers*: Swati Khandelwal, "Hacker Hijacks ISP Networks to Steal $83,000 from Bitcoin Mining Pools," http://thehackernews.com/2014/08/hacker-hijacks-isp-networks-to-steal_7.html.

106   *a Greece-based botnet used Facebook to infect 250,000 computers*: Mohit Kumar, "Facebook Takes Down Bitcoin-Stealing Botnet That Infected 250,000 Computers," *Hacker News,* July 9, 2014.

106   *the $148 million attack on Target in December 2013*: Tom Gara, "An Expensive Hack Attack: Target's $148 Million Breach," August 5, 2014, http://blogs.wsj.com/corporate-intelligence/2014/08/05/an-expensive-hack-attack-targets-148-million-breach/.

107   *Let's compare the average U.S. price of a gallon of gasoline*: Weekly average U.S.-wide gasoline prices from the Energy Information Administration, http://www.eia.gov/dnav/pet/pet_pri_gnd_dcus_nus_w.htm; and bitcoin prices from the *CoinDesk* Bitcoin Price Index, http://www.coindesk.com/price.

107   *New York University professor David Yermack concluded that bitcoin*: David Yermack, "Is Bitcoin a Real Currency?," NBER Working Paper No. 19747, December 2013.

108   *You need look no further*: CoinDesk Bitcoin Price Index.

110   *This included a harrowing "flash crash"*: Paul Vigna, "BitBeat: A Bitcoin 'Flash Crash' as Volume Spike Briefly Takes Price to $309," *Wall Street Journal, MoneyBeat* blog, August 18, 2014, http://blogs.wsj.com/moneybeat/2014/08/18/bitbeat-a-bitcoin-flash-crash-as-volume-spike-briefly-takes-price-to-309/.

110   *In a scathing presentation to the New York*: Mark T. Williams, "Testimony of Mark T. Williams," New York State Department of Financial Services, January 28–29, 2014, http://www.dfs.ny.gov/about/hearings/vc_01282014/williams.pdf.

110   *"I wouldn't say hoarding is a bad thing"*: Bobby Lee, interviewed by Michael J. Casey in Shanghai, July 19, 2014.

110   *Gil Luria, the Wedbush analyst*: Gil Luria, "Embracing Volatility: Trading as Bitcoin's First Killer App," research report by Wedbush Securities, August 20, 2014.

113   *"If they can do that there, they can do it anywhere"*: Mark McGowan, "The Great Cyprus Bank Robbery by Financial Terrorists," March 17, 2013, https://www.youtube.com/watch?v=YDXtHsz2q6Q.

113   *The price went from $33 at the end of February to $230 on April 9*: CoinDesk Bitcoin Price Index.

113   *The bitcoin price plunged to $68 on April 16*: Ibid.

113   *In late June 2013, reports emerged that the FBI*: John Biggs, "The DEA Seized Bitcoins in a Silk Road Drug Raid," *TechCrunch,* June 27, 2013, http://techcrunch.com /2013/06/27/the-dea-seized-bitcoins-in-a-silk-road-drug-raid/.

113   *A month later, the Securities and Exchange Commission filed charges*: Jessica B. Magee, lead attorney, SEC Complaint, July 23, 2013, http://www.sec.gov/litigation /complaints/2013/comp-pr2013-132.pdf.

114   *they had acquired a massive stock of bitcoin then worth $11 million*: Nathaniel Popper and Peter Lattman, "Never Mind Facebook; Winklevoss Twins Rule in Digital Money," April 11, 2013, *New York Times, Dealbook* blog, http://dealbook.ny times.com/2013/04/11/as-big-investors-emerge-bitcoin-gets-ready-for-its-close-up/?_php=true&_type=blogs&_r=0 ; also see David Benoit and Andrew R. Johnson, "Winklevoss Twins Launch IPO for Bitcoin-Tracking Stock," *Wall Street Journal, All Things Digital* blog, July 1, 2013, http://allthingsd.com/20130701/win klevoss-twins-launch-ipo-for-bitcoin-tracking-stock/.

114   *Not even the dramatic October 2 news*: Danny Yadron,"FBI Makes Arrest, Seizes Online Market 'Silk Road,'" *Wall Street Journal, Law* blog, October 2, 2013, http:// blogs.wsj.com/law/2013/10/02/fbi-makes-arrest-seizes-online-market-silk-road/.

114   *"recognizes the innovation virtual currencies provide"*: Jennifer Shasky Calvery, statement to U.S. Senate Subcommittee on Economic Policy, November 19, 2013, http://www.fincen.gov/news_room/testimony/html/20131119.html.

115   *In January of 2013, a Chinese company called Avalon*: Bitcoin core developer Jeff Garzik is believed to have had one of the first deliveries. Vitalik Buterin, "Working Avalon ASIC Confirmed, Hashing At 68 GH/s," *Bitcoin Magazine,* January 31, 2013, http://bitcoinmagazine.com/3231/working-avalon-asic-confirmed/.

115   *In a watershed moment,* Bloomberg Businessweek *ran*: Max Raskin, "Meet the Bloomberg Millionaires," *Bloomberg Businessweek,* April 10, 2013, http://www. businessweek.com/articles/2013-04-10/meet-the-bitcoin-millionaires.

115   *By December, bitcoin was over $1,100*: For price, *CoinDesk* Bitcoin Price Index; for market capitalization, CoinMarketCap.com, http://www.coinmarketcap.com.

115   *BTC China exchange, which at one point even surpassed Mt. Gox in volume*: Emily Spaven, "BTC-China Beats Mt. Gox and Bitstamp to Become the World's No. 1 Bitcoin Exchange," *CoinDesk,* November 4, 2013, http://www.coindesk.com/btc -china-beats-mt-gox-bitstamp-become-worlds-1-bitcoin-exchange/.

116   *the People's Bank of China was not happy*: Robin Sidel, Chao Deng, and William Horobin, "Central Banks Warn of Bitcoin Risks," *Wall Street Journal,* December 5, 2013, http://online.wsj.com/news/articles/SB100014240527023034978045792 39451297424842.

116   *By January 2014, the price was down to $770*: *CoinDesk* Bitcoin Price Index.

116   *The day after the conference, Charlie Shrem, one of* Businessweek's *"bitcoin millionaires"*: Christopher M. Matthews and Robin Sidel, "Two Charged in Alleged Bitcoin-Laundering Scheme," *Wall Street Journal,* January 27, 2014.

116   *announced that it would also no longer allow customers*: Michael Carney, "Mt.

Gox Suspends Bitcoin Withdrawals (Temporarily?), Market Falls amid Concerns of Impropriety," *Pando Daily,* February 7, 2014, http://pando.com/2014/02/07/mt-gox-suspends-bitcoin-withdrawals-temporarily-market-falls-amid-concerns-of-impropriety/.

116   *on February 28 it announced that it would file for bankruptcy*: Robin Sidel, Eleanor Warnock, and Takashi Mochizuki, "Almost Half a Billion Worth of Bitcoins Vanish," *Wall Street Journal,* February 28, 2014.

117   *China cemented that concern with a more formal ruling in April banning banks*: Michael J. Casey, "BitBeat: China Dings Bitcoin Again," *Wall Street Journal, MoneyBeat* blog, April 25, 2014, http://blogs.wsj.com/moneybeat/2014/04/25/bitbeat-china-dings-bitcoin-again/.

117   *The Internal Revenue Service came out with a much-awaited ruling*: John D. McKinnon and Ryan Tracy, "IRS Says Bitcoin Is Property, Not Currency," *Wall Street Journal,* March 25, 2014.

118   *Although Financial Services superintendent Benjamin Lawsky*: Paul Vigna, "NY Financial Regulator Releases Draft of 'BitLicense' for Bitcoin Businesses," *Wall Street Journal, MoneyBeat* blog, July 17, 2014, http://blogs.wsj.com/moneybeat/2014/07/17/ny-financial-regulator-releases-draft-of-bitlicense-for-bitcoin-businesses/.

118   *Lawsky indicated he was willing to change*: Paul Vigna, "BitBeat: BitLicense Gets Extension; Lawsky: 'We Don't Have a Monopoly on the Truth,'" *Wall Street Journal, MoneyBeat* blog, August 21, 2014, http://blogs.wsj.com/moneybeat/2014/08/21/bitbeat-bitlicense-gets-extension-lawsky-we-dont-have-a-monopoly-on-the-truth/.

118   *Chinese exchanges, margin-trading facilities introduced*: Michael J. Casey, "Bit Beat: So Much for That Boring Bitcoin Market," *Wall Street Journal, MoneyBeat* blog, August 13, 2014, http://blogs.wsj.com/moneybeat/2014/08/13/bitbeat-so-much-for-that-boring-bitcoin-market/.

5. Building the Blockchain

121   *we'll borrow an idea developed by software engineer*: Yevgeniy Brikman, "Bitcoin by Analogy," on Brikman's blog *Don't Panic,* April 24, 2014, http://brikis98.blogspot.com/2014/04/bitcoin-by-analogy.html.

124   *The blockchain is managed*: Much of what is explained is taken from the Bitcoin wiki at bitcoin.org and from conversations with multiple developers.

130   *nonce is derived from a passage by Lewis Carroll*: See Angela Tung, "10 Whimsical Words Coined by Lewis Carroll," *Week,* January 25, 2013, http://theweek.com/article/index/239253/10-whimsical-words-coined-by-lewis-carroll.

131   *At the exact moment that these words were being written*: Per the home page at the time of Blockchain.info, http://blockchain.info.

132   *including one from start-up BlockCypher*: Michael J. Casey, "BitBeat: A Solution to That 10-Minute Transaction Wait?," *The Wall Street Journal, MoneyBeat* blog, September 5, 2014, http://blogs.wsj.com/moneybeat/2014/09/05/bitbeat-a-solution-to-that-10-minute-transaction-wait/.

6. The Arms Race

138   *One of those newcomers was Jason Whelan*: Details of Whelan's experience taken from e-mail correspondence, May 29, 2014, and June 2, 2014.

143   *At a data center on the outskirts*: Material on CoinTerra's operations in Utah taken from a visit to the facilities by Michael J. Casey, June 7, 2014.

145   *By that time, the network, which was then producing*: Hashrate data from Blockchain.info, https://blockchain.info/charts/hash-rate; computing-power comparison uses total petaflop estimate at http://www.bitcoinwatch.com/ and compares to total power of five hundred top supercomputers detailed at http://www.top500.org.

145   *Back in April 2013, various press reports*: For example, see Mark Gimein, "Virtual Bitcoin Mining Is a Real-World Environmental Disaster," Bloomberg, April 12, 2013, http://www.bloomberg.com/news/2013-04-12/virtual-bitcoin-mining-is-a-real-world-environmental-disaster.html.

147   *Months later, Guy Lane*: Lane's BitCarbon methodology is explained at http://www.bitcarbon.org/bitcarbon/.

147   *If every miner used these rigs*: Discussion of outdated energy-consumption estimates at http://rationalwiki.org/wiki/Talk:Bitcoin/Archive1#Outdated_energy_consumption_estimate.

148   *data-center consultants were advising bitcoin miners*: Michael J. Casey, "BitBeat: For Bitcoin Miners, a Hot Problem This Summer," *Wall Street Journal, MoneyBeat* blog, April 29, 2014, http://blogs.wsj.com/moneybeat/2014/04/29/bitbeat-for-bitcoin-miners-a-hot-problem-this-summer/.

148   *Adam Smith opined on a similar matter in the eighteenth century*: Paul Krugman, "Adam Smith Hates Bitcoin," *New York Times, Conscience of a Liberal* blog, April 12, 2013, http://krugman.blogs.nytimes.com/2013/04/12/adam-smith-hates-bitcoin/.

148   *One such vulnerability was thrust*: Account of the hardfork in the blockchain comes from a thread on the #bitcoin-dev list at the Bitcoin Forum, March 11, 2013, http://bitcoinstats.com/irc/bitcoin-dev/logs/2013/03/11.

151   *One $10,000 case of double-spending*: Vitalik Buterin, "Bitcoin Network Shaken by Blockchain Fork," *Bitcoin Magazine*, March 12, 2013, http://bitcoinmagazine.com/3668/bitcoin-network-shaken-by-blockchain-fork/.

152   *According to coinometrics.com*: The cost of a 51 percent attack is regularly updated on the Coinometrics Web site, http://www.coinometrics.com/bitcoin/brix.

152   *in June 2014, the pool GHash.IO*: Michael J. Casey, "BitBeat: Mining Pool Rejects Short-Term Fixes to Avert '51% Attack,'" *Wall Street Journal, MoneyBeat* blog, June 16, 2014, http://blogs.wsj.com/moneybeat/2014/06/16/bitbeat-a-51-attack-what-is-it-and-could-it-happen/.

152   *In a controversial paper*: Ittay Eyal and Emin Gün Sirer, "Majority Is Not Enough: Bitcoin Mining Is Vulnerable," research paper published by arXiv.org of Cornell University, November 15, 2013, http://arxiv.org/pdf/1311.0243v5.pdf.

152   *The paper upset many in the bitcoin community*: Phone interview with Sirer by Michael J. Casey, March 9, 2014.

153   *As Nakamoto explained in his white paper*: Satoshi Nakamoto, "Bitcoin: A Peer-to-Peer Electronic Cash System," August 2008, bitcoin.org, https://bitcoin.org/bitcoin.pdf.

153   *CEX.IO has at times*: Casey, "BitBeat: Mining Pool Rejects Short-Term Fixes."

154   *As of late August 2014*: Per "Top 100" on bitcoinrichlist.com, http://bitcoinrichlist.com/top100.

154   *Hence the reports of ostentatious bitcoin-based*: See Robin Sidel, "Bitcoins Buy a Villa in Bali," *Wall Street Journal*, March 19, 2014; and Michael J. Casey and Paul Vigna, "From Space Travel to Pizza, Your Bitcoin Goes Far These Days," *Wall Street Journal, MoneyBeat* blog, January 16, 2014, http://blogs.wsj.com/moneybeat/2014/01/16/from-space-travel-to-pizza-your-bitcoin-goes-quite-far-these-days/.

155   *"multi-sig" wallets from innovators such as BitGo*: Michael J. Casey, "Bitcoin Security Startup BitGo Gets More Funds; Ex-Verisign CEO Joins Team," *Wall Street Journal, MoneyBeat* blog, June 16, 2014, http://blogs.wsj.com/moneybeat/2014/06/16/bitcoin-security-startup-bitgo-gets-more-funds-ex-verisign-ceo-joins-team/.

155   *Core bitcoin developer Jeff Garzik*: See Daniel Cawrey, "Jeff Garzik Announces Partnership to Launch Bitcoin Satellites into Space," *CoinDesk*, April 23, 2014, http://www.coindesk.com/jeff-garzik-announces-partnership-launch-bitcoin-satellites-space/; also see Catherine Bleish, "An Interview with Jeff Garzik, Bitcoin in Space," *Bitcoin Magazine*, June 17, 2014, http://bitcoinmagazine.com/14069/interview-jeff-garzik-bitcoin-space/.

157   *Of these altcoins, litecoin*: Litecoin explanations taken from various sources, including https://litecoin.org/.

157   *In the case of nextcoin*: Nextcoin explanations taken from various sources, including http://nxt.org.

159   *"financial weapons of mass destruction," as Warren Buffett called them*: From 2002 Annual Report of Berkshire Hathaway Inc., edited excerpts, http://www.fintools.com/docs/Warren%20Buffet%20on%20Derivatives.pdf.

7. Satoshi's Mill

161   *Stanford would later donate land he owned*: Stanford University, *History of Stanford*, http://www.stanford.edu/about/history/.

161   *Decades later, two young students at that school*: David Jacobson, "Founding Fathers," *Stanford Magazine*, July/August 1998.

162   *We wandered into one specialty shop*: Sarah Needleman, "More Small Businesses Embrace Bitcoin," *Wall Street Journal*, June 26, 2013.

162   *If the Bay Area is the most important region*: Many of the details in this chapter come from a trip to 20Mission and interviews conducted by Paul Vigna in June 2014.

162   *"There is a sense you're part of a movement"*: Taariq Lewis, interviewed by Paul Vigna, June 15, 2014.

164   *Dan Held was twenty-five years old when he attended his first bitcoin meetup*: Dan Held, interviewed by Paul Vigna, June 14, 2014.

165 *"It's a very specific type of brain that's obsessed with bitcoin"*: Adam Draper, interviewed by Paul Vigna, June 13, 2014.

165 *It's Kenna, 20Mission's founder, who best*: Jered Kenna, interviewed by Paul Vigna, June 15, 2014.

167 *which he later sued for $2 million over what Tradehill claimed*: Jeremy Quittner, "Dwolla Put Us out of Business, Bitcoin Exchange Says in Suit," *American Banker*, March 6, 2012, http://www.americanbanker.com/issues/177_45/tradehill-dwolla-bitcoin-exchange-digital-currency-lawsuit-1047273-1.html.

168 *Allan Grant is a cofounder of hired.com*: Billy Gallagher, "Hired Raises $15M in Series A at Valuation Around $60M," *TechCrunch*, March 24, 2014, http://techcrunch.com/2014/03/24/hired-raises-15m-series-a/.

170 *Chris Cassano, a twenty-five-year-old from Florida*: Chris Cassano, interviewed by Paul Vigna, June 12, 2014.

171 *He posted a description of it on Kickstarter*: Chris Cassano, "Piper: A Hardware-Based Paper Wallet Printer and More," Kickstarter, July 10, 2013, https://www.kickstarter.com/projects/299052466/piper-a-hardware-based-paper-wallet-printer-and-mo.

171 *"Money's great, too"*: Nathan Lands, interviewed by Paul Vigna, June 13, 2014.

173 *According to surveys conducted by news site* CoinDesk: "State of Bitcoin Q2 2014 Report Reveals Expanding Bitcoin Economy," *CoinDesk*, July 10, 2014, http://www.coindesk.com/state-of-bitcoin-q2-2014-report-expanding-bitcoin-economy/.

174 *Andreessen Horowitz, has made major investments*: Gregory Zuckerman, "Web Pioneer Keeps Faith, and Cash, in Bitcoin," *Wall Street Journal*, March 21, 2014.

174 *put money from his AME Ventures into*: Michael J. Casey, "Bitcoin Processor Raises $30 Million," *Wall Street Journal*, May 13, 2014.

174 *Stratton Sclavos, the former CEO of Verisign*: Michael J. Casey, "Bitcoin Security Startup BitGo Gets More Funds; Ex-Verisign CEO Joins Team," *Wall Street Journal*, *MoneyBeat* blog, June 16, 2014, http://blogs.wsj.com/moneybeat/2014/06/16/bitcoin-security-startup-bitgo-gets-more-funds-ex-verisign-ceo-joins-team/.

174 *Jim Breyer of Accel Partners*: Emily Spaven, "Circle Launches with $9M from Jim Breyer, Accel, and General Catalyst in Biggest Ever Bitcoin Funding," *CoinDesk*, October 31, 2013, http://www.coindesk.com/circle-9m-jim-breyer-accel-general-catalyst-biggest-bitcoin-funding/.

175 *London-based wallet company Blockchain ran its entire*: Kim Lachance Shandrow, "Blockchain.info CEO: We Pay Our Employees in Bitcoin. And Someday You Might, Too," *Entrepreneur*, June 2, 2014, http://www.entrepreneur.com/article/234463.

176 *Before the old guard of the Valley VC community*: Draper, interviewed by Vigna.

178 *Scott Robinson is the marketing director*: Interviews with Scott Robinson, Andrew Lee, Kent Liu, Joshua Schechter, as well as details of Plug and Play's expo day, were all collected by Paul Vigna, June 12, 2014.

182 *The meandering history of the domain name*: Paul Vigna and Michael J. Casey, "BitBeat: The Men Who Owned Bitcoin.com," *Wall Street Journal*, *MoneyBeat*

blog, http://blogs.wsj.com/moneybeat/2014/04/22/bitbeat-the-men-who-owned-bitcoin-com/.

183   *In a post on the* StrictlyVC *blog*: Connie Loizos, "A Bitcoin Bear in Silicon Valley, It's True," *StrictlyVC,* March 7, 2014, http://www.strictlyvc.com/2014/03/07/bitcoin-bear-silicon-valley-true/.

184   *"If you went back to 1993 and you asked"*: Chris Dixon, phone interview with Michael J. Casey, June 25, 2014.

8. The Unbanked

186   *Roughly 2.5 billion people in the world*: Asli Demirguc-Kunt and Leora Klapper, "Measuring Financial Inclusion," World Bank Policy Research Working Paper 6025, April 2012.

187   *To illustrate, let's go back briefly*: Songyi Lee, Johann Barbie, and Jonathan Zobro, interviewed by Paul Vigna, June 12, 2014, as well as subsequent interview with Songyi Lee, June 23, 2014.

187   *Mali is one of the poorest nations on the planet*: See *The Statesman's Yearbook* (2014).

189   *The World Bank estimates that the global remittance business*: "Migration and Development Brief," World Bank, April 11, 2014, http://siteresources.worldbank.org/INTPROSPECTS/Resources/334934-1288990760745/MigrationandDevelopment Brief22.pdf.

189   *fees for money sent from the United States*: Prices for a myriad of "corridors" can be found at http://remittanceprices.worldbank.org/en.

190   *The problem isn't limited to the emerging markets*: Data about financial inclusion by country can be found on the World Bank's financial inclusion index, called the Global Findex, http://datatopics.worldbank.org/financialinclusion/.

191   *Between 1990 and 2010, the percentage of*: "Poverty Overview," World Bank, April 7, 2014, http://www.worldbank.org/en/topic/poverty/overview.

192   *With regard to literacy, the developing world*: "World Development Indicators, 2014," World Bank, http://wdi.worldbank.org/table/2.13.

192   *"I remember I was in the Caribbean once"*: Pelle Braendgaard, speaking at the Inside Bitcoins conference, New York, April 7, 2014.

193   *Ericsson ConsumerLab forecasts that*: "Sub-Saharan Africa, Ericsson Mobility Report Appendix," Ericsson ConsumerLab, http://www.ericsson.com/res/docs/2014/emr-june2014-regional-appendices-ssa.pdf.

193   *is now selling very basic smartphones*: Lorraine Luke, "India, Indonesia to Get $25 Smartphones," *Wall Street Journal,* http://online.wsj.com/articles/mozilla-to-sell-25-smartphones-1402466959.

194   *an escape route for their $12 trillion hoard of savings*: Grace Zhu, "Chinese Banks Match Tech Firms in Race for Deposits," *Wall Street Journal,* February 24, 2014, http://online.wsj.com/news/articles/SB10001424052702304834704579402573128666330.

195   *When combined with the central bank's*: Bobby Lee, interviewed by Michael J. Casey in Shanghai on July 19, 2014.

197 *"Many people in the U.S. don't"*: Eric Gu, interviewed by Michael J. Casey in Shanghai on July 20, 2014.

198 *"I tried everything"*: Jamal Ifill, interviewed by Paul Vigna, June 27, 2014.

198 *At $25,000, the island's per capita GDP*: See *The Statesman's Yearbook* (2014).

199 *Friends call him Mr. Bit, and it's not clear*: Much of the information for this section, including interviews with Gabriel Abed, Dr. Leroy McClain, David Simpson, and Jamal Ifill, was collected by Paul Vigna in Barbados, June 24–28, 2014.

200 *taking advantage of relatively low electricity costs there*: Mark Lyndersay, "On Bitcoin and Beyond," *Tech News T&T*, June 24, 2014, http://technewstt.com/bd942/.

202 *Patrick Byrne, the CEO of Salt Lake City*: Patrick Byrne, interviewed by Michael J. Casey, June 8, 2014.

204 *"I have no compassion for these women"*: Francesco Rulli, Fereshteh Forough, and Roya Mahboob, interviewed by Michael J. Casey and Paul Vigna, June 19, 2014.

208 *BitPagos's service is so attractive*: Based on interviews with BitPagos CEO Sebastian Serrano by Michael J. Casey, January 25 and June 2, 2014.

209 *To Mike Abridello, a U.S. expatriate*: Based on phone interview with Mike Abridello by Michael J. Casey, June 13, 2014.

210 *"Those are only the official flows"*: Dilip Ratha, interviewed by Paul Vigna, May 22, 2014.

211 *To use M-Pesa, people sign up*: Frederik Eijkman, Jake Kendall, and Ignacio Mas, "Bridges to Cash: The Retail End of M-Pesa," *Savings and Development*, http://aisberg.unibg.it/bitstream/10446/27458/1/EIJKMAN%202-2010.pdf.

212 *one relief group, Concern Worldwide*: Dipankar Datta, Anne Ejakait, and Monica Odak, "Mobile Phone–Based Cash Transfers: Lessons from the Kenya Emergency Response," *Humanitarian Exchange Magazine*, October 2008, http://www.odihpn.org/humanitarian-exchange-magazine/issue-40/mobile-phone-based-cash-transfers-lessons-from-the-kenya-emergency-response.

213 *Perhaps inevitably, then, someone like Duncan*: Elizabeth Rossiello, interviewed by Paul Vigna, May 9 and 18, 2014.

215 *a hacker house called iHub*: http://www.ihub.co.ke/.

216 *from what Peruvian economist Hernando de Soto calls*: See Hernando de Soto, *The Mystery of Capital* (Basic Books, 2000).

217 *Jonathan Mohan, who works at Ethereum*: Jonathan Mohan, speaking at the Inside Bitcoins conference, New York, April 7, 2014.

9. The Everything Blockchain

220 *Joseph Gleason, better known as Fireduck*: Joseph Gleason, "Anyone Want to Run My Bitcoin Casino," Bitcoin Forum, April 17, 2012, posted under "fireduck," http://www.reddit.com/r/Bitcoin/comments/segz0/anyone_want_to_run_my_bitcoin_casino; identified as Joseph Gleason via Gleason's Web site, http://1209k.com/bitcoin/faq.php.

220   *Gamblers would send bitcoin to one*: Jon Matonis, "Bitcoin Casinos Report 2012
      Earnings," *Forbes*, January 22, 2013, http://www.forbes.com/sites/jonmatonis
      /2013/01/22/bitcoin-casinos-release-2012-earnings/.

221   *Then, a few months after those share offerings*: Erik Voorhees, "Re: S.DICE—
      SatoshiDICE 100% Dividend-Paying Asset on PMEx," Bitcoin Forum, July 17, 2013,
      https://bitcointalk.org/index.php?topic=101902.msg2751536#msg2751536.

222   *Mike Hearn, who worked for three years on security*: Mike Hearn, "The Future of
      Money," Turing Festival speech, YouTube, August 23, 2013, https://www.youtube.
      com/watch?v=Pu4PAMFPo5Y.

224   *"smart contracts," an idea first floated by Nick Szabo*: Nick Szabo, "Formalizing
      and Securing Relationships on Public Networks," September 1997, http://szabo
      .best.vwh.net/formalize.html.

227   *David Johnston is a senior board member*: David Johnston, interviewed by Mi-
      chael J. Casey, January 25, 2014.

229   *For Daniel Larimer, one basic conceptual obstacle*: Daniel Larimer, interviewed by
      Michael J. Casey, April 8, 2014.

231   *In mid-2013, journalist Vitalik Buterin also got*: Vitalik Buterin, interviewed by
      Michael J. Casey, January 26, 2014.

231   *Buterin first laid out his vision in a white paper*: Vitalik Buterin, "Ethereum
      White Paper," January 2014, https://www.ethereum.org/pdfs/EthereumWhitePa-
      per.pdf.

232   *The team also planned a fund-raiser*: Michael J. Casey, "BitBeat: Ethereum Presale
      Hits $12.7 Million Tally," *Wall Street Journal*, *MoneyBeat* blog, http://blogs.wsj.
      com/moneybeat/2014/08/05/bitbeat-ethereum-presale-hits-12-7-million-tally/.

234   *Here, once again at the vanguard*: "The Ripple Protocol: Executive Summary for
      Financial Institutions," Ripple.com, https://ripple.com/files/ripple-FIs.pdf.

235   *David Andolfatto, the chief economist at*: David Andolfatto, "Bitcoin and Beyond:
      The Possibilities and the Pitfalls of Virtual Currencies," Federal Reserve Bank of St.
      Louis, March 31, 2014, http://www.stlouisfed.org/dialogue-with-the-fed/bitcoin-
      and-beyond.cfm.

236   *The issue of Ripple's profit motives*: Jed McCaleb, "Selling My XRP," *XRPtalk*, May
      22, 2014, https://xrptalk.org/topic/2629-selling-my-xrp/.

237   *But then things got nasty when*: Jesse Powell, "Ripple Board Member Resigns,"
      Reddit, May 24, 2014, http://www.reddit.com/r/Ripple/comments/26ccz3/ripple_
      board_member_resigns/.

237   *Fences were mended three months later*: Monica Long, "Settlement of Jed's XRP,"
      Ripple Forum, https://ripple.com/forum/viewtopic.php?f=1&t=7641.

237   *Larsen doesn't downplay that Ripple Labs*: Chris Larsen, interviewed by Michael J.
      Casey, May 5, 2014.

238   *Jed McCaleb would use an entirely new*: Michael J. Casey and Paul Vigna, "Mt.
      Gox, Ripple Founder Unveils Stellar, a New Digital Currency Project," *Wall Street
      Journal*, *MoneyBeat* blog, July 31, 2014, http://blogs.wsj.com/moneybeat/2014/07
      /31/mt-gox-ripple-founder-unveils-stellar-a-new-digital-currency-project/.

238 *MaidSafe is founded on the notion that many people*: "Distributed Platform Overview," MaidSafe, http://maidsafe.net/overview.

239 *purports to avoid the "ecological disaster" that's brewing*: David Irvine, interviewed by Michael J. Casey and Paul Vigna, April 8, 2014.

239 *For an internal currency that MaidSafe*: Michael J. Casey and Paul Vigna, "BitBeat: MaidSafe's Manic Offer Highlights Hot Bitcoin 2.0," *Wall Street Journal, MoneyBeat* blog, April 24, 2014, http://blogs.wsj.com/moneybeat/2014/04/24/bit beat-maidsafes-manic-offer-highlights-hot-bitcoin-2-0/.

240 *the Securities and Exchange Commission imposed*: "SEC Charges Bitcoin Entrepreneur with Offering Unregistered Securities," U.S. Securities and Exchange Commission, June 3, 2014, http://www.sec.gov/News/PressRelease/Detail/PressRelease/1370541972520#.VA2lhBBdWsA.

241 *"You think it's hard to figure out what bitcoin"*: Jacob Farber, speaking at the Inside Bitcoins conference, New York, April 7, 2014.

242 *Realcoin, founded by prolific bitcoin investor Brock Pierce*: Michael J. Casey, "Dollar-Backed Digital Currency Aims to Fix Bitcoin's Volatility Dilemma," *Wall Street Journal, MoneyBeat* blog, June 8, 2014, http://blogs.wsj.com/moneybeat/2014/07/08/dollar-backed-digital-currency-aims-to-fix-bitcoins-volatility-di lemma/.

242 *An even more centralized version of a similar concept is Bitreserve*: Paul Vigna and Michael J. Casey, "BitBeat: BitReserve Vows Bitcoin-Like Costs, No Bitcoin-Like Risk," *Wall Street Journal, MoneyBeat* blog, May 15, 2014, http://blogs.wsj.com/moneybeat/2014/05/15/bitbeat-bitreserve-vows-bitcoin-like-costs-no-bitcoin-like-risk/.

243 *"It's like we're Henry Ford and we're working with this"*: Nicholas Cary, interviewed by Michael J. Casey and Paul Vigna, June 6, 2014.

245 *"This is not Satoshi's dream"*: Chris Odom, speaking at the North American Bitcoin Conference, Miami Beach, January 25, 2014.

10. Square Peg Meets Round Hole

246 *Gavin Andresen opened the door*: Details of events surrounding the Mt. Gox transaction malleability attack taken from interviews Michael J. Casey had with Gavin Andresen on February 11 and 14, 2014, and with Jeff Garzik on February 14, 2014.

248 *"Contrary to Mt. Gox's statement, Bitcoin is not at fault"*: Gavin Andresen, "Contrary to Mt. Gox's Statement, Bitcoin Is Not at Fault," Bitcoin Foundation, blog post, https://bitcoinfoundation.org/2014/02/contrary-to-mt-goxs-statement-bitcoin-is-not-at-fault/.

249 *The price of bitcoin, at $703*: Source: Bitcoin Price Index, *CoinDesk,* http://www.coindesk.com/price.

251 *At its worst moment*: Price details from Bitcoin Price Index, *CoinDesk,* http://www.coindesk.com/price/; market capitalization information from http://www.coinmarketcap.com.

251   *"Probably ten thousand of the best developers"*: Chris Dixon, phone interview with Michael J. Casey, June 25, 2014.

252   *In their 2006 book*: Ori Brafman and Rod Beckstrom, *The Starfish and the Spider*: *The Unstoppable Power of Leaderless Organizations* (Portfolio, 2006).

253   *as per a schema on network structure*: Paul Baran, "On Distributed Communication," The Rand Corporation, August 1964, http://www.rand.org/content/dam/rand/pubs/research_memoranda/2006/RM3420.pdf.

254   *In June 2013, the California Division of Financial Institutions*: Jon Matonis, "Bitcoin Foundation Receives Cease and Desist Order from California," *Forbes,* June 23, 2013, http://www.forbes.com/sites/jonmatonis/2013/06/23/bitcoin-foundation-receives-cease-and-desist-order-from-california/.

254   *In February 2014, West Virginia Democratic senator*: Senator Joe Manchin, "Manchin Demands Federal Regulators Ban Bitcoin," letter addressed to Treasury Secretary Jacob Lew, Federal Reserve chairwoman Janet Yellen, et al., http://www.manchin.senate.gov/public/index.cfm/2014/2/manchin-demands-federal-regulators-ban-bitcoin.

255   *As Gareth Murphy, the director of markets*: Amir Mizroch, "Irish Central Banker Lays Down the Law at Bitcoin Gathering," *Wall Street Journal, Digits* blog, July 3, 2014, http://blogs.wsj.com/digits/2014/07/03/irish-central-banker-lays-down-the-law-at-bitcoin-gathering/.

255   *This set the stage for a much-anticipated Senate hearing*: Jennifer Shasky Calvery, "Statement of Jennifer Shasky Calvery, Director, Financial Crimes Enforcement Network, United States Department of the Treasury," Senate Committee on Banking, Housing, and Urban Affairs, November 19, 2013, http://www.fincen.gov/news_room/testimony/html/20131119.html.

256   *Some states, such as Texas, took a deliberately accommodating stance*: Texas banking commissioner George T. Cooper argued that virtual currencies did not meet the definition of money and so could not fall under the state's money-transmission rules. See the statement of April 3, 2014, at http://www.dob.texas.gov/public/uploads/files/Laws-Regulations/New-Actions/sm1037.pdf.

256   *That led a bunch of storefronts in tech-friendly Texan locales such as Austin*: Dave Byknish and Paul Shelton, "Austin Gets 2nd Bitcoin ATM; It's at a Gun Store," kxan.com, March 2, 2014, http://kxan.com/2014/03/02/austin-gets-2nd-bitcoin-atm-its-at-a-gun-store/.

256   *New York's Department of Financial Services' ambitious superintendent*: Benjamin M. Lawsky, "Notice of Intent to Hold Hearing on Virtual Currencies, Including Potential NYDFS Issuance of a 'BitLicense,'" November 14, 2013, http://www.dfs.ny.gov/about/press2013/virtual-currency-131114.pdf.

256   *In February the following year*: Statements of witnesses, New York Department of Financial Services Web site, http://www.dfs.ny.gov/.

257   *After the hearings, Lawsky took to Reddit*: Benjamin M. Lawsky, "As Requested, I'm Ben Lawsky, Superintendent of the NY Dept of Financial Services, Here for an AMA on Bitcoin/Virtual Currency," Reddit.com, February 20, 2014, posting

as BenLawsky, http://www.reddit.com/r/IAmA/comments/1ygcil/as_requested_
im_ben_lawsky_superintendent_of_the.

258   *Fed chairwoman Janet Yellen pointed out*: Steven Russolillo, "Yellen on Bitcoin:
Fed Doesn't Have Authority to Regulate It in Any Way," *Wall Street Journal, MoneyBeat* blog, February 27, 2014.

258   *Miami-based lawyer Andrew Ittleman*: Interviewed by Michael J. Casey, May 29,
2014.

259   *Eventually, a formal ruling came down in April 2014*: Paul Vigna, "Bitcoin Prices
Down 10% After Chinese Banks Cut Off Local Exchanges," *Wall Street Journal,
MoneyBeat* blog, April 10, 2014, http://blogs.wsj.com/moneybeat/2014/04/10/bit
coin-prices-down-10-after-chinese-banks-cut-off-local-exchanges/.

259   *After that, the European Banking Authority*: Viktorai Dendrinou, "EU Cautions
Banks over Virtual Currencies," *Wall Street Journal,* July 4, 2014.

259   *The Bitcoin Foundation's chief government-liaison officer*: Jim Harper, "Will Europe
Listen to 'Europe'?," Bitcoin Foundation blog, July 4, 2014, https://bitcoinfounda
tion.org/2014/07/will-europe-listen-to-europe/.

259   *Back in the United States, on March 25*: John D. McKinnon and Ryan Tracy, "IRS
Says Bitcoin Is Property, Not Currency," *Wall Street Journal,* March 25, 2014.

260   *A few months later, in July*: Paul Vigna, "NY Financial Regulator Releases Draft of
'Bitlicense' for Bitcoin Businesses," *Wall Street Journal, MoneyBeat* blog, July 17,
2014, http://blogs.wsj.com/moneybeat/2014/07/17/ny-financial-regulator-releases-
draft-of-bitlicense-for-bitcoin-businesses/.

261   *Meanwhile, Perianne Boring*: Perianne Boring, "Chamber of Digital Commerce
BitLicense Comments," August 18, 2014, http://www.digitalchamber.org/assets/
chamber—bitlicense-comments-final.pdf.

261   *A petition quickly circulated*: Letter and signatories available on Chamber of
Digital Commerce Web site, http://www.digitalchamber.org/ny-bitlicense.html.

261   *Some suggested more drastic action and started lobbying*: Open-Source Financial Developers Association, "Stop BitLicense from Harming Small Businesses
and Tech Innovation in NY," petition to Governor Andrew Cuomo via change.
org, http://www.change.org/p/governor-andrew-m-cuomo-and-the-new-york-
state-legislature-stop-bitlicense-from-harming-small-businesses-and-tech-in
novation-in-ny.

261   *Most dramatically, Circle CEO Jeremy Allaire*: Jeremy Allaire, "Thoughts on the
New York BitLicense Proposal," August 13, 2014, Circle Internet Financial blog,
https://www.circle.com/2014/08/13/thoughts-new-york-bitlicense-proposal.

262   *Conceding that the NYDFS didn't have "a monopoly on the truth"*: Paul Vigna,
"BitBeat: BitLicense Gets Extension; Lawsky: 'We Don't Have a Monopoly on the
Truth,'" *Wall Street Journal, MoneyBeat* blog, August 21, 2014, http://blogs.wsj.
com/moneybeat/2014/08/21/bitbeat-bitlicense-gets-extension-lawsky-we-dont-
have-a-monopoly-on-the-truth/.

262   *As Harper of the Bitcoin Foundation points out*: Jim Harper, interviewed by Michael J. Casey, August 8, 2014.

263   *somewhere between $5 trillion and $32 trillion*: $5 trillion estimate in 2007 from
the Organization for Economic Cooperation and Development in "Places in the
Sun," *Economist,* February 22, 2007; $32 trillion is top end of $21 trillion–$32
trillion range estimated by the Tax Justice Network in its report "The Price of
Offshore Revisited," released July 22, 2012, http://www.taxjustice.net/cms/upload/
pdf/The_Price_of_Offshore_Revisited_Presser_120722.pdf.

263   *Bulgaria, whose tax agency*: Ali Najjar, "Bulgarian NRA Offers Bitcoin Tax
Guidelines," *CoinReport,* April 2, 2014, https://coinreport.net/bulgaria-bitcoin-
tax-guidelines/.

263   *The Swiss Financial Market Supervisory Authority announced*: Emily Spaven,
"Swiss Government Report: Bitcoin Too 'Insignificant' for Legislation," June 25,
2014, *CoinDesk,* http://www.coindesk.com/switzerland-government-report-bitcoin-
insignificant-legislation/.

263   *This hands-off approach has turned*: Michael J. Casey, "BitBeat: Crypto Innovators Find Fertile Ground in Soft-Touch Switzerland," *Wall Street Journal, Money-
Beat* blog, August 4, 2014, http://blogs.wsj.com/moneybeat/2014/08/04/bitbeat
-crypto-innovators-find-fertile-ground-in-soft-touch-switzerland/.

264   *In August 2014, Chancellor of the Exchequer*: Anna Irrera, "U.K. to Examine Virtual Currency Regulation," *Wall Street Journal, Digits* blog, August 6, 2014, http://
blogs.wsj.com/digits/2014/08/06/uk-to-examine-virtual-currency-regulation/.

264   *The first fully regulated bitcoin investment fund*: Nermin Hajdarbegovic, "First
Regulated Bitcoin Investment Fund to Launch on Island of Jersey," July 10, 2014,
CoinDesk, http://www.coindesk.com/first-regulated-bitcoin-investment-fund-
launch-island-jersey/.

264   *the Isle of Man announced*: Robert Paul Davis, "Isle of Man Welcomes Digital Currency Exchanges 'No License Required,'" *CoinDesk,* March 28, 2014, http://www.
coindesk.com/isle-man-welcomes-digital-currency-exchanges-license-required/.

264   *The Canadian government broke its silence*: Samuel Rubenfeld, "Canada Enacts Bitcoin Regulations," *Wall Street Journal, Risk & Compliance* blog, June 23, 2014,
http://blogs.wsj.com/riskandcompliance/2014/06/23/canada-enacts-bitcoin-reg
ulations/.

264   *As for Mexico, in July*: Tanaya Macheel, "The Case for Merging Mexico's Peso with
Block Chain Technology," *CoinDesk,* July 26, 2014, http://www.coindesk.com/
case-merging-mexicos-peso-block-chain-technology/.

265   *"All the banks are crazy scared"*: Aurélien Menant, interviewed by Michael
J. Casey, July 20, 2014.

265   *twenty-eight-year-old American CEO, Autumn Radtke*: Newley Purnell, "Singapore
Investigates Death of American Startup CEO," *Wall Street Journal, Digits* blog,
March 7, 2014, http://blogs.wsj.com/digits/2014/03/07/singapore-investigates-
death-of-american-startup-ceo/.

265   *Monetary Authority of Singapore said in March*: Sanat Vallikappen, "Singapore to
Regulate Bitcoin Operators for Laundering Risk," March 13, 2014, Bloomberg,

http://www.bloomberg.com/news/2014-03-13/singapore-to-regulate-bitcoin-op
erators-for-money-laundering.html.

265 *According to one report, giant, state-owned conglomerate Temasek*: Jon Southurst,
"Singapore Government-Owned Investment Firm 'Experiments' with Bitcoin,"
CoinDesk, June 27, 2014, http://www.coindesk.com/singapore-government-owned-
investment-firm-experiments-bitcoin/.

268 *Reuters reported that only Karpelès knew the passwords*: Sophie Knight, "At Mt.
Gox Bitcoin Hub, 'Geek' CEO Sought Both Control and Escape," Reuters, April 21,
2014, http://www.reuters.com/article/2014/04/21/us-bitcoin-mtgox-karpeles-in
sight-idUSBREA3K01D20140421.

268 *Roger Ver and his high school buddy Jesse Powell*: Details of Powell and Ver's experience at Mt. Gox in June 2011 taken from interview of Jesse Powell by Paul Vigna, March 3, 2014.

268 *Interacting on bitcoin forums with other bitcoiners*: Adam B. Levine, "The Ghost in
the Machine at MtGox," February 27, 2014, *Let's Talk Bitcoin,* http://letstalkbit
coin.com/the-ghost-in-the-machine-at-mtgox/.

269 *Many theories would later develop*: Many of the theories were outlined in a blog
post by Cameron Winklevoss at Winklevoss Capital's Web site on March 14, 2014,
https://winklevosscapital.com/what-may-have-happened-at-mt-gox/.

269 *This appears to be a play on a popular meme*: Douglas Adams, *Life, the Universe
and Everything* (Harmony Books, 1982).

270 *Adam Levine, a bitcoin talk-show host*: Adam B. Levine, interviewed by Michael
J. Casey, February 28, 2014.

270 *BitGo's highly secure multi-sig wallet came out at this time*: Michael J. Casey, "Bitcoin Is Entering the Multi-Sig Era," in "BitBeat: Rep. Stockman Wants IRS to Reconsider Bitcoin Decision," *Wall Street Journal, MoneyBeat* blog, April 8, 2014,
http://blogs.wsj.com/moneybeat/2014/04/08/bitbeat-rep-stockman-wants-irs-to-
reconsider-bitcoin-decision/.

270 *Meanwhile, the Winklevoss twins progressed with a request*: Michael J. Casey,
"Lawyer for Winklevoss Twins' Bitcoin ETF Says SEC Review Going Smoothly,"
Wall Street Journal, MoneyBeat blog, January 17, 2014, http://blogs.wsj.com/mon
eybeat/2014/01/17/lawyer-for-winkelvoss-twins-bitcoin-etf-says-sec-review-go
ing-smoothly/.

270 *Later, Atlas ATS launched a network*: Michael J. Casey, "Perseus, Atlas Launch
Global Bitcoin Trading Platform," *Wall Street Journal,* March 12, 2014.

271 *Bitcoin enthusiast Barry Silbert launched his own bitcoin fund*: Michael J. Casey
and Paul Vigna, "SecondMarket Seeks to Open Bitcoin Fund to Ordinary Investors," *Wall Street Journal,* March 19, 2014.

271 *Silbert also started building his own exchange*: Michael J. Casey and Robin Sidel,
"Firms Bank on a Bitcoin Bounceback," *Wall Street Journal,* February 26, 2014.

271 *Their most radical solution*: Danny Yadron, "Tech Renegade: From Print-at-Home
Guns to Untraceable Currency," *Wall Street Journal,* December 31, 2013.

271 *"A bunch of start-ups are coming in"*: Cody Wilson, interviewed by Michael J. Casey, March 20, 2014.

272 *Elsewhere, Wilson was quoted describing it*: Andy Greenberg, "'Dark Wallet' Is About to Make Bitcoin Money Laundering Easier Than Ever," April 29, 2014, http://www.wired.com/2014/04/dark-wallet/.

272 *the Bitcoin Foundation's chief scientist, called it "fantastic"*: Kadhim Shubber, "Gavin Andresen: Rising Transaction Fees Could Price Poor out of Bitcoin," *CoinDesk*, May 16, 2014, http://www.coindesk.com/gavin-andresen-rising-trans action-fees-price-poor-bitcoin/.

272 *However, the freelance journalist*: Ryan Selkis, "Dark Wallets Are a Regulatory Nightmare for Bitcoin," *TwoBitIdiot* blog, May 1, 2014, http://two-bit-idiot.tumblr. com/post/84454892629/dark-wallets-are-a-regulatory-nightmare-for-bitcoin.

11. A New New Economy

275 *has by many measures only got more intense since that crisis*: Luke Johnson, "Elizabeth Warren: 'Too Big to Fail Is Worse Than Before Financial Crisis," *Huffington Post,* November 12, 2013, http://www.huffingtonpost.com/2013/11/12/elizabeth-warren-too-big-to-fail_n_4260871.html.

276 *the widest wealth gap since the Great Depression*: Scott Neuman, "Study Says America's Income Gap Widest Since Great Depression," NPR, September 10, 2013, http://www.npr.org/blogs/thetwo-way/2013/09/10/221124533/study-says-ameri cas-income-gap-widest-since-great-depression.

276 *As former U.S. vice president Al Gore put it*: Al Gore, "The Turning Point: New Hope for the Climate," *Rolling Stone,* June 18, 2014, http://www.rollingstone.com /politics/news/the-turning-point-new-hope-for-the-climate-20140618.

276 *People have figured out that if they have idle assets*: "The Rise of the Sharing Economy," *Economist,* March 9, 2013, http://www.economist.com/news/leaders/21573104 -internet-everything-hire-rise-sharing-economy.

278 *A phrase from Mastercoin's David Johnston*: David Johnston, "Johnston's Law," http://www.johnstonslaw.org/.

279 *among a host of overhyped Super Bowl XXXIV ads*: Dashiell Bennett, "8 Dot-Coms That Spent Million on Super Bowl Ads and No Longer Exist," *Business Insider,* February 2, 2011, http://www.businessinsider.com/8-dot-com-super-bowl-advertisers-that-no-longer-exist-2011-2?op=1.

279 *for which Eastman Kodak provides a cautionary tale*: Mike Spector and Dana Mattiolo, "Kodak Teeters on the Brink," *Wall Street Journal,* January 5, 2012.

279 *But Wall Street lobbyists fought*: David Enrich, "Banks Return with a Goal: Pushing Back," *Wall Street Journal,* January 26, 2011.

280 *U-Haul, the venerable truck-rental company*: Information about U-Haul's lending program can be found at http://www.uhaulinvestorsclub.com/AboutUs.

280 *"The world is not short of currencies"*: Francesco Guerrera, "Bitcoin's Crisis Is Turning Point for Currency," *Wall Street Journal, MoneyBeat* blog, February

17, 2014, http://blogs.wsj.com/moneybeat/2014/02/17/bitcoins-crisis-is-turning-point-for-currency/.

281 *D.C. lobbying firm Peck Madigan Jones to lobby Congress*: Olga Kharif and Eliza-beth Dexheimer, "MasterCard Lobbyist Adds Bitcoin to List of Topics," Bloom-berg, April 30, 2014, http://www.bloomberg.com/news/2014-04-30/mastercard-lobbyist-adds-bitcoin-to-list-of-topics.html.

281 *Jason Oxman, the CEO*: Jason Oxman, interviewed by Michael J. Casey, June 24, 2014.

281 *supports payments at retail outlets via QR codes*: Donna Tam, "PayPal Offers QR Codes Retail-Store Purchases," CNET, October 8, 2013, http://www.cnet.com /news/paypal-offers-qr-codes-for-retail-store-purchases/.

282 *Facebook is widely believed to be working*: Samuel Gibbs, "Facebook Prepares to Launch e-Money Transfer Service in Europe," *Guardian,* April 14, 2014, http:// www.theguardian.com/technology/2014/apr/14/facebook-e-money-transfer-ser vice-europe.

282 *only now coming to the United States*: John Ginovsky, "EMV a Work in Progress in U.S.," *ABA Banking Journal,* August 24, 2014, http://www.ababj.com/blogs-3/ making-sense-of-it-all/item/4859-emv-a-work-in-progress-in-u-s/.

283 *Square, which posted a $100 million loss in 2013*: Alistair Barr, Douglas MacMillan, and Evelyn M. Rusli, "Mobile-Payments Start-Up Square Discusses Possible Sale," *Wall Street Journal,* April 21, 2014.

285 *"Now the crowd has their own business model"*: Jeremiah Owyang, interviewed by Paul Vigna, July 11, 2014.

286 *A comprehensive 2011 study of U.S. society by the Pew Research Center*: "Millennials in Adulthood," Pew Research Social & Demographic Trends, March 7, 2014, http:// www.pewsocialtrends.org/2014/03/07/millennials-in-adulthood/.

286 *Separate Pew data from the same study*: Ibid.

286 *Gil Luria, an analyst at Wedbush Securities*: Michael J. Casey, "WedBush Securities Analysts Gil Luria and Aaron Turner Make Some Big Claims," in "BitBeat: Bit-coin Continues to Grow—Gingerly—in China," *Wall Street Journal, MoneyBeat* blog, May 28, 2014.

287 *Glorivee Caban knows a thing or two*: Glorivee Caban, interviewed by Michael J. Casey, August 7, 2014.

287 *Visa, MasterCard, and Western Union*: Employee tallies taken from 2013 annual reports for Visa Inc., MasterCard Inc., and Western Union Holding Inc.

288 *Andreessen Horowitz venture capitalist*: Chris Dixon, phone interview with Mi-chael J. Casey, June 25, 2014.

288 *Asked to describe the job market*: Daniel Larimer, interviewed by Michael J. Casey, April 8, 2014.

289 *As Tyler Cowen noted in his book*: See Tyler Cowan, *Average Is Over: Powering America Beyond the Age of the Great Stagnation* (Dutton, 2013).

289 *Yale's Robert Shiller*: Joe Weisenthal, "Robert Shiller: Bitcoin Is an Amazing

Example of a Bubble," *Business Insider,* January 24, 2014, http://www.businessin sider.com/robert-shiller-bitcoin-2014-1#ixzz3Cmp0YFyx.

289   *New York University's Nouriel Roubini*: Erik Holm, "Nouriel Roubini: Bitcoin Is a 'Ponzi Game,'" March 10, 2014, *Wall Street Journal, MoneyBeat* blog, http://blogs. wsj.com/moneybeat/2014/03/10/nouriel-roubini-bitcoin-is-a-ponzi-game/.

289   *Former U.S. treasury secretary*: Lawrence Summers, phone interview by Michael J. Casey, April 30, 2014.

290   *In 2014, the U.S. Federal Election Commission*: Michael J. Casey, "Bitcoin Campaign Donations Get Green Light from FEC," *Wall Street Journal, MoneyBeat* blog, May 8, 2014, http://blogs.wsj.com/moneybeat/2014/05/08/bitcoin-campaign-donations-get-green-light-from-fec/.

291   *According to Make Your Laws*: https://makeyourlaws.org/fec/bitcoin/pacs.

Conclusion: Come What May

293   *to peg it at a low number, about 1 percent*: Ben Popper, "Meet the Man Building the Fort Knox of Bitcoin," *Verge,* August 29, 2014, http://www.theverge.com/2014/8/29 /6082195/the-fort-knox-of-bitcoin-xapo-wences-casares; also, Rob Wile, "Over-stock CEO: We're Now Averaging $15,000 a Day in Bitcoin Sales," *Business Insider,* August 13, 2014, http://www.businessinsider.com/overstock-patrick-byrne-talks-bitcoin-sales-2014-8.

293   *only about half of U.S. citizens were aware*: Paul Vigna and Michael J. Casey, "BitBeat: More People Know About Bitcoin, but Few Willing to Use It," *Wall Street Journal, MoneyBeat* blog, August 27, 2014, http://blogs.wsj.com/moneyb eat/2014/08/27/bitbeat-more-people-know-about-bitcoin-but-few-willing-to-use-it/.

294   *Economists such as Boston University's*: Mark T. Williams, "Finance Professor: Bitcoin Could Evolve into an Existential Threat Worthy of a Science Fiction Movie," *Business Insider,* February 13, 2014, http://www.businessinsider.com/bitcoin -sovereign-attack-2014-2?op=1; Paul Krugman, "Golden Cyberfetters," *New York Times, Conscience of a Liberal* blog, September 7, 2011, http://krugman.blogs. nytimes.com/2011/09/07/golden-cyberfetters/.

296   *We already know that Canada*: David George-Cosh, "Canada Puts Halt to Mint-Chip Plan, Could Sell Digital Currency Program," *Wall Street Journal, Canada Real Time* blog, April 4, 2014, http://blogs.wsj.com/canadarealtime/2014/04/04 /canada-puts-halt-to-mintchip-plans-could-sell-digital-currency-program/.

296   *Ecuador is planning to introduce*: Daniel A. Media, "Introducing the World's First National Digital Currency," *Quartz,* September 4, 2014, http://qz.com/258989/in troducing-the-worlds-first-national-digital-currency/.

297   *creation of the Web browser Netscape*: Eric Niiler, "Netscape's IPO Anniversary and the Internet Boom," NPR, August 9, 2005, http://www.npr.org/templates /story/story.php?storyId=4792365.

298   *why the Betamax videocassette recorder was technically*: Bill Hammack, "How

Sony's Betamax lost to JVC's VHS videocassette recorder," EngineerGuy.com, June 17, 2014, https://www.youtube.com/watch?v=ddYZITaxlTQ.

299 *the headache of capital-gains-tax tracking*: Notice 2014-21, Internal Revenue Service, March 25, 2014, http://www.irs.gov/pub/irs-drop/n-14-21.pdf.

300 *Some of the more cryptocurrency-friendly states*: The Web site *BitLegal* offers comprehensive reports on the legal status of bitcoin around the world, http://www.bit legal.net/index.php.

302 *Wences Casares, the CEO of bitcoin wallet*: Interviewed by Michael J. Casey, September 12, 2014.

303 *Zurich-based investment manager and high-tech*: Richard Olsen, interviewed by Michael J. Casey, December 11, 2013, and June 13, 2014.

304 *when the dollar goes digital, "national borders are"*: Eswar Prasad, interviewed by Michael J. Casey, February 7, 2014.

306 *such as the Bretton Woods system of pegged*: M. J. Stephey, "Bretton Woods System," *Time*, October 21, 2008, http://content.time.com/time/business/article/0, 8599,1852254,00.html.

309 *"If suddenly the entire world starts"*: Roger Ver, speaking at the North American Bitcoin Conference, Miami Beach, January 26, 2014.

Index